PUBLIC
POLICYMAKING

PUBLIC POLICYMAKING

An Introduction

Third Edition

JAMES E. ANDERSON

Texas A&M University

HOUGHTON MIFFLIN COMPANY ■ BOSTON ■ NEW YORK

Senior Sponsoring Editor: Paul Smith
Project Editor: Helen Bronk
Production/Design Coordinator: Jennifer Meyer
Senior Manufacturing Coordinator: Marie Barnes
Marketing Manager: Clint Crockett

Portions of this book were published previously in *Public Policy-Making,* Third Edition, by James Anderson (New York: Holt, Rinehart and Winston, 1984).

Cover Design: Linda Manly Wade, Wade Design.

Photo Credits
Page 1: Ron Edmonds/AP/Wide World Photos. *Page 47:* Tom Horan/Sygma. *Page 91:* Robert Trippett/SIPA Press. *Page 133:* Robert Trippett/SIPA Press. *Page 177:* Terry Ashe/The Gamma Liaison Network. *Page 213:* Robert Trippett/SIPA Press. *Page 271:* John Duricka/AP/Wide World Photos. *Page 315:* P. Aventurier/The Gamma Liaison Network.

Printed in the U.S.A.

Library of Congress Catalog Card Number: 96-76854

ISBN: 0-395-75396-1

123456789-QM-00 99 98 97 96

CONTENTS

4 ■ Policy Adoption   133

5 ■ Budgeting and Public Policy   177

6 ■ Policy Implementation   213

PREFACE

Public Policymaking: An Introduction, Third Edition, presents an overview of the policymaking process as a sequence of functional activities, beginning with problem identification and agenda-setting and concluding with the evaluation and revision or termination of policy. This approach still constitutes a reasonable and workable approach to the study and analysis of public policymaking. The text also surveys a number of other major approaches to the study of policy formation, describes and analyzes the political environment of policymaking in the United States, includes quite a bit of information about the content of public policies, and treats some of the practical aspects of policymaking, such as political feasibility and cost-benefit analysis.

Although the book is comprehensive in that it covers all of the stages or phases of the policymaking process, by no means does it yield "everything anyone really needs to know" about public policymaking. As the word "introduction" in its title indicates, it serves as a starting point for the study of public policy. Once again, I have updated and expanded the annotated bibliography to assist readers desiring to explore the policy process more fully.

In this new edition I have made changes reflecting new developments in the policymaking process (especially at the national level in the United States), recent additions to political science literature and learning on policymaking, and my continuing professional development. I note some of these changes here. New case studies on airline deregulation and the Family and Medical Leave Act have been included. The discussion of budgeting has been expanded and the story about the budget deficit struggle has been updated. Material has been added on such topics as problem definition, agenda-setting, policy evaluation, interest groups, administrative agencies, and multiple advocacy. The discussion of problems in policy research has been shifted from the epilogue (now Chapter 8) to Chapter 1, where it fits in better.

I have included some references to changes in government and the policy process that resulted from the Republican takeover in 1994 of both houses of Congress. Some readers, I suppose, will be disappointed that the coverage of this topic is not more extensive. However, writing in the fall of 1996, it seems clear to me that, while important changes did occur, as in the House subcommittee system and the rejection of seniority in the choice of some House committee chairs, overall there was no "revolution" in governmental structure or policymaking practices. The American system once again demonstrated its resilience and capacity to temper change, and the general outlines of the policymaking process remains as before.

I have tried to be evenhanded and impartial in my treatment of the many topics covered in the book, even though such matters as abortion rights, budget deficits, the performance of Congress, and cost-benefit analysis have produced sharp controversies in society. Many rational-choice theories have also generated controversy among political scientists. Although I am fully equipped with values, preferences, and biases, I have been guided, and I think with considerable success, by the principle of "intended neutrality." Analysis rather than advocacy and teaching rather than preaching have been my goals.

In my treatment of the policymaking process, I have undoubtedly included information that could be regarded as ordinary knowledge, as knowledge not requiring the skills of political or social scientists to develop and report. It is difficult, however, at least for me, to draw a neat line between ordinary knowledge and scientific knowledge. Indeed, knowledge produced by scientific research may with time become ordinary, as in the instances of the germ theory of disease, the view of administration as a political process, and rejection of the quaint belief that judges merely find or discover law. Consequently, I have not hesitated to include information that may seem obvious or commonplace, especially to experts, when it adds meaning and clarity to the discussion of public policymaking.

I wish to express my appreciation for the assistance given by several people in the preparation of this edition. A number of persons provided suggestions for revision or reviewed a draft of the revised manuscript. They include: Stephen C. Brooks, University of Akron; James A. Dunn, Rutgers the State University of New Jersey-Camden; Gary Gregg, Clarion University; George A. Krause, University of South Carolina; Keith Mueller, University of Nebraska; Glenn McNitt, State University of New York-New Paltz; Max Neiman, University of California-Riverside; Michael J. Scicchitano, University of Florida; Richard D. Sylves, University of Delaware; Mark E. Tompkins, University of South Carolina. These reviewers provided a multitude of useful, challenging, and positive comments and recommendations. Though sometimes I did not agree with their advice, and at other times I was unable to act on it, collectively they did much to help make this a better book.

Various colleagues in the Texas A&M Department of Political Science supplied needed information, though perhaps they were not always aware of the purpose of my questions and requests. Avis Munson and Laura Nelson ably handled the technical and typing aspects of manuscript preparation. At Houghton Mifflin, Jean Woy, Paul Smith, and Helen Bronk steered the project to completion. Finally, Alberta (Mrs. Anderson) dutifully listened to my gripes and complaints, evaluated some of my ideas, and provided advice and encouragement. Without her the task of revision would have been more difficult, as would my life.

J.A.

1

THE STUDY OF PUBLIC POLICY

*The State of the Union message provides the president with an opportunity to
outline his programs and help set the Congressional agenda.*

U nemployment was not identified as a significant social problem until late in the nineteenth century.[1] Even then, and until the Great Depression of the 1930s, unemployment was viewed in the United States as basically a personal problem, as something that was unfortunate for those affected, perhaps, but not a matter warranting redress by the government. Millions of American workers (no one knew precisely how many) were thrown out of work after World War I by the conversion from a wartime to a peacetime economy. At a conference on unemployment sponsored by the national government to consider what might be done about this situation, President Warren G. Harding expressed the government's position in his opening remarks: "There has been vast unemployment before and there will be again. There will be depression and inflation just as surely as the tides ebb and flow. I would have little enthusiasm for any proposed remedy which seeks palliation or tonic from the Public Treasury."[2] Not surprisingly, no action on unemployment occurred.

The Depression, which for a decade caused continuing high rates of unemployment (one-fourth of the labor force was out of work in the winter of 1932–1933), helped to change such attitudes. Unemployment came to be regarded as a public problem that government was properly expected to prevent or ameliorate. New Deal responses to the unemployment problem included the unemployment insurance program, aid in finding jobs, and extensive public works and other programs to create jobs. The latter included the Works Progress Administration (WPA), which was criticized by conservatives as a "leaf-raking" program and a "boondoggle." Since the 1930s, the U.S. government has been committed to combating unemployment through a variety of policies and programs.

A major addition to the arsenal of government unemployment programs in the 1960s was job (or work) training. Initially intended to protect workers against the adverse effects of automation, in time the emphasis shifted to assisting those who found it difficult to compete effectively for available jobs—low-skilled workers, unemployed youth, and minority group members.[3] Among the work-training programs created were skill training, on-the-job training, adult basic education, and work experience. Subsequently, a program was authorized providing funding for temporary, full-time public service jobs for the unemployed with state and local agencies. In 1973 most of these job-training and public-employment measures were consolidated under the Comprehensive Employment and Training Act (CETA). Although much of the financing for them was provided by the national government, responsibility for the program administration was assigned to state and, particularly, local governments.[4]

For a decade CETA was the mainstay of government unemployment policy. Spending on CETA programs ran as high as $10 billion annually in the late 1970s before being cut back by the Reagan administration. However,

CETA had begun to produce substantial controversy soon after its enactment. Complaints were common about the act's complexity and waste, inefficiency, and administrative incompetence in the conduct of its programs. Public-service employment was often derided as a "make-work, dead-end jobs" program. Politically, CETA suffered from a weak constituency (the disadvantaged) and a poor public image.

One of Ronald Reagan's first actions after becoming president in 1981 was to propose elimination of most job-training and public-employment programs. A staunch conservative, he viewed them as ineffective and beyond the proper province of government. The public-employment program, which was in trouble before Reagan took office, was quickly eliminated. Congress balked, however, at doing away with the job-training programs, of which the Democrats were especially supportive.

Within the year, though, in one of the shifts in policy position at which he was adept, President Reagan changed his stance on job training. His administration's restrictive economic policies, which brought down the high inflation that had been afflicting the country, also elevated the unemployment rate. In the fall of 1982 it exceeded 10 percent, the highest rate the nation had experienced since the Great Depression. The president now publicly endorsed job training, not from a change of heart but rather because political realities and the approaching 1982 congressional elections made it politic to call for action on unemployment.

Although the Republicans fared poorly in the 1982 elections, both parties became committed to formulating a new job-training policy. Much of the work in developing the new legislation was handled within a policy community consisting of those most interested in employment and job-training programs, notably the House and Senate labor committees; various labor, community, and client groups; and the Department of Labor. For the first time business groups also became deeply involved. The primary bill in the Senate was jointly sponsored by Senator Dan Quayle (R, Indiana) and Senator Ted Kennedy (D, Massachusetts), which was emblematic of the bipartisan support for job-training legislation.

Enacted into law early in 1983, the Job Training Partnership Act (JTPA) retained many of the CETA training programs. Some important changes were made, however, that reflected compromises between Democrats and Republicans in Congress and responded to recommendations by the Reagan administration. The states, rather than the local governments, as had been the case under CETA, were now accorded primary responsibility for overseeing job-training programs. Governors could divide their states into service-delivery areas (SDA) to receive federal funds and provide services. Within each SDA a Private Industry Council (PIC), dominated by representatives of the business community, would have responsibility for managing the local service and training programs. These programs were to be especially targeted at youths, welfare recipients, and high-school dropouts. The popular Job Corps program for disadvantaged urban youths was continued, along with the summer youth employment program. Under JTPA, however, only limited payment of subsistence allowances to trainees was permitted and employment of trainees in public-service jobs was banned. In all, the administration got much of what it wanted and President Reagan signed JTPA into law, chiding the Democrats for not acting more quickly on the job-training problems.

In the early 1990s, federal expenditures supporting JTPA grew to more than $4 billion annually and went to more than 600 local SDAs plus 56 state and territorial programs. More participants received on-the-job training and were placed in private-sector jobs, at lower cost, than had been the case under CETA programs.

All was not well with the JTPA program, however. Criticism and complaints about JTPA developed early and persisted. A General Accounting Office (GAO) report in 1989 asserted that school dropouts were underserved by the program and, moreover, often did not receive remedial education. Much of the training was for jobs with limited potential and, in a practice referred to as "creaming," resources were often focused on those most likely to be hired after participation in the program.[5] A subsequent GAO report indicated problems in the management of JTPA, including improper expenditure of funds, excessive job training for some enrollees, and inadequate monitoring of the program by state officials.[6] A member of Congress who supported JTPA stated that some program administrators converted federal funds into "pure subsidies to local businesses, paying half the wages for a constant stream of new employees who train on the job as car washers, dishwashers, or broom pushers for six months until the subsidy runs out, their training ends, and a new trainee replaces them."[7] This was obviously an abuse of the program.

Such problems and complaints gained JTPA a place on the congressional agenda. In 1992, following a four-year struggle, legislation was enacted making revisions in JTPA. While preserving the public–private partnership in job training, the new law provided for more control by the Department of Labor over use of federal funds, encouraged the states to provide literacy and lifelong learning programs, provided that at least half the youths in the program had to be school dropouts, and limited on-the-job training to a six-month period. JTPA is now the national government's primary job-training program. It is, however, a limited program in that its annual funding is sufficient to provide training for only a small portion of those who are eligible.

More emphasis was placed on job training in 1988, when Congress adopted the Family and Child Support Act reforming the welfare system (Aid to Families with Dependent Children). Its major goal is to shift people from the welfare rolls to productive employment. The states are directed to set up and administer Job Opportunities and Basic Skills (JOBS) programs, which provide education, job training, and work experience for members of welfare families. The national government provides money to help fund the JOBS program and the costs of child care necessary to enable welfare mothers to participate in the program. By the mid-1990s the JOBS program was fully operative, providing training to several hundred thousand enrollees. There is some cooperation between JTPA and JOBS.

Job-training programs, for the most part, attract bipartisan support. Democrats like them because they provide assistance to people, help people become independent, and reduce poverty. Republicans see job-training programs as a means of reducing people's dependency on government and moving them off of the welfare rolls.

As this account of job-training policies illustrates, public policymaking is a complex and continuing process, involving many participants with differing roles and interests. Numerous questions about the policymaking process can be based on the job-training experience, including: Why does a condition or situation come to be viewed as a public problem? Why does the government decide to act on a problem? Why does it decide to adopt a given policy (or course of action) on a problem? How can we determine whether a policy is successful? This book is intended to assist you in developing responses to such questions and to better understand the nature and nuances of the policy process.

In the remainder of this chapter, several topics will be discussed. I will first respond to the question, "Why study public policy?" Attention will then turn to the nature of public policy, typologies of public policies, and some approaches to the study of public policymaking, including the one used in this book. The intent is to provide the reader with an understanding of the nature and scope of public policy and with a perspective on how, from the standpoint of political science, the policymaking process can be examined.

WHY STUDY PUBLIC POLICY?

Political scientists, in their teaching and research, have customarily been most interested in political institutions, such as legislatures or international organizations; in political processes, such as the electoral and judicial processes; and in elements of the political system, such as public opinion and interest groups. This is not to say, however, that political scientists have been totally indifferent to public policies. Foreign policy and policy on civil rights and liberties have traditionally been viewed as appropriate for their attention. So, too, has the subject that Professor Robert H. Salisbury calls "constitutional policy," or the "decisional rules by which subsequent policy actions are to be determined."[8] Among the procedural and structural "givens" that make up constitutional policy are legislative apportionment, the city-manager form of government, and federalism. These practices help shape decisions and public policies. Some political scientists with a normative bent also think about what governments *should do*, with the identification of "correct" or "proper" public policies. Their value-oriented approach, however, places them outside the mainstream of political science, which as a "science" is supposed to be rigorous, objective, and value-neutral.

In the last few decades, however, political scientists have been giving more attention to the study of public policy and specifically to describing, analyzing, and explaining its causes and effects. Professor Thomas Dye summarizes the various objectives of policy study:

> This focus involves a description of the content of public policy; an analysis of the impact of social, economic, and political forces on the content of public policy; an inquiry into the effect of various institutional arrangements and political processes on public policy; and an evaluation of the consequences of public policies on society, in terms of both expected and unexpected consequences.[9]

Students of public policy consequently seek answers to such questions as these: What effect do urbanization and industrialization have on welfare policies? How does the organization of Congress help shape agricultural or welfare policies? What role do interest groups have in forming environmental policy? What is the actual content of antitrust policy? Who benefits, and who does not, from current tax policies? What are the problems in implementing programs for disposal of hazardous waste? Although such questions are often difficult to answer, especially with precision, they direct our attention to the actual operation of the policy process and its societal consequences.

We now come to the question posed in the heading of this section: Why study public policy? One response is that it is important, that we are all affected in many ways by public policies, and thus we should know something about them, including why they are so difficult to enact, budget, and implement. We certainly should. A more systematic response is needed, however, which can be framed as the scientific, professional, and political reasons for studying public policies.[10] The same motivation does not drive all who engage in the study or analysis of public policy.

Scientific Reasons

Public policies can be studied to gain greater understanding of their origins, the procedures by which they are developed and implemented, or their consequences for society. This, in turn, will increase our understanding of political processes and political behavior. Policy may be regarded as either a dependent or an independent variable for this sort of analysis. When we consider policy as a dependent variable, as the product of various political

DEPENDENT VARIABLE

forces, we focus on the environmental considerations and political actors contributing to its adoption and content. For instance, how is policy affected by the distribution of power among the national, state, and local levels of government? Were pressure groups or public opinion important in getting a policy adopted? If public policy is viewed as an independent variable, our focus shifts to the impact of policy on the structure and operation of the political system and its environment. One may then seek answers to such questions as these: How does policy affect the public's support for the political system? How does policy affect social well-being? Do policymaking processes vary depending upon the kind of policy involved? Do distributive (e.g., pork-barrel) policies help ensure the reelection of legislators?

INDEP

I use the term *policy studies* to designate the study of public policy undertaken to gain greater basic understanding of political behavior and the governmental process.

Professional Reasons

for paper

Don K. Price distinguishes between the "scientific estate," which seeks only to discover knowledge, and the "professional estate," which strives to apply scientific knowledge to the solution of practical social problems.[11] Here, we encounter those practitioners of "policy analysis" whose numbers both inside and outside the government have multiplied greatly in recent years. Policy analysis has an applied orientation and is intended to determine the most efficient (or best) alternative (i.e., the one that will yield the largest net social benefit) for dealing with a current problem, such as reducing air pollution or collection and disposal of household garbage.[12] A variant of policy analysis is evaluation research, which assesses the societal effects of a particular public policy. The policy evaluator wants to know, for instance, whether a job-training program has increased the prospects for employment and the earnings of its enrollees, and, if so, by how much.

Policy analysis draws heavily from economic theory and statistical and mathematical techniques of analysis. Cost-benefit analysis, for example, is widely used in determining (perhaps "estimating" is a better word here) the efficiency (which is of course a value) of proposed alternatives or actual policies. In appraising the efficiency of government actions, the policy analyst focuses on their influence on society generally, on whether society as a whole gains or loses, rather than on their distributional consequences. Which groups receive the benefits and which pay the costs of, say, a consumer-protection policy are not of real interest to the analyst. In sum, professional policy analysis seeks to identify and promote adoption of good public policies, as measured by the efficiency criterion. Achieving a basic understanding of political and other human behavior is, at best, a secondary consideration. (Cost-benefit analysis is further discussed in Chapter 7.)

Political Reasons

As we have seen, some political scientists do not believe that political scientists should strive to be neutral or impartial in studying public policy. (This view is shared by some members of other social-science disciplines.) Rather, they contend that the study of public policy should be directed toward helping ensure that governments adopt favored public policies to attain the "right" goals. They reject the notion that the study of public policy should be value-free, contending rather that political science should not be silent or impotent on how best to deal with current political and social problems. In short, they engage in policy advocacy and are undeterred by society's substantial disagreement over what constitutes "correct" policies or the "right" goals of policy. Research engaged in by policy advocates is often skewed by the desire to develop "evidence" to support their cause. Policy study, in contrast, is motivated by the intent to be impartial.

In this book, I draw on the scientific policy studies approach to develop a basic understanding of the policymaking process, which is here viewed as an inherently political process involving conflict and struggle among people (public officials and private citizens) with conflicting interests, values, and desires on policy issues. In describing and analyzing the policymaking process, the scientific policy studies approach has three basic aims. First, its primary goal is to explain the adoption of a policy rather than to identify or prescribe "good" or proper policy. Analysis, rather than advocacy, is its style. Second, it rigorously searches for the causes and consequences of public policies by applying social-scientific methodology, which is not restricted to the use of quantitative data and methodology. At a minimum, it does require that one should strive to be rational, empirical, and objective. Third, this approach aims to develop reliable theories about public policies and their politics. Thus policy studies can be both theoretical and somewhat relevant to the more practical aspects of policymaking. It has been said that nothing is as practical as a good theory.

WHAT IS PUBLIC POLICY?

In general usage, the term *policy* designates the behavior of some actor or set of actors, such as an official, a governmental agency, or a legislature, in an area of activity such as public transportation or consumer protection. Public policy also may be viewed as whatever governments choose to do or not to do. Such definitions may be adequate for ordinary discourse, but because we set out in this book to do a systematic analysis of public policy, a more precise definition or concept is needed to structure our thinking and to facilitate effective communication with one another.

The literature of political science contains many definitions of public policy. Sooner or later, it seems, almost everyone who writes about public policy yields to the urge to offer a definition, and does so with greater or less success in the eyes of critics. I will note a few such definitions here and remark upon their utility for analysis. To be really useful and to facilitate communication and understanding, an operational definition or concept (I use these two words somewhat interchangeably) should indicate the essential characteristics or features of the matter being defined or conceptualized.

One definition holds that public policy, "broadly defined," is "the relationship of a governmental unit to its environment."[14] Such a definition is so broad as to leave most students uncertain of its meaning; it could encompass almost anything. Another states that "public policy is whatever governments choose to do or not to do."[15] Roughly accurate, this definition does not adequately recognize that what governments decide to do and what they actually do may diverge. Moreover, it could be taken to include such actions as routine personnel appointments or grants of driver's licenses, which are not usually thought of as policy matters. Professor Richard Rose suggests that policy be considered "a long series of more-or-less related activities" and their consequences for those concerned, rather than a discrete decision.[16] Although somewhat ambiguous, his definition does embody the useful notion that policy is a course or pattern of activity and not simply a decision to do something. Finally, political scientist Carl J. Friedrich regards policy as

> a proposed course of action of a person, group, or government within a given environment providing obstacles and opportunities which the policy was proposed to utilize and overcome in an effort to reach a goal or realize an objective or a purpose.[17]

To the notion of policy as a course of action, Friedrich adds the requirement that policy is directed toward accomplishing some purpose or goal. Although the purpose or goal of governmental actions may not always be easy to discern, the idea that policy involves purposive behavior seems a necessary part of its definition. Policy, however, should designate what is actually done rather than what is merely proposed in the way of action on some matter.

Taking into account the problems raised by these definitions, I offer this as a useful concept of policy: A relatively stable, purposive course of action followed by an actor or set of actors in dealing with a problem or matter of concern. This statement focuses on what is actually done instead of what is only proposed or intended, and it differentiates a policy from a decision, which is essentially a choice among competing alternatives.

Public policies are those developed by governmental bodies and officials. (Nongovernmental actors and factors may of course influence public-policy development.) The special characteristics of public policies stem from their being formulated by what political scientist David Easton has called the "authorities" in a political system, namely, "elders, paramount chiefs, executives, legislators, judges, administrators, councilors, monarchs, and the like." These are, he says, the persons who "engage in the daily affairs of a political system," are "recognized by most members of the system as having responsibility for these matters," and take actions that are "accepted as binding most of the time by most of the members so long as they act within the limits of their roles."[18] In short, public policies are those produced by government officials and agencies.

It would be helpful now to consider some of the implications of my concept of public policy as a relatively stable, purposive course of action followed by government in dealing with some problem or matter of concern. First, the definition links policy to purposive or goal-oriented action rather than to random behavior or chance occurrences. Public policies in modern political systems do not, by and large, just happen. They are instead designed to accomplish specified goals or produce definite results, although these are not always achieved. Proposed policies may be usefully thought of as hypotheses suggesting that specific actions be taken to achieve particular goals. Thus, to increase farm income, the national government utilizes income subsidies and production controls. These programs have indeed enhanced the incomes of many farmers, but not all.

In actuality, the goals of a policy may be somewhat loosely stated and cloudy in content, thus providing general direction rather than precise targets for its implementation. Those who want action on a problem may differ both as to what should be done and how it should be done. Ambiguity in language then can become a means for reducing conflict, at least for the moment. Compromise to secure agreement and build support may consequently yield general phrasing and lack of clarity in the statement of policy goals.

Second, policies consist of courses or patterns of action taken over time by governmental officials rather than their separate, discrete decisions. It is difficult to think of such actions as a presidential decision to honor a movie actor or a Social Security Administration decision to award disability benefits to Joe Doaks as public policies. A policy includes not only the decision to adopt a law or make a rule on some topic but also the subsequent decisions that are intended to enforce or implement the law or rule. Industrial health and safety policy, for example, is shaped not only by the Occupational Safety and Health Act of 1970 but also by a stream of administrative rules and judicial decisions interpreting, elaborating, and applying (or not applying) the act to particular situations.

Third, public policies emerge in response to *policy demands*, or those claims for action or inaction on some public issue made by other actors—private citizens, group representatives, or legislators and other public officials—upon government officials and agencies. Such demands may range from general insistence that a municipal government "do something" about traffic congestion to a specific call for the national government to prohibit theft of pet dogs and cats for sale to medical and scientific research organizations. In short, some demands simply call for action; others also specify the action desired.

In response to policy demands, public officials make decisions that give content and direction to public policy. These decisions may enact statutes, issue executive orders or edicts, promulgate administrative rules, or make judicial interpretations of laws. Thus the decision by Congress to enact the Sherman Antitrust Act in 1890 was a policy decision; another was the 1911 Supreme Court ruling that the act prohibited only unreasonable restraints of trade rather than all restraints of trade. Each was of major importance in shaping that course of action called antitrust policy. (The Sherman Act also prohibits monopolization and attempts to monopolize.) Such decisions may be contrasted with the innumerable relatively routine decisions that officials make in the day-to-day application of public policy. The Department of Veterans Affairs, for example, makes hundreds of thousands of decisions every year on veterans' benefits; most, however, fall within the bounds of settled policy and can be categorized as routine decisions.
DEF.

Policy statements in turn are formal expressions or articulations of public policy. Among these are legislative statutes, executive orders and decrees, administrative rules and regulations, and court opinions, as well as statements and speeches by public officials indicating the government's intentions and goals and what will be done to realize them. Policy statements are sometimes notably ambiguous. Witness the conflicts that arise over the meaning of statutory provisions or judicial holdings, or the time and effort expended analyzing and trying to divine the meaning of policy statements by national political leaders, such as the president of the United States or the chair of the Federal Reserve Board. Different levels, branches, or units of government may also issue conflicting policy statements, as on such matters as environmental pollution or liability for consumer products.

A. Fourth, policy involves what governments actually do, not just what they intend to do or what they say they are going to do. If a legislature enacts a law requiring employers to pay no less than a stated minimum wage but nothing is done to enforce the law, and subsequently little change occurs in economic behavior, it seems reasonable to contend that public policy actually takes the form of nonregulation of wages.

A concept of relevance here is that of *policy output,* or the action actually taken in pursuance of policy decisions and statements. This concept focuses *DEF*
our attention on such matters as amounts of taxes collected, miles of highway built, welfare benefits paid, restraints of trade eliminated, traffic fines collected, and foreign-aid projects undertaken. These can usually be enumerated with little difficulty. Examining policy outputs, we may find that a policy *DEF.*
differs somewhat or even greatly from what policy statements indicate it should be. Policy outputs should be distinguished from *policy outcomes,* which focus on a policy's societal consequences. For example, do longer prison terms reduce crime rates?

5.   Fifth, a public policy may be either positive or negative. Some form of overt governmental action may deal with a problem on which action is demanded (positive), or governmental officials may decide to do nothing on some matter on which government involvement was sought (negative). In other words, governments can follow a policy of laissez-faire, or hands off, either generally or on some aspects of economic activity. Such inaction may have major consequences for a society or some groups, as in the late 1970s, when the national government decided to cease regulating commercial airline rates and routes.

Inaction becomes a public policy when officials decline to act on a problem—that is, when they decide an issue negatively. This choice differs from nonaction on a matter that has not become a public issue, has not been brought to official attention, and has not been considered or debated. A slightly ludicrous example is the lack of governmental action on the taking of earthworms—the activity has no seasons and no bag limits. Is this a public policy? The answer is no, because it is not an issue and no decisions have been made.

6.   Finally, public policy, at least in its positive form, is based on law and is authoritative. Members of a society usually accept as legitimate the facts that taxes must be paid, import controls must be obeyed, and highway speed limits must be complied with, unless one wants to run the risk of fines, jail sentences, or other legally imposed sanctions or disabilities. Thus public policy has an authoritative, legally coercive quality that the policies of private organizations do not have. Indeed, a major characteristic distinguishing government from private organizations is the monopoly over the legitimate use of coercion. Governments can legally incarcerate people; private organizations cannot.

Some public policies may be widely violated even though they are authoritative, such as national prohibition in the 1920s and the 55-mile-an-hour speed limit today in some states. Moreover, enforcement may be limited, piecemeal, or sporadic. Are these still public policies? The answer is yes, because they either were or currently are on the statute books and enforcement was provided for. Whether such policies are effective or wise is another matter. Authoritativeness is a necessary but not a sufficient condition for effective public policy.

CATEGORIES OF PUBLIC POLICIES

Governments at all levels in the United States—national, state, and local—have been increasingly active in developing public policies. Every year a large volume of laws and ordinances flows from the nation's national, state, and local legislative bodies. That volume of laws in turn is greatly exceeded by the

TABLE 1.1 Major Congressional Legislation, 1994

Improving America's Schools Act
Bankruptcy Reform Act
Uruguay Round Agreements Act
Veteran Benefits Improvement Act
California Desert Protection Act
Federal Acquisition Streamlining Act (on government purchasing practices)
Interstate Banking and Branching Efficiency Act
Violent Crime Control and Law Enforcement Act
Community Development and Regulatory Improvement Act
Social Security Independence and Program Improvements Act
Independent Counsel Reauthorization Act
Goals 2000: Educate America Act
School-to-Work Opportunities Act
Department of Agriculture Reorganization Act

Source: U.S. Statutes at Large, 1994.

quantity of rules and regulations produced by administrative agencies acting on the basis of legislative authorizations. This proliferation of public policies has occurred in such traditional areas of governmental action as foreign policy, transportation, education, welfare, law enforcement, business and labor regulation, and international trade. Much activity has also come in areas that received little attention until the last two or three decades: economic stability, environmental protection, equality of opportunity, medical care, nuclear energy, and consumer protection.

In 1994, Congress adopted more than 200 public laws. Some of the major statutes enacted, as measured by such loose criteria as the estimated number of people affected and the likely effect on society and economy, are listed in Table 1.1. The table suggests the varied matters with which Congress deals. Some, such as those involving "improvements," represent changes in or supplements to current policies; others are new additions to the collection of public policies. All the policies incorporate biases that favor some groups and disadvantage others in varying degrees, which is indeed an intrinsic characteristic of public policies. Few public policies make everybody better off.

Given the large number and complexity of public policies in the United States, the task of trying to make sense of them is enormous. I summarize in this section a number of general typologies that political scientists and others have developed for categorizing public policies. These typologies will prove much more useful in distinguishing among and generalizing about policies than some of the more traditional and widely used categorization schemes, such as by issue area (labor, welfare, civil rights, and foreign affairs), institution (legislative policies, judicial policies, and departmental policies), and time (New Deal era, post–World War II, and late nineteenth century). Although the latter categories are convenient for designating various sets of policies and organizing discussions about them, they are not helpful in developing generalizations, because they do not reflect the basic characteristics and content of policies. The discussion of typologies should also provide the reader with a notion of the scope, diversity, and different purposes of public policies.

Substantive and Procedural Policies

First, policies may be classified as either substantive or procedural. Substantive policies involve what government is going to do, such as constructing highways, paying welfare benefits, acquiring bombers, or prohibiting the retail sale of liquor. Substantive policies directly distribute to people advantages and disadvantages, benefits and costs. Procedural policies, in contrast, pertain to how something is going to be done or who is going to take action. So defined, procedural policies include laws providing for the creation of administrative agencies, determining the matters over which they have jurisdiction, specifying the processes and techniques that they can use in carrying out their programs, and providing for presidential, judicial, and other controls over their operations.

A procedural policy of great importance is the federal Administrative Procedure Act (APA) of 1946. This statute, a response to the growth of administrative agency discretion in the twentieth century, prescribes procedures to be used by agencies in notice and comment or informal rule-making. For example, APA requires notice of the proposed rule-making, opportunity for interested persons to participate in the proceeding through oral or written submissions, publication of a proposed rule at least thirty days before it becomes effective, and opportunity for interested persons to petition for issuance, amendment, or repeal of a rule. The act's requirements for adjudication are much more detailed, but in both instances it is intended to ensure fairness in agency decision-making. Another example of a procedural policy is the requirement that an environmental impact statement be prepared by agencies proposing major actions affecting the environment by the National Environmental Policy Act (NEPA). Its purpose is to cause agencies to give consideration to environmental effects before making their decisions. In itself NEPA adds nothing to the substance of policy; it neither prohibits nor requires particular agency actions toward the environment.

Procedural policies may have important substantive consequences. That is, how something is done or who takes the action may help determine what is actually done. See Chapter 6 for a number of propositions on the possible influence of organizational decisions on substantive policy. Frequently, efforts are made to use procedural issues to delay or prevent adoption of substantive decisions and policies. An agency's action may be challenged on the ground that improper procedures were followed, as under APA, when it is really the substance of the action that is being resisted. Some Washington lawyers have become highly skilled in manipulating procedural rules to delay agency action. Thus, because of procedural delays and complications (most of them produced by the maneuverings of the defendant company), it took the Federal Trade Commission thirteen years to complete a case compelling the manufacturer to remove the word "liver" from a product named "Carter's Little Liver Pills." (The product has no effect on one's liver.)

Distributive, Regulatory, Self-Regulatory, and Redistributive Policies

This typology differentiates policies by their effect on society and the relationships among those involved in policy formation.[19]

Distributive policies involve allocation of services or benefits to particular segments of the population—individuals, groups, corporations, and communities. Some distributive policies may provide benefits to one or a few beneficiaries, as in the Chrysler loan guarantee of the late 1970s, which kept the company from bankruptcy, and the subsidies for the operation of American merchant ships. Others may provide benefits for vast numbers of persons, as is true for agricultural income-support programs, tax deductions for home mortgage interest payments, free public school education, and job-training programs.

Distributive policies typically involve using public funds to assist particular groups, communities, or industries. Those who seek benefits usually do not compete directly with one another, although in some instances they do, as in the selection of the site for the Superconducting Super Collider, where there could be only one winner. Nor do their benefits represent a direct cost to any specific group; rather, the costs are assessed to the public treasury, which is to say all taxpayers. Thus, distributive policies appear to create only winners and no specific losers, although obviously someone does pay their financial cost.

A standard example of distributive policy involves the rivers and harbors improvement and flood control legislation, customarily referred to as pork-barrel legislation, carried out by the Army Corps of Engineers. In 1986, Congress authorized construction of 262 projects for such purposes as port development, flood control, water supply, and control of beach erosion. Approximately three-quarters of the estimated cost of $16.3 billion was assigned to the national government, with the remainder to be paid by local governments and users of the projects.[20]

These projects are scattered all around the country and have little connection with one another, which supports Professor Theodore J. Lowi's contention that distributive policies "are virtually not policies at all but are highly individualized decisions that only by accumulation can be called a policy."[21] Each locality and its supporters seek authorization and funding for their own project without challenging the right of others to do likewise. Most projects consequently have some friends and no enemies in Congress, and presidents usually leave them alone. President Jimmy Carter upset the apple cart in 1977, when he successfully eliminated some water projects on the ground that they were wasteful and unnecessary. Many members of Congress were antagonized by this action, either because they favored the targeted projects or resented presidential intervention in an area long under congressional domination. A few of the projects later were restored.

Regulatory policies impose restrictions or limitations on the behavior of individuals and groups. That is, they reduce the freedom or discretion to act of those who are regulated, whether bankers, utility companies, meat-packers, or saloon-keepers. In this sense they clearly differ from distributive policies, which increase the freedom or discretion of the persons or groups affected.

When we think of regulatory policies we usually focus on business regulatory policies, such as those pertaining to control of pollution or regulation of transportation industries. Among others, these sorts of policies were the focus of the movement for deregulation. The most extensive variety of regulatory policies, however, is that which deals with criminal behavior against persons and property. What are called social regulatory policies deal with such topics as affirmative action, school prayer, gun control, pornography, and abortion.[22]

The formation of regulatory policy usually features conflict between two groups or coalitions of groups, with one side seeking to impose some sort of control on the other side, which customarily resists, arguing either that control is unnecessary or that the wrong kind of control is being proposed. Amid this opposition, regulatory decisions involve clear winners and losers, although the winners usually get less than they initially sought. (When the winners are public interest groups, they may not gain direct material benefits from policies which, like the Clean Air Act, provide broad social benefits.) It is often difficult, however, to identify all the purposes and consequences of regulatory policies. Let us consider how regulatory policies vary.

Some regulatory policies set forth general rules of behavior, directing that actions be taken or commanding that others not be taken. The Sherman Act in effect tells businesses, "Thou shalt not monopolize or attempt to monopolize or act to restrain trade." These prohibitions are enforced by actions brought in the federal courts against violators. In contrast, public-utility regulation handled by state governments involves detailed control of entry into the business, standards of service, financial practices, and rates charged by electric, telephone, and other utility companies. Comparatively, antitrust regulation entails much less restriction of business discretion than does public-utility regulation.

Consumer-protection policies illustrate other variations in regulatory policies. Some statutes, such as the Pure Food and Drug Act of 1906 and the Drug Amendments of 1962, set standards for quality that drug manufacturers must comply with. Thus, before new drugs can be put on the market, they must be shown to meet the standards for safety in use and efficacy for the purposes intended. Other consumer legislation, such as the Consumer Credit Protection Act of 1968, requires creditors to provide borrowers with accurate information on interest and other financing costs for credit purchases. The first sort of policy is intended to prevent products that do not meet designated standards from entering the marketplace; the second type is meant to provide consumers with enough information to make informed decisions.

Some regulatory policies, such as those which restrict entry into a business such as television broadcasting or electric power distribution, are implemented by decisions that confer benefits on some and deny them to others. Of the several applicants for a television broadcast license for a city that may be before the Federal Communications Commission, only one can be propitiated. Here, Lowi states, "regulatory policies are distinguishable from distributive in that in the short run the regulatory decision involves a direct choice as to who will be indulged and who deprived."[23] Decisions are also made by applying some kind of general rule to particular institutions.

Self-regulatory policies are similar to regulatory policies in that they involve restricting or controlling some matter or group. Unlike regulatory policies, however, self-regulatory policies are usually sought and supported by the regulated group as a means of protecting or promoting the interests of its members. Several hundred professions and occupations, ranging from tree surgeons and auctioneers to lawyers and physicians, are licensed in one or more states; about sixty are licensed in a majority of states. Commonly licensed health professionals include chiropractors, dentists, dental hygienists, emergency medical technicians, optometrists, pharmacists, physicians, podiatrists, practical and registered nurses, psychologists, sanitarians, and social workers.[24]

The usual policymaking pattern here is for a professional or occupational group acting on its own to seek licensing legislation from the state legislature. Outside the ranks of the interested group, interest in the matter usually is slight. The result is enactment of a licensing law, whose implementation is delegated to a board dominated by members from the licensed group. In time, entry into the licensed occupation or profession may be restricted and the prices charged for its specialized services may increase. It is unclear to what extent licensing improves the quality of services available to the public.[25]

Supervised self-regulation may also occur. Under the Agricultural Marketing Agreement Act of 1937, the producers and handlers of fruits, vegetables, and specialty crops such as almonds sold on the fresh market collectively act to obtain marketing orders from the Agricultural Marketing Service (AMS).

Put into effect with the approval of two-thirds of the producers of a commodity, these orders are binding on all producers and may authorize research and promotional programs, set standards for quality, and control movement of such products as oranges and grapefruit to market so as to ensure "orderly marketing." Marketing orders, which are managed by producer-dominated administrative committees and are subject to AMS supervision, are intended to improve the economic situation of producers.[26]

Redistributive policies involve deliberate efforts by the government to shift the allocation of wealth, income, property, or rights among broad classes or groups of the population, such as haves and have-nots, proletariat and bourgeoisie. "The aim involved is not use of property but property itself, not equal treatment but equal possession, not behavior but being."[27] In American society redistributive policies ultimately involve disagreements between liberals (pro) and conservatives (con) and tend to be highly productive of conflict.

The usual pattern in redistributive policy shifts resources from haves to have-nots. It is possible, however, for the flow to reverse. Farm subsidy payments under the agricultural price-support programs go mostly to large commercial farmers; small-scale farmers derive few benefits, yet everyone who pays taxes contributes to financing of the programs. Typically, however, such instances are not debated as redistributive,[28] perhaps because of reluctance to acknowledge that sometimes the haves benefit at the expense of the have-nots.

Redistributive policies are difficult to enact because they involve the reallocation of money, rights, or power. Those who possess money or power rarely yield them willingly, regardless of how strenuously some may discourse upon the "burdens" and heavy responsibility attending their possession. Because money and power are good coinage in the political realm, those who possess them have ample means to resist their diminution.

Policies that have (or have had) some redistributive influence include the graduated income tax, Medicare and Medicaid, the War on Poverty, the Voting Rights Act, and legislative reapportionment. The Johnson administration's War on Poverty represented an effort to shift wealth and other resources to blacks and poor people. Encountering much resistance from conservatives and lacking strong presidential support, it was gradually dispersed and dismantled. Although most of the individual antipoverty programs (such as Head Start and the community action or service programs) still function, they have lost much of their redistributive quality. The Voting Rights Act, which on the whole has been enforced with considerable strength by the Justice Department, has helped to produce a substantial increase in black voter registration, voting, and state and local officeholding in the South.

The graduated income tax, which is based on the principle of ability to pay (those who have more income can fairly be expected to pay at progressively higher rates) has now lost much of its redistributive potential. The top marginal rate once was as high as 91 percent. In the early 1980s the rates ranged from 14 to 50 percent over a dozen income brackets, which still held out the possibility of considerable redistribution. The Tax Reform Act of 1986, enacted by Congress with strong support from President Reagan, who believed that high marginal tax rates both infringed on individual liberty and discouraged economic growth, provided for only two tax brackets at 15 and 28 percent. Brackets of 31, 36, and 39.6 percent were added in the 1990s, however. Whether rates will stay at these levels will depend partly upon the government's future revenue needs.[29] Low marginal tax rates do, however, have much political appeal.

Redistributive policies are not only difficult to obtain, they are also hard to retain, as my discussion of the income tax indicates. Equality of result or condition (that is, equality in income or standard of living) is not overly appealing to most Americans, whatever they think about equality of opportunity.

Material and Symbolic Policies

Public policies may also be described as either material or symbolic, depending upon the kind of benefits they allocate.[30] Material policies actually either provide tangible resources or substantive power to their beneficiaries, or impose real disadvantages on those who are adversely affected. Legislation requiring employers to pay a prescribed minimum wage, appropriating money for a public-housing program, or providing income-support payments to farmers is material in content and effect.

Symbolic policies, in contrast, have little real material impact on people. They do not deliver what they appear to deliver; they allocate no tangible advantages and disadvantages. Rather, they appeal to people's cherished values, such as peace, patriotism, and social justice. A prime example of a symbolic policy is the Kellogg-Briand Pact of 1928, by which the United States and fourteen other countries agreed to outlaw war. Comment on its impact seems unnecessary.

Burning of the United States flag as a symbolic form of political protest has agitated members of Congress for several years. In 1989 the Flag Protection Act provided criminal penalties for any person who "knowingly mutilates, defaces, physically defiles, burns, maintains on the floor or ground, or tramples upon any flag of the United States." Quickly challenged, the act was declared unconstitutional by the U.S. Supreme Court as an infringement on the freedom of expression protected by the first amendment. The Court's ruling touched off a public and political furor. An effort in the early 1990s to amend the Constitution to prohibit desecration of the flag failed. However, in 1995, the House, stimulated by the new Republican majority, approved (312 to 120) an amendment authorizing the national and state governments to ban "physical desecration of the flag of the United States."[31] There is much symbolism at stake in this struggle.

Occasionally a policy that appears to be mostly symbolic may turn out to have important consequences. The Endangered Species Act of 1973, which is intended to help ensure the survival of rare animals and plants, initially appeared to be a statement of good intentions with few costs. Little opposition attended its enactment. As implemented, however, the act has had important effects, sometimes being used to block construction projects, timber cutting, and other activities that would threaten or destroy the habitats of endangered species, such as spotted owls and California gnatcatchers.

Most policies are neither entirely symbolic nor wholly material. The symbolic and material categories should instead be viewed as the poles of a continuum, with most policies being ranged along the continuum depending upon how symbolic or material they are in practice. The Sherman Act, as an instrument for "trust busting," for breaking up large monopolistic companies, has long been symbolic. With the exception of AT&T, no trusts have been broken up since the Progressive Era. On the other hand, beginning with the Carter administration and continuing on into the Clinton administration, the Sherman Act has been applied with some vigor against collusive behavior such as price fixing, bid rigging, and market allocation. Here it has had substantial material impact.

Policies that are ostensibly material as labeled by legislative language may be rendered essentially symbolic by administrative action or by the legislature's failure to provide adequate funds for their implementation. The public-housing goals of the Housing Act of 1949 and later laws were made substantially symbolic by the subsequent failure of Congress to provide the authorized level of funding for housing construction.[32] On the other hand, policies may move from the more symbolic to the more material category. Professor Bruce I. Oppenheimer argues that policy for controlling oil pollution was largely symbolic during the years 1947 to 1966.[33] Legislation was on the books but little was done to enforce it. After 1966, the control of oil pollution became much more effective as a consequence of growing public concern about pollution, increased enforcement activity, and additional congressional legislation, such as the 1986 Oil Pollution Act.

The material–symbolic typology is especially useful to keep in mind when analyzing effects of policy because it directs our attention beyond formal policy statements. It also alerts us to the important role of symbols in political behavior.

Policies Involving Collective Goods or Private Goods

Public policies may also involve the provision of either collective (indivisible) goods or private (divisible) goods.[34] The nature of collective goods is such that

DEF.

if they are provided for one person, they must be provided for all. A standard example is national defense: there is no effective way to provide it for some citizens and exclude others from its benefit, enjoyment, or other consequences, nor to calculate that some citizens benefit more from it than others. Thus, an economically rational person would never voluntarily pay for national defense, choosing rather to be a free rider and let others stand the costs. Hence defense must be provided, if we want it, by government and financed by taxation. Other examples of collective goods are clean air, public safety, traffic control, and mosquito abatement.

Private goods, in contrast, may be broken into units and purchased or charged by the individual user or beneficiary, and are available in the marketplace. Others may be excluded from their use. Various social goods provided by government (garbage collection, postal service, medical care, museums, public housing, and national parks) have some characteristics of private goods. Charges and fees are sometimes, but not always, levied on users. Whether such goods, which conceivably could be provided by the market economy, will be provided by the government is a function of political decisions influenced by tradition (parks), notions of the proper functions of government (the post office), the desire of users or beneficiaries to shift some of their costs to others (federal crop insurance), and the like.

Some might still argue that only collective goods should be the subject of public policy. The tendency, however, has been more and more to convert private goods into social goods by government action. Many consider ill health, unemployment, environmental pollution, industrial accidents and disease, and misrepresentation in the marketplace to be collective rather than individual problems—matters affecting the entire population, hence involving public goods for which the entire society should pay. Generally, the more something is thought to have the qualities of a public good, the more likely people are to accept its provision by government. If it seems clear that some benefit more directly than others, there may also be a desire to levy charges, fees, or taxes on the direct beneficiaries to cover part of the cost. Thus we encounter user fees at national parks, tuition at public colleges, rent in public-housing projects, and tolls for some bridges and highways.

The privatization movement, encouraged in the 1980s by the Reagan administration, represented a counterforce to the long-run tendency to expand the scope of social goods. Based on free-market economic theory, privatization supports transferring many government assets or programs to the private sector and contracting with private companies to handle many public services, whether the collection of garbage or the operation of prisons. "The private sector, it is argued, will perform these functions more efficiently and economically than the public sector."[35]

The results of the privatization movement at the national level are mixed. A successful example is the sale of Conrail, which operated several railroads in the Northeast and Midwest, to a private corporation. Nothing, however, came out of proposals by the Reagan administration and others to sell public lands in the western states to private buyers.[36] Even western ranchers and other supporters of the "sagebrush rebellion," which promoted transferring ownership of public lands to state and local governments, lost interest in privatization. Their access to public grazing lands with low lease rates would have been jeopardized by privatization. Congress was also quite skeptical about the sale of public lands.

Liberal and Conservative Policies

Finally, discussions of public policies are frequently conducted in the format of liberals versus conservatives. These labels, however, are slippery and difficult to define. Just what distinguishes "liberal" from "conservative"? Lowi argues that in the latter part of the nineteenth century and the early years of the twentieth it was possible to make a fairly precise distinction.[37] Generally, liberals favored using government to bring about social change, usually in the direction of greater equality, whether of political power or economic well-being. Conservatives, in turn, were opposed to using government for such purposes, if not always in disagreement with the purposes themselves. Liberals spoke of the need for public policies to correct injustices and shortcomings in the existing social order. Conservatives either found the current order satisfactory or contended that change should occur slowly and gradually by "natural" social processes. By and large, those who advocated economic regulatory programs were liberals. Conservatives supplied the opposition. Later, when welfare programs became an issue, support for them came from liberals, resistance from conservatives.

Lowi contends, however, that by the late 1960s the traditional distinction between liberals and conservatives had broken down. "The old dialogue has passed into the graveyard of consensus. Yet it persists. Old habits die hard. Its persistence despite its irrelevance means that the liberal–conservative debate has become almost purely ritualistic."[38] The nineteenth-century notion of a minimal government that would "do only those things people could not do better for themselves" (and not many things were put in this category) has been replaced by positive government, by government with extensive responsibilities for meeting human needs and problems. The traditional criteria thus no longer neatly distinguish between liberals and conservatives.

The disappearance of the traditional liberal–conservative distinction is illustrated by Table 1.2. Government ("liberal") policies are located above the centerline; private ("conservative") policies are located below it. Policies that are likely to produce change ("liberal") are toward the left side of the table; those tending to maintain current practices ("conservative") are toward the right side. Were the old criteria involving attitudes toward using government and promoting change still determinative, liberal policies would be concentrated in the upper left corner of the table and conservative policies would be

TABLE 1.2   Selected Public and Private Policies Arranged According to Their Probable Effect on Society

Voting Rights Act	Affirmative Action	Job-training programs	Sales taxes	Social Security	Farm price supports	Import quotas
Low tarriffs	Graduated income tax	Pell grants	Aid to small business	Monetary policy	Occupational licensing	No "trust busting"
Trucking deregulation	Air-pollution regulation	Merit systems	Motor-vehicle licensing	Defense contracting	Taxicab regulation	Public-utility regulation
	Head Start program	Inheritance taxes	Railroad-safety regulation		Land-use zoning	
		Medical research				
Competition in agriculture	Competitive business (e.g., computers)	High interest rates	Brand-name advertising	Price leadership in industry	Collusive behavior	
Public-interest groups	Equal-opportunity employers	Limitations on medical advertising	Oligopolistic industry (e.g., tobacco)	Trade associations	"Old boy" hiring practices	
Discount pricing	Health maintenance organizations	Redlining on bank loans	Patent infringement litigation	Vertical price maintenance	Non-portable fringe benefits	
			Airline hub-and-spoke systems			

Above the line: Public policies ("liberal")
Below the line: Private policies ("conservative")
Toward the left: Policies likely to produce change ("liberal")
Toward the right: Policies likely to maintain the status quo ("conservative")

Source: Adapted from Theodore J. Lowi, *The End of Liberalism: The Second Republic of the United States,* 2nd ed. (New York: W. W. Norton, 1979), p. 45.

nested at the lower right corner. This is not the configuration one sees, however, for both public and private policies range from left to right across the table; both may be used either to promote or to restrict change. In other words, government is variously used for both "liberal" and "conservative" purposes—that is, both to promote and to restrict change. The same is true for private policies or actions. This is the basis for Lowi's conclusion that the traditional distinction between liberals and conservatives no longer is valid.

Admittedly, Table 1.2 is somewhat impressionistic. A couple of conclusions about public policies can, however, be derived from it. Public policies can be either productive of change or designed to help maintain the current order. Vigorous programs for equal employment opportunity are designed to bring about change and protective tariffs help maintain the status quo. Public policies can also derive their support from either liberal or conservative officials and groups. In the nineteenth century, conservatives were not opposed to all uses of government for economic purposes. Protective tariffs and governmental action to restrain labor unions drew support mostly from conservatives, who in other instances might claim laissez-faire as the best policy. An element of pragmatism has always colored the actions of most conservatives and liberals when they are advancing the interests of groups that they favor.

This proclivity leads Lowi to another contention: "The most important difference between liberals and conservatives, Republicans and Democrats—however they define themselves—is to be found in the interest groups they identify with."[39] Whether one identifies with the interests of business or labor, the well-to-do or the poor, the "establishment" or ethnic minorities, is what really matters. Support for one or another of these groups can be based on principle, whether it involves a desire for greater equality, the need to ameliorate social conflict, or a wish to maintain the status quo. Principles, to be legitimate, do not need to be accepted as proper or appropriate by all, nor do they have to be adhered to in any and every case. Relatively few of us are constant, consistent ideologues, whether our ideology is described as conservative, neoconservative, liberal, libertarian, or socialist. In short, if we can say something like "conservatives tend to support policies, public or private, which advance the interests of business, and liberals tend to favor policies that protect the interests of consumers and minorities," we have said something meaningful.

The great changes that have occurred in our society and economy during the past century, and especially since the 1930s, make it clear why the liberal–conservative conflict shifted away from the issue of whether there should be governmental intervention and toward the issues of when intervention should occur, in what form, and on whose behalf. Sociologist Robert McIver states,

> Wherever technology advances, wherever private business extends its range, wherever the cultural life becomes more complex, new tasks are imposed

upon government. This happens apart from, or in spite of, the particular philosophies that governments cherish. . . . In the longer run the tasks undertaken by the governments are dictated by changing conditions, and governments on the whole are more responsive than creative in fulfilling them.[40]

The Reagan administration took office in 1981 with the goal of substantially reducing the national government's role in the economic life of the nation. Though the administration had some initial success in securing adoption of its economic program, resistance grew with time, especially in the Democratic-controlled House. Although President Reagan was overwhelmingly reelected in 1984, the Republicans lost control of the Senate in 1986, further contributing to Reagan's political difficulties.

During its eight years in office, the Reagan administration was most successful in altering national tax policies. (It also had success, especially in its early years, in increasing defense spending.) For the most part, the administration was able to make only limited or marginal changes in domestic policies. Most of the major economic deregulatory legislation (as for airlines and railroads) that has been enacted came during the Carter years. Sweeping changes in domestic public policies and governmental intervention in the economy, such as those in the 1930s during the New Deal, usually require major changes in the distribution of political power in society. This shift did not occur in the 1980s. As a consequence, McIver's viewpoint still seems valid.

APPROACHES TO POLICY STUDY

Political and social scientists have developed many models, theories, approaches, concepts, and schemes for analyzing policymaking and its related component, decision-making. Indeed, political scientists have often displayed more facility and verve for theorizing about public policymaking than for actually studying policy and the policymaking process. Nonetheless, theories and concepts are needed to guide the study of public policy, to facilitate communication, and to suggest possible explanations for policy actions. Those who aspire to systematically study the policymaking process need some guidelines and criteria of relevance to focus their effort and to prevent aimless meandering through the fields of political data. What we find when we engage in research depends partly upon what we are looking for; policy concepts, models, and theories give direction and structure to our inquiry.

In this section I will survey several theoretical approaches to the study of public policy. But first we must distinguish between policymaking and decision-making, a distinction students of public policy do not always see with clarity, if at all. Decision-making, which will be treated in Chapter 4, involves making a discrete choice from among two or more alternatives, such as whether or not to read further in this book. Theories of decision-making deal with the criteria and processes used in making such choices. A policy, as I defined it earlier, is "a relatively stable, purposive course of action followed by an actor or set of actors in dealing with a problem or matter of concern." Policymaking thus typically encompasses a flow and pattern of action that extends over time and includes many decisions, some routine and some not so routine. Rarely will a policy be synonymous with a single decision. Here is a mundane illustration: it would not be accurate for a person to state that it was his policy to bathe on Saturday nights, if in fact he did so infrequently, however elegant and thoughtful the decision-making process that led to his doing so on a rare Saturday. It is the course of action, the pattern or regularity, that defines policy, not an isolated event. In the example, the policy is best thought of as going dirty.

The theoretical approaches discussed here include political systems theory, group theory, elite theory, institutionalism, and rational-choice theory. Although most of these approaches were not developed specifically for analyzing policy formation, they can readily be bent to that purpose. They are useful to the extent that they direct our attention to important political phenomena, help clarify and organize our thinking, and suggest explanations for political activity or, in our case, public policies. Limitations and criticisms are mentioned as the discussion proceeds.

Political Systems Theory

Public policy may be viewed as a political system's response to demands arising from its environment. The political system, as Easton defines it, comprises those identifiable and interrelated institutions and activities (what we usually think of as governmental institutions and political processes) in a society that make authoritative allocations of values (decisions) that are binding on society. The environment consists of all phenomena—the social system, the economic system, the biological setting—that are external to the boundaries of the political system. Thus at least analytically one can separate the political system from all the other components of a society.[41]

Inputs into the political system from the environment consist of demands and supports. Demands are the claims for action that individuals and groups make to satisfy their interests and values. Support is rendered when groups and individuals abide by election results, pay taxes, obey laws, and otherwise accept the decisions and actions undertaken by the political system in response to demands. The amount of support for a political system indicates the extent to which it is regarded as legitimate, or as authoritative and binding on its citizens.

Outputs of the political system include laws, rules, judicial decisions, and the like. Regarded as the authoritative allocations of values, they constitute

FIGURE 1.1   A Model of the Political System

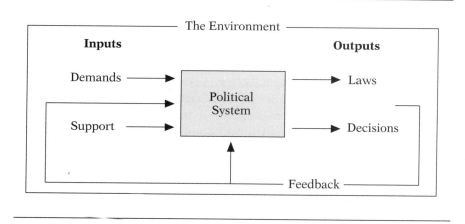

public policy. The concept of feedback indicates that public policies (or outputs) made at a given time may subsequently alter the environment and the demands arising therefrom, as well as the character of the political system itself. Policy outputs may produce new demands, which lead to further outputs, and so on in a never-ending flow of public policy (see Figure 1.1).

The usefulness of systems theory in studying public policy is limited by its highly general and abstract nature. It does not, moreover, say much about the procedures and processes by which decisions are made and policy is developed within the "black box" called the political system. Indeed, systems theory depicts government as simply responding to demands made upon it, and its results are sometimes characterized as "input-output studies." (For an illustration, see the discussion on p. 57). Nonetheless, this approach can be helpful in organizing inquiry into policy formation. It also alerts us to some important facets of the political process, such as these: How do inputs from the environment affect the content of public policy and the operation of the political system? How in turn does public policy affect the environment and subsequent demands for policy action? How well is the political system able to convert demands into public policy and preserve itself over time?

2. Group Theory

According to the group theory of politics, public policy is the product of the group struggle. One writer states, "What may be called public policy is the equilibrium reached in this [group] struggle at any given moment, and it represents a balance which the contending factions or groups constantly strive to weight in their favor."[42] Many public policies do reflect the activities of groups. Examples include the AFL-CIO and minimum-wage legislation, farm groups and agricultural subsidies, the National Rifle Association and gun-control policies, and the National Education Association and federal aid to public schools.

Group theory rests on the contention that interaction and struggle among groups are the central facts of political life. A group is a collection of individuals that may, on the basis of shared attitudes or interests, make claims upon other groups in society. It becomes a political interest group "when it makes a claim through or upon any of the institutions of government."[43] And many groups do just that. The individual is significant in politics only as a participant in or a representative of groups. It is through groups that individuals seek to secure their political preferences.

A main concept in group theory is that of access. To have influence and to be able to help shape governmental decisions, a group must have access, or the opportunity to express its viewpoints to decision-makers.[44] Obviously, if a group is unable to communicate with decision-makers, if no one in government will listen to it, the chances that it will be able to affect policymaking are slim. Access may result from the group's being organized, from its having status, good leadership, or resources such as money for campaign contributions. Social lobbying—the wining, dining, and entertaining of legislators and other public officials—can be understood as an effort to create access by engendering a feeling of obligation to the groups involved. Then, when a group wishes to discuss policy matters with an official, it will have an opportunity to present its case. Contributions to legislators by political action committees (PAC) are also often justified as a way of acquiring or maintaining access.

In the nature of things, some groups will have more access than others. Public policy at any given time will reflect the interests of those who are dominant. As groups gain and lose power and influence, public policy will be altered in favor of the interests of those gaining influence against the interests of those losing it.

The role of government ("official groups") in policy formation is described by one proponent of group theory:

> The legislature referees the group struggle, ratifies the victories of the successful coalitions, and records the terms of the surrenders, compromises, and conquests in the form of statutes. Every statute tends to represent compromises because the process of accommodating conflicts of group interests is one of deliberation and consent. The legislative vote on any issue tends to represent the composition of strength, i.e., the balance of power, among the contending groups at the moment of voting. . . . Administrative agencies of the regulatory kind are established to carry out the terms of the treaties that the legislators have negotiated and ratified. . . . The judiciary, like the civilian

bureaucracy, is one of the instrumentalities for the administration of the agreed rules.[45]

Group theory focuses on one of the major dynamic elements in policy formation, especially in pluralist societies such as the United States, but it seems both to overstate the importance of groups and to understate the independent and creative role that public officials can play in the policy process. Indeed, many groups have been generated by public policies. The American Farm Bureau Federation, which developed around the agricultural extension program, is a notable example, as is the National Welfare Rights Organization. Public officials also may acquire a stake in particular programs and act as an interest group supporting their continuance. In the United States some welfare-agency employees, including social workers, prefer current programs, with their emphasis on supervision and services (as well as benefits), to a guaranteed annual income, which would probably eliminate some of their jobs.

Another shortcoming of group theory is that in actuality many people (e.g., the poor and disadvantaged) and interests (such diffuse interests as natural beauty and social justice) are either not represented or only poorly represented in the group struggle. As Professor E. E. Schattschneider remarks about the underorganization of the poor, "The flaw in the pluralist heaven is that the heavenly chorus sings with a strong upper-class accent."[46] Those who are not represented will have little voice in policymaking and thus their interests are likely to be slighted therein.

Finally, from a methodological perspective, it is misleading and inefficient to try to explain politics and policymaking solely in terms of interests and the group struggle. This bias leads to neglect of many other factors, such as ideas and institutions, which abound and which independently affect the development of policy. The reductionism or unicausal explanation that results when all political phenomena are crammed into the group concept should therefore be avoided.

Elite Theory

Approached from the perspective of elite theory, public policy can be regarded as reflecting the values and preferences of a governing elite. The essential argument of elite theory is that public policy is not determined by the demands and actions of the people or the "masses" but rather by a ruling elite whose preferences are carried into effect by public officials and agencies.

Professors Thomas Dye and Harmon Zeigler provide a summary of elite theory:

1. Society is divided into the few who have power and the many who do not. Only a small number of persons allocate values for society; the masses do not decide public policy.
2. The few who govern are not typical of the masses who are governed. Elites are drawn disproportionately from the upper socioeconomic strata of society.
3. The movement of non-elites to elite positions must be slow and continuous to maintain stability and avoid revolution. Only non-elites who have accepted the basic elite consensus can be admitted to governing circles.
4. Elites share a consensus on the basic values of the social system and the preservation of the system. [In the United States, the elite consensus includes private enterprise, private property, limited government, and individual liberty.]
5. Public policy does not reflect demands of the masses but rather the prevailing values of the elite. Changes in public policy will be incremental rather than revolutionary. [Incremental changes permit responses to events that threaten a social system with a minimum of alteration or dislocation of the system.]
6. Active elites are subject to relatively little direct influence from apathetic masses. Elites influence masses more than masses influence elites.[47]

So stated, elite theory is a provocative theory of policy formation. Policy is the product of elites, reflecting their values and serving their ends, one of which may be a desire to provide in some way for the welfare of the masses. Dye argues that development of civil-rights policies in the United States during the 1960s can be suitably explained by elite theory. These policies were "a response of a national elite to conditions affecting a small minority of Americans rather than a response of national leaders to majority sentiments." Thus, for example, the "elimination of legal discrimination and the guarantee of equality of opportunity in the Civil Rights Act of 1964 was achieved largely through the dramatic appeals of middle-class black leaders to the conscience of white elites."[48] This interpretation presents a narrow perspective on both who is affected by or interested in civil-rights policies and the explanation for adoption of the Civil Rights Act of 1964. Certainly leadership in Congress and the executive branch was very important, but so too were civil-rights protests and marches, public opinion, and support from an array of nonblack organizations. The civil-rights movement of the 1960s was far more than an effort by black leaders to appeal to the conscience of white elites.

Elite theory does focus our attention on the role of leadership in policy formation and on the reality that, in any political system, a few govern the many. Whether the elites rule and determine policy, with little influence from the masses, is a difficult proposition to handle. It cannot be proved merely by assertions that the "establishment runs things," which has been a familiar plaint in recent years. Political scientist Robert Dahl argues that to defend the proposition successfully one must identify "a controlling group, less than a majority in size, that is not a pure artifact of democratic rules. . . a minority of individuals whose preferences regularly prevail in cases of differences of preferences on key political issues."[49] It may be that elite theory has more utility for analysis and explanation of policy formation in some political systems, such as developing or Eastern European countries, than in others, such as the pluralist democracies of the United States and Canada. Sociologist William Domhoff has long argued, however, that there is an American upper class, based on the ownership and control of large corporations, which is in fact a governing class.[50]

4. Institutionalism

The study of government institutions (or organizations) is one of the oldest concerns of political science. This is not surprising, since political life generally revolves around governmental institutions such as legislatures, executives, courts, and political parties; public policy, moreover, is authoritatively determined and implemented initially by these institutions.

Traditionally, the institutional approach concentrated on describing the more formal and legal aspects of governmental institutions: their formal structure, legal powers, procedural rules, and functions or activities. Formal relationships with other institutions might also be considered, such as legislative–executive relations. Usually little was done to explain how institutions actually operated as opposed to how they were supposed to operate, to analyze public policies produced by the institutions, or to discover the relationships between institutional structure and public policies.

Subsequently, political scientists turned their attention in teaching and research to the political processes within governmental or political institutions, concentrating on the behavior of participants in the process and on political realities rather than formalism. In the study of the legislatures, interest shifted from simply describing the legislature as an institution to analyzing and explaining its operation over time, from its static to its dynamic aspects. Thus in the academic curriculum the course on the legislature often came to be about the legislative process.

Institutionalism, with its emphasis on the formal or structural aspects of institutions, can nonetheless be usefully employed in policy analysis. An institution is, in part, a set of regularized patterns of human behavior that persist over time and perform some significant social function or activity. It is their differing patterns of behavior that really distinguish courts from legislatures, from administrative agencies, and so on. These regularized patterns of behavior, which we often call rules or structures, and the like, can affect decision-making and the content of public policy. Rules and structural arrangements are usually not neutral in their effects; rather, they tend to favor some interests in society over others and some policy results over others. It is contended that some of the Senate rules (and traditions, which often have the effect of rules), such as those relating to unlimited debate and action by unanimous consent, favor the interests of minorities over majorities. Many actions in the Senate, such as bringing bills up for consideration and closing off debate on them, are done by unanimous consent. Thus one senator, so inclined, can block action by the Senate.

In the American federal system, which allocates governmental power among the national and state governments, several arenas of action are created. Some groups may have more influence if policy is made at the national level, whereas others may benefit more from state policymaking. Civil-rights groups, for example, have received a better response in Washington, D.C., than in the capitals of the southern states. Groups advocating adoption of English as the nation's official language, however, have fared better at the state level. Between 1983 and 1989, seventeen state legislatures enacted such laws, but the Congress was unsympathetic. Indeed, the Voting Rights Act provides that in some states ballots must be printed in foreign languages as well as English.

In summary, institutional structures, arrangements, and procedures often have important consequences for the adoption and content of public policies. They provide part of the context for policymaking, which must be considered along with the more dynamic aspects of politics, such as political parties, groups, and public opinion, in policy study. By itself, however, institutional theory can provide only partial explanations of policy.

Rational-Choice Theory

The rational-choice theory, which is sometimes called social-choice, public-choice, or formal theory, originated with economists and involves applying the principles of microeconomic theory to the analysis and explanation of political behavior (or nonmarket decision-making). It has now gained quite a few adherents among political scientists.

Perhaps the earliest use of rational-choice theory to study the political process is Anthony Downs's *Economic Theory of Democracy*.[51] In this influential book, Downs assumes that voters and political parties act as rational decision-makers who seek to maximize attainment of their preferences. Parties formulated whatever policies would win them most votes, and voters sought to maximize the portion of their preferences that could be realized through government action. In attempting to win elections, political parties moved toward the center of the ideological spectrum to appeal to the greatest number of voters and maximize their voting support. Thus, rather than providing voters with "meaningful alternatives," parties will become as much alike as possible, thereby providing an "echo rather than a choice."

Let us now look more closely at the major components of rational-choice theory. One of its basic axioms is that political actors, like economic actors, act rationally in pursuing their own self-interest. Thus economist James Buchanan, a leading proponent of rational-choice theory, contends that politicians are guided by their self-interest rather than an altruistic commitment to such goals as statesmanship or the national interest. "This should be no surprise," says Buchanan, "because governments are made up of individuals, and individuals operate from self-interest when they are engaged in a system of exchange, whether this is in the market economy or in politics."[52] Individuals who are engaged in decision-making exchanges or transactions, such as voting, also have preferences that vary from person to person. Being rational, individuals are able to comprehend and rank their preferences from most to least desired. In making decisions (whether economic or political), they are guided by these preferences and will seek to maximize the benefits they gain. In short, people are self-interested utility maximizers, not the uninformed, confused, or irrational choice-makers often depicted in analyses of political behavior.

A second basic axiom of rational-choice theory involves methodological individualism. The individual decision-maker is the primary unit of analysis and theory. The individual's preferences or values are assumed to be more important than other values—collective, organizational, or social. Conversely, rational-choice theorists argue that the actions of organizations and groups can be satisfactorily explained in terms of the behavior of a model individual. Nothing substantial will be lost by so doing in explaining the behavior of all persons.

For example, a rational-choice explanation of why Congress delegates discretionary power to administrative agencies begins with the assumption that the preference of members of Congress is to get reelected.[53] To this end, legislators delegate power to agencies, knowing that in exercising that power the agencies will create problems for their constituents. Legislators will then be called on by their constituents to assist them with their bureaucratic problems and, in return for assistance, the grateful constituents will vote to reelect the legislators. The pursuit of self-interest by the members of Congress thus explains the delegation of power and the growth of bureaucracy.

Some rational-choice theorists have begun to explore the effects of incomplete or imperfect information and uncertainty on policymaking.[54] Political decision-makers are said to be possessed of differing amounts of information (a condition called information asymmetry) and are uncertain about the outcomes or consequences of laws and policies when they are implemented. In Congress, legislative committee members, as policy specialists and the basic developers of legislation, are best informed about the relationship between a proposed policy and its likely consequences. In comparison, the rank-and-file members of Congress, who make the final decisions on the enactment of legislation, have only limited knowledge of the policy–consequences relationships. Conceivably this information asymmetry would permit committee members to act strategically and secure the enactment of policies of benefit primarily to themselves (and their constituents). Various rules and practices in Congress, however, help ensure that legislators will have incentives both to specialize in analyzing public problems and crafting policies and to make information generally available to the members of Congress. The problem is to identify the institutional arrangements that help reduce uncertainty. This "information-theories" variant of rational choice continues to assume that legislators are utility maximizers with differing interests. Their utility, however, is determined by policy outcomes rather than by policies per se. About outcomes, as we have seen, there is uncertainty.

Rational-choice studies of political behavior are often characterized by rigid and narrow assumptions, mathematical equations, abstractions, and remoteness from reality. Even William C. Mitchell, an early enlistee in the rational-choice movement, remarks that as it appears in textbooks, rational-choice theory "hardly involves government, politicians, bureaucrats, and interest groups. Little of the exposition . . . has anything to do with the fiscal or regulatory lives of the community or state."[55] A more positive view holds that "in its pure form it is one, but only one, useful, partial explanation of politics."[56]

Rational-choice theory both alerts us to the importance of self-interest as a motivating force in politics and policymaking, and provides a better understanding of decision-making processes. Many contend, however, that politics is not as devoid of altruism and concern for the public interest as the rational-choice theorists assume. The adoption of "good public policy," for example, is frequently a goal of members of Congress.[57] And public-interest groups, such as the National Wildlife Federation, are motivated by more than immediate self-interest.

Commentary

Although individual political scientists often manifest strong preference for one or another of these theoretical approaches (or others, such as incrementalism, which is presented as a decision-making theory in Chapter 4), I cannot authoritatively state which is the "best" or the most satisfactory. Each approach focuses one's attention on different aspects of policymaking and politics, and thus seems more useful for understanding some situations or events than others.

Group theory and elite theory are mutually exclusive explanations of how the policy process operates and, most important, of who controls or dominates and benefits from it. Or, succinctly: Who rules? Sharp intellectual struggles have been waged between group (or pluralist) theorists and elite theorists about who controls decision-making on public policy in American communities. Much heat if not light was generated by this controversy, which has quieted down without the issue having been fully resolved.[58]

Systems theory and institutionalism both focus on the process of policy-making, albeit in different ways, and are not incompatible. Institutionalism can be used to help explain what goes on within the "black box" (the political system), which is neglected by systems theory. Because neither theory directly confronts the question of who rules, either group or elite theory could be combined with them to some degree. Rational-choice theory, because of its narrow focus, must stand pretty much by itself. Institutions appear as the individual writ large; little attention is given to the policy environment, how issues are brought to the attention of government, or how policy preferences are developed. Like institutionalism, however, rational-choice theory does show much interest in how rules and structures help determine the outcomes of decision-making. Rational-choice scholars often occupy themselves with demonstrating how the manipulation of rules can produce preferred decisions.

On the question of who rules, rational-choice theory asserts that democratically elected officials will promote their own interest rather than the people's. This conviction frequently leads to the normative (and conservative) conclusion that less government is better government. Group theorists feel that the interests of dominant groups (however determined) prevail, and for elite theorists the few (a ruling class) govern in their own interest, perhaps with some concern for the condition of the masses.

The various theories thus raise some controversial questions about politics and the policymaking process. They also tend to skew research findings. Not surprisingly, pluralists find groups in control, elite theorists detect dominance by an elite, and rational-choice theorists find that self-interest dominates. These theories are therefore not merely neutral alternatives for guiding analysis. What one finds in policy research depends in important part on what one is looking for, just as those who go about town "looking for trouble" are more apt to find it than are more peaceful citizens.

It seems wise not to be bound too dogmatically or rigidly to one model or approach. A good rule for the policy student is to be eclectic and flexible, and to draw from theories or concepts that seem most useful for the satisfactory and fair-minded description and explanation of political events and policies. The objective explanation of political behavior rather than the validation of one's preferred theoretical approach should be the goal of political inquiry.

Each of the theories discussed, if drawn upon skillfully and selectively, can contribute to a better understanding of policymaking.

METHODOLOGICAL DIFFICULTIES IN STUDYING PUBLIC POLICY

Methodological problems afflict all research, although social scientists appear both more self-conscious about their methodology and more intellectually inclined to batter themselves for methodological infirmities than do natural and physical scientists. Policy research, especially given the complexity of its subject matter, has its full share of methodological problems. Such problems may impede or limit policy research, and may make it more than a little frustrating at times, but they neither prevent it nor negate the need for it. An awareness of some of these problems, however, may help prevent wasted efforts, needless errors, unsound conclusions, and insomnia.

Solid, conclusive evidence, facts, or data, as one prefers, on the motives, values, and behavior of policy-makers, the nature and scope of public problems, the impact of policies, and other facets of the policy process are often difficult to acquire or simply not available. The urge to convert assumptions or speculations about what happened into facts is something to be resisted, along with the uncritical acceptance of the often self-serving statements or incomplete explanations emanating from public officials and other participants in the policy process. Sometimes numerical measures of political phenomena such as policy impacts are used without sufficient care in determining their validity. Is the number of infant deaths (in their first year) per 1,000 live births a good indicator of the general level of health care in a society that has much income inequality? Do salary levels and similar data really measure the professionalism of civil servants? The acquisition of hard facts about who did what, why, and with what effect should be the goal of research. We need to be able to say with some certainty why members of Congress respond to constituency interests on some issues and not others, or what role the media play in setting agendas.

In explaining behavior in the policy process, one needs empirical data that will permit the demonstration or sound inference of cause-and-effect relationships. Once a person gets involved in quantitative data-based analysis, it is important to resist the notion that collecting empirical data is of prime importance and that the more data one has, the more one can explain. One can drown in a sea of data as well as thirst for lack thereof. To account for or explain behavior, theory is needed that will guide analysis in potentially fruitful directions, as well as good judgment in the selection of policy measures. As much as possible, hypotheses about cause-and-effect relationships need to be developed and tested on the basis of the best available evidence.

The notion that policy analysis is worthwhile only when it involves the analysis of quantitative data with statistical techniques—the higher powered the better—should also be resisted. There is no reason to assume that if something cannot be counted, it does not count. Some policy areas and problems have not been very amenable to rigorous quantitative measurement and analysis, although this may not always continue to be the case. Many aspects of social welfare and economic regulatory policies currently fit into this category. How does one measure the comparative influence of pressure groups, agency values, and economic analysis on rulemaking by EPA or OSHA? The prosecution of insider traders by the Securities and Exchange Commission? The total benefits of a public-housing program? And how does one appraise the power of ideas, as distinct from interests, in developing programs for the handicapped? Such questions present real puzzles.

Yet it should be stressed that explicit theory, quantitative data, and careful, rigorous analysis have not been as frequently utilized in studying policy as would be possible or desirable. Thus political scientist Marver H. Bernstein's hoary contention that regulatory agencies pass through a four-stage life cycle (gestation and birth, youth, maturity, and old age), frequently culminating in their "capture" (which is not well-specified) by the regulated groups, is often cited as though it were a clearly supported phenomenon.[59] Bernstein provides impressionistic support but by no means strong proof for his life-cycle theory. (He does not follow a single commission through all of the stages of the cycle.) It still lacks systematic empirical support. Conventional wisdom of this sort frequently rests on a rather frail intellectual foundation. Another example, also in the regulatory area, is economist George Stigler's theory of economic regulation. It holds that, as a rule, regulation is sought by the affected industry and operated for its benefit.[60] This theory will not do much to explain a raft of consumer protection, industrial health and safety, and environmental programs, or the deregulation legislation of the late 1970s and early 1980s.

Many perceptive and informative studies of policy formation employ little or no statistical analysis. Examples are Charles O. Jones's *Clean Air;* Alan Stone's *Economic Regulation and the Public Interest;* Barbara J. Nelson's *Making an Issue of Child Abuse;* and I. M. Destler's *American Trade Politics.*[61] The quality of analysis and careful use of sound data (or information) are more important than whether and to what extent quantitative analysis is employed when it comes to determining the worth of a study. To be rigorous, analysis does not have to be quantitative, and not all quantitative analysis is rigorous. Those who use quantitative techniques have been known to quarrel with enthusiasm and even a touch of rancor over the reliability of appropriateness of their techniques and the validity of their findings. (In Chapter 2 there is a discussion on whether socioeconomic or political variables better explain policy.) Also, to be fair-minded, one should avoid developing a phobia for quantitative or statistical analysis, as some did in reaction to the behavioral movement in political science. Much can be learned through quantitative analysis.

Data gained by interviews and questionnaires administered to public officials and other players in the policy process are often invaluable and may not otherwise be available to researchers. Care is required, however, in using both such techniques and the data acquired. Questions must be properly framed to elicit the needed information. Questions which are "loaded" and therefore bias responses, or which are so general as to create strong doubt about their intent, need to be avoided. Officials and others may not always respond fully or candidly to questions, their memories may be hazy, and they may overstate their own role in events. Data gained from these sources obviously should not be viewed as gospel. Rather, they should be checked against other sources, used with care, and regarded as representing particular viewpoints on some event. Good judgment is called for.

Many studies of policymaking take the form of case studies; that is, they focus on particular programs, statutes, or areas of public policy. Case studies have been the butt of much criticism because, being narrowly based, they do not permit sound generalization. "What is a case study a case of?" is a common gibe. Preferred studies are those dealing with all the cases in a universe, such as all regulatory commissions or sunset laws, or a meaningful sample thereof, such as Supreme Court decisions on the rights of the accused or the benefit decisions made by a welfare agency. These afford a better basis for generalizations. Case studies, however, do have a variety of uses.[62] They can be used to test theories, to develop new theories, to provide detailed, contextual analysis of events, to analyze deviant cases that contradict our generalizations, and to help provide an "intuitive feel" for the subtleties and nuances of the policy process and the practice of politics. There is plenty of room in the study of policy for both case studies and more general and comparative studies. To draw on a Republican analogy, policy study should be viewed as a "big tent."

THE PLAN OF THIS BOOK

The central concern of this book is the policy process, which is a shorthand way of designating the various processes and practices by which public policies are formed. There is not, however, a single process by which policies are made. They do not come off of an assembly line as do automobiles or television sets. Rather, variations in the subjects of policies will produce variations in the style and techniques of policymaking. Foreign policy, taxation, railroad regulation, health-care financing, professional licensing, and reform of local government each are characterized by a distinguishable policy process—different participants, procedures, techniques, decision rules, and the like. Policymaking may also vary depending upon whether its primary organizational location is the legislature, the executive, the judiciary, or administrative agencies. Policymaking within administrative agencies is more likely to be characterized by hierarchy, secrecy (or low visibility), and the involvement of experts or professionals than is legislative policymaking.[63] And certainly one will discover differences in the formation of tax policy in the United States, Great Britain, and Mexico.

This variability does not mean, however, that there are no common functions or elements, and that it is impossible to formulate generalizations on policy formation. Given the diversity and complexity in policymaking processes, the development of some sort of "general theory" that has broad explanatory power is an unrealistic aspiration."[64] But we can achieve a useful start toward what political scientists call "theory building" by striving to develop sound generalizations about such topics as who is involved in policy formation, on what sorts of issues, under what conditions, in what ways, and to what effect. Nor should we neglect to ask about how policy problems develop or obtain a place on governmental agendas. Such questions are not as simple as they may first appear.

To provide a conceptual framework to guide the examination of the policy process in the ensuing chapters, I view it as a sequential pattern of activities or functions that can readily be distinguished analytically although they may be empirically more difficult to pull apart. The following categories or stages are employed (see their portrayal in Table 1.3). Some illustrative questions are included.

1. *Problem identification and agenda setting.* The focus here is on how the problems that may become the targets of public policies are identified and specified. Why only some problems, out of all that exist, receive consideration by policy-makers requires an examination of agenda setting; that is, how governmental bodies decide what problems to address. What is a public problem? Why does some condition or matter become a public problem? How does a problem get on a governmental agenda? Why do some problems not achieve agenda status?

2. *Formulation.* This encompasses the creation, identification, or borrowing of proposed courses of action, often called alternatives or options, for resolving or ameliorating public problems. Who participates in policy formulation? How are alternatives for dealing with a problem developed? Are there difficulties and biases in formulating policy proposals?

3. *Adoption.* This involves deciding which proposed alternative, including taking no action, will be used to handle a problem. In American legisla-

TABLE 1.3 The Policy Process

Policy Terminology	Stage 1: Policy Agenda	Stage 2: Policy Formulation	Stage 3: Policy Adoption	Stage 4: Policy Implementation	Stage 5: Policy Evaluation
Definition	Those problems, among many, that receive the serious attention of public officials	Development of pertinent and acceptable proposed courses of action for dealing with a public problem	Development of support for a specific proposal so that a policy can be legitimized or authorized	Application of the policy by the government's administrative machinery	Efforts by the government to determine whether the policy was effective and why or why not
Common sense	Getting the government to consider action on the problem	What is proposed to be done about the problem	Getting the government to accept a particular solution to the problem	Applying the government's policy to the problem	Did the policy work?

Source: Adapted from James E. Anderson, David W. Brady, and Charles Bullock III, *Public Policy and Politics in the United States*, 2d ed. (Monterey, Calif.: Brooks/Cole, 1984).

tures this function is performed by majorities. How is a policy alternative adopted or enacted? What requirements must be met? Who are the adopters? What is the content of the adopted policy?

4. *Implementation.* (A synonym is administration.) Here attention is on what is done to carry into effect or apply adopted policies. Often further development or elaboration of policies will occur in the course of their administration. Who is involved? What, if anything, is done to enforce or apply a policy? How does implementation help shape or determine the content of policy?

5. *Evaluation.* This entails activities intended to determine what a policy is accomplishing, whether it is achieving its goals, and whether it has other consequences. Who is involved? Who is advantaged and disadvantaged by a policy? What are the consequences of policy evaluation? Are there demands for changes in or repeal of the policy? Are new problems identified? Is the policy process restarted because of evaluation?

Within this simplified framework, the formation and implementation of policies are seen as political in that they involve conflict and struggle among individuals and groups, officials and agencies, with conflicting ideas, interests, values, and information on public-policy issues. Policymaking is "political"; it involves "politics." That is, its features include conflict, negotiation, the exercise of power, bargaining, and compromise—and sometimes such nefarious practices as deception and bribery. There is no good reason to resist or disparage this conclusion, or to imitate those who derogate policies that they do not like with such statements as, "It's nothing but politics." Although it is sometimes implied or even asserted that if enough analysis were done, if enough facts and data were gathered, all "right-thinking" people would agree on the appropriate course of action to handle a problem, this is not the way the world works. Quite reasonable people often disagree on policy issues because they have differing interests, values, and affiliations. Politics is the way a democratic society resolves such differences.

The policy-process approach to policy study has several advantages. First, policymaking frequently, but by no means always, follows the stages that I have described. Its sequential nature thus helps one capture and comprehend the flow of action in the actual policy process. However, the formulation and adoption stages may blend together, as when proposed legislation on welfare reform is modified during consideration in committees and on the House and Senate floors in order to win votes needed for its enactment. Administrative agencies issue rules elaborating policy, as in the case of public-lands policy, while implementing it (see Chapter 6). The adoption of a policy, such as restrictions on abortion, solves a problem for some people while it creates a problem for others, who then restart the policy process in an effort to modify or repeal the disliked policy. Even in such instances, the sequential-process approach can be used to analytically distinguish the various activities involved.

Second, the sequential process approach is flexible and open to change and refinement.[65] Additional stages can be introduced if experience indicates that they would strengthen description and analysis. Perhaps budgeting should be recognized as a separate stage of the process. Various forms of data collection and analysis, whether quantitative (statistical), historical, legal, or normative (value-oriented), are compatible with it. It can be used to study a single policy (e.g., the Americans with Disabilities Act) or to compare the enactment and implementation of several civil rights laws. Group, institutional, and other approaches to policy study can be fitted into it. The group approach may help explain policy adoption; institutionalism can cast light on its implementation. Systems theory may help alert us to some of its consequences.

Third, the sequential-process approach helps present a dynamic and developmental, rather than static and cross-sectional, view of the policy process. It is concerned with the evolution of policy and requires that one think about what moves action on policy from one stage of the process to another. Moreover, it helps emphasize relationships, or interactions, among the participants in policymaking. Political parties, interest groups, legislative procedures, presidential commitments, public opinion, and other matters can be tied together as they help explain the formulation of a policy. Further, one can seek to discover how action at one stage of the process affects action at later stages. For example, how does the design and content of legislation ease or complicate its implementation?

Fourth, the sequential approach is not "culture bound." It can readily be used to study policymaking in foreign political systems. It also lends itself to manageable comparisons, such as how problems reach governmental agendas, or how policies are adopted in various countries. A few such comparisons are included in this book.[66]

The structure of the remainder of the book looks like this: Chapter 2 surveys the environment or context of policymaking and the official and unofficial participants in the policy process. Chapter 3 examines the nature of policy problems and agendas, agenda-setting processes, and the formulation of policy proposals. Chapter 4 is concerned with decision-making and the adoption of public policies. A case study on airline regulation and deregulation examines the rise, elaboration, and termination of an important public policy over several decades. Chapter 5 takes up the budgetary process because of its important effects on the implementation of public policies. The struggle to balance the budget is also considered. Chapter 6 discusses several aspects of policy implementation and explores why people comply with policies. Chapter 7 deals with policy impacts, the evaluation of policies, and policy termination, which occasionally may follow evaluation. In Chapter 8 I present some conclusions and comments on the American policy process.

Notes

1. John A. Garraty, *Unemployment in History* (New York: Harper & Row, 1978), chap. 7.
2. Quoted in Robert Aaron Gordon, *Economic Instability and Growth: The American Record* (New York: Harper & Row, 1974), p. 22.
3. Roger H. Davidson, *The Politics of Comprehensive Manpower Legislation* (Baltimore: John Hopkins University Press, 1972), pp. 3–4.
4. This account is based on Donald C. Baumer and Carl E. Van Horn, *The Politics of Unemployment* (Washington: Congressional Quarterly Press, 1985), esp. chaps. 1 and 6.
5. General Accounting Office, *Job Training Partnership Act: Service and Outcomes for Participants with Different Needs* (Washington: USGAO, June 1989), pp. 2–6.
6. General Accounting Office, *Job Training Partnership Act: Inadequate Oversight Leaves Program Vulnerable to Waste, Abuse, and Mismanagement* (Washington: USGAO, July 1991), pp. 2–5.
7. Representative William D. Ford (D, Michigan) quoted in *Congressional Quarterly Weekly Report,* Vol. 50 (August 15, 1992), p. 2452.
8. Robert H. Salisbury, "The Analysis of Public Policy: A Search for Theories and Roles," in Austin Ranney, ed., *Political Science and Public Policy* (Chicago: Markham, 1968), pp. 13–18.
9. Thomas R. Dye, *Understanding Public Policy,* 7th ed. (Englewood Cliffs, N.J.: Prentice-Hall, 1992), p. 3.
10. Austin Ranney, "The Study of Policy Content: A Framework for Choice," in Ranney, ed., *Political Science and Public Policy* (Chicago: Markham, 1968), p. 59.
11. Don K. Price, *The Scientific Estate* (Cambridge, Mass.: Harvard University Press, 1965), pp. 122–135.
12. This discussion of policy analysis is informed by Robert D. Behn, "Policy Analysis and Policy Politics," *Policy Analysis,* VII (Spring 1981), pp. 199–226.
13. Dye, op. cit., p. 7.
14. Robert Eyestone, *The Threads of Public Policy: A Study in Policy Leadership* (Indianapolis: Bobbs-Merrill, 1971), p. 18.
15. Thomas R. Dye, *Understanding Public Policy,* 5th ed. (Englewood Cliffs, N.J.: Prentice-Hall, 1984), p. 1.
16. Richard Rose, ed., *Policy Making in Great Britain* (London: Macmillan, 1969), p. x.
17. Carl J. Friedrich, *Man and His Government* (New York: McGraw-Hill, 1963), p. 79.
18. David Easton, *A Systems Analysis of Political Life* (New York: Wiley, 1965), p. 212.
19. The basic typology is from Theodore J. Lowi, "American Business, Public Policy Case Studies, and Political Theory," *World Politics,* XVI (July 1964), pp. 677–715. The self-regulatory category is from Salisbury, op. cit., pp. 151–175.
20. *Congressional Quarterly Weekly Report,* Vol. 44 (October 18, 1986), p. 2625.
21. Lowi, op. cit., p. 690.

22. Raymond Tatalovich and Byron W. Daynes, eds., *Social Regulatory Policy: Moral Controversies in American Politics* (Boulder, Colo.: Westview Press, 1988).
23. Lowi, op. cit., pp. 690–691.
24. Kenneth J. Meier and E. Thomas Garman, *Regulation and Consumer Protection*, 2nd ed. (Houston: Dome Publications, 1995), pp. 41–42.
25. For a thorough discussion of licensing, see *ibid.*, chap. 3.
26. James E. Anderson, "Agricultural Marketing Orders and the Process and Politics of Self-Regulation," *Policy Studies Review,* II (August 1982), pp. 97–111.
27. Lowi, op. cit., p. 691. On redistributive policies, see Randall B. Ripley and Grace A. Franklin, *Congress, the Bureaucracy, and Public Policy,* 6th ed. (Pacific Grove, Calif.: Brooks/Cole, 1991), chap. 6.
28. Randall B. Ripley, *Policy Analysis in Political Science* (Chicago: Nelson Hall, 1985), pp. 68–69.
29. Paul E. Peterson and Mark Rom, "Lower Taxes, More Spending, and Budget Deficits," in Charles O. Jones, ed., *The Reagan Legacy: Promise and Performance* (Chatham, N.J.: Chatham House, 1988), pp. 218–221.
30. On the symbolic aspects of policies, see Murray Edelmann, *The Symbolic Uses of Politics* (Urbana: University of Illinois Press, 1964), chap. 2; and Charles D. Elder and Roger W. Cobb, *The Political Uses of Symbols* (New York: Longman, 1983).
31. *Congressional Quarterly Weekly Report,* Vol. 53 (July 1, 1995), p. 1933.
32. Richard O. Davis, *Housing Reform During the Truman Administration* (Columbia: University of Missouri Press, 1966), chap. 10.
33. Bruce I. Oppenheimer, *Oil and the Congressional Process* (Lexington, Mass.: Heath, 1974), pp. 130–145.
34. Cf. L. L. Wade and R. L. Curry, Jr., *A Logic of Public Policy* (Belmont, Calif.: Wadsworth, 1970), chap. 5.
35. Ronald C. Moe, "Exploring the Limits of Privatization," *Public Administration Review* XLVII (November–December 1987), p. 453.
36. R. McGregor Cawley, *Federal Land, Western Anger* (Lawrence: University Press of Kansas, 1993).
37. This discussion draws on Lowi, op. cit., chap. 3.
38. Ibid., p. 57.
39. Ibid., p. 72. His emphasis.
40. Robert McIver, *The Web of Government* (New York: Macmillan, 1947), pp. 314–315.
41. David Easton, "An Approach to the Analysis of Political Systems," *World Politics,* IX (April 1957), pp. 383–400; and Easton, *A Systems Analysis of Political Life* (New York: Wiley, 1965).
42. Earl Latham, *The Group Basis of Politics* (New York: Octagon Books, 1965), p. 36.
43. David Truman, *The Governmental Process* (New York: Knopf, 1951), p. 37.
44. Alan C. Isaak, *Scope and Methods of Political Science* (Chicago: Dorsey Press, 1988), pp. 269–270.
45. Latham, op. cit., pp. 35–36, 38–39.

46. E. E. Schattschneider, *The Semisovereign People* (New York: Holt, Rinehart and Winston, 1960), p. 35.
47. Thomas R. Dye and L. Harmon Zeigler, *The Irony of Democracy*, 8th ed. (Monterey, Calif.: Brooks/Cole, 1990), p. 7.
48. Dye, op. cit., pp. 59–63.
49. Robert A. Dahl, "A Critique of the Ruling Elite Model," *American Political Science Review*, LII (June 1958), p. 464.
50. G. William Domhoff, *Who Rules America?* (Englewood Cliffs, N.J.: Prentice-Hall, 1967); G. William Domhoff, *The Power Elite and the State: How Policy Is Made in America* (New York: Walter deGruyter, 1990).
51. Anthony Downs, *An Economic Theory of Democracy* (New York: Harper & Row, 1957).
52. Roger Lewin, "Self-Interest in Politics Earns a Nobel Prize," *Science* CCXXXIV (November 21, 1986), p. 941.
53. Morris P. Fiorina, *Congress: Keystone of the Washington Establishment*, 2nd ed. (New Haven: Yale University Press, 1989).
54. This discussion leans heavily upon Keith Krehiel, *Information and Legislative Organization* (Ann Arbor: University of Michigan Press, 1992); and Thomas W. Gilligan and Keith Krehbiel, "Asymmetric Information and Legislative Rules with a Heterogeneous Committee," *American Journal of Political Science*, XXXIII (May 1989), pp. 459–490.
55. William C. Mitchell, "Textbook Public Choice: A Review Essay," *Public Choice*, XXVIII (1982), p. 99.
56. Louis F. Weschler, "Methodological Individualism in Politics," *Public Administration Review*, XLIII (May–June 1982), p. 294.
57. See Richard J. Fenno, Jr., *Congressmen in Committees* (Boston: Little, Brown, 1973). Fenno indicates that members of Congress are variously influenced by the desires to be reelected, to help enact good public policy, and to acquire influence in the House.
58. See Philip J. Trounstine and Terry Christensen, *Movers and Shakers: The Study of Community Power* (New York: St. Martin's, 1982).
59. Marver H. Bernstein, *Regulating Business by Independent Commission* (Princeton: Princeton University Press, 1955), pp. 74–95.
60. George Stigler, "The Theory of Economic Regulation," *Bell Journal of Economic and Management Science* (Spring 1971), pp. 3–21.
61. Charles O. Jones, *Clean Air* (Pittsburgh: University of Pittsburgh Press, 1975); Alan Stone, *Economic Regulation and the Public Interest* (Ithaca, N.Y.: Cornell University Press, 1977): Barbara J. Nelson, *Making an Issue of Child Abuse* (Chicago: University of Chicago Press, 1984); and I. M. Destler, *American Trade Politics*, 2nd ed. (Washington: Institute of International Economics, 1992). All are political scientists.
62. See Harry Eckstein, "Case Study and Theory in Political Science," in Fred I. Greenstein and Nelson W. Polsby, eds., *The Handbook of Political Science*, Vol. 7, *Strategies of Inquiry* (Reading, Mass.: Addison-Wesley, 1975), pp. 79–137.
63. Francis E. Rourke, *Bureaucracy, Politics, and Public Policy*, 3rd ed. (Boston: Little, Brown, 1984), pp. 145–158.

64. See David Easton, *The Political System* (New York: Knopf, 1953), chap. 2.
65. See, generally, Richard Rose, "Concepts for Comparison," *Policy Studies Journal,* I (Spring 1973), pp. 122–127.
66. For criticisms of the sequential process approach, see Paul A. Sabatier, "Political Science and Public Policy," *PS: Political Science and Politics,* XXIV (June 1991), pp. 144–147; and Charles E. Lindblom and Edward J. Woodhouse, *The Policy Making Process,* 3rd ed. (Englewood Cliffs, N.J.: Prentice Hall, 1993), pp. 10–12.

2

THE POLICY-MAKERS AND THEIR ENVIRONMENT

Congressional committee hearings, such as the Senate Foreign Relations Committee's hearings on Bosnia, examine and critique actions by the executive.

I n the American political system, political power is fragmented and dispersed by constitutional prescription and political practice. Many points of official decision-making exist, and a multitude of officials share in the exercise of political power and the formation of public policy. At the national level the Framers of the Constitution provided for the separation of power, distributing it among the legislative, executive, and judicial branches of the national government. Thus, Article I provides that "all legislative Powers herein granted shall be vested in a Congress of the United States. . . ." Article II states that "the executive Power shall be vested in a President of the United States of America." In turn, Article III declares that "the judicial Power of the United States, shall be vested in one supreme court and such inferior Courts as the Congress may from time to time ordain and establish." This separation was reinforced by the provision of different selection processes for officials in each branch. Thus, the House of Representatives was to be chosen by the voters, the Senate by the state legislatures (changed to the voters by the Sixteenth Amendment), the president by the Electoral College, and the judges by the president with the consent of the Senate. The Constitution also prohibits anyone from being a member of more than one branch at the same time.

The separation of powers was not rigidly imposed, however. By the corollary principle of checks and balances, the Framers gave each branch some means for interfering with—checking—the exercise of power by the other two branches. Thus Congress is given primary responsibility for the enactment of legislation, but the president is authorized to recommend matters for its attention and to veto laws, although the veto can be overcome by a two-thirds vote in both houses. Many presidential appointments, including those to the federal courts, require Senate approval. The Supreme Court can declare actions by the other branches unconstitutional, but Congress can regulate the jurisdiction of the courts and the kinds of cases they may hear. What the Framers really created was a set of separate institutions sharing power.

The Framers' intent was to use the principles of separation of powers and checks and balances to prevent the abuse of power and the intrusion by government on individual liberty. Whatever their influence in these respects, these principles have had other consequences. One is the decentralization of power. Another is creation of the need for cooperation and deference among the branches in order for the government to act effectively. Indeed, if each branch were to insist on the fullest exercise of its prerogatives, the government would end in deadlock. A third is to make American government inefficient in its operation. Much time and effort is often required to make policy decisions, and the content of the resulting policy is often diluted and moderated.

Conventional wisdom holds that the national government performs more effectively when both houses of Congress and the presidency are controlled by the same party. However, divided governments, where one party controls the White House (usually the Republicans) and the other party controls one or both houses of Congress, existed for all but six years during the 1969–1996 period. This condition is thought to contribute to gridlock, a situation in which partisan, ideological, and other differences make it difficult for the government to deal effectively with important problems. If one believes that the government should act decisively on all problems soon after they reach the policy agenda, something of a case could be made for the gridlock contention. In actuality, it has frequently taken the government many years, even decades, to adopt legislation on such contentious matters as federal aid to education, medical care, civil rights, and welfare reform.

Further doubt on the divided government–gridlock contention is cast by Professor David Mayhew's study of the 1946–1990 era.[1] Using as his criteria the enactment of important legislation and the conduct of major congressional investigations of alleged misconduct in the executive branch, he finds that there are no major differences in governmental output between periods of divided and unified government. Mayhew was not concerned with whether presidents got what they wanted from Congress or with the ideological hue of legislation. His study stands as a challenge to the validity of the argument that unified party control is necessary for effective national governance.

Power in the American political system is further dispersed by the principle of federalism, which created separate national and state governments, each deriving its power from the Constitution. Essentially, the Constitution assigns delegated and implied powers to the national government and reserved powers to the state governments. The basic arrangement is summarized by the Tenth Amendment: "The powers not delegated to the United States by the Constitution, nor prohibited by it to the States, are reserved to the States respectively, or to the people."

Article I, Section 8 of the Constitution delegates to Congress such powers as to tax and spend for the general welfare, to regulate interstate and foreign commerce (the "commerce clause"), to coin money and regulate the value thereof, to establish post offices and post roads, to raise and support armies and a navy, and to declare war. Congress is also authorized "to make all laws which shall be necessary and proper for carrying into execution" these and other powers assigned to the national government. The "necessary and proper" clause has been used to significantly enhance the scope of the national government's power.

As currently interpreted, the Constitution does not reserve any specific policy areas for the states. Consequently, the national government can deal with any or all matters where action can be justified as exercises of its delegated and implied (necessary and proper) powers. Constitutional "habits" persist, however, and help impose political limits on the national government. Constitutional support could likely be found for a national uniformed police force but that would not make it politically acceptable to most Americans.

The reach and power of the national government has undergone continual expansion since the Constitution's adoption, albeit more rapidly in some eras than others. Today the national government is vastly more active and powerful than it was in 1800, 1900, or even 1950. National policies now apply to many areas once regarded as the domain of the states; examples include public education, social welfare, and highway construction and maintenance.

Much of what the national government does is constitutionally based on the commerce clause—the authority to regulate interstate and foreign commerce. Since the 1930s, the commerce clause has been given an expansive interpretation by the Supreme Court. In 1995, however, the Court, by a 5–4 majority, declared unconstitutional the Gun-Free School Zones Act of 1990. This law, which made possession of a gun within one thousand feet of a school a federal crime, was held to be "a criminal statute that by its terms has nothing to do with 'commerce' or any sort of economic enterprise, however broadly one might define those terms."[2] Not since 1936, when it struck down a law regulating wages and hours in the coal industry, had the Court declared a congressional action unconstitutional as in excess of the commerce clause. What the Court's 1995 ruling portended for the future was unclear. One possibility was constitutional challenges to other federal gun-control laws.

Notwithstanding the national government's growth, the state governments (and their local governments) continue to be important policy-makers in many areas, including law enforcement, definition and protection of property rights, public education (both higher and lower), land-use regulation, construction and maintenance of highways and streets, occupational licensing, mental-health services, and public sanitation services. Indeed, some observers contend that there has been a "resurgence of the states" as a consequence of institutional, legislative reapportionment, increased cooperation among the states, and distrust and lack of confidence in the national government.[3]

In the nineteenth century the dominant conception of national–state relationships was that called "dual federalism." Each level of government had its distinct functions that it handled independently of the other. In the twentieth century dual federalism gave way to "cooperative federalism," where all levels of government—national, state, and local—cooperate in the development and implementation of public policies. Thus the state and local governments play a major role in the enforcement of national environmental pollution-control and welfare programs. One would be hard pressed to identify a policy area in which they have no involvement or effect.

Although the Constitution does not require the states to employ the principle of separation of powers in organizing their governments, they all do so. And only the state of Nebraska has chosen to have a one-house legislature. The states have created many local governments (more than 83,000 separate entities in 1992) to handle the local administration of state functions, such as law enforcement and public education, and to provide for local self-government. In practice, local governments frequently operate with only limited supervision and control by the state agencies and officials. Along with the states they constitute additional arenas for policymaking and implementation.

The existence of all these governments—national, state, and local—permits interest groups and others to engage in "arena shopping." Those dissatisfied with policy at one level of government may seek favorable action at another level, as did civil-rights groups in the 1950s and 1960s. In recent years business groups have become dissatisfied with the diversity of state laws on product liability and the large monetary awards sometimes granted by state courts to injured consumers.[4] Although product liability has traditionally been handled by the states, business groups have turned to Washington for help. Their goal, unsuccessful to date, is a less stringent national product-liability law that would limit awards for actual and punitive damages, make it more difficult for plaintiffs to win damage suits, and preempt state laws.

Describing and analyzing policymaking at all three levels of government is a task too enormous for one book. Hence, in the remainder of this book, I focus on the national government's action on domestic issues, but I do not wholly exclude foreign policy, American state and local governments, or other political systems. This chapter will begin by examining the environment in which policymaking occurs and which helps to shape its actions—something that tends to be overlooked by rational-choice theory but to which we are alerted by systems theory. Then we survey the official and unofficial participants in the policymaking process.

THE POLICY ENVIRONMENT

Policymaking cannot adequately be studied apart from the environment or context in which it occurs. According to systems theory, demands for policy actions stem from problems and conflicts in the environment and are transmitted to the political system by groups, officials, and others. At the same time, the environment both limits and directs what policy-makers can effectively do. The environment, broadly viewed, includes geographic characteristics such as climate, natural resources, and topography; demographic variables such as population size, age distribution, and spatial location; political culture; social structure, or the class system; and the economic system. Other nations also become an important part of the environment when foreign and defense policies are involved. The discussion here will focus on a pair of these environmental factors that have received much attention from political scientists (although not always from a policy-studies perspective): political culture and socioeconomic conditions.

Political Culture

Every society has a culture that differentiates its members' values and life-styles from those of other societies. The anthropologist Clyde Kluckhohn defined culture as "the total life way of a people, the social legacy the individual acquires from his group. Or culture can be regarded as that part of the environment that is the creation of man."[5] Most social scientists seem to agree that culture shapes or influences social action but does not fully determine it. Culture is only one of many factors that may give form and direction to human behavior.

We are interested here in the portion of the general culture of a society that can be designated political culture: widely held values, beliefs, and attitudes on what governments should try to do, how they should operate, and relationships between the citizen and government.[6] Political culture is transmitted from one generation to another by socialization, a process in which the individual, through many experiences with parents, friends, teachers, political leaders, and others, learns politically relevant values, beliefs, and attitudes. Political culture, then, is acquired by the individual, becomes a part of his or her psychological makeup, and is manifested in his or her behavior. Within a society, variations among regions and groups may result in distinctive subcultures. In the United States, variations are noticeable in political culture (subcultures) between North and South, black and white, and young and old.

Political scientist Daniel J. Elazar contends that we have three identifiable political cultures—individualistic, moralistic, and traditionalistic—and mutations thereof scattered throughout the United States.[7] The individualistic political culture emphasizes private concerns and views government as a utilitarian device to be used to accomplish what the people want. Politicians are interested in holding office as a means of controlling government's favors or rewards. The moralistic political culture views government as a mechanism for advancing the public interest. Government service is considered public service. More governmental intervention in the economy is accepted, and there is much public concern about policy issues. Moralistic political culture is strong in states like Minnesota and Wisconsin, whereas individualistic political culture is dominant in Illinois and New York. The traditionalistic political culture takes a paternalistic and elitist view of government, and favors its use to maintain the existing social order. Real political power centers in a small segment of the population, and most citizens are expected to be relatively inactive in politics. Traditionalistic political culture has been strong in some southern states, which have been marked by low levels of political participation. Such variations in political culture clearly compound the tasks of political description and analysis.

No attempt is made here to fully describe the political culture of the United States, or that of any other society. Rather, the discussion is confined to indicating and illustrating some of the implications and significance of political culture for policy formation.

The sociologist Robin M. Williams identifies a number of "major value orientations" in American society, including individual freedom, equality, progress, efficiency, and practicality.[8] Values such as these—and others, such as democracy, individualism, and humanitarianism—clearly have significance for policymaking. For example, the general American style in regulating economic activity has been practical or pragmatic rather than ideological. It has emphasized particular solutions to present problems rather than long-range planning or ideological consistency. Moreover, demand for individual freedom has created a general presumption against restricting private activity and in favor of the broadest scope possible for private action. Stress on individualism and private property finds expression in the notion (often departed from in practice) that people should generally be free to use their property as they see fit. Land-use controls and municipal zoning demonstrate that this notion is subject to limitations. The American emphasis on individualism has both slowed the development of welfare programs and, once they have come into being, helped to keep them limited and made them subject to much criticism and complaint. Large numbers of Americans believe that people should be expected to take care of themselves.

Differences in public policy and policymaking in various countries can be accounted for at least partially by variations in political culture. Public programs for medical care are of longer standing and are more numerous and extensive in Western Europe than in the United States because there public expectation and acceptance of such programs have been greater. Again, more people in Great Britain approve of governmental ownership than in the United States, where support for it is quite narrow.[9] Thus we find considerably more governmental ownership of business and industry in Great Britain. Americans much prefer governmental regulation to ownership when control seems necessary.

Professor Karl W. Deutsch suggests that people's time orientation—their view of the relative importance of past, present, and future—has implications for policy formation. A political culture oriented more to the past than to the present or future may better encourage preserving monuments than making innovations, and may help stimulate the enactment of legislation on old-age pensions years before expanding public higher education. Great Britain adopted an old-age pension law in 1908, but did not significantly expand public higher education until after 1960. In contrast, Deutsch notes that the United States, with a more future-oriented culture, adopted legislation providing support for land-grant colleges in 1862 and for Social Security in 1935.[10]

Gabriel A. Almond and Sidney Verba differentiated among parochial, subject, and participant political cultures.[11] In a parochial political culture, citizens have little awareness of or orientation toward either the political system as a whole, the input process, the output process, or the citizen as a political participant. The parochials expect nothing from the system. It is suggested that some African chiefdoms, kingdoms, and tribal societies as well as modern Italy illustrate parochial political cultures. In a subject political culture like that of Germany the citizen is oriented toward the political system and the output process, yet has little awareness of input processes or of the individual as a participant. He or she is aware of governmental authority and may like or dislike it, but is essentially passive. The person is, as the term implies, a subject. In a participant political culture, which Almond and Verba say exists in the United States, citizens have a comparatively high level of political awareness and information along with explicit orientations toward the political system as a whole, its input and output processes, and meaningful citizen participation in politics. They also understand how individuals and groups can influence decision-making.

Some of the implications of these differences in political culture for policy formation seem readily apparent. Obviously, citizen participation in policy formation in a parochial political culture is essentially nonexistent, because government matters little to most citizens. Individuals in a subject political culture may believe that they can do little to influence public policy, whether they like it or not. This belief may lead to passive acceptance of governmental action that may be authoritarian in style. In some instances, frustration and resentment may build until redress or change is sought through violence. In the participant political culture, individuals may organize themselves into groups and otherwise seek to influence governmental action to rectify their grievances. Government and public policy are thus viewed as controllable by citizens. It can also be assumed that more demands will be made on government in a participant political culture than in either a parochial or a subject culture.

Let us return to an earlier point. Political culture helps shape political behavior; it "is related to the frequency and probability of various kinds of behavior and not their rigid determination."[12] Common values, beliefs, and attitudes inform, guide, and constrain the actions of both decision-makers and citizens. Political cultural differences help ensure that public policy will be more likely to favor economic competition in the United States, where individual opportunity is a widely held value, but it is more likely to tolerate industrial cartels in West Germany, where economic competition has not been highly valued. Some political scientists shy away from using political culture as an analytic tool because they see it as too imprecise and conjectural, and subject to varying interpretations. Although this argument has some merit, political culture does have utility for the analysis and explanation of policy.

Socioeconomic Conditions

The term *socioeconomic conditions* is used here because it is often impossible to separate social and economic factors as they impinge on or influence political activity. The levels of educational attainment in a society, for instance, have both social and economic effects.

Public policies often arise out of conflicts among groups of people, private and official, with differing interests and desires.[13] This origin especially applies to regulatory and redistributive policies. One of the prime sources of conflict, particularly in modern industrial societies, is economic activity. Conflicts may develop between the interests of big business and small business, employers and employees, wholesalers and retailers, bankers and securities dealers, hospitals and medical-insurance companies, farmers and agricultural-commodity importers, and consumers and manufacturers.

Groups that are underprivileged or dissatisfied with their relationships with other groups in the economy may seek governmental assistance to improve their situation. Thus it has been labor groups, dissatisfied with the wages sometimes resulting from bargaining with corporate employers, that have sought minimum-wage legislation. Consumer groups, who feel disadvantaged in the marketplace, have sought protection against unwholesome foods and hazardous products. In a private conflict it is customarily the weaker or disadvantaged party, at least in a comparative sense, who seeks to expand the conflict by bringing government into the fray. The dominant group, which can achieve its goals satisfactorily by private action, has no incentive to bring government into the conflict and instead usually seeks to privatize the conflict by contending that governmental action is unnecessary, improper, or unwise.

Satisfactory relationships between groups may be disrupted or altered by economic change or development. Those who feel adversely affected or threatened may then demand government action to protect their interests or establish a new equilibrium. Rapid industrialization and the growth of big business in the United States in the latter part of the nineteenth century produced new economic conditions. Farmers, small-business operators, reform elements, and other aggrieved groups called for government action to control big business (also known as "the trusts"). The eventual results were the enactment by Congress of the Sherman Act in 1890 and the Clayton and Federal Trade Commission acts in 1914. More recently, American manufacturing companies, economically threatened by an increasing volume of less costly imported products, have sought and sometimes obtained both voluntary and mandatory import quotas. The Omnibus Trade and Competitiveness Act of 1988 authorizes retaliation against countries discriminating against the sale of American products while themselves benefiting from American market opportunities.

It is a truism that a society's level of economic development will impose limits on what government can do in providing public goods and services to its citizens. Nonetheless, this fact is occasionally overlooked by those who assume that the failure of governments to act on problems is invariably due to official recalcitrance or unresponsiveness or citizens' reluctance to pay higher taxes, rather than limited resources. Clearly, one factor affecting what governments can provide in the way of welfare programs is the availability of economic resources. A scarcity of economic resources will of course be more limiting in many of the developing countries than in an affluent society such as the United States, although even American governments do not have the funds to do everything that everyone wants. National health-insurance legislation, which seemed highly likely to be adopted in the 1970s, lost its appeal in an era of large budget deficits. So, too, has there been delay in improving and repairing highways, bridges, and other parts of the transportation infrastructure because of the large costs entailed.

Within the United States, economic resources are very unequally distributed among state and local governments, affecting their capacity to deal with such social problems as inadequate public education, poverty, overcrowded prisons, and congested traffic. Consequently, among the states variations are substantial in welfare spending and within the states educational expenditures (as measured by expenditures per student) vary among school districts. Pressed for funds, cities devote most of their resources to police and fire protection and street maintenance while cutting back on "amenities" such as libraries, parks, and recreation programs. In some states, unequal funding among school districts is a divisive and seemingly intractable political issue.

Social change and conflict also stimulate demands for governmental action. The growing interest in the United States in women's rights and the increased use (and acceptance) of marijuana, especially by middle-class people, has produced demands for alterations in public policies. In consequence, greater protection has been provided for women's rights, including the right to terminate pregnancies by abortion, equal employment opportunity, and, in some states, comparable pay for comparable work and parental-leave programs. Penalties have also been reduced for use and possession of small amounts of marijuana. Those with conflicting interests and values have strongly, sometimes vehemently, opposed such demands. Because such conflicts are difficult to resolve, public officials often find themselves hard pressed to devise acceptable policy solutions.

The ways in which socioeconomic conditions influence or constrain public policies in the states have been extensively analyzed by political scientists. Controversy has developed over the relative influence of political and socioeconomic variables on policy. One of the most prominent examinations of this question is Thomas R. Dye's study of policy outputs in the fifty states,[14] which is in accord with systems theory. Dye contends that the level of economic development (as measured by such variables as per capita personal income, percentage of urban population, median education, and industrial employment) had a dominant influence on state policies (as measured by expenditures) on such matters as education, welfare, highways, taxation, and public regulation. Comparing the effects of economic development with those of the political system, he found that political variables (voter participation, interparty competition, political-party strength, and legislative apportionment) had only a weak relationship to public policy. Dye summarized the findings of his sophisticated statistical analysis:

> Much of the literature in state politics implies that the division of the two-party vote, the level of interparty competition, the level of voter participation, and the degree of malapportionment in legislative bodies all influence public policy. Moreover, at first glance the fact that there are obvious policy differences between states with different degrees of party competition, Democratic dominance, and voter participation lends some support to the notion that these system characteristics influence public policy. . . .
>
> However, partial correlation analysis reveals that these system characteristics have relatively little independent effect on policy outcomes in the states. Economic development shapes both political systems and policy outcomes, and most of the association that occurs between system characteristics and policy outcomes can be attributed to the influence of economic development. Differences in the policy choices of states with different types of political systems turn out to be largely a product of differing socioeconomic levels rather than a direct product of political variables. Levels of urbanization, industrialization, income, and education appear to be more influential in shaping policy outcomes than political system characteristics.[15]

Notice that Dye did not argue that political variables had no influence whatsoever on state policies; rather, in his estimation they were clearly subordinated to socioeconomic factors in explaining differences in state public policies.

Richard Dawson and James Robinson also sought to demonstrate that socioeconomic variables have a stronger impact on policy than political factors.[16] They analyzed the effect of interparty competition and selected economic variables on public welfare policy, trying to determine whether party competition significantly influenced welfare policy (especially expenditures). They concluded that environmental factors had a greater effect than party competition. "The level of public social welfare programs in the American states seems to be more a function of socioeconomic factors, especially per capita income."[17] The conclusions of these and similar studies were quickly accepted by some political scientists. One declared that such research provides "a devastating set of findings and cannot be dismissed as not meaning what it plainly says—that analysis of political systems will not explain policy decisions made by those systems."[18]

But is public policy really primarily an outcome of some kind of socioeconomic determinism? Are studies such as those cited really conclusive on this issue? Two scholars cautioned against "simple acceptance" of such a conclusion.[19] Not discounting socioeconomic factors' influence on policy outputs, they pointed out a number of problems and limitations in these studies.

First, there is a tendency to exaggerate the strength of the economy–policy relationship. Thus they state, "Dye reports 456 coefficients of simple correlations between policy measures and his four economic measures of income, urbanism, industrialization and education, but only 16 of them (4 percent) are strong enough to indicate that an economic measure explains at least one-half the interstate variation in policy."[20] This result leaves quite a bit unexplained statistically. Second, the political variables used in such studies have been limited in scope, focusing on only a few aspects of the political process. Third, there is a tendency to overlook variations in the influence of economic factors on policymaking. Officials in local governments appear more strongly influenced by economic factors than are state officials. Further, local officials are not equally influenced by the character of the local economy. I report here the findings of another study:

> Where the locality has adopted reformed government structures there is less of an economy–policy linkage than where local government has an unreformed structure. The principal features of a reformed local government structure are a professional city manager, nonpartisan elections for local offices, and a council selected at-large rather than by wards. These features seem to depoliticize the social and economic cleavages within a community, permitting local officials to make their policy decisions with less concern for economics.[21]

Another limitation is that most of these studies only consider statistical relationships among various political and socioeconomic variables and public policies. If, when condition A exists, policy B usually occurs, and the relationship is not caused by some third factor, then we can predict that when A exists, B will occur. Such a prediction is not an explanation, however, and we are still left with the task of explaining how political decisions are actually made. If per capita income is directly related to the level of welfare spending, then we must try to account for the relationship. This task is neither insignificant nor easy. Obviously policy decisions are made by public officials and not socioeconomic variables. No one has identified the means by which socioeconomic variables are translated into public policies.

Two conclusions can be fairly drawn from this discussion. One is that to understand how policy decisions are made and why some decisions are made rather than others, we must take into account social and economic as well as political factors. The second is that whether socioeconomic factors are more important than political factors in shaping public policy remains an open question. Though Dye's findings have been criticized, they have not been directly refuted. Most research along this line has been focused on the American states, and it is less than conclusive. Political scientists continue to spend most of their time studying the policy effects of political variables, with which they are most comfortable.

THE OFFICIAL POLICY-MAKERS

Official policy-makers are those who have the legal authority to engage in the formation of public policy. (I recognize, of course, that some who have the legal authority to act may in fact be significantly influenced by others, such as important constituents or pressure groups.) These include legislators, executives, administrators, and judges. Each performs policymaking tasks that are at least somewhat different from the others.

It is useful to differentiate between primary and supplementary policy-makers. Primary policy-makers have direct constitutional authority to act; for example, Congress does not have to depend upon other government units for authorization to enact legislation. Supplementary policy-makers, such as national administrative agencies, however, operate on the basis of authority granted by others (primary policy-makers). This puts secondary policy-makers in a dependency relationship. Administrative agencies, such as the Federal Trade Commission and the Bureau of Land Management, that derive their operating authority from congressional legislation will typically need to be at least somewhat responsive to congressional interests and requests. Congress may retaliate against unresponsive agencies by imposing restrictions on their authority or reducing their budgets. On the other hand, Congress has little need to be solicitous about agency interests.

The conflict between president and Congress during the second Nixon administration over whether the president could refuse to spend appropriated funds and thus act on his own to terminate previously authorized programs illustrates the importance of the distinction between primary and supplementary policy-makers. If the president lacked constitutional authority for impounding (or not spending) funds, as many in Congress contended, then Congress could ultimately control spending. This conflict over constitutional authority was essentially about whether the president could act here as a primary policy-maker, which would increase the independence and power of the executive vis-à-vis Congress. The issue was resolved in favor of Congress by several federal court decisions. Also, the Congressional Budget and Impoundment Control Act of 1974 provided that presidential decisions to impound appropriated funds were subject to control by Congress (see Chapter 5). Given the different interests and constituencies of the two branches, it is clear that who prevails on such matters can have profound policy implications.

The following survey of official policy-makers is intended only to be suggestive, that is, to convey a notion of their general role in policy formation, not to catalogue all their powers and activities.

Legislatures

The easy response to the question, "What do legislatures do?" is that they legislate—that is, they are engaged in the central political tasks of lawmaking and policy formation in a political system. It cannot be assumed, however, that a legislature, merely because it bears that formal designation, actually has independent decision-making functions. This is a matter to be determined by empirical investigation rather than by recourse to definition.

Unlike those in most other countries, legislatures at all levels in the United States do typically legislate in an independent decisional sense. At the national level, policies on such matters as taxation, civil rights, social welfare, consumer protection, economic regulation, and environmental protection tend to be shaped in substantial degree by Congress through the enactment of substantive and appropriations legislation. The committee and subcommittee system and legislative norms (accepted rules of conduct) encouraging members to concentrate on particular policy areas have provided Congress with its own policy specialists. Specialization, in turn, gives members more opportunity to influence policy in their areas of expertise, whether tax policy, welfare programs, or banking regulation.

The capacity of Congress to engage effectively in policymaking has been much enhanced by its expanded staff assistance. As the issues that members are called upon to resolve become more complex, so their need for technical and expert assistance becomes greater. Congressional staff assistance falls into three categories:

1. *Personal staff:* These people work for the individual members of Congress, either in Washington or in their home districts and states. More than 11,000 persons serve as staff aides to members. The average House member has a staff of seventeen; senators' staffs are typically larger. Some staffers handle routine office duties and constituency matters; others have

important legislative responsibilities. Legislative assistants, for instance, write speeches, draft bills, monitor committee hearings, negotiate with other staffs and lobbyists, suggest policy initiatives, and otherwise assist members in handling their policymaking responsibilities.

2. *Committee and subcommittee staffs:* Members of these staffs proliferated in the last two or three decades and now number in the thousands. The professional members of committee staffs, usually subject-matter experts, often have much influence on the development of legislation—drafting bills, developing political support, working with agency officials, fashioning compromises on disputed provisions, and the like. A committee's staff is divided between the majority and minority members, with the majority getting the lion's share. Complaints that committee staffs had become too large and were contributing to congressional inefficiency culminated in action in 1995 by the new Republican majority to reduce by one-third the size of House committee staffs.

3. *Institutional staff:* Agencies providing information services to Congress include the Congressional Research Service (part of the Library of Congress), the General Accounting Office, and the Congressional Budget Office. These agencies, which are expected to perform in a nonpartisan and objective manner, provide members of Congress with research studies, policy evaluations, and budgetary data. Another agency, the Office of Technology Assessment, was abolished in 1995 by Congress.

All of this staff assistance helps increase the policymaking capacity of Congress and reduces its dependency upon others—the executive, administrative agencies, and interest groups—for information. Also, some staff members may act as policy entrepreneurs, scouting for matters on which Congress could legislate or problems that might be investigated, or working to hinder proposals with which they disagree. Some members of Congress, especially senators, overburdened with committee and subcommittee assignments or other duties may become overly dependent upon staff and become their captives.

Democratic government in modern societies is representative government. Only in small communities can people directly govern themselves. Consequently, at the national level, democratic theory assigns to Congress the task of representing the people in the governing process.[22] People expect their representatives to allocate benefits (public buildings, highways, research facilities) to their districts and states; to assist them in resolving their difficulties with Social Security, veterans benefits, and regulatory and other government programs; and to represent their interests in the course of making policy on matters both large and small. It is this third aspect of representation that is of concern to us in this book.

In enacting legislation, the members of Congress try to take care of state and local interests as well as promote broad national or public interests.

Former Speaker of the House Thomas ("Tip") O'Neill often said that "all politics are local." Some critics allege that many of the members of Congress are much too caught up in local, or parochial, interests, acting more as local ambassadors than national legislators. Certainly many members of Congress do experience many demands and pressure from some of their constituents and narrowly based interests. However, they are also under pressure from the White House and from congressional leaders to act on behalf of more general and national interests. As a result, members find themselves squeezed between conflicting demands. Professor Walter A. Rosenbaum portrayed the effects of this condition on energy policymaking in this manner: "Thus, representatives and Senators must fashion a national energy policy within a vortex of competing political powers and pressures: national interest versus local interests, and commitments to party or congressional leaders versus loyalty to local power centers."[23] Legislators, of course, also have their own values and policy preferences to think about in making decisions.

Congressional representation of the people on the whole is uneven. The politically active, the powerful, and the well-to-do are more likely to have their needs and interests responded to than are the politically quiescent, the weak, and the poor or disadvantaged. These and other factors—such as the pounding Congress has taken on radio and television talk shows and the perception that it has not dealt adequately with major problems such as the budget deficit—have generated cynicism and distrust toward Congress and the government. In a nationwide opinion survey taken in mid-1995, 79 percent of the respondents agreed with the statement, "The government is run by a few big interests looking out for themselves." Only 41 percent believed that "people like themselves have at least some say in what the government does."[24]

In the states, the legislature's role often varies with the type of issue. Many state legislatures, because of their limited sessions, rather "amateur" membership, and inadequate staff assistance, often cannot act with much independence on complex, technical legislative matters. They may simply enact bills agreed upon elsewhere. In a fairly typical case several years ago, the Texas legislature passed a law on pooling (or unitization) for the common development of oil fields. It was introduced after being agreed to and drafted by representatives of the major and independent petroleum producers' organizations and enacted with little change; the legislature did not really have the capacity to do otherwise. On other issues, such as criminal legislation, the legislature clearly does "legislate." It does not require any special skills to make decisions, for example, on the penalty for embezzlement or automobile theft. Such questions do not admit of scientific or technical determination.

The British Parliament has been said merely to consent to laws that are originated by political parties and interest groups, drafted by civil servants, and steered through the House of Commons by "the government" (the prime minister and the cabinet). This view, however, is oversimplified. The government usually gets what it wants from Commons partly because it knows what

Commons will accept and requests only measures that are acceptable. Conversely, what is recommended by the government helps make it acceptable to its members in Commons. In the course of approving legislation, Commons performs the vital functions of deliberating, scrutinizing, criticizing, and publicizing governmental policies and activities and their implications for the public. The legislative process in Congress also performs these functions.

To conclude, legislators are more important in policy formation in democratic than in authoritarian countries. In the latter, the legislature may simply be a form of political theater used to convey the impression of public representation in policymaking. In the democratic category, legislatures generally have a larger role in presidential systems (like the United States) than parliamentary systems (like Great Britain). Some countries, such as Oman and Saudi Arabia, have no legislature; public policies are executive or monarchic products handed down to the people.

The Executive

We continue to live in an "executive-centered era," in which the effectiveness of government substantially depends upon executive leadership and action in both the formation and execution of policy. This is clearly true for the United States. Our attention now turns to the president.

The president's authority to exercise legislative leadership is both clearly established by the Constitution and legislation, and accepted as a practical and political necessity. The fragmentation of authority in Congress stemming from the committee system and the lack of strong party leadership generally renders that body incapable of developing a comprehensive legislative program. In the twentieth century, Congress has come to expect the president to present to it a program of proposed legislation. Whether the Congress does what the president recommends is another matter. The president cannot command Congress; he can urge and persuade and appeal to the public for support, but he cannot compel.

Presidents have had varying degrees of success in their dealings with Congress. In the past half-century, Lyndon Johnson was most successful, winning 82 percent of the votes on issues on which he took a stand. Jimmy Carter, in contrast, had great difficulty in getting what he wanted from Congress, even though his own party controlled it. After getting much of what he wanted from Congress during his first year in office, Ronald Reagan's ability to influence Congress began to decline. In 1987 and 1988, Congress supported Reagan on fewer than half the issues on which he took a clear position, the poorest presidential performance on this measure in more than three decades. During his term in office, George Bush managed to win 51 percent of the votes on issues on which he took a stand.[25] Bill Clinton's relationship with Congress, which had been pretty successful during his first two years in office, took a nosedive in 1995 after the Republicans gained control of both houses of Congress in the 1994 congressional elections.

Although the presidency may be a lonely place, the president does not act alone on policy matters. The Executive Office of the President (EOP) comprises several staff agencies whose raison d'être is advising and assisting the president in handling his responsibilities, including development and implementation of policy. The White House Office includes many personal aides and advisers, such as the chief of staff, the special assistant on national security affairs, the press secretary, and the counsel to the president. The Office of Management and Budget assists the president in preparing the annual budget, supervising expenditures, and managing the executive branch. Set up in 1947 to help the president coordinate foreign, military, and domestic policies relating to national security, the National Security Council has become a major player in developing and conducting foreign policy. The Council of Economic Advisors, staffed by a handful of professional economists, provides the president with information and advice on issues of micro- and macroeconomic policy. These agencies and other EOP units have taken shape in response to expanded presidential duties and responsibilities in recent decades. Collectively, they have enhanced the president's capacity to act, and frequently to act effectively, as a policy-maker.[26] They help ensure that the president will make informed decisions, if not always wise decisions.

Congress has delegated a substantial amount of policymaking authority to the president. Foreign-trade legislation gives the president discretionary authority to raise or lower tariff rates on imported goods. Presidents have used this authority to significantly lower rates on most imports. The Taft-Hartley Act authorizes the president to intervene in labor-management disputes that threaten the national health and safety. Such presidential interventions have been infrequent, however, because they tend to be both controversial and unwelcome. Perhaps the most extensive delegation of power came with the Economic Stabilization Act of 1970, which gave the president a blank check to impose wage and price controls for combating inflation. President Nixon said he did not want this authority and would not use it if it were granted. Concerned about the state of the economy and its importance for his reelection, he subsequently changed his mind and surprised the nation with a 90-day price–wage freeze in August 1971. This decree was followed by systems for mandatory and voluntary controls, until the whole effort was abandoned in 1974.

In foreign and military policy, which often merge, the president has greater constitutional authority and operating freedom than in domestic policy. Foreign policy of the United States is largely a product of presidential leadership and action. American policy toward Vietnam, as we well know, was shaped by the presidents in office between 1950 and 1975. The decision to seek more open and friendly relations with the People's Republic of China in the early 1970s was President Nixon's, and the decision to drive the Iraqi armed forces out of Kuwait was President Bush's. Much of foreign policy is the domain of the executive, not only in the United States but elsewhere in the world.

In recent decades, though, Congress has sought to expand its role in foreign policy. One manifestation was the War Powers Resolution of 1973, which was stimulated by the Vietnam War. Enacted over President Nixon's veto, the resolution requires the president to consult with Congress in "every possible instance" involving use of American armed forces in hostile situations. The president must report to Congress within forty-eight hours after using the forces. Unless Congress provides otherwise, military action must be halted within sixty to ninety days. Presidents have been highly critical of the resolution as an improper intrusion in their constitutional domain, and their compliance with it has been spotty at best.[27] Congress was also the source of much opposition to the Reagan administration's military and financial involvements in Central America. No longer can presidents count on bipartisan support for military and foreign-policy actions as they could in the first decade or two after World War II. By no means is Congress simply a rubber stamp for presidential initiatives. The Somali case is illustrative.

In early December 1992, a few weeks before he left office, President Bush sent several thousand U.S. troops to Somalia as part of a multi-nation humanitarian effort to relieve famine in that nation.[28] He explained that the troops were being sent only to ensure that food supplies moved to the starving people; the troops would not be used to "dictate political outcomes" or to "engage in hostilities." Subsequently, the conduct of the Somali operation became the responsibility of the Clinton administration. Unfortunately, hostilities did erupt. In June 1993 twenty-three Pakistani peacemakers were killed. Four U.S. soldiers were killed in August when their vehicle struck a land mine. Then, early in October, eighteen U.S. soldiers died and scores more were wounded during a botched raid on a Somali warlord.

As these events occurred, Congressional support for the Somali mission dissipated and Congress, with strong bipartisan support, began to consider legislation calling for the withdrawal of the American troops. So pressured, President Clinton announced that the troops would be withdrawn by March 31, 1994. He and Congress were then able to agree on a compromise that was enacted into law. The legislation provided that no funds could be used for military operations in Somalia after March 31, 1994, unless authorized by Congress. However, funds could be used after that date to support protection from American diplomatic facilities and citizens. All troops were to be under U.S. rather than United Nations control. Several days before the March 31 deadline, almost all of the U.S. troops departed from Somalia.

Reflective of the important policymaking role of the American executive is that in evaluating an executive—whether the president, a governor, or a mayor—our emphasis is on policymaking rather than administrative accomplishments. Presidents, for their part, are more interested in policy initiation and adoption rather than administration, because it enables them to build more visible and measurable records of achievement.

Administrative Agencies

Administrative systems throughout the world differ in such characteristics as size, complexity, hierarchic organization, and degree of autonomy from the other branches of government. Although it was once common doctrine in political science that administrative agencies only carried into effect, more or less automatically, policies determined by the "political" branches of government, now it is axiomatic that politics and administration are blended, and that administrative agencies are often significantly involved in the formation of public policies. This is particularly apparent, given the concept of policy as encompassing what government actually does over time concerning a problem or situation. Administration can make or break a law or policy that was made elsewhere. In the eighteenth century, Catherine II of Russia decreed that a large part of the institution of serfdom was to be abolished. However, the landowning aristocracy, which really controlled the administration of the government, was largely able to prevent this decision's implementation. In the United States, the effectiveness of state and national pollution-control laws has often been blunted by heel-dragging and inadequate enforcement by the administering agencies.

Especially in complex, industrial societies, the technicality and complexity of many policy matters, the need for continuing control of matters, and legislators' lack of time and information have caused the delegation of much discretionary authority, which often includes extensive rule-making power, to administrative agencies. Consequently, agencies make many decisions and issue many rules that have far-reaching political and policy consequences. Illustrations include the choice of weapons systems by the Department of Defense, the development of air-safety regulations by the Federal Aviation Agency, the location of highways by state highway departments, and the regulation of motor vehicles by the National Highway Traffic Safety Administration and the Environmental Protection Agency. Professor Norman C. Thomas comments, "It is doubtful that any modern industrial society could manage the daily operation of its public affairs without bureaucratic organizations in which officials play a major policymaking role."[29]

Administrative agencies are an important source of legislative proposals and ideas in the American political system. Because of their experience and specialized knowledge, agency officials are able to identify needed changes in existing policies, perhaps to eliminate loopholes, as well as new problems, that, in their view, are appropriate targets for legislation. Specific proposals to deal with such matters, including statutory language, may either be conveyed directly to Congress or channeled through the White House as part of the president's legislative program.

Agencies also actively lobby and otherwise strive to win acceptance of legislation they favor, or kill that which they oppose.[30] Officials frequently testify before congressional committees on legislative and budgetary issues. They provide requested information to members and help them prepare speeches. Projects and federal grants-in-aid may be allocated to states and districts with an eye to building support for the agency. Many agencies have congressional liaison offices to regularize contacts with Congress. The Department of State, for example, has an assistant secretary for legislative affairs; the Environmental Protection Agency has an associate director for congressional and legislative affairs. There are also myriad informal contracts between the agencies and Congress. Much of this can accurately be called lobbying: "the stimulation and transmission of a communication, by someone other than a citizen acting on his own behalf, directed to a governmental decision-maker with the hope of influencing his decision."[31]

In years past, the Congress has occasionally become irritated about administrative lobbying and has adopted legislation banning it.[32] This ban essentially has been ignored. Extensive administrative–congressional communication has become accepted as a legitimate part of the policymaking process.

The Courts

Nowhere do the courts play a greater role in policy formation than in the United States. The courts, notably the national and state appellate courts, have often greatly affected the nature and content of public policy by exercising the powers of judicial review and statutory interpretation in cases brought before them.

Judges are often thought to be nonpolitical, merely "following the law" or previous decisions, but in fact they are often deeply involved in policy politics (as distinguished from party or partisan politics). Their selection, whether by appointment or election, typically hinges on their party affiliation and their policy preferences and values. Once in office, values and preferences deeply affect their decisions. Thus Professors Robert Carp and Claude Rowland, in their exhaustive study of federal district judges, found that judges appointed by President Lyndon Johnson, who deliberately appointed civil-rights supporters to the bench, in actuality were considerably more likely to render pro–civil-rights decisions than were judges appointed by Presidents Dwight Eisenhower and Richard Nixon.[33] That the Reagan and Bush administrations took great care to appoint staunch Republican conservatives to federal judgeships is familiar recent history.[34]

Essentially, judicial review is the power of courts to determine the constitutionality of actions by the legislative and executive branches, and to declare them null and void if they are found to be in conflict with the Constitution. Clearly, the Supreme Court was making policy when, in various cases before 1937, it held that no legislature, state or national, had constitutional authority to regulate minimum wages. After 1937, the Constitution was found (i.e., interpreted) to permit such legislation. Clearly, too, the Court has helped shape public policy by holding that segregated school systems, official prayers in public schools, and malapportionment of state legislatures are unconstitutional. The course of policy is strongly affected by such decisions.

Although the Court has used its power of judicial review somewhat sparingly, the very fact that it has such power may affect the policymaking activities of the other branches. Congress may hesitate to act on a matter if there is some expectation that its action will be found unconstitutional. State supreme courts also have the power of judicial review but frequently have less discretion in its exercise because most state constitutions are detailed and specific.

The courts are often called upon to interpret and decide the meaning of statutory provisions that are ambiguously or unclearly stated and open to conflicting interpretations. When a court accepts one interpretation rather than another, it gives effect to the policy preference of the winning party. In 1984, in the *Grove City* case, the meaning or intent of Title IX of the 1972 Education Act Amendments was at issue.[35] This provision prohibited discrimination on the basis of sex by educational institutions receiving federal aid "for any program or activity." Did this ban on discrimination apply to the entire institution being aided, as many members of Congress and civil-rights groups contended? Or did it apply only to the specific "program or activity" receiving funding, as the Reagan administration argued? A majority on the Supreme Court took the latter position, much restricting the effect of the 1972 statute and three other civil-rights laws with similar provisions.

After this ruling, a legislative campaign was initiated to correct what many critics thought was an improper interpretation of the 1972 law. It culminated in the Civil Rights Restoration Act of 1988, enacted into law over President Reagan's veto.[36] The act overcame the Court's *Grove City* decision by clearly specifying that if one part of an institution received federal funds then the ban on sex discrimination applied to the entire institution. This was the view of the 1972 law's scope that had prevailed prior to the Court's decision.

The judiciary has also played a major role in forming economic policy in the United States. A substantial portion of the law relating to such matters as property ownership, contracts, corporations, and employer–employee relationships has been developed and applied by the courts in the form of common law and equity. These are systems of judge-made law fashioned over the years on a case-to-case basis. They originated in England but American judges have adapted them to American needs and conditions. Much of this law was developed by the state courts, and much of it is still applied by them.[37]

Today the courts are not only becoming more involved in policy formation, they are also playing a more positive role, specifying not only what government cannot do but also what it must do to meet legal or constitutional requirements. For instance, in *Roe* v. *Wade* (1973), the Supreme Court declared unconstitutional a Texas statute prohibiting abortion as a violation of the privacy protected by the First and Fourteenth Amendments.[38] The right to an abortion was held to be a "fundamental right," one that could not be readily regulated or limited by governments. The majority went on to specify the standards future abortion laws would have to meet to comply with the Constitution. During the first trimester of pregnancy, abortion was left to the decision of a woman and her physician. During the second trimester, abortion could be regulated to protect the mother's health. During the third trimester, however, after the fetus gained viability, abortion could be prohibited, except when necessary to protect the mother's life or health. This ruling clearly had a legislative-like quality. It also touched off a major, continuing political controversy.

In 1989 the Court, which had become more conservative because of three Reagan appointees, partially overruled *Roe* v. *Wade*. In *Webster* v. *Reproductive Health Services*, the Court upheld a Missouri state law that prohibited the performance of abortions in public hospitals and clinics and the use of state funds for counseling women about abortion.[39] Also, testing was required before performing an abortion after twenty weeks to determine whether the fetus was viable outside the womb. This decision, by giving state legislatures more authority to regulate abortions, made the abortion issue even more contentious and thrust it back into the legislative arena in the fifty states. The Supreme Court came to grips with abortion again in 1992 in *Planned Parenthood of Southeastern Pennsylvania* v. *Casey*. At issue was state law imposing various restrictions on a woman's right to end a pregnancy. The five-justice majority reaffirmed a woman's right to have an abortion in the early stages of pregnancy but upheld all provisions of the state law except one requiring spousal notification. Only two justices, however, continued to view abortion as a fundamental right.[40] The Court's 1992 decision did nothing to reduce the intensity of the abortion issue.

Several factors would seem to guarantee continued judicial involvement on policy formation: the growing influence of government on people's lives; the failure or refusal of the legislative branches to act on some problems; the dissatisfaction that often arises when they do act; the willingness of the courts to become involved; and the increasing litigiousness in at least some segments of the population. Americans have become quite adept at converting political issues into legal issues that the courts are then called on to decide.

Although courts in such other Western countries as Canada, Australia, and West Germany have some power of judicial review, they have had less influence on policy than American courts. In the developing countries the courts appear to have no meaningful role. The American practice of settling through judicial action many important policy issues, including such technical matters as standards for clean air and industrial health and safety, remains unique.

UNOFFICIAL PARTICIPANTS

The official policy-makers are joined by many other participants in the policy process, including interest groups, political parties, research organizations, communications media, and individual citizens. They are designated here as unofficial participants because, however important or dominant they may be in various situations, they themselves do not usually have legal authority to make binding policy decisions. They provide information, they exert pressure, they seek to persuade, but they do not decide. That is the prerogative of official policy-makers.

Interest Groups

Interest groups appear to take an important part in policymaking in practically all countries. Depending upon whether they are democratic or dictatorial, modern or developing, countries may differ in how groups are constituted and how legitimate they are. Thus, groups appear to be more numerous and to operate much more openly and freely in the United States or Great Britain than in Austria or Nigeria. In all systems, however, groups may perform an interest-articulation function; that is, they express demands and present alternatives for policy action. They may also supply public officials with much information, often technical, and perhaps not available from other sources, about the nature and possible consequences of policy proposals. In doing so they contribute to the rationality of policymaking.

Interest groups, such as those representing organized labor, business, and agriculture, are a major source of demands for public policy action in the United States. Because American society is pluralist, pressure groups are many and quite diverse in their interests, size, organization, and style of operation. They have expanded greatly in number in the last couple of decades. This does not mean, however, that some societal interests may not be poorly represented by groups. Migrant workers and poor people are cases in point. Typically, interest groups want to influence policy on a specific subject, such as the minimum wage, ethanol, or health-care financing. Because several groups often have conflicting desires on a policy issue, public officials confront the need to choose from among, or reconcile, conflicting demands. Groups that are well organized and active are likely to fare better than those whose potential membership is poorly organized and inarticulate. The group struggle is not a contest among equals.[41]

In recent years, "single-issue" interest groups have proliferated. They focus on one issue or set of related issues such as gun control, milk prices, and legislation on abortion. The National Rifle Association and the National Abortion and Reproduction Rights Action League are illustrative. The proliferation of subcommittees in Congress with narrow jurisdictions stimulated the development of such groups and contributed to their importance by permitting concentration of their efforts. Among the single-issue groups that substantially affected public policy in the past were those advocating abolition of slavery, suffrage for women, and nationwide prohibition.

Public-interest groups also are important players in the policy process. Whereas most pressure groups represent interests of direct, material benefit to their members, public-interest groups usually represent interests that in their absence would go unrepresented, such as those of consumers, nature lovers, environmentalists, and "good-government" proponents. Frequently these interests involve intangible matters such as honesty, beauty, and safety.[42] The members of public-interest groups usually do not benefit selectively and materially from the interests they advocate, and indeed may not benefit at all in an immediate sense. Members of groups advocating the abolition of the death penalty do not expect to be in personal jeopardy. Public-interest groups include the Sierra Club and the National Wildlife Federation, which support environmental protection and wilderness programs; Common Cause, which advocates more open and accountable government; and the Pacific Legal Foundation (PLF), which engages in litigation supporting free enterprise and economic development. Not all public-interest groups are liberal in their policy inclinations, as is sometimes assumed, and as the PLF indicates.

At the national level, many associations of state and local governmental officials routinely seek to influence the content of national policies. Three factors seem to have been especially significant in generating this "intergovernmental lobby."[43] One is the increasing professionalism in state and local governments. The second is growth in federal grants-in-aid to state and local governments, which amounted to $225 billion in 1995, or approximately 23 percent of their expenditures. Third are the many regulations and requirements that these and other federal programs impose on the states and localities, and that are open to modification.

Some of these associations represent elected or appointed officials with executive and legislative duties, such as the National Conference of State Legislators, the U.S. Conference of Mayors, and the National Association of

Counties. Others involve functional specialists in highways, education, recreation, and other matters, such as the American Association of State Highway and Transportation Officials, the Council of Chief State School Officers, and the National Association of County Park and Recreation Officials. They gain influence from their expertness and the support of state and local politicians. Many individual states, cities, counties, and public universities also have their own Washington lobbyists or representatives. As with other interest groups, the intergovernmental lobby is not a monolithic force: its component groups frequently disagree among themselves. Thus the highway officials want more funding for interurban highways, and city officials see a need for more spending on mass-transit systems.

The amount of influence that interest groups have upon decisions depends on a number of factors, including (subject to the rule of ceteris paribus—other things being equal) the size of the membership, its monetary and other resources, its cohesiveness, the skill of its leadership, its social status, the presence or absence of competing organizations, the attitudes of public officials, and the site of decision-making in the political system. (On this last item, recall the discussion of institutionalism in Chapter 1.) With other things again being equal, a large, well-regarded group (e.g., the American Legion) will have more influence than a smaller, less well-regarded group (e.g., Friends of the Earth), and a labor union with a large membership will have more influence than one with few members. Also, as a consequence of the factors enumerated here, a group may have strong or controlling influence on decisions in one policy area and little in another. Whereas the National Association of Manufacturers has much influence on some economic issues, it has little impact in the area of civil rights.

Much of the work in promoting pressure-group interests in the policy process is performed by group representatives, or lobbyists. Although "lobbyist" is the more popular term, "group representative" seems more descriptive, given the many and varied activities in which these people engage. Table 2.1, which is based on a survey of more than seven hundred group representatives, conveys a notion of both the array of activities undertaken by group representatives and the relative importance they attribute to the various activities. Once a group makes a decision to try to influence government on some matter, it is then confronted with deciding how it can best accomplish that goal. Should emphasis be on lobbying—directly seeking to inform and persuade officials? Should emphasis be on mobilizing group members back home to contact officials—what is often called "grass-roots lobbying"? Should emphasis be on providing written information and testimony to officials? How should the efforts of competing groups be countered? Typically, there is no clear road to success.

The relatively open and fluid pressure system in the United States is markedly different from the neocorporatist pattern of group relationships in some Western European countries, such as Austria, Norway, Sweden, and the

TABLE 2.1 Importance Rating of Group Representatives' Tasks

Task description	% reporting task was of great or considerable importance
Government regulations	
1 Monitoring changes in rules, regulations, or laws	62
2 Providing written information to officials	52
3 Maintaining general relations with officials	64
4 Maintaining informal, substantive contacts with officials	62
5 Drafting legislation or rules	27
6 Alerting client organization about issues	84
Interest group networks	
7 Mobilizing grass-roots support	41
8 Maintaining contacts with allies	50
9 Monitoring interest groups	29
10 Political fund-raising (PACs)	19
11 Maintaining contacts with adversaries	18
12 Resolving conflicts within organization	23
Public presentation	
13 Testifying at official proceedings	27
14 Preparing official testimony	47
15 Commenting for press, publications, or speeches	44
16 Developing policy positions or strategies	83
Litigation	
17 Pursuing litigation aimed at changing policy	17
18 Working on and filing amicus briefs	5

Source: John P. Heinz, Edward O. Laumann, Robert L. Nelson, and Robert H. Salisbury, *The Hollow Core: Private Interests in National Policymaking* (Cambridge, Mass.: Harvard University Press, 1993), p. 99.

Netherlands, which combine democratic politics with a formally structured group system.[44] In the neocorporate scheme of things, access to policy-makers is controlled by the government. Policies are adopted after close consultation, bargaining, and compromise between the government and groups that are the officially recognized representatives of farmers, labor unions, and employers. Groups can withdraw from this partnership with the government but they may lose influence as a consequence. Some groups, such as those representing consumer and environmental interests, find it difficult to gain access to the government. Neocorporatism has found little support in the United States.

Political Parties

In the United States, political parties are interested primarily in contesting elections in order to control the personnel of government. They care more, in short, about power than about policy. Elections are contested more on the basis of constituency, service, media imagery, and negative attacks on opponents rather than on policy differences. This situation has often led to the complaint that the Republican and Democratic parties do not present a meaningful choice for the voters and consequently, that for public-policy formation, it makes little difference which party is in office. Although the parties are not highly policy-oriented, such complaints ignore both the fact that many people do believe that the parties are different and the substantial impact that the parties do have on policy. Moreover, in the 1990s the parties in Congress became more united and policy-oriented. This was especially true for the House of Representatives.

Clearly, the parties appeal to different segments of society. The Democratic Party draws disproportionately from big-city, labor, minority, and ethnic voters; the Republican Party draws disproportionately from rural, small-town, and suburban areas, Protestants, and business people and professionals. In the South, where for many decades it was the heavily dominant party, the Democratic Party has yielded much ground to the Republican Party in national elections since the 1960s. The parties often come into conflict on such issues as welfare programs, labor legislation, business regulation, public housing, taxation, and agricultural price-support legislation. The reader should not have much difficulty in differentiating between the parties on these issues. Given such policy inclinations and the fact that party members in Congress often vote in accordance with party policy positions, which party controls Congress or the presidency has important policy implications.

In the American state legislatures, political parties vary greatly in importance from one state to another. In one-party states, it is obvious that parties exercise little discipline over legislative voting, and the party has little, if any, effect on policymaking, as in the Alabama and Louisiana legislatures. In such states, factions within the dominant party may be more important. By contrast, in states such as Connecticut and Michigan both parties are active and cohesive and have considerable influence on legislative decision-making. When conflict over policy occurs in such states, the parties' function is to provide alternatives. In many cities an effort has been made to eliminate political party influence on policy by running nonpartisan elections for city officials. Policy is supposed to be made "objectively." An unintended conse-quence of the policy of nonpartisanship in city elections is reduced interest and participation in politics.

In modern societies generally, political parties often perform the function of interest aggregation; that is, they seek to convert the particular demands of interest groups into general policy alternatives. The way in which parties "aggregate" interests is affected by the number of parties. In predominantly two-party systems, such as the United States and Great Britain, the parties' desire to gain widespread electoral support "will require both parties to include in their policy 'package' those demands which have very broad popu-lar support and to attempt to avoid alienating the most prominent groups."[45] In multiparty systems, on the other hand, parties may do less aggregating and act as the representatives of fairly narrow sets of interests, as they appear to do in France and Spain. Generally, though, parties have a broader range of policy concerns than do interest groups; hence, they act more as brokers than as advocates for particular interests in policy formation. In some one-party systems, such as that of Mexico, they are the predominant force in policymaking.

Research Organizations

Private research organizations, frequently and inelegantly referred to as "think tanks," are another set of important players in policymaking. One researcher estimates that approximately a thousand private, not-for-profit research organizations exist in the United States, with one hundred being located in the Washington, D.C., area.[46] These organizations are staffed with full-time policy analysts and researchers, some of whom are ex-government officials, who perhaps hope to return to office once their party regains power in Washington. Their studies and reports provide basic information and data on policy issues, develop alternatives and proposals for handling problems, and evaluate the effectiveness and consequences of public policies. Some prominent research organizations are the Heritage Foundation, the Cato Institute, the American Enterprise Institute, the Brookings Institution, the Institute for International Economics, the Urban Institute, and the Council on Foreign Relations. Collectively, they add much substance to policy debates.

Many of these research organizations have policy biases and distinct ideological leanings. The orientations of the American Enterprise Institute and the Economic Policy Institute, for example, are widely regarded as conservative and liberal, respectively. The Brookings Institution and Re-sources for the Future occupy a middle-of-the-road position. In addition to their policy-analysis activities, these organizations may also engage in policy advocacy. The Heritage Foundation, which is staunchly conservative, played an important role in launching the Reagan administration in 1981 and in shaping its policies on issues such as environmental protection, social welfare, and economic regulation. For a time its study *Mandate for Leadership* was a bestseller in Washington. Other research organizations, taking their cue from the Heritage Foundation, developed "policy blueprints" to influence the Bush administration in 1988; none appeared to make much difference. The Heritage Foundation has continued to be a strong advocate of conservative policy positions. Many new research organizations, mostly conservative or libertarian in orientation, have entered the policy lists as advocates in recent years.[47]

Many universities have policy or research centers that produce policy studies and evaluations on national, state, and local issues. Several, for instance, house groups concentrating on coastal and marine resources. Individual university researchers also occasionally produce studies of direct value to policy-makers, sometimes under contract with government agencies, and participate in issue networks comprising many researchers, officials, and others interested in particular policy areas.

Communications Media

The communications media—newspapers, news magazines, radio, and television—participate in policymaking as suppliers and transmitters of information; as agenda setters, in that they help determine what people think about; and, whether intentionally or otherwise, as shapers of attitudes. For many people the evening television news is the primary source of information on public affairs. In a 1992 survey, 69 percent of the respondents said that they got most of their news information from television; 56 percent said they were inclined to believe television over other news sources.[48] Those seeking more profound coverage and information rely more heavily on newspapers and news magazines. Complaints about bias in media coverage and reporting of public affairs are common, as are allegations that public officials are managing or manipulating the news. Whatever their validity, such complaints attest to the importance the media are thought to have in politics and policymaking.

With good reason, Washington officials are quite sensitive to what is reported by the national media, which means newspapers such as *The New York Times* and the *Washington Post* and the major television networks. A survey found that more than 70 percent of senior federal officials believed a positive press increased the likelihood that they would attain their goals and negative coverage would reduce their chances of doing so. Here the perceived power of the media does not involve changing policy but rather influences the capacity of officials to convert their ideas into policy. However, the substance of policy may also be affected.[49] Unfavorable coverage of the Reagan administration's attempts to tighten eligibility requirements for Social Security disability benefits, for example, contributed to the eventual abandonment of the effort.

Officials, of course, are not simply acted upon by the media but also strive to use the press for their own purposes. With interviews, press releases, and news "leaks," they seek to use the media to test and influence the attitudes among both the general public and other officials toward particular proposals or actions. Those who oppose a decision may "leak" premature or adverse information in an effort to kill it. This tactic was applied in the Bush administration to a proposal for securing funds to bail out bankrupt savings and loan institutions by imposing a tax on all savings and loan depositors. The proposal was abandoned and the costs of the bailout were imposed on taxpayers.

President Reagan was often referred to as the "great communicator" because of his ability to use radio and television addresses to shape public opinion in support of his purposes. He used this ability in 1986 to put income-tax reform on the national agenda and build support for its enactment. Speaker of the House O'Neill, who was not personally inclined to support tax reform, felt the pressure generated by the president's speeches. "I have to have a bill, the Democratic party has to have a [tax] bill . . . ," he was quoted as saying. "If we don't we'll be clobbered over the head by the President of the United States."[50] Used appropriately, the presidency can indeed be a "bully pulpit," as Theodore Roosevelt once observed.

The Individual Citizen

In discussions of policymaking, the individual citizen is often neglected in favor of legislatures, interest groups, and more prominent participants. This bias is unfortunate, however, for the individual often does seem to make a difference. Although the task of policymaking is generally assigned to public officials, in various instances citizens can still participate directly in decision-making. In some of the American states (notably California) and some countries (such as Switzerland), citizens still can and do vote directly on legislation. Moreover, in most states, constitutional amendments are submitted to the voters for approval. In many local jurisdictions, bond issues and increases in tax rates must be authorized directly by the voters. In Texas, approval by voters in local governmental units is required for local sales taxes, sale of liquor by the drink, and operation of bingo games. A great many citizens, of course, do not directly avail themselves of these opportunities to shape policy because of inertia or indifference.

This apathy frequently leads to the comment that citizen participation in policymaking, even in democratic politics, is slight. Many people do not vote, engage in party activity, join pressure groups, or even display much interest in politics. Survey research indicates, moreover, that many voters are influenced comparatively little by policy considerations when voting for candidates for public office. Granting this inaction, however, it still does not hold that citizens have no influence on policy except in the limited situations mentioned in the preceding paragraph. Let us review some possibilities.

Even in authoritarian regimes, the interests or desires of common citizens are consequential for public policies.[51] The old-style dictator will pay some attention to what his people want just to keep down unrest. A Latin American dictator is supposed to have said, "You can't shoot everyone." Modern authoritarian regimes such as the People's Republic of China also seem to want to meet many citizen wants even as they exclude citizens from more direct participation in policy formation. Also, several years before its collapse the Soviet regime increased production of consumer goods and even indicated a desire to surpass the United States in providing consumer benefits. It did not succeed.

Elections in democratic countries may indirectly reinforce official responsiveness to citizen interests. Professor Charles E. Lindblom summarizes:

> The most conspicuous difference between authoritarianism and democratic regimes is that in democratic regimes citizens choose their top policy makers in genuine elections. Some political scientists speculate that voting in genuine elections may be an important method of citizen influence on policy not so much because it actually permits citizens to choose their officials and to some degree instruct these officials on policy, but because the existence of genuine elections put[s] a stamp of approval on citizen participation. Indirectly, therefore, the fact of elections enforces on proximate policy makers a rule that citizens' wishes count in policy-making.[52]

The "rule" Lindblom refers to is sometimes expressed in the aphorism that citizens have a right to be heard and that officials have a duty to listen. The effect of such considerations on policy-makers is worth thinking about; although public sentiments are not amenable to rigorous measurement in the present state of political science, they do appear to have an effect on political behavior.

Some presidential elections in the United States have been classified as "critical" because they produce major realignments in voter coalitions and shifts in public policy. The presidential election of 1932 is a prime example. The Republican and Democratic candidates differed substantially on how they proposed to deal with the crisis of the Great Depression. The voters gave Franklin D. Roosevelt and the Democrats an overwhelming victory. The flood of New Deal legislation that followed produced major changes in government–economy relationships and in government's role in American society generally. In such instances, large numbers of newly elected officials, chosen because of their stand on the critical question, enact legislation consistent with their party's stand. Through the electoral process the voters help to produce basic changes in public policy. Other critical elections were those of 1860 and 1896.[53]

Initially some observers thought the election of 1980, in which the Republican Party elected Reagan and gained control of the Senate, might have been a critical election, but it turned out not to be. The Democratic gains in the 1982 congressional elections indicated that no basic realignment in voters' allegiances had occurred. The Democratic Party remains the majority party among voters having a party preference. "Landslide" elections are thus not necessarily critical elections. Following the Republican victories in the 1994 congressional elections, speculation again arose as to whether this marked the beginning of a realignment.[54]

Some citizens, through their intellectual and agitational activities, contribute new ideas and directions to the policy process. Thus Rachel Carson, with *Silent Spring*, and Ralph Nader, with *Unsafe at Any Speed*, considerably influenced policy on pesticide control and automobile safety, respectively. In a 1947 article in *Foreign Affairs* under the byline X, George Kennan outlined a proposal for a policy of containment to prevent expansion of the Soviet Union's influence and domination. This became the basic United States approach in dealing with the Soviet Union in the international arena. Only in the last few years before the collapse of the Soviet Union did the United States begin to develop new responses to the Soviets. The effect of Kennan's article was much greater than he anticipated.

Others may substantially affect policy action through their political activism. Social Security legislation in the 1930s was certainly affected by the activities of Dr. Francis Townsend, who advocated that every person over sixty should be paid a monthly pension of $200, and the large following he gathered. In the 1960s, Reverend Martin Luther King, Jr., provided leadership for the civil-rights movement and impetus for civil-rights legislation. Fifteen years of effort by Howard A. Jarvis culminated in the adoption of Proposition 13 in California in 1977. That proposition, adopted through the initiative process, provided for substantial reduction in property taxes and touched off a "tax revolt" that inspired similar actions in other states. Its effects are still being felt.

LEVELS OF POLITICS

Not all the participants in policymaking discussed above are involved in every policymaking or decision-making situation. Some matters arouse much attention and attract a wide range of participants. Others are less visible or affect only a few people and consequently stir little attention and participation.

Professor Emmette S. Redford identifies three levels of policies based on the scope of participation normally characteristic of each and, to a lesser extent, the kind of issue involved: micropolitics, subsystem policies, and macropolitics.[55]

Micropolitics involves efforts by individuals, companies, and communities to secure favorable governmental action for themselves. Subsystem politics is focused on functional areas of activity—such as air-pollution control, coal-mine safety regulation, or river and harbor improvements—and involves relationships among congressional committees, administrative agencies (or bureaus), and interest groups. Macropolitics occurs when "the community at large and the leaders of government as a whole are brought into the discussion and determination of [public] policy."[56] The controversies over the Clinton initiatives to reduce the budget deficit and to reform the health-care system are examples of macropolitics.

Micropolitics

Micropolitics often occurs when an individual seeks a favorable ruling from an administrative agency or a special bill offering an exemption from a requirement of the immigration laws, when a company seeks a favorable change in the tax code or a television broadcasting license, or when a community seeks a grant for the construction of an airport or opposes the location of a public-housing project in its area. In each of these instances one finds the specific, differentiated, and intense interest of one or a few in a society of many individuals, companies, and communities. They require or seek a decision applicable to one or a few. Typically, only a few persons and officials are involved in or even aware of such decision-making situations, however important they may be for those seeking action, and whatever the ultimate consequences of such decisions or a cluster of them may be.

In the short run at least, micropolitical decisions appear to be distributive and can be made without considering limited resources. That is, such decisions appear to affect only those immediately interested and are usually made on the basis of mutual noninterference, each claimant seeking its own benefits (or subsidies) and not opposing or interfering with others' efforts to do likewise. Benefits received by one individual or group do not appear to be won at the expense of other individuals or groups.

Micropolitics is exemplified by the congressional enactment of private legislation.[57] Almost every year Congress enacts several bills into law which apply only to a person, company, or governmental unit specifically designated in the law. A private law may exempt someone from a provision of the Immigration and Nationality Act, or provide for the payment of a monetary claim against the government, as when a government agency has caused damage to someone's property. Such legislation arouses little attention on its way through the legislative process and becomes law with the public unaware of its existence. Each party in the House does have a three-member "objector committee" whose task is to screen private bills for controversial provisions. For whatever reason, many more private bills are introduced during a session than become law.

As governmental programs become more numerous and complex, and as they make more benefits available for, or impose more requirements or restrictions on, individuals, groups, companies, and communities, both the opportunity and the incentive to engage in micropolitics increases. As this happens, the likelihood of favoritism and unequal treatment for persons and groups increases. Those who have more political resources (e.g., information, influential contacts, money) are more likely to become the beneficiaries of micropolitics, whatever the justness or soundness of their cause.

Subsystem Politics

In a frequently quoted passage, political analyst Ernest S. Griffith in 1939 called attention to the existence of political subsystems and the value of studying them:

> One cannot live in Washington for long without being conscious that it has whirlpools or centers of activity focusing on particular problems . . . it is my opinion that ordinarily the relationship among these men—legislators, administrators, lobbyists, scholars—who are interested in a common problem is a much more real relationship than the relationship between congressmen generally or between administrators generally. In other words, he who would understand the prevailing pattern of our present governmental behavior, instead of studying the formal institutions or even generalizations of organs, important though all these things are, may possibly obtain a better picture of the way things really happen if he would study these "whirlpools" of special social interests and problems.[58]

In the years since Griffith made that statement, political scientists and others have devoted much attention to examining political subsystems (also variously called subgovernments, policy clusters, and policy coalitions).

For many years, subsystems were usually designated as iron triangles (or cozy little triangles, or triple alliances). An iron triangle involves a pattern of stable relationships among some congressional committees (or subcommittees), an administrative agency or two, and the relevant interest groups centered on a policy area.[59] All have a direct, material interest in the policy matters being treated. A classic iron triangle was focused on rivers and harbors development activity. It comprised the Army Corps of Engineers (who still handle many civilian water projects), the congressional committees with jurisdiction over public works, and the National Rivers and Harbors Congress, an interest group. This triangle, which was resistant to wider participation, dominated policymaking on water projects. As with other triangles, the participants preferred policy to be made cooperatively and quietly.

The national government was often (and sometimes continues to be) described as heavily populated with iron triangles.[60] Although these arrangements provided participants with continuing access and much influence on the content of policy, those who were excluded—policy experts (often within the academic community), groups adversely affected by their policies, and others—were very critical of them. Iron triangles were charged with contributing to governmental fragmentation, causing lack of policy coordination, and acting contrary to the public interest. Moreover, the governmental agencies involved were frequently alleged to have been captured by the dominant groups; the Civil Aeronautics Board (now defunct) and the Interstate Commerce Commission (also defunct) were called captives of the commercial airlines and railroads, respectively. Although frequently bandied about, the notion of capture has not been well explained. Usually it appears to mean that, for whatever reasons, an agency has become—the person alleging capture feels—too responsive to the interests of an industry.

The iron-triangle concept came under attack several years ago by political scientist Hugh Heclo, who contended that it was "not so much wrong as it was disastrously incomplete."[61] The concept, he said, "suggests a stable set of participants coalesced to control fairly narrow public programs which are in the direct economic interest of each party to the alliances." Heclo's view was that other, larger sorts of arrangements also exist, which he referred to as "issue networks." He went on to explain that an issue network includes many participants who constantly move into and out of the network, including public officials, interest-group representatives, political activists, and technical or policy experts from universities, research organizations, and elsewhere. Within these somewhat cloudlike or amorphous configurations, no one seems to be in control of the policies and issues. What then does an issue network look like? Let Heclo answer:

> It is difficult to say, precisely, for at any given time only one part of a network may be active, and through time the various connections may intensify or fade among the policy intermediaries and the executive and congressional bureaucracies. For example, there is no single health policy network but various sets of people knowledgeable and concerned about cost control mechanisms, insurance techniques, nutritional programs, pre-paid plans, and so on. At any one time these experts in designing a nationwide insurance system may seem to be operating in relative isolation, until it becomes clear that previous efforts to control costs have already created precedents that have to be accommodated in any new system, or that the issue of federal funding for abortions has laid land mines in the path of any workable plan.[62]

Many of those involved in a network will not have direct material interests at stake; rather, their ideas and beliefs about proper public policy will be the basis for their participation. Figure 2.1 portrays the issue network focused on the price-support provisions of the 1985 farm bill.

Political scientists have enthusiastically embraced the concept of issue networks, despite a dearth of empirical data on the actual presence and operation of networks. The political science literature is replete with references to networks and to how they have replaced iron triangles in the policy process. In reality, some iron triangles probably survive, especially in distributive policy.

It would seem, however, that there is no need to assume that only one kind of subsystem can exist at a time. (That was not Heclo's position.) Why not rather assume that subsystems take various forms that can be arrayed along a continuum? At one pole we could put iron triangles, with their limited participation, resistance to external influences, and preoccupation with material interests. At the other pole we could put the issue network with its amorphousness, wide and changing participation, issue experts, and unclearness about who is in control. Other forms of subsystems could be appropriately arrayed between the poles.[63]

What I call a policy community is broader and more open in participation than an iron triangle but less amorphous and more under identifiable control than an issue network. Thus the antitrust community includes primarily the Antitrust Division of the Department of Justice and the Federal Trade Commission, the House and Senate Judiciary committees (or their antitrust subcommittees), the relevant appropriations subcommittees, writers of books and journal articles on antitrust, the private antitrust bar, and the federal courts that rule on antitrust cases. This community has much influence on the nature and implementation of antitrust policy as long as important new legislation is not involved. Significant changes in antitrust policy were achieved through variations in the interpretation and enforcement of laws by executive and judicial members of the antitrust community in the 1980s. The Reagan administration's attempt to have these changes enacted into statutory law failed, however. Clinton administration antitrust officials soon acted to reverse some of the Reagan and Bush administrations' antitrust practices.

Within a subsystem, especially if it is large and complex, advocacy coalitions may develop.[64] An advocacy coalition is a set of people within a subsystem who share basic values, perceptions of problems, and policy preferences, and who cooperate to advance attainment of their policy goals and interests. Often there are two or more advocacy coalitions in a subsystem. The policy area of air-pollution control provides an illustration.

The air-pollution control subsystem is complex, comprising the Environmental Protection Agency, various congressional committees, other agencies with overlapping jurisdictions, polluting companies, state and local pollution-control agencies, makers of pollution-control equipment, many health and

FIGURE 2.1   The 1985 Farm Bill Issue Network: Price Supports

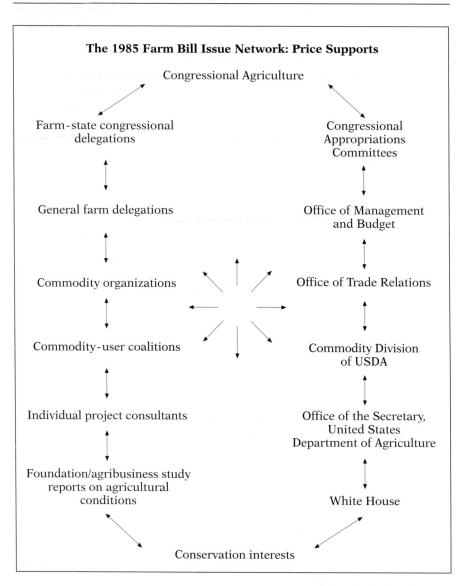

Source: William P. Browne, "Policy and Interests: Instability and Change in a Classic Issue Subsystem," in Allen J. Cigler and Burdett A. Loomis, eds., *Interest Group Politics,* 2nd ed. (Washington, D.C.: CQ Press, 1986), p. 198.

environmental groups, other countries (as on acid rain), and more. Two advocacy coalitions are identifiable in this subsystem: the clean-air and the economic-feasibility coalitions. The clean-air coalition consists of more EPA air-pollution officials, environmental and health groups, some labor unions, some state and local air-pollution control officials, some researchers, and some members of Congress. This coalition asserts the primacy of health over economic development, contends that the market cannot adequately deal with pollution problems, and favors a traditional regulatory approach to pollution control. The economic-feasibility coalition includes industrial sources of air pollution, energy companies, their allies in Congress, a few labor unions, some state and local pollution-control officials, and a number of economists. The economic-feasibility coalition stresses the need to balance health and economic development and efficiency, doubts that the health problems are as serious as some contend, and favors more deference to market arrangements and the use of economic incentives to reduce pollution.

Inside the air-pollution control subsystem, rulemaking and implementation actions will be shaped by the interaction of these advocacy coalitions, and will rest ultimately upon the EPA's legal authority. What advocacy coalitions obviously want to do is help shape the exercise of discretionary authority of the agency or agencies that are the focal point of their subsystem. The adoption of major air pollution control legislation, such as the Clean Air Act Amendments of 1990, however, will take place in the macro-political arena.

Whatever their form or style, subsystems are influential in policy development and implementation in the American political system. Perhaps issue networks are more important in new or unsettled areas of public policy, such as the disposal of hazardous waste, computer network communications, and the control of terrorism. Political communities or iron triangles are likely to be more common in stable areas of policy such as shipping regulation, vocational education, and veterans' benefits. There has been a tendency for subsystems to become broader in scope. Thus, the iron triangle, once centered on rivers and harbor projects, gave way to a wider policy community as many environmental groups became interested in this policy area. As a consequence, political life was made more complex for the Army Corps of Engineers, which has become more amenable to environmental interests.

Subsystems, of course, are part of the larger (macro) political system. As such, they are subject to penetration and control by the president, Congress, and other non-subsystem actors. Some things that subsystems need can come only from the larger political system—namely, legislation, appropriations, and political-level appointments. Those who are aggrieved by subsystem action may carry appeals for redress to the larger system. Consequently, subsystem autonomy is a conditional phenomenon. It may last only so long as subsystem actions are routine, accepted, and within the bounds of existing legislative authority. Even then, an external event, such as a change in presidential administrations or congressional majorities, may focus unwanted attention on some subsystems.

Macropolitics

Some policy issues will attract enough attention or become sufficiently controversial to be ripe for action in the macropolitical arena. Certain issues are "born" to be macropolitical, such as escalation of the war in Vietnam, President Reagan's proposal for a major reduction in personal income taxes, the Los Angeles earthquake of 1993, and the Clinton administration's proposal for health-care reform. Because of their controversy and major consequences they attracted wide interest and participation.

Many other issues may be moved from the subsystem to the macropolitical level by the action of public officials or other interested parties, perhaps because of dissatisfaction with subsystem actions. Moreover, policy proposals developed within subsystems often require approval by the larger political system. Then, because of their importance or magnitude, they draw extensive interest and participation. So it went with the Job Partnership Training Act and the 1988 legislation strengthening the Fair Housing Act. In other instances, however, bills emerging from subsystems may move through Congress with little attention or deliberation.

Some matters may begin political life at the micropolitical level and then escalate into macropolitical issues because of their symbolic, scandalous, or substantive characteristics. Consider the snail darter (a species of minnow), which was accorded protection under the Endangered Species Act (ESA) of 1973. Its designation as endangered by the U.S. Fish and Wildlife Service was a routine instance of policy implementation. What followed was not, as this summary reveals:

> The discovery of the snail darter in the Little Tennessee River in eastern Tennessee in August 1973, its subsequent listing as endangered in October 1975, and the designation of its critical habitat in April 1976 led to a major conflict with the Tennessee Valley Authority's Tellico project, a multipurpose water resource development project that was to provide economic development, hydroelectric, flood control, and recreation benefits. The conflict turned into litigation that went as high as the Supreme Court, resulting in front page headlines across the nation in mid-1978. The Supreme Court ruling that the ESA prohibited completion of the project led to amendments to the act that established an interagency panel to review projects for possible exemptions from the act's provisions. In January 1979, the panel ruled that the Tellico project should not be exempted because the project was "ill-conceived and uneconomic . . ." However, by attaching a rider onto an omnibus public works appropriation bill, Tennessee congressmen were able to sneak through a provision that directed the TVA to complete the project. Citing political problems and the difficulty of vetoing a bill that would fund numerous other projects, President Carter signed the bill "with regret" in September 1979.[66]

Thus did the snail darter and the Endangered Species Act become the focus of a macropolitical struggle. Several other listings of endangered species have also instigated macropolitical conflicts. Most, however, have been handled within the bounds of a subsystem centered around endangered species policy.

The central participants in macropolitics include the president, party and congressional leaders (who often overlap), and the executive departments. The communications media, who often drum up public attention on an issue, and various group leaders usually are also deeply involved. This level of politics attracts most attention in studies of policymaking because it is often quite visible and salient as well as sharply conflictual and sometimes sensational.

Decisions made in the macropolitical arena may differ considerably from what they would have been if made at one of the other levels. Among other things, when an issue moves, say, from the subsystem to the macropolitical arena, the conflict is expanded in scope. More players take part, and, E. E. Schattschneider suggests, expanding the conflict often changes the substance of the settlement, that is, the policy decision.[67] Broad public interests are likely to receive fullest consideration at the macropolitical level.

A distinctive characteristic of macropolitics is presidential involvement. Whether the president more adequately represents national interests than does the Congress, as some contend, is open to debate. What is certainly true, however, is that those interests that are represented by the president enjoy an advantage in the macropolitical arena. Because of the centrality and visibility of his office, his capacity to formulate policy alternatives, and the resources he can draw upon in support of his proposals, the president can be the policy leader here if he so chooses. His actions will substantially affect the content and direction of public policies, as a comparison of the differing influences of the Johnson, Nixon, and Reagan administrations on antipoverty policy indicates.

In Chapter 3, we look at the emergence and definition of public problems, agenda setting, and the formulation of policy proposals, especially as they occur in the macropolitical arena.

Notes

1. David R. Mayhew, *Divided We Govern: Party Control, Lawmaking, and Investigations, 1946–1990* (New Haven, Conn.: Yale University Press, 1991). See also Charles O. Jones, *The Presidency in a Separated System* (Washington, D.C.: Brookings Institution, 1994)
2. *United States v. Lopez* (1995). Reported in *The New York Times*, April 27, 1995, pp. 1, A13.

3. Ann O. M. Bowman and Richard C. Kearney, *The Resurgence of the States* (Englewood Cliffs, N.J.: Prentice-Hall, 1986), pp. 10–22.
4. *Congressional Quarterly Almanac, 1992*, XLVII (Washington, D.C.: Congressional Quarterly, Inc., 1993), pp. 210–211.
5. Clyde Kluckhohn, *Mirror for Man* (Greenwich, Conn.: Fawcett, 1963), p. 24.
6. For an extended discussion of political culture, see Gabriel A. Almond and Sidney Verba, *The Civic Culture* (Boston: Little, Brown, 1965); and Donald J. Devine, *The Political Culture of the United States* (Boston: Little, Brown, 1972).
7. Daniel J. Elazar, *American Federalism: A View from the State* (New York: Harper & Row, 1984), chap. 4.
8. Robin M. Williams, Jr., *American Society*, 3rd ed. (New York: Knopf, 1974), chap. 11.
9. Devine, op. cit., pp. 210–211.
10. Karl W. Deutsch, *Politics and Government* (Boston: Houghton Mifflin, 1970), p. 207.
11. Almond and Verba, op. cit., pp. 11–26.
12. Deutsch, op. cit., p. 207.
13. Cf., E. E. Schattschneider, *The Semi-Sovereign People* (New York: Holt, Rinehart and Winston, 1960), chap. 1.
14. Thomas R. Dye, *Politics, Economics, and the Public Policy Outcomes in the Fifty States* (Chicago: Rand-McNally, 1966). Dye uses the term "policy outcome" to designate what I described as policy outputs in Chapter 1.
15. Ibid., p. 293. See also Thomas R. Dye, *Understanding Public Policy*, 7th ed. (Englewood Cliffs, N.J.: Prentice-Hall, 1992), chap. 12; and Michael Lewis-Beck, "The Relative Importance of Socio-economic and Political Variables in Public Policy," *American Political Science Review*, Vol. 62 (June 1977), pp. 559–566.
16. Richard Dawson and James Robinson, "The Relation Between Public Policy and Some Structural and Environmental Variables in the American States," *Journal of Politics*, XXV (May 1963), pp. 265–289.
17. Ibid., p. 289.
18. Robert H. Salisbury, "The Analysis of Public Policy," in Austin Ranney, ed., *Political Science and Public Policy* (Chicago: Markham, 1968), p. 164.
19. Ira Sharkansky and Richard I. Hofferbert, "Dimensions of State Policy," in Herbert Jacob and Kenneth N. Vines, ed., *Politics in the American States*, 2nd ed. (Boston: Little, Brown, 1972), esp. pp. 318–323.
20. Ibid., p. 320.
21. Ibid., p. 321. Cf. Robert L. Lineberry and Edmund P. Fowler, "Reformism and Public Policies in American Cities," *American Political Science Review*, LXI (September 1967), pp. 701–716.
22. Leroy N. Rieselbach, *Congressional Politics: The Evolving Legislative System*, 2nd ed. (Boulder, Colo.: Westview, 1995), p. 13.
23. Walter A. Rosenbaum, *Energy, Politics, and Public Policy*, 2nd ed. (Washington: CQ Press, 1987), p. 51.
24. *The New York Times*, August 12, 1995, p. 8.
25. Norman J. Ornstein, Thomas E. Mann, and Michael J. Malbin, *Vital Statistics on Congress, 1993–1994* (Washington, D.C.: Congressional Quarterly, 1994), pp. 195–196.

26. William M. Lunch, *The Nationalization of American Politics* (Berkeley: University of California Press, 1987), pp. 122–123. See also John Hart, *The Presidential Branch*, 2nd ed. (Chatham, N.J.: Chatham Press, 1995).
27. Louis Fisher, *Presidential War Power* (Lawrence: University Press of Kansas, 1995), chap. 7.
28. This discussion draws on ibid., pp. 153–154; and *Congressional Quarterly Weekly Report*, Vol. 51 (October 16, 1993), pp. 2823–2827.
29. Norman C. Thomas, *Rule 9: Politics, Administration, and Civil Rights* (New York: Random House, 1966), p. 6.
30. Rieselbach, op. cit., pp. 212–214.
31. Lester W. Milbrath, *The Washington Lobbyists* (Chicago: Rand-McNally, 1963), p. 8.
32. Abraham Holtsman, *Legislative Liaison: Executive Leadership in Congress* (Chicago: Rand-McNally, 1970), chap. 3.
33. Robert A. Carp and C. K. Rowland, *Policy-Making and Politics in the Federal District Courts* (Knoxville: University of Tennessee Press, 1983).
34. See, for example, Ronald Stidham and Robert A. Carp, "Judges, Presidents, and Policy Choices: Exploring the Linkage," *Social Science Quarterly*, Vol. 68 (June 1987), pp. 395–404.
35. *Grove City College v. Bell*, 465 U.S. 555 (1984).
36. *Congressional Quarterly Weekly Report*, Vol. 46 (January 23, 1988), pp. 160–163; Vol. 46 (March 26, 1988), pp. 774–776.
37. Emmette S. Redford, *American Government and the Economy* (New York: Macmillan, 1965), pp. 53–54.
38. *Roe v. Wade*, 410 U.S. 113 (1973). Also *Griswold v. Connecticut*, 381 U.S. 479 (1958).
39. *Webster v. Health Reproductive Services*, 492 U.S. 490 (1989). Also *The New York Times*, July 4, 1989, pp. A1, A8–A12.
40. *Planned Parenthood of Southeastern Pennsylvania v. Casey*, 112 S. Ct. 931 (1992).
41. See generally, John P. Heinz, Edward O. Laumann, Robert L. Nelson, and Robert H. Salisbury, *The Hollow Core: Private Interests in National Policy Making* (Cambridge, Mass.: Harvard University Press, 1993).
42. This discussion is based on Kay Lehman Scholzman and John T. Tierney, *Organized Interests and American Democracy* (New York: Harper & Row, 1986), pp. 28–35.
43. Thomas J. Anton, *American Federalism and Public Policy* (New York: Random House, 1989), pp. 94–95; Scholzman and Tierney, op. cit., pp. 55–57.
44. Graham K. Wilson, *Business and Politics: A Comparative Introduction*, 2nd ed. (Chatham, N.J.: Chatham House, 1990), chap. 6.
45. Gabriel A. Almond and G. Bingham Powell, Jr., *Comparative Politics: A Developmental Approach* (Boston: Little, Brown, 1966), p. 103.
46. James A. Smith, *The Idea Brokers: Think Tanks and the Rise of the New Policy Elite* (New York: The Free Press, 1991), p. xiv.
47. Louis Jacobson, "Tanks on the Roll," *National Journal*, Vol. 27 (July 8, 1995), pp. 1767–1771.
48. Stanley and Niemi, op. cit., p. 1994.
49. Martin Linsky, *Impact: How the Press Affects Federal Policy-Making* (New York: Norton, 1986), pp. 114–115.

50. Steven B. Roberts, "A Most Important Man on Capitol Hill," *New York Times Magazine*, September 22, 1984, p. 48.

51. This discussion draws on Charles E. Lindblom, *The Policy-Making Process* (Englewood Cliffs, N.J.: Prentice-Hall, 1968), p. 44.

52. Ibid., p. 45.

53. For further discussion, see James R. Sundquist, *Dynamics of the Party System: Alignment and Realignment of Party Systems in the United States* (Washington: Brookings Institution, 1972); David W. Brady, "Critical Elections, Congressional Parties and Clusters of Policy Changes," *British Journal of Political Science*, VIII (January 1978), pp. 79–99; and Warren E. Miller and J. Merrill Shanks, "Policy Directions and Presidential Leadership: Alternative Interpretations of the 1980 Presidential Election," *British Journal of Political Science*, XII (July 1982), pp. 299–358.

54. Walter Dean Burkham, "Realignment Lives: The 1994 Earthquake and Its Implications," in Colin Campbell and Burt A. Rockman, eds., *The Clinton Presidency: First Appraisals* (Chatham, N.J.: Chatham House, 1995), chap. 12.

55. Emmette S. Redford, *Democracy in Administrative State* (New York: Oxford University Press, 1969), p. 107.

56. Ibid., p. 53.

57. Walter J. Oleszek, *Congressional Procedure and the Policy Process*, 3rd ed. (Washington: CQ Press, 1989), pp. 117–118.

58. Ernest S. Griffith, *The Impasse of Democracy* (New York: Harrison-Hilton Books, 1938), p. 182.

59. The subsystem concept is discussed in J. Leiper Freeman, *The Political Process*, rev. ed. (New York: Random House, 1965). See also Jeffrey M. Berry, *The Interest Group Society*, 2nd ed. (Chicago: Scott Foresman, 1989), chap. 8.

60. Many introductory American government textbooks contain discussions of iron triangles. See, for example, Theodore J. Lowi and Benjamin Ginsbery, *American Government: Freedom and Power* (New York: Norton, 1990), pp. 308–310.

61. Hugh Heclo, "Issue Networks and the Executive Establishment," in Anthony King, ed., *The New American Political System* (Washington: American Enterprise Institute, 1978), pp. 87–124.

62. Ibid., p. 104.

63. For a similar suggestion, independently arrived at, see John Creighton Campbell with Mark A. Baskin, Frank R. Baumgartner, and Nina P. Halpern, "Afterword on Policy Communities: A Framework for Comparative Research," *Governance: An International Journal of Policy and Administration*, II (January 1989), pp. 86–94.

64. This discussion relies on Paul A. Sabatier, "Policy Change over a Decade or More," in Paul A. Sabatier and Hank Jenkins-Smith, eds., *Policy Change and Learning: The Advocacy Coalition Approach* (Boulder, Colo.: Westview, 1993), chap. 2.

65. Cf. Frank R. Baumgartner and Bryan D. Jones, *Agendas and Instability in American Politics* (Chicago: University of Chicago Press, 1993), chaps. 2, 3.

66. Steven Lewis Yaffee, *Prohibitive Policy: Implementing the Federal Endangered Species Act* (Cambridge, Mass.: MIT Press, 1982), p. 165.

67. Schattschneider, op. cit., chap. 4.

3

POLICY FORMATION:
PROBLEMS, AGENDAS,
AND FORMULATION

*Protests and demonstrations are used to influence government action. The "Satur-
day for Kids" march on Washington in January 1996 attracted 200,000 marchers.*

U ntil the New Deal years, government paperwork (forms, reports, information requests) was not perceived as a public problem. Up to that time the national government had only limited direct contact with citizens. The great expansion of governmental programs in the 1930s, however, "dramatically increased the need for data and unleashed a wave of forms and surveys upon the land."[1] World War II programs generated more needs for information, and complaints about the burdens imposed on citizens and companies became more frequent. Paperwork was transformed into a public problem.

Congress responded to this new problem with the Federal Reports Act, which authorized agencies to collect from citizens information that was necessary for agency operations, unless other agencies were already gathering the information. The law rested on the assumption that agency officials could properly decide what information they needed and that any burdens imposed upon citizens were an acceptable inconvenience.[2]

The Federal Reports Act did not render paperwork popular, however. Complaints and criticisms continued and grew in volume as paperwork requirements escalated in the 1960s and early 1970s with the proliferation of national social welfare and economic regulatory programs. Soon after he became president in August 1974, Gerald Ford put regulatory reform and paperwork reduction on the national policy agenda. His public speeches and statements contained many remarks about needless paperwork, the "paperwork mountain," and the high costs of paperwork. At his request, Congress created a Commission on Federal Paperwork, which subsequently found that federal paperwork cost "more than $100 billion a year, or about $500 for each person in the country."[3] By now, paperwork was no longer merely an inconvenience; it had become a costly and unnecessary burden whose benefits for the administrative process were slighted. Information collection lost quite a bit of its legitimacy.

The Carter administration continued the campaign to control paperwork, first through an executive order and then by urging Congress to legislate on the problem. The result was the Paperwork Reduction Act, signed into law late in 1980 by President Jimmy Carter, despite strong objections from several executive departments and agencies. The act specified that all agency requests for information had to be cleared through the Office of Management and Budget and that OMB should act to reduce the burden of information collection by 25 percent by October 1, 1983. Apparently this goal was met.[4] The struggle against paperwork has continued, however, and the Paperwork Reduction Act periodically has been renewed, most recently in 1995, when it had strong bipartisan support in Congress. Further reductions in the paperwork burden were called for. However, two Senate amendments that would have reduced the paperwork burden imposed by Congress on federal agencies were dropped from the final act.[5]

In this chapter we begin to analyze the policy-making process as a sequence of functional activities, as illustrated by the issue of federal paperwork reduction. Three interrelated aspects of policy formation are discussed: the nature of public problems, agendas and the process of agenda setting, and the formulation of proposed policies to deal with problems. The adoption of policies is taken up in Chapter 4. Before going on, let me clarify the meaning of a couple of terms. Policy formation denotes the total process of creating or developing and adopting a policy. Policy formulation, in contrast, refers more narrowly to the crafting of proposed alternatives or options for handling a problem, such as what should be done to reduce the number of high school dropouts or the volume of federal paperwork.

The legislature is the primary institutional focus of this chapter, although the other branches of government also get involved in setting agendas and formulating policy proposals. The U.S. Supreme Court, for instance, sets its own agenda when it determines which of the thousands of cases appealed to it will be heard and decided. Again, much policy (or rule) formulation occurs in the context of the administrative process, as agencies exercise their delegated authority to make rules on air pollution, motor-vehicle safety, trade practices, and other matters.

It should be kept in mind that defining problems, setting agendas, and formulating proposals, together with adoption of policies, are functional categories. Although they can be readily separated for analysis, in actuality they frequently are interrelated and smudged together. For instance, those who want action on a problem may try to define it broadly, as affecting large numbers of people, to help ensure that it gets on a legislative agenda. Again, those formulating a policy proposal will often be at least partly guided in their efforts by the need to build support for the adoption of their proposal. Particular provisions may be included, modified, or excluded in an attempt to win the support or reduce the opposition of some groups or officials.

POLICY PROBLEMS

Older studies of policy formation devoted little attention to the nature and definition of public problems. Instead, problems were taken as "givens," and analysis moved on from there. However, it is now conventional wisdom that policy study that does not consider the characteristics and dimensions of the problems that stimulate government action is less than complete.[6] It is important to know both why some problems are acted on and others are neglected and why a problem is defined in one way rather than another. This helps one determine where power lies in the political system. Moreover, whether a problem is foreign or domestic, a new item or the outgrowth of an existing policy, or limited or sweeping in scope helps to determine the nature of the ensuing policy-making process. Evaluating a policy also requires information on the substance and dimensions of the target problem in order to appraise the policy's effectiveness.

For our purposes, a policy problem can be defined as a condition or situation that produces needs or dissatisfaction among people and for which relief or redress through governmental action is sought. Such conditions as dirty air, unwholesome food, the practice of abortion, urban congestion, crowded prisons, and global warming are conditions that may become problems if they produce sufficient anxiety or dissatisfaction to cause people to seek a remedy. For this to happen people must have some criterion or standard by which the troubling condition is judged to be both unreasonable or unacceptable and appropriate for government to handle. Something in effect needs to tell us that we do not need to put up with free-roaming dogs in the city, for instance, or that inflation will have unacceptable economic effects. If people think that a condition is normal, inevitable, or their own responsibility, then nothing is likely to happen because it is not perceived as a problem. If, let us say, a group of people is afflicted by depressed economic conditions but regards these conditions as inevitable or legitimate and neither does anything about them nor somehow elicits actions by others in their behalf, then according to the stated definition, no problem exists. Conditions do not become public problems unless they are defined as such, articulated by someone, and then brought to the attention of government. This action can be and frequently is taken by legislators and other government officials who are often scouting around for problems that they can claim credit for solving.

As stated, to be converted into a problem a condition must also be seen as an appropriate topic for governmental action and, further, as something for which there is a possible governmental remedy or solution. Those who oppose government action to ban smoking in public places may argue that tobacco smoke is not harmful, or that smoking is a matter of individual choice and should not be regulated. Such argumentation is variously designed to prevent the controversial condition from being viewed as a problem, to keep it off a government agenda, or, failing that, to prevent adoption of a smoking regulation. Professor Aaron Wildavsky contends that officials are unlikely to deal with a problem unless it is coupled with a solution. As he states, "A problem is a problem only if something can be done about it."[7]

Hurricanes and earthquakes as such are not likely to become public problems because government can do nothing to prevent them. However, the conditions of human distress and property destruction caused by hurricanes do become public problems. Relief programs, building regulations, and early-warning systems are devised to prevent or reduce hurricanes' adverse consequences. Quite a few conditions will not be transformed into problems because they do not qualify as matters that government can handle appropriately and effectively. "Putting a man on the moon became a problem for policy-makers only after it became technically possible to do so in the late 1950s."[8]

Conditions can be defined as problems, and redress for them can be sought by persons other than those who are directly affected.[9] In the mid-1960s, poverty was identified as a public problem and the Johnson administration declared a War on Poverty more because of the actions of public officials and publicists than those of the poor themselves. Legislators are frequently looking for problems that they can mitigate or solve so as to enhance their reputations and/or help themselves win reelection. Of course, there is always the possibility that others will define a problem differently than those directly affected. Indeed, problems are often defined differently by individuals and groups possessing varying interests and values.

Although many problems are persistent, how they are defined may change as values and conditions change. We can use alcoholism (drunkenness) as an illustration. In the nineteenth century, drunkenness was viewed as a personal problem, as the product of one's evil, wicked, or sinful ways, and therefore as one's just punishment. In the early decades of the twentieth century, it became more common to view drunkenness as a social problem that arose from the response by some individuals to the social, family, and other pressures that played upon them. Counseling and other social services were seen as appropriate responses. More recently, alcoholism (no longer called drunkenness) has been defined as an illness (i.e., a pathological condition) requiring medical treatment and deserving health-insurance coverage, whatever its immediate social causes. This medical definition reduces the individual's responsibility and the stigma attached to the condition. Public policy, however, has not fully caught up with the modern definition, and many problem drinkers continue to be dealt with through the regular law-enforcement processes, especially if they combine drinking and driving. Mothers Against Drunk Driving (MADD) takes a tough enforcement stance on this issue.

Conditions that at one time are accepted as the normal order of things may later, because of social change, be treated as problems.[10] For centuries, wife-beating, child abuse, and other forms of family violence were private matters except, perhaps, when the regular criminal laws, as against homicide, were violated. They are no longer so treated. Changes in public attitudes, media attention, the women's movement, and other factors changed our notions about acceptable conduct in family matters. A variety of national and state laws pertaining to family violence now are on the statute books. There is still uncertainty as to the pervasiveness of family violence, however.

The definition of problems is often a political process whose outcome will help determine appropriate solutions. Is access to public transportation for the physically handicapped a transportation problem or a civil-rights problem? Identifying it as a transportation problem means that the handicapped should have adequate transportation available to them, by regular modes or any practical means, such as special van service. Defining it as a civil-rights problem, however, means that the handicapped should have equal access to regular transportation facilities, which might require installing elevators at subway stations, fitting buses with loading ramps for wheelchairs, and making other expensive modifications in transportation facilities. After some wavering between the two alternatives, public policy moved toward the availability-of-transportation solution in the 1980s under the Reagan administration.[11]

Another facet of problem definition is causation. A condition may be defined as a problem, but what causes the condition? Many problems—crime, poverty, inflation, and air pollution—have multiple causes. For example, inflation, the upward movement of prices at an unacceptable rate as measured by the consumer price index, is a public problem. But what is its cause? Is it the underproduction of goods and services? Excess demand for goods and services (i.e., too many dollars chasing too few goods)? Too much money in circulation? The product of inflationary psychology, where people expect prices to continue to climb? To deal effectively with a problem one must treat its causes rather than its symptoms. For many problems, the underlying causes are not easy to diagnose or evaluate. Identifying the causes of a problem and getting agreement on them may be a hard task for policy-makers. Defining the problem then itself becomes a problem.

The nature and scope of some public problems may be difficult to specify because they are diffuse or "invisible." Because measurement may be quite imprecise, policy-makers may be uncertain about the magnitude of the problem and in turn about effective solutions, or even whether there is a need for governmental action. In the 1980s, growing numbers of homeless people were sleeping in public and private shelters, in the streets, under bridges, and in other places not suitable for human habitation. Estimates of the number of homeless people in the United States ranged from 250,000 to 3 million.[12] Anywhere from 10 to 47 percent of them were thought to be chronically mentally ill. These wide ranges reflect the difficulty in getting an accurate count of the homeless and their characteristics. The causes of homelessness are also poorly understood. The Stewart B. McKinney Homeless Assistance Act of 1987 called for better collection of data on the homeless by the states while also expanding federal assistance for services to this group. Other problems that are difficult to measure include child abuse, learning disabilities among schoolchildren, illegal immigration, and the amount of income not reported on federal income tax returns.

Another dimension of public problems is their tractability, or amenability to solution. Some problems, for instance, require much less behavioral change than others. Thus, the elimination of discrimination in voting registration in Southern states was fairly quickly accomplished under the Voting Rights Act. Essentially what was required to correct the problem was either altering the behavior of a comparatively small number of voting registrars or bypassing them by the appointment of federal registrars. School desegregation was much more difficult because it involved large numbers of people and strongly established social patterns. Desegregation was strongly resisted, sometimes in violent ways. More than four decades after *Brown v. Board of Education* (1954) some Southern schools continue to have manifestations of racial discrimination.[13]

Tractability is also affected by whether problems are tangible or intangible. Tangible problems, such as scarce jobs, poorly managed public-housing projects, or an overburdened criminal justice system, can be eased by improving the incentives and resources available to people and agencies. Other inner-city problems—racism, inadequate job skills, or despair—are intangible, involving values. According to Professor James Q. Wilson, such problems "are hard to address by money alone because they make whites less likely to invest or extend opportunities and blacks less likely to take advantage of opportunities."[14]

Our subject is not merely problems but *public* problems, which leads to this question: What characteristics or qualities make a problem public? Most people would agree that John Smith's car being out of gasoline is a private problem, however disturbing to Smith it may be, whereas the widespread shortage of gasoline in a community or region is perceived as a public problem. What distinguishes private problems from public problems? Essentially, public problems are those which affect a substantial number of people and have broad effects, including consequences for persons not directly involved.[15] Problems that have limited effects, being of concern only to one or a few persons who are directly affected, can normally be viewed as private.

Admittedly, this is not a very sharp set of definitions. An illustration will help clarify the difference between private and public problems. Assume that Mary Smith is unhappy with her personal tax burden under the current laws. Acting on her own, she may seek a favorable administrative ruling from the tax collector to reduce her burden or try to induce her representative to do so. She may decide in the future to invest in tax-exempt municipal bonds or otherwise try to reduce her tax obligation. Our imaginary citizen has a problem, but at this point it is essentially private. As another alternative, she may seek to publicize her problem and enlist the support of others who share or sympathize with her situation. They organize for political action. A bill may be introduced in the legislature at their request and a campaign for its passage may be launched, which in turn is likely to draw opposition. Directly or indirectly, many people become involved or perceive themselves as affected. A public problem is now evident.

Many of the problems that are acted on by governments are really private problems. To a large extent, the micropolitical level of politics discussed in Chapter 2 focuses on private problems. Private bills passed by Congress that apply only to the persons named in them deal with private problems, such as immigration difficulties. Much of the time of many members of Congress and their staffs is also devoted to "casework," providing assistance to individual constituents in their personal problems with administrative agencies. This activity does help "humanize" government by making it more responsive to the problems of private citizens.

Before leaving this discussion of problems, it should be stressed that whether a condition or situation is regarded as a problem depends not only on its objective dimensions, but also, quite importantly, upon how it is perceived by people or, put differently, how it is socially constructed. A wealthy person who has never lacked a good job may see little threat in a rising rate of unemployment, and indeed may view it as necessary to prevent inflation. However, an industrial worker for whom unemployment is always a possibility may regard it as a clear threat. One's perceptions are shaped by one's values, situation, and experience. There is no single correct way to assess a condition or to define a problem, although many people will have strong views and preferences on some matters. Problem definitions often compete for acceptance.[16]

Whether there was in fact an "energy crisis" in the form of a shortage of fuel, especially oil and natural gas, in the 1970s and whether this was a public problem requiring governmental action depended upon its being defined and accepted as such. Moreover, how it was defined, including what its causes were, helped determine what was viewed as an appropriate response. The Nixon, Ford, and Carter administrations, acting on the belief that there was indeed an energy crisis, took actions to alleviate it, including petroleum price controls, conservation measures, programs to develop new sources of energy, and eventually deregulation of oil and natural-gas prices. The Reagan administration, in sharp contrast, denied the existence of an energy crisis and moved to dismantle many of the programs set up in the 1970s. Critics of the administration contended that it took a shortsighted view of the problem. The notion of an energy crisis has now faded into history, but perhaps only temporarily.

This review leads to another question: Why are some matters, apart from their scope or effect on society, seen as public problems requiring governmental action while others are not? Some answers to this question are provided in the following discussion of the policy agenda and the process of agenda setting.

THE POLICY AGENDA

One frequently reads about demands being made by this group or that individual or some public official for action by a governmental body on some problem, whether it be rough streets or crime therein, disintegration of the family, or waste and fraud in defense contracting. Of the thousands and thousands of demands made upon government, only a small number will receive serious consideration by public policy-makers. In other words, each problem must compete for official attention because legislators and executives have limited time and resources. Decisions to consider some problems mean that others will not be taken up, at least for the time being. The demands that policy-makers choose to or feel compelled to act on at a given time, or at least appear to be acting on, constitute the policy agenda,[17] which is thus distinguishable from political demands generally. It should also be distinguished from the term *political* (or *policy*) *priorities*, which designates a ranking of agenda items, with some matters being considered more urgent or pressing than others. Sometimes a problem will be labeled as a "crisis," as in "the health care crisis," in an effort to secure higher agenda status and help ensure action.

To achieve agenda status, a public problem must be converted into an issue, or a matter requiring governmental attention (see Figure 3.1). Political scientist Robert Eyestone states, "An issue arises when a public with a problem seeks or demands governmental action, and there is public disagreement over the best solution to the problem."[18] A rising crime rate may be defined as a public problem, but disagreement over what, if anything, government should do about it creates an issue. In recent years important public issues have included such matters as prayer in public schools, illegal drug traffic, illegal immigration, research on and treatment of AIDS, and how the United States should deal with the situation in Bosnia. Many stands may be taken or alternatives proposed on such issues, thereby demonstrating the inadequacy of the old saw that there are two sides to every issue.

Of the number of policy agendas that can be identified in a political system, Professors Roger W. Cobb and Charles D. Elder specify two basic types: the systemic agenda and the institutional, or governmental, agenda. The systemic agenda as they define it "consists of all issues that are commonly perceived by members of the political community as meriting public attention and as involving matters within the legitimate jurisdiction of existing governmental authority."[19] A systemic agenda will exist for every national, state, and local political system. Some items may appear simultaneously on many systemic agendas, such as environmental protection, drug abuse, and crime in the streets. Other issues, such as the international trade deficit or the building of a new convention center in a city, will appear only on the national and a local agenda, respectively.

The systemic agenda is essentially a discussion agenda. Most of the items on it will be general or abstract rather than specific or detailed. Action on a problem requires that it be brought to the attention of a governmental body with authority to take appropriate measures. An institutional or governmental agenda consists of the problems to which legislators or public officials feel

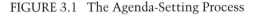

FIGURE 3.1   The Agenda-Setting Process

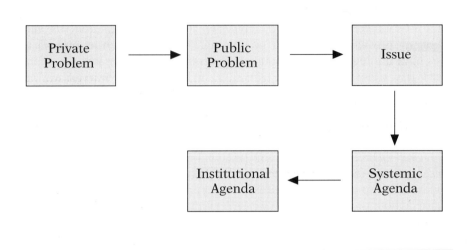

obliged to give serious and active attention. Only some of the issues that concern policy-makers are likely to be widely discussed by the public. The general public's cognizance of policy issues is often rather low, with awareness and information mostly confined to a narrow segment of the population, that is, the "attentive public." Many of the issues dealt with by legislatures, involving minor legislation and technical or uncontroversial changes in current laws, are essentially unknown to the rank-and-file citizens.

Because policy decisions can be made at a variety of points in the political system, there are also several institutional agendas. At the national level one can identify legislative, executive, administrative, and judicial agendas. An institutional agenda is basically an action agenda and thus will be more specific and concrete in content than a systemic agenda. Whereas crime in the streets may be of systemic concern, Congress will be confronted with more fully developed proposals for action in this policy area, such as a program of financial aid to local law-enforcement agencies or a proposal for constructing additional prisons. Appearance on an institutional agenda does not guarantee that a topic will be acted upon, although it clearly increases its chances. Professor John W. Kingdon makes a useful distinction between subjects on the governmental (or institutional) agenda that are getting attention and those on the "decision" agenda, which "are up for an active decision."[20]

Institutional agenda items can range from mandatory to discretionary.[21] Congress can be used to illustrate this classification scheme. Much congressional time is given to considering matters it is required to handle, including reauthorization of public programs (such as the foreign-aid program); the president's budget requests; and, for the Senate, approval of treaties and presidential appointments. Other matters, notably proposals for new legislation, whether initiated by members themselves, pressure groups, or other sources, are more discretionary. The leaders and members of Congress have more control over whether these will be given consideration. Some new matters, which technically are discretionary, may appear mandatory because of strong presidential pressure or a compelling crisis, such as income tax reform in the 1980s or the budget crisis in the 1990s.

The number of people affected and the intensity of their interest will vary across the issues on an agenda. Some matters will attract much interest from the broad range of citizens and officials; others will attract the attention primarily of policy specialists and those who have a direct stake in them. Professor Barbara Sinclair suggests that an agenda "is best conceptualized as roughly pyramidal" in form. A "limited number of highly salient issues" will be at the top; as one moves toward the base there will be "an increasing number of progressively less and less salient issues."[22] Those at the top would likely qualify for Kingdon's decision agenda, although many of them will attract little attention from the public or the media.

To conclude, a policy agenda is not a thing of precision or fixed content. It would probably not be possible to secure complete agreement on the content of any policy agenda, at least if it is somewhat complex, whether it is that of Congress or a city council. Clues to the content of the congressional agenda, for example, are provided by presidential messages, legislation singled out by party leaders for attention, issues discussed in the communications media, and the like. Inability to enumerate all the items on a policy agenda does not destroy the usefulness of the concept for studying policy.

THE AGENDA-SETTING PROCESS

How, then, do problems reach the agendas of governmental organizations, such as Congress? A prominent answer to this query has been supplied by Professor John Kingdon.[23] In an analysis that has captivated many political scientists, he holds that agenda setting can be viewed as comprising three mostly independent streams of activity (problems, proposals, and politics), which occasionally converge, opening a "policy window" and permitting some matters to reach a governmental agenda.

The problems stream consists of matters on which policy players, either inside or outside of the government, would like to secure action. In the health area, for instance, people may be worried about the cost of health care, access to care, the adequacy of disease-prevention programs, or the need for more biomedical research.

The policy-proposals stream comprises possible solutions for problems. Public officials, congressional committee staffs, bureaucrats, academics, group representatives, and others develop proposals. "They each have their pet ideas or axes to grind; they float their ideas up and the ideas bubble around in . . . policy communities. In a selection process, some ideas or proposals are taken seriously and others are discarded."[24] Solutions that survive await problems to which to attach themselves. Sometimes, according to Kingdon, those with "pet" solutions look for problems that can be solved with them.

The politics stream includes such items as election results, changes in presidential administrations, swings in public moods, and pressure-group campaigns. Occasionally, these three streams converge and, for a short time, a policy window is open, that is, "an opportunity for advocates of proposals to push their pet solutions, or to push attention to their special problems" will come available. Sometimes the window opens predictably, as when a law comes up for renewal; in other instances, it happens unpredictably.[25]

Kingdon's theory appears to make agenda setting a rather chancy process; much depends upon timing and luck. Without denying that timing and luck play a part in agenda setting, especially for large or basic changes in public policy, my view is that the process is more predictable, controllable, and orderly than he implies. That stated, I turn to my more structured view of agenda setting.[26]

At any given time, many problems and issues will be competing for the attention of public officials, who will also have their own preferred ideas to push. Only a portion of these problems will succeed in securing agenda status, however, because officials lack the time, resources, interest, information, or will to consider many of them. Agenda building is thus a competitive process, and a number of factors can determine whether an issue gets on an agenda, including how the problem at issue is defined.

One factor is suggested by political scientist David B. Truman, who says that interest groups seek to maintain themselves in a state of reasonable equilibrium and that if anything threatens this condition, they react accordingly.

> When the equilibrium of a group (and the equilibrium of its participant individuals) is seriously disturbed, various kinds of behavior may ensue. If the disturbance is not too great, the group's leaders will make an effort to restore the previous balance. . . . This effort may immediately necessitate recourse to the government. Other behaviors may occur if the disturbance is serious to the point of disruption.[27]

Thus American steel producers and shoe manufacturers, seeing cheaper imported steel and shoes as contrary to a satisfactory price and profit situation, seek limitations on imports. Companies threatened by unfriendly takeovers have likewise sought governmental restrictions on corporate acquisitions. Moreover, when one group gets what it wants from government, this gain may cause a reaction by other groups, as with organized labor's continued efforts to secure first the repeal of and then modifications to some of the restrictions in employee relations and collective bargaining imposed on them by the Taft-Hartley Act of 1947. For years, automobile manufacturers were similarly successful in delaying imposition of fuel-economy standards set by legislation on energy conservation. Interest groups thus successfully strive to place issues on an institutional agenda but by no means do they account for all issues achieving agenda status.

Political leadership is another important factor in setting agendas. Political leaders, whether motivated by thoughts of political advantage, the public interest, or their political reputations, may seize upon problems, publicize them, and propose solutions. Of particular importance here is the president because of his prominent role as an agenda setter in American politics. Presidents can use the State of the Union, the budget, and special messages to set the congressional agenda. Media events may accompany these messages and bring them to the attention of the general public as well. Presidential initiative here tends to be limited by the notion that Congress can handle only a few major initiatives at a time. Jimmy Carter was criticized for flooding Congress with legislative proposals and thereby reducing his effectiveness as a legislative leader. In contrast, Ronald Reagan focused on tax cuts and expenditure reductions during his initial year in office.

In his study of presidential agenda setting, Professor Paul Light found that in selecting major domestic issues on which to advocate action, presidents are motivated by three primary considerations.[28] The first is electoral benefits, which are especially important during a president's first term. Certain issues are seen as critical to electoral success, and as vital in building and maintaining electoral coalitions. There is also a feeling that issues stressed during a campaign should be acted on. The second concern is historical achievement. Because history surrounds the office, and the Washington community and others constantly compare presidents, a president often becomes mindful of greatness, of his place in history. Issues are singled out that the presidents want to "mark" their administration. The third consideration is good policy. Presidents enter office with ideological leanings and personal commitments that may dispose them to act on some matters even in the face of congressional hostility and bureaucratic resistance. The importance of some issues, moreover, makes such action imperative. Light concludes, "Presidents do have notions of what constitutes good public policy." This was certainly true for Ronald Reagan, although many people did not agree with what he considered good policy.

Members of Congress also sometimes serve as agenda setters. In a study of agenda setting in the U.S. Senate, Professor Jack L. Walker concludes that there are some "activist legislators, motivated by a desire to promote social change, and anxious to gain reputations as reformers [who] constantly search for issues that might be transformed into new items on the Senate's discretionary agenda."[29] Senator Alan Simpson (R, Wyoming) was instrumental in putting immigration-reform legislation on the Congressional agenda and securing its enactment. In the House, Representative Henry Waxman (D, California) has been a strong proponent of legislation to control acid rain and other forms of air pollution. Members of Congress and others who push policy proposals in this manner are often referred to as "policy entrepreneurs." They are especially important in promoting action on policy issues that entail diffuse benefits for large numbers of people.

Governmental entities also often serve as agenda setters for one another. The case of highway speed limits is a good example. When Congress in 1974 enacted the National Maximum Speed Law, which provided that states would lose some federal highway funds if they did not reduce speed limits to 55 miles per hour, it ensured that the speed limits issue would appear on the agendas of states' legislation. This occurred again in the late 1980s, when Congress permitted the speed limit on rural interstate highways to be increased to 65, and in 1995 when the maximum speed law was repealed. Supreme Court decisions have often helped put items on the Congressional agenda.[30] Congress has tried (unsuccessfully) to overcome the Court's decision that prayer in public schools is unconstitutional by proposing a constitutional amendment. Several provisions have also been included in legislation to restrict use of federal funds to pay for abortions as a consequence of the Court's decision in *Roe* v. *Wade* (see p. 69). More frequently, Court decisions interpreting and applying legislation trigger congressional responses to overcome their effects. The Civil Rights Act of 1991 offset several Court decisions, making it more difficult for job discrimination victims to successfully sue for damages.

Items may achieve agenda status and be acted upon as a result of some sort of crisis, natural disaster, or sensational event, such as a hurricane or an airplane disaster. Such an event serves to dramatize an issue and attract wide attention, causing public officials to feel compelled to respond. There may be awareness, discussion, and continuing advocacy of action on some matter, but without broad interest being stirred, some sort of "triggering" even seems needed to push the matter onto a policy agenda for decision.[31] Thus the Soviet launching of the first Sputnik into orbit in 1957 helped push space research and exploration onto the policy agenda in the United States, notwithstanding the Eisenhower administration's initial professed lack of concern about this accomplishment. The killing of five schoolchildren and the wounding of several others in Stockton, California, in early 1989 by a deranged person wielding an assault rifle sparked public outcry against the sale of such weapons; President Bush subsequently acted to ban their importation but not their domestic production.

Protest activity, which may include actual or threatened violence, is another means by which problems may be brought to the attention of policymakers and put on a policy agenda.[32] During the 1960s, such actions as the sit-in movement, the voters' rights march in Selma, Alabama (and the brutal reaction by the Selma police), and the 1963 march on Washington helped keep civil-rights issues at the top of the national policy agenda. Riots in many northern cities were also contributory. In more recent years, groups concerned with women's rights have utilized various kinds of demonstrations in their efforts to move their concerns onto policy agendas, and with some success. Gays and lesbians have also taken to the streets and engaged in protest activities to call attention to their problems.

Some problems or issues may attract the attention of the communications media and, through their reportage, either be converted into agenda items or, the more likely result, if already on an agenda, be given more salience. A classic example is the highly colored and often inaccurate reporting of the Pulitzer and Hearst newspapers in the 1890s in making Spain's treatment of its colonies, particularly Cuba, a major issue and thus doing much to cause the United States eventually to declare war on Spain.[33] More recently, the media helped make nuclear safety a continuing concern by extensive coverage of such major events as the meltdown at the Three Mile Island nuclear power plant in Pennsylvania in 1979, and the explosion of a nuclear reactor at Chernobyl in the Soviet Ukraine in 1986, as well as many lesser nuclear-safety incidents.

Whether the news media are motivated by a desire to "create" news, report all that is newsworthy, stimulate sales, or serve the public interest is not the question here. Whatever their motives, as important opinion shapers they help structure policy agendas. Although notions about proper news-media operations and the compelling force of some events limit somewhat the discretion the media have in selecting the events (the "news") they bring to the public's attention, they nonetheless do have much leeway. The media do not so much tell people and policy-makers what to think as they do what to think about.

Changes in statistical indicators may also produce awareness of problems and help move them onto agendas.[34] Governmental agencies and others regularly collect data on many activities and events, such as consumer prices, the foreign-trade balance, highway deaths, disease rates, infant-mortality rates, and industrial-accident rates. Health-care cost containment has been an important issue in Washington because statistics indicate that costs of health care are rising rapidly. Conversely, as the rate of increase in the consumer price index remained low in the mid-1990s, so, too, did public concern about inflation. Although the Federal Reserve Board continued to worry about inflation (reflecting its policy orientation), most Washington officials became more interested in other problems.

Political changes, including election results, changes in administrations, and shifts in the public mood, may make possible moving onto an agenda items that previously were unlikely candidates for inclusion.[35] Lyndon Johnson's landslide election in 1964, together with the election of favorable majorities in both houses of Congress, opened the doors for enacting a flood of social-welfare legislation. These doors partly closed two years later when the voters, reacting negatively to the administration's ventures in Vietnam, turned many of Johnson's supporters out of office. Political change can also reduce the agenda opportunities for some items. The Reagan administration's preference for cutbacks in the government's role in society made major new spending and regulatory programs difficult to obtain, and few were proposed. The Republican takeover of Congress in 1995 brought to the fore many proposals for reducing or eliminating national government programs.

Finally, items may gain agenda status in rather arcane or peculiar ways. Take the instance of occupational safety and health. Robert Hardesty, one of President Lyndon Johnson's speech-writers, had a brother who worked in the Department of Health, Education, and Welfare's Bureau of Occupational Safety and Health, a research unit. At his urging, Hardesty would occasionally insert references to occupational safety and health in the president's speeches. Although HEW and the labor movement were indifferent to occupational safety, the Department of Labor saw in the speech references an opportunity to propose a program that would win presidential approval. A draft occupational safety and health bill was included in a package of legislative ideas which Labor sent to the White House in late 1967. With little urging from Labor, it was accepted and became part of the Johnson administration's 1968 legislative program. It did not win congressional approval that year but it stayed on the agenda and became law as the Occupational Safety and Health Act of 1970.[36]

Although I have not presented all the alternatives, my purpose here is to indicate a variety of ways in which problems can reach a policy agenda.[37] It should also be apparent that all public problems do not reach a policy agenda, because policy-makers do not feel compelled to handle some problems (or potential problems). To help account for their inaction, the concept of nondecisions is a useful analytical and explanatory tool.

NONDECISIONS

Nondecision-making is defined by Professors Peter Bachrach and Morton S. Baratz as "a means by which demands for change in the existing allocation of benefits and privileges in the community can be suffocated before they are even voiced; or kept covert; or killed before they gain access to the relevant decision-making arena; or failing all these things, maimed or destroyed in the decision-implementing stage of the policy process."[38] Problems may be kept off a systemic or institutional agenda in various ways. At the local level, particularly, force may be utilized, as in the South during the 1950s and 1960s by white groups to stifle black demands for equal rights. Another possibility is that prevailing values and beliefs—political culture—may also operate to deny agenda status to problems or policy alternatives. Our beliefs about private property and capitalism kept railroad nationalization from ever becoming a real agenda item—even late in the nineteenth and early in the twentieth centuries, when railroad policy was being developed—except when facets of railroad operations, such as passenger service (witness Amtrak), became unprofitable for private enterprise.

A third possibility is suggested by Professor E. E. Schattschneider. "The crucial problem in politics," he states, "is the management of conflict. No regime could endure that did not cope with this problem. All politics, all leadership, all organization involves the management of conflict. All conflict allocates space in the political universe. The consequences of conflict are so important that it is inconceivable that any regime would survive without making an attempt to shape the system." To survive, then, political leaders and organizations must prevent problems or issues that would threaten their existence from reaching the political arena (that is, from achieving agenda status). The kinds of problems that they resist will depend upon what kinds of leaders and organizations they are—whether, for example, they are conservative Republicans or independent commissions. They will in any case resist considering some problems, for, as Schattschneider contends, "all forms of political organization have a bias in favor of the exploitation of some kinds of conflicts and the suppression of others because organization is the mobilization of bias. Some issues are organized into politics while others are organized out."[39]

In studying public policy-making it is important to know why some problems are dealt with and others are neglected or suppressed. Recall that public policy is determined not only by what government does do but also by what it deliberately does not do. Take the situation of migratory farm workers, whose problems usually receive short shrift from public officials. Why? What does an answer to this question tell us about who gets what and why from the policy process? Is the neglect of migrant workers at least partly due to nondecision-making? Notwithstanding the somewhat imprecise nature of the concept of nondecision, it has utility for analyzing the policy process.

THE LOSS OF AGENDA STATUS

Problems that may reach agendas may also, of course, disappear from agendas. Action may be taken on a problem, or a decision may be made not to act, not to have a law on a matter. Policy-makers may then feel that the problem has been taken care of and turn their attention to other issues. In the late 1970s, whether to impose charges on commercial users of inland waterways, such as the Mississippi and Ohio rivers, was briefly a hot issue.[40] Once legislation imposing user charges was enacted, however, the issue quickly fell from sight. Other factors that may push items off an agenda include changes in the conditions that give rise to a problem, the appearance of new and more pressing problems, or people becoming accustomed to a condition and no longer labeling it a problem (as in the case of noise caused by the landing of Concorde airplanes around Washington, D.C.).

Policy analyst Anthony Downs suggests that an "issue-attention cycle" causes some public problems to fade from public view.[41] The cycle has five stages that vary in duration:

1. The pre-problem stage. At this time a quite undesirable social condition exists but has not received much public notice. Some specialists and interest groups may have become concerned about it.
2. Alarmed discovery and euphoric enthusiasm. Something causes the public to become aware of and alarmed about the problem. There is a strong desire to quickly solve the problem, which reflects the notion that most obstacles to improvement are external. Hence the solution does not appear to necessitate fundamental change in society.
3. Realization of the cost of significant progress. Awareness spreads that solving the problem will entail high costs. People realize that part of the problem stems from arrangements, such as the millions of cars that cause traffic congestion, that benefit many people. The nation's most pressing social problems usually involve intended or unconscious exploitation of one social group by another.
4. Gradual decline in the intensity of public interest. As people realize how difficult and costly it will be to solve the problem, some become discouraged, others feel threatened, and some become bored. Attention to the issue wanes, and moreover, by now another issue may be reaching stage 2.
5. The post-problem stage. The issue moves into a "twilight realm" of less attention. The agencies, policies, and programs created to help solve it persist and usually have some impact. A supportive subsystem may develop.

Not all major problems go through the "issue-attention cycle." Those which do likely possess three qualities in some degree: First, they affect a numerical minority, as in poverty and unemployment. Second, they involve social arrangements beneficial to a majority or a powerful minority. Thus, car owners and highway lobbies benefit from the ban on using motor-fuel taxes for mass-transit systems that would aid the urban poor. Third, there are no longer exciting events associated with problems, such as television coverage of race riots or NASA space shots. The space program, the War on Poverty, the farm program, and labor-management relations policy all seem to have experienced this cycle. Downs predicted that environmental protection was an issue unlikely to fade quickly because its support was constantly being re-newed. Time appears to have validated his opinion. What will happen to the "war on drugs"? Reduction of the national budget deficit?

TWO CASES IN AGENDA SETTING

To cast additional light on the agenda-setting process, we briefly consider how two regulatory problems of quite different scope, content, and effect achieved agenda status. The first is coal-mine safety, which directly affects only a small segment of the labor force and is likely to be unfamiliar to most readers. The second is environmental pollution control, which has been an important item on government agendas since the early 1970s.

Coal mining has long been a highly hazardous occupation marked by high rates of accidental injury and death. Underground (or shaft) coal mines, which until after World War II produced most of the nation's coal, tend to be deep, dark, dusty, and dangerous. Regulatory activity to protect miners was first undertaken by the state governments early in this century.[42] Because of dissatisfaction with the ineffectiveness of state regulation, however, federal regulation was sought by miners and their supporters. After decades of struggle, it was finally gained with the Coal Mine Safety Act of 1952.

Enforcement of the act was entrusted to the Bureau of Mines in the Department of the Interior. The bureau, which also had responsibility for promoting the economic well-being of the mining industry, was often criticized as too responsive to the mine owners' interests. Frequent accidents and deaths continued to occur in the coal mines. For nearly two decades nothing really effective was done to strengthen policy on mine safety, even though technology was available to improve safety conditions without a major decline in production. One reason for the inactivity was that underground coal mining is concentrated in a few areas of the country, such as West Virginia and southern Illinois, and most people are both relatively unaffected by and unaware of the miners' problems. Also, mine union leaders were more interested in economic issues.

This situation changed, however, on November 20, 1968, when an explosion occurred at the Consolidated Coal Company's No. 9 mine in Farmington, West Virginia. Seventy-nine miners were trapped below the surface, and all died before rescue workers could reach them. This major tragedy, well reported by the national news media, focused the nation's attention on the miners' plight, including not only explosions and other accidents but also black-lung disease, caused by continued inhalation of coal dust. Demanding remedies, the miners staged protest meetings, engaged in wildcat strikes, and conducted other activities, including a march on the West Virginia state capitol. In March 1969, the West Virginia legislature enacted legislation providing compensation for victims of black-lung disease.

The miners and their leaders continued to press for national legislation as well, repeatedly threatening a nationwide coal strike if action was not forthcoming. President Nixon responded by sending Congress a special message, along with a draft bill, on coal-mine safety. The bill was stronger than one proposed a year earlier, prior to the explosion, by President Johnson. In October 1969 the Senate passed a mine-safety bill by a 73 to 0 vote and a few weeks later the House did so by a 389 to 4 vote. Signed into law by President Nixon, the federal Mine Safety and Health Act of 1969 provided for health standards and stronger safety standards for mines and authorized a black-lung compensation program. The Bureau of Mines continued to have responsibility for enforcing the health and safety standards.[43]

Mine safety did not drop off the congressional agenda with the adoption of the new law, however, as frequently happens in such matters, although it did become less salient. Interested members of Congress continued to monitor the mine-safety act's enforcement by the Bureau of Mines, which was criticized as being too responsive to the mining industry, too willing to trade safety for more production, and generally lax in enforcing the law. Early in 1973, several bills providing for transfer of mine safety away from the Bureau of Mines were introduced in Congress. Before action could be taken on them, however, the Secretary of the Interior unexpectedly set up a new Mine Enforcement and Safety Administration (MESA) in the department to handle the mine-safety program separately from the Bureau of Mines.[44] This ploy was obviously intended to ward off congressional action.

Because accidents and deaths continued to occur in the coal mines, some members of Congress transferred their unhappiness with the quality of mine-safety enforcement from the Bureau of Mines to MESA. The Department of the Interior was viewed as lax on health and safety matters. Discontent peaked in 1977, and mine safety returned to the congressional decision agenda. Amendments to the federal Coal Mine Safety Act transferred mine-safety enforcement from MESA to a new Mining Safety and Health Administration (MSHA) in the Department of Labor, which was viewed as a more hospitable locale for the program. The 1969 act was also revised in an effort to expedite setting health and safety standards and imposing penalties for their violation. Metal and nonmetal mines were also put under the jurisdiction of MSHA. Strongly supported by organized labor, the 1977 legislation was strenuously opposed by the coal-mining industry.

Enforcement of the mine-safety legislation, which was never stringent, waned in the 1980s under the Reagan administration.[45] A former coal-mine operator was appointed to head MSHA, and revisions were made in mine-safety regulations that generally accorded with coal-industry recommendations. Also, legislation was proposed by the administration that, it was said, would reduce the regulatory burden on mine operators without reducing safety protection for workers. No action was taken by Congress.

In 1987, as a consequence of multiple-death mine accidents and studies critical of mine-safety enforcement, the issue once again hit the congressional agenda. Hearings were held by both House and Senate committees. At a hearing before the Senate Labor and Human Resources Committee, witnesses decried the laxity of enforcement and supported the creation of a new, independent agency to handle all mine-safety enforcement duties. The committee chair, Senator Orrin Hatch (R, Utah), and its ranking Democratic member, Senator Edward Kennedy (D, Massachusetts), joined in assailing MSHA for weakening safety standards and enforcement programs. No legislation resulted. The Reagan administration, however, did agree to hire about one hundred additional mine inspectors, and a rule that had reduced criminal convictions of negligent operators was rescinded.[46]

The number of coal-mine deaths has declined in recent years, in part because the number employed in underground mines has declined as more of the nation's coal is produced by surface (or strip) mining. Less hazardous for miners, surface mining is more hazardous for the environment, which is a problem that President Carter and Congress sought to deal with by the Surface Mining Control and Reclamation Act of 1977.

Critics of MSHA, taking advantage of the anti-regulatory atmosphere created by the new Republican majorities in Congress, put the agency on the agenda again in 1995. Supported by the owners and operators of coal mines in eastern Kentucky, which were "among the most dangerous and latest targets" of MSHA, legislation was launched to reduce MSHA's inspection and enforcement powers and then abolish it through a merger with the Occupational Safety and Health Administration.[47] Called reform legislation, it readily cleared the House Economic and Educational Opportunities Committee, but it was not further acted upon during that session of Congress.

Similar stories could be compiled for a number of other relatively "obscure" public problems and the policies that deal with them. Such problems and policies constitute much of the substance of modern government. Now, however, it is time to turn to a problem which has attracted widespread public and official attention—environmental pollution control.

Environmental pollution has long been a condition in American society. The nation's air, waters, and soil have commonly been used as free or inexpensive means for disposing of wastes. Not until the 1960s, however, did pollution become widely perceived as a major public problem. Whereas belching factory smokestacks once were thought to be emblematic of economic progress, now they are generally viewed as deplorable matters requiring control. The national and state governments have enacted a large volume of legislation intended to control pollution and protect the environment, often in the face of considerable resistance from economic development interests.

Several factors have contributed to making pollution control an important item on the policy agendas. Early on, a number of triggering events raised public awareness about the adverse consequences of pollution. The publication in 1962 of Rachel Carson's *Silent Spring* called attention to the detrimental effects of the extensive application of chemical pesticides on wildlife and human beings.[48] An oil-well blowout off the California coast near Santa Barbara in 1969 polluted miles of beaches and received extensive coverage by the news media. The first Earth Day, which occurred on April 22, 1970, elicited the participation of millions of people on college campuses and elsewhere. It represented a tremendous expression of popular interest in protecting the environment.

Environmentalist J. Clarence Davies argues that underlying the attention to pollution is the affluence of American society. He explains,

> The massive growth in production and in the availability of resources which have characterized the American economy . . . affect the problem of pollution in several ways. The increase in production has contributed to an intensification of the degree of actual pollution; the increase in the standard of living has permitted people the comparative luxury of being able to be concerned about this; and the availability of ample public and private resources has given the society sufficient funds and skilled manpower to provide the potential for dealing with the problem.[49]

People who are compelled to continually worry about whether they will be able to secure the basic necessities of life are likely to have little time or inclination to fret about pollution. In the developing countries concern about the problem is still limited; indeed, it is probably not perceived as a problem by many of their inhabitants. In an affluent society, in comparison, favorable conditions of life contribute to a growing belief in the need to control pollution. More time for leisure leads to greater demand for recreational resources and aesthetic pleasures, and a higher level of education enables people to more readily understand the nature and dangers of pollution and the need to protect the natural environment. There is considerable accuracy to the contention that pollution control is a "middle-class issue," a characteristic that contributes to government's willingness to respond favorably.

Pollution and its consequences, however, do affect everyone, and that helps make it an attractive public issue. Pollution control, in turn, can be depicted as an activity that does something for everyone, which enhances its political appeal. Politicians supporting pollution control can portray themselves as on the side of the angels and as protectors of the public interest. Although many business groups and industries are opposed to tough environmental-protection programs, they are handicapped by the issue's broad appeal and attractiveness. Not much support can be won by appearing to favor dirtier air or water. Rather, opposition to stringent control must be indirectly expressed, as by contending that the cost of controlling pollution will increase the cost of doing business and add to inflation. This sort of argumentation has an abstract quality that reduces its public effectiveness.

Another factor contributing to the political attractiveness of environmental protection is its strong link to public health. Pollution is not benign.

Chemicals and other wastes discharged into the environment have a variety of adverse consequences for the health of people (and other creatures), consequences that if not always well understood are much feared. Much like lyrics of the old song, "Everybody wants to go to heaven, but nobody wants to die."

Finally, government action to control pollution has created a dynamic that produces demands for additional and stronger action. We can draw on Davies again for an explanation:

> The issue is given publicity and "respectability" by governmental recognition, and the public learns that something can be done to alleviate the problem. Once an official agency has been established to control pollution, that agency becomes a focal point for bringing the issue to the attention of the general public as well as of other government officials. The members of the agency have a vested interest in drawing attention to the problem. If they are successful, private interest groups will take up the call for action and new groups will be created for the specific purpose of doing something about pollution. This public concern will in turn strengthen the hand of the governmental agency. The concern with pollution thus becomes institutionalized and the pressure to take action becomes constant.[50]

For more than two decades, control of environmental pollution has had a prominent spot on national systemic and institutional agendas. New environmental issues keep coming to the fore: acid rain (or deposition), global warming, and depletion of the ozone layer. In the same week in August 1988, both *Time* and *Newsweek* featured cover stories on the problem of ocean pollution.[51] The huge crude-oil spill that occurred when the oil tanker *Exxon Valdez* ran aground in Alaska's Prince William Sound in March 1989 further focused public and official attention on the need to control environmental pollution. So also did the United Nations Conference on Environment and Development (the "Earth Summit") in Rio de Janeiro in June 1992. Events like these help ensure that pollution control will remain on policy agendas at all levels of government in the United States for years to come.

THE FORMULATION OF POLICY PROPOSALS

Policy formulation involves developing pertinent and acceptable proposed courses of action (often called alternatives, proposals, or options) for dealing with public problems. Policy-makers may be confronted with several competing proposals for dealing with a problem; or they may have to struggle with devising their own alternative. Policy formulation does not always culminate in a law, executive order, or administrative rule. Policy-makers may decide not to take positive action on a problem, but instead to leave it alone, to let matters work themselves out. Or they may be unable to agree on what to do. For example, because Reagan administration officials could not agree on how to revise an executive order on affirmative action in hiring by governmental contractors, the existing order was left intact. In short, that a public problem reaches a policy agenda does not mean positive action will be taken or, if it is, that it will be soon in coming. Decades of complaints, recommendations, studies, and failed attempts preceded the enactment by Congress of the Family Support Act of 1988 to reform the nation's welfare system. (FSA satisfied the demand for welfare reform only for a short while.) Awareness of a problem does not guarantee positive governmental action, although unawareness or lack of interest pretty much ensures inaction.

Who Is Involved?

In this discussion of who is involved in developing policy proposals, we focus primarily on the national level in the United States. In the twentieth century, the president, together with his chief aides and advisers in the Executive Office of the President, has been the leading source of initiative in forming major policy proposals (at the state level, governors usually play the same role). The origins of these proposals are many. Some may have originated in the EOP agencies; more likely, however, they bubbled up from the bureaucracy or had been floating around Congress and the Washington community for some time and were taken over by the president.

The members of Congress and the public have come to expect the president to present policy recommendations to Congress for consideration. Years ago, President Dwight Eisenhower was the target of much criticism, even from members of his own party, when in his first year in office he chose not to submit a legislative program to Congress. Moreover, the members of Congress have come to expect the chief executive to present them with draft bills embodying his recommendations. What the members of Congress want is "some real meat to digest," not merely some good ideas to consider. "Don't expect us to start from scratch on what you want," a committee chair told an Eisenhower official. "That's not the way we do things here—you draft the bills, and we work them over."[52] As this quotation implies, Congress does not always proceed kindly in handling the president's proposals (far from it), but presidential recommendations do, among other things, help Congress set its agenda and indicate where the president stands on some major issues, which is useful information to members of Congress.

GOVERNMENTAL AGENCIES   Many policy proposals are developed by officials—both career and appointed—in the administrative departments and agencies. Continually working with governmental programs in agriculture, health, welfare, law enforcement, foreign trade, and other areas, they become aware of new policy problems and develop proposals to deal with them. These plans are then transmitted to the executive and, if in accord with the president's policies and programs, sent on to Congress. Agency officials, because of their specialization, expertise, and continued involvement in particular policy areas, are in a good technical position to engage in formulating policy.

Many agency proposals are designed to modify or strengthen existing laws, typically to the benefit or advantage of the proposing agency. During their administration, loopholes, weaknesses, or omissions may have been identified. A large, complex piece of legislation, the Tax Reform Act of 1986, contained numerous technical errors when it was passed, typical of such legislation. Two years were required for Congress to pass "corrective" legislation: the Technical and Miscellaneous Tax Act of 1988. The reason for the delay lay not in correcting the technical errors, which were readily taken care of. Rather, problems arose in reaching agreement on new substantive provisions, some raising revenue and others providing tax breaks for various individuals, companies, and groups that senators and representatives wanted to put into the tax law. The need to correct the 1986 law provided them with an opportunity and a legislative vehicle for additional tax action.

PRESIDENTIAL ORGANIZATIONS   Temporary organizations, sometimes called "adhocracies," may be established by the president to study particular policy areas and to develop policy proposals.[53] These include presidential commissions, task forces, interagency committees, and other arrangements. Except for interagency committees, their memberships may include both legislative and executive officials as well as private citizens.

The President's Commission on Privatization, set up in 1987 by President Reagan, recommended that various services provided by the United States Postal Service and some federal prisons be turned over to private contractors. The commission also supported previous proposals by the administration to sell some governmental petroleum reserves and marketing administrations for electric power. Advisory commissions of this sort are variously employed to develop policy proposals, to win support for those proposals through the endorsement of their usually prestigious members, or to create the appearance of government concern with some problem.

Presidential commissions, however, may not always produce the sorts of policy recommendations preferred by their appointer. The Brady Commission was appointed by the Reagan administration to investigate the stock-market collapse of October 19, 1987, and to make recommendations for preventing future recurrences. The commission, to the administration's surprise, recommended tighter governmental control, preferably by the Federal Reserve Board, of trading activities on the stock and futures markets. Finding such advice uncongenial, the administration appointed an interagency committee, which drew its members from the various financial regulatory agencies, to review the recommendations of the Brady Commission and others. The interagency committee (formally, the White House Working Group on Financial Markets), composed of conservative administration officials, subsequently favored making only minimal changes in regulatory policies, which was in line with presidential preferences.[54] Doing little or nothing is often a preferred policy option, notably among conservatives, on economic regulatory problems.

President Lyndon Johnson made extensive use of task forces to develop legislative proposals, appointing more than one hundred of these groups during his tenure.[55] He believed that task forces, composed of outstanding private citizens and top administration officials, would be more innovative and imaginative in developing proposals for new policies than would the national bureaucracy. He was quite pleased with the results. His successors in the 1970s and 1980s made little use of task forces, perhaps because they were less activist in their policy inclinations.

Another arrangement takes the form of a committee of executive officials and members of Congress appointed jointly by the president and legislative leaders to deal with a pressing problem. In 1987, such a committee worked out the Bipartisan Budget Agreement on reducing the budget deficit. (This subject is discussed in Chapter 5.) The arrangement was very informal. More formal and more publicized was the Budget Commission, composed of private citizens appointed by the House, Senate, and President Bush to devise a longer-term proposal for balancing the federal budget. The commission was unable to agree on a plan, however, partly because it had to work in public sessions. Divided along party lines, it issued two reports. The Republican version supported President Bush's policies; the Democratic version said Bush's policies "led nowhere." The commission's influence was nil.

LEGISLATORS   In the course of congressional hearings and investigations, through contacts with administrative officials and interest-group representatives, and on the basis of their own interests and activities, legislators receive suggestions for action on problems and formulate proposed courses of action. The capacity of members of Congress to engage in formulating policy has been strengthened by the creation of the Office of the Legislative Counsel and the Congressional Research Service (a part of the Library of Congress). Increased staff resources for both individual members and committees also have had a positive effect.

In some policy areas, Congress has done much of the formulation: environmental protection, agriculture, welfare reform, and energy conservation are examples. Both the Clean Air Act of 1970 and the Clean Air Act Amendments of 1990, in final form, were substantially legislative products.[56] They represent markedly different styles in formulation. The landmark 1970 act takes up forty-seven pages in the statute books. Focused mostly on setting goals for the reduction of air pollution, it accorded much discretion to the Environmental Protection Agency and industry in achieving them. In contrast, the 1990 amendments run more than three hundred pages in length and are studded with many specific requirements, timetables, and "hammers" (tough provisions intended to compel action). All of the detail is intended to limit the discretion of administrative officials in implementing the act. In part this reflects distrust of Republican-appointed administrators and federal judges by Democratic congressional majorities. But also, it signifies the willingness and capacity of Congress to enact more detailed legislation and to engage in what some call "micromanagement of the implementation process."

INTEREST GROUPS   Interest groups have a major role in policy formation, often going to the legislature with specific proposals for legislation. They may also work with executive and legislative officials to develop and enact an officially proposed policy, perhaps with some modifications to suit their interests. Environmental, agricultural, and pesticide manufacturers were major players in formulating the legislation in 1988 that amended and reauthorized the Federal Insecticide, Fungicide, and Rodenticide Act (FIFRA). The act is intended to protect the public against harm from hazardous pesticides used on farm crops. Another example is the Israeli lobby, which consists of a number of groups and has been very influential and successful in shaping American financial aid to Israel.

At the state level, interest groups may play a big part in formulating legislation, especially on complex and technical issues, because state legislators frequently lack the time and staff needed to cope with such matters. It is reported that the Illinois legislature customarily enacts legislation in labor–management relations only after it has been agreed to by representatives of organized labor and industry.[57] Thus, by custom, private groups may become the actual formulators of policy.

Competing proposals for handling a problem may emanate from several of these sources. Let us take as an example reform of the national health-care system, which has been on and off the national policy agenda for decades. Containing costs and expanding coverage have been major issues. Beginning in the late 1980s, a spate of health-care proposals emerged. The National Leadership Commission on Health Care, a private entity that included three former presidents among its members, advocated using incentives to encourage employers to provide workers with insurance, and levying a tax to provide insurance for those lacking employer coverage.[58] The Heritage Foundation, a conservative "think tank," favored requiring that every family purchase basic health-care coverage. Personal tax credits and subsidies for the needy would be used to offset insurance and other health-care costs. The American Medical Association offered a plan requiring employers to provide health insurance for full-time workers and their families and calling for tax incentives to make insurance more affordable. State "risk pools" and Medicaid would provide coverage for others. A bipartisan group of presidential appointees and members of Congress, the Pepper Commission, wanted to require most employers to provide basic health insurance for workers and their families. For others, a new public plan would yield coverage. Provision was also made for long-term care. The commission did not indicate how all of this would be paid for. The National Association of Social Workers called for universal national health insurance, administered by the national government, run by the states, and financed by taxes on personal incomes and employer payrolls. Additional reform proposals were presented by other groups and organizations.

Policy-makers were thus not confronted simply with a choice between a single new health-care program and the status quo. Rather, private and official organizations had formulated a variety of proposals reflecting their various interests and concerns. No proposal was adopted, however. Just as each plan had some support, so did it also encounter opposition. The competing pressures for change were sufficiently strong that they canceled one another out.

Health-care reform remained on the national agenda and became a major issue during the 1992 presidential election campaign. The Clinton administration established a Task Force on National Health Care Reform chaired by Hillary Rodham Clinton. Assisted by some five hundred public- and private-sector health-care specialists, in the course of several months the task force drafted a complex, thirteen-hundred-page bill involving mandatory employer-based coverage, health-insurance purchasing cooperatives, limits on consumer expenses, and partial funding by a tobacco tax increase. Various other health-care reform plans, including one for national health insurance, were introduced by members of Congress. Strong opposition to the Clinton plan developed. Once again the status quo prevailed because none of the proposals were able to win majority support.[59] In 1995 President Clinton and the Republican-controlled Congress turned their attention to holding down the costs of the Medicare and Medicaid programs.

POLICY FORMULATION
AS A TECHNICAL PROCESS

Policy formulation involves two markedly different sorts of activities. One is to decide generally what, if anything, should be done about a problem. Thus in the illustration above we find the question, "What kind of national health-insurance system should we have?" In other instances the question may be: "What sorts of restrictions should be imposed on the practice of abortion?" or "What should be the minimum-wage level and who should be covered by it?" Answers to these questions take the form of general principles or statements.

Once such questions have been resolved, the second type of activity comes into play. Legislation or administrative rules must be drafted that, when adopted, will appropriately carry the agreed-upon principles or statements into effect. Often new legislation must be appropriately tied into existing statutes. This is a technical and rather mundane but nevertheless highly important task. The way a bill is written and the specific provisions it includes can substantially affect its administration and the actual content of public policy. Poor drafting can result in a statute like the one enacted by the Kansas legislature early in this century. It provided that when two trains met on the same track each should get off onto a siding until the other had passed.

An interesting illustration of what can result from careless formulation is provided by the National Defense Education Act of 1958, enacted after the launching of the Soviet Sputnik and intended to help the United States "catch up with the Russians" in scientific and engineering education. This illustration also provides a glimpse into how the fear of communism affected politics and policy-making in the United States during the early years of the Cold War. A provision in the act stating that students receiving graduate-fellowship assistance had to sign a noncommunist affidavit, or "loyalty oath," quickly produced a great deal of controversy. Liberals criticized the oath requirement as an affront to the patriotism of students and as unnecessary, among other things. To them it was an important public problem requiring redress. Conservatives defended the loyalty oath as a necessary means of preventing financial aid from going to communists (who were then much out of favor in the United States) and wondered why any loyal American would balk at signing such an oath. In short, they saw no problem. Some universities announced they would not participate in the fellowship program if the oath requirement were retained. Apparently, few graduate students who qualified for fellowships, practical souls that they were, declined to sign the oath and give up the money. Eventually, the oath was replaced by a milder and more acceptable "loyalty affirmation." Symbolic language is important.

Despite the controversy sparked by the oath requirement, there had been no discussion of it either in the committee hearings or during the floor debates on the act. No one had advocated its inclusion. How, then, did it find its way into the law? The answer to this question is not very dramatic, but so it goes with answers to many public-policy questions. The person drafting the formal language of the act copied some of its fellowship provisions from an existing statute; one of these provisions (it can be called "boilerplate") was the loyalty-oath requirement. It had caused no dispute under the earlier law. But when it was discovered in the 1958 act, the fun began. One moral that can be drawn from the story is that often it is easier to get a provision into a law than it is to remove it later. Bill drafters frequently borrow language from laws already on the books when they write new legislation.

The writing of laws and rules has to be done skillfully because, as soon as these laws or rules go into effect, people will begin looking for loopholes or trying to bend the meaning of the language to their advantage. Clarity in phrasing and intent also may help protect laws and rules against unfavorable judicial interpretations and provide clear guidance to those assigned the task of implementation. Congress and most of the state legislatures now have bill-drafting services to assist them in writing legislation. They also draw on the expert services of committee staffers, bureaucrats, and interest-group representatives.

When faced with the need to interpret a law that is unclear in meaning (or intent), judges have traditionally sought guidance from the law's legislative history: committee reports, hearings, and congressional debates. Consequently, efforts are sometimes made in Congress to construct legislative histories that will support given interpretations. The president of the American League of Lobbyists says, "Often a bill is written too broadly and Congress says, 'we'll fix it up with legislative history.' Lobbyists frequently suggest terminology, phrases, ideas, and concepts."[60]

Some conservative judges, most notably Justice Antonin Scalia of the U.S. Supreme Court, have begun to express strong skepticism about using legislative history (or content) to derive congressional intent. Scalia contends that it is a judge's duty to interpret the text of statutes, not to attempt to discover legislators' intentions.[61] Should this "plain-meaning" mode (or textualist approach) of statutory interpretation catch on—and it has quite a bit of support among conservative judges, many of whom were appointed to the federal bench during the 1981–1992 period—it will put much pressure on congressional bill drafters to produce legislation with a minimum of loose, sloppy, or ambiguous provisions.

FORMULATING POLICY: THE ECONOMIC RECOVERY TAX ACT

The Economic Recovery Tax Act of 1981 was a primary part of the Reagan administration's program to control inflation and reduce the size of the national government. Other parts of the Reagan program included the reduction of domestic expenditures, a monetary policy featuring gradual growth in the money supply, and economic regulatory reform. In this account our attention is on the administration's 1981 tax cut, its roots, and the process by which it evolved and won adoption.

During his campaign for the Republican presidential nomination in the early months of 1980, Ronald Reagan became committed to the theory known as supply-side economics. Essentially, this theory holds that many of the economic problems confronting the American people were the consequence of high income-tax rates that reduced people's incentive to work, save, and invest. Significant tax reduction was therefore necessary to unleash the economy's productive capacity. Supply-side economics thus contrasted with traditional Keynesian economics with its focus on influencing aggregate demand for goods and services. (Reagan reportedly was also still peeved because of the high tax rate he had to pay in the 1940s when he was a popular Hollywood actor.)

A prominent feature of the supply-side strategy was the Kemp-Roth tax-cut proposal, named after two of its leading advocates: Representative Jack Kemp (R, New York) and Senator William Roth (R, Delaware). The Kemp-Roth proposal, first introduced in Congress in 1977, called for a 30 percent reduction in marginal income-tax rates (the rate a person pays on the last dollar of income taxed) spread over a three-year period. The proposal attracted support from conservatives, but until 1980 it never came close to enactment by Congress. Support of the Kemp-Roth proposal by Reagan, however, resulted in its being written into the 1980 Republican Party platform.

In February 1981, a few weeks after taking office, President Reagan unveiled the tax-reduction legislation that had been quickly put together by a few top administration officials. The administration's tax bill had two main features: (1) a 10 percent cut in income-tax rates, to take effect July 1, 1981, with additional 10 percent cuts on July 1 in each of the two succeeding years; and (2) liberalized depreciation allowances for business investment, permitting depreciation for tax purposes of vehicles over three years, machinery and equipment over five years, and buildings over ten years. This was known as the 10–5–3 proposal. That the administration's tax proposal was based on supply-side economics and the Kemp-Roth proposal is quite evident.

Although pressure was applied by various interest groups and congressional sources for other tax changes, these were resisted by the administration, which wanted to secure quick passage of its "clean" bill. Once that was done, the administration promised to introduce a second tax bill that might incorporate such other tax changes as tuition tax credits, lowered inheritance taxes, and indexed income-tax rates to reduce the "bracket creep" caused by inflation.

The president initially barred any compromises on his tax proposal. In the Senate, where the Republicans were in the majority, there was never much doubt that his basic tax proposal would pass. The Senate has traditionally added special provisions called "sweeteners" to tax bills, however, and once again senatorial interest in doing so was ample. In the House, where the Democrats were in the majority, the administration needed to pick up some Democratic votes to put together a majority coalition for its bill. Indeed, the Democratic leadership in the House disliked Reagan's approach to tax reduction, charging that the president's bill favored the wealthy and would result in huge budget deficits.

The task of preparing a Democratic alternative to the Reagan tax proposal fell to Representative Dan Rostenkowski (D, Illinois), Chairman of the House Ways and Means Committee, and the committee's Democratic majority. They developed a proposal that included a 15 percent cut in income taxes spread over two years, focusing the cuts on low- and middle-income persons, increased business depreciations (but less than in the administration's proposal), and other changes in taxation. Generally, their proposal provided greater tax relief for individuals than for businesses.

In May, the administration sought to work out a compromise with Rostenkowski because it was uncertain that its "clean" bill could pass. Rostenkowski, however, was unable to get authorization to bargain from the Ways and Means Democrats. The administration, impatient to secure action on taxation, then turned its attention to the conservative Democrats (the "Boll Weevils") in the House. In fact, some White House aides had been talking with the Boll Weevils at the same time as other officials were dealing with Rostenkowski.

To win the support of the conservative Democrats, the administration now offered to include in its proposal some tax cuts that had been targeted for the second bill. Examples included tax breaks for small oil and gas royalty holders, lower inheritance taxation, and savings incentives. Also, the income-tax cut was scaled back to 25 percent, and business depreciation was reduced somewhat. Business groups remained unenthusiastic about the proposal, and so a few days later the administration added more special tax advantages for business.

In the meantime, the Democratic majority on the Ways and Means Committee had continued working on its alternative, which they hoped would defeat the administration's proposal when the legislation reached the House floor. In mid-July, by an 18 to 17 vote, the Democratic majority approved a provision reducing the windfall-profits tax on oil that had been adopted in 1978. This move was their effort to secure the support of the conservative Democrats, many of whom were from oil-producing states. Not to be outbid, the administration hastily revised its proposal. More sweeteners were added, including tax breaks for oil producers, increased charitable deductions, annual indexation of income-tax rates, and relief from estate and gift taxes. Generally, these changes were intended to pick up a handful of swing votes. "Both Republicans and Democrats admitted that their bills were more products of a political bidding war than blueprints for sound economic policy."[62]

A couple of days before the House was scheduled to act on the tax legislation, President Reagan addressed the nation on television and urged the public to support his proposal. Almost immediately, the members of Congress were inundated by a tidal wave of communications, mostly supporting the president's position. When the question came up in the House, the members voted 238 to 195 to adopt the Republican tax proposal rather than the

Democratic alternative; 190 Republicans were joined by 48 conservative Democrats in supporting the administration. (Only one Republican representative voted against the administration.)

The Senate completed its action on the administration's tax proposal on the same day as the House. Of the 118 amendments to the tax bill considered by the Senate, 80 were adopted. The special-interest quality of some of the amendments is illustrated by one that permitted taxpayers in southern Alabama to claim a $10 tax credit for every pecan tree planted to replace one destroyed by Hurricane Frederick. (This provision was later abandoned.) There were, however, only a few major differences between the House and Senate bills, such as the scope of tax breaks for oil producers and increases in tax credits for child care. Annual indexation of income-tax rates, which appeared in both bills, was added at the insistence of Senator Robert Dole (R, Kansas), chairman of the Senate Finance Committee. According to one explanation, "Dole figured there was so much junk being put in the tax bill that there might as well be some real reform, too."[63]

The differences between the House and Senate tax bills were readily resolved by a conference committee. Signed into law by the president in mid-August, the Economic Recovery Tax Act of 1981 included a three-year, 25 percent cut in income-tax rates; indexation of tax rates after 1984; new-business depreciation allowances; and an array of tax breaks on such items as oil production, estates and gifts, interest income, charitable contributions, deposits into retirement accounts, income from new tax-exempt savings certificates, foreign earned income, child care, and the income of two-earner married couples. It was estimated that the act would reduce federal tax revenues by amounts ranging from $39 billion in 1982 to $280–290 billion in 1987.[64]

In this case study, one sees how in actuality the formulation and adoption of policy become interwoven. Formulators must be concerned not only with developing a preferred or satisfactory policy alternative but also with winning its approval. An affirmative decision is the payoff of the policy process; its price may be concession and compromise, taking less or giving more than one would really prefer. Despite the bargaining over the Economic Recovery Tax Act, the Reagan administration's basic tax-reduction proposal survived relatively intact; however, to secure its adoption the administration had to agree to myriad amendments. To put it another way, the administration had to share the formulation function with Congress and various interest groups. The result was tax legislation that reduced revenues substantially more than the administration had originally intended. In 1982 Congress, apprehensive about large prospective budget deficits, enacted legislation increasing taxes by $98 billion over a three-year period, in part by eliminating or reducing some of the 1981 tax cuts. The new statute was entitled the Tax Equity and Fiscal Responsibility Act.

FORMULATING POLICY: THE FAMILY AND MEDICAL LEAVE ACT

In the third week of his administration, President Bill Clinton signed into law the Family and Medical Leave Act, the product of an eight-year legislative struggle. This account of FLMA's legislative odyssey examines its origins and some of the actions that contributed to its final form.[65]

In 1984, a federal district court held that a California law requiring employers to grant four months' leave to female employees for temporary disability related to pregnancy or childbirth violated the Civil Rights Act of 1964 and other federal statutes guaranteeing equal treatment of men and women in the workplace. Because men could not take maternity leave, the state law was held to discriminate against them. (The court's decision was later overruled.)

Many women activists were outraged by the court's decision. Also disturbed by it was Congressman Howard Berman (D, California), who, as a California state legislator, had been instrumental in securing enactment of the state's maternity-leave law. Having decided that there was now a need for a national maternity-leave law, Berman called on Donna Lenhoff at the Women's Legal Defense Fund for help. She assembled a group of women activists located in the Washington area to consider the problem. They concluded that what was needed was a law covering all medical and family circumstances, not just maternity, and that treated all workers alike. But Berman expressed doubts about the political viability of such a law.

Impetus for the idea of family leave, however, was provided by hearings before the House Select Committee on Children, Youth, and Families where expert witnesses spoke of the importance of parental leaves to care for newborn children. An informal working group, drawing representatives from the Children's Defense Fund, the American Council of Jewish Women, the Association of Junior Leagues, the U.S. Catholic Conference, and other organizations, began considering the need for a bill requiring leave for temporary medical disability and for the care of newborn or newly adopted children. Although all of the industrial European nations had family-leave programs that provided at least partial compensation for leave takers, the group decided not to include compensation in their proposal because they knew it would be exceedingly difficult to obtain from a Congress that was becoming obsessed with budget deficits.

Over the next several months, discussions and negotiations were carried on about family-leave legislation by interested members of Congress and group representatives. It was determined that a bill providing for a national leave policy should be introduced by Representative Pat Schroeder (D, Colorado). The Parental and Disability Leave Act, which she introduced in April

1985, featured broad coverage, requiring that all businesses provide up to eighteen weeks of unpaid leave for mothers or fathers of newborn or newly adopted children. Up to twenty-six weeks of unpaid leave was mandated for employees with non-work-related temporary disabilities or sick children. Health insurance and other benefits were to be continued during the leave period, after which the worker was entitled to return to the same or a comparable job. As we will see, many changes were made in the bill as it moved through Congress.

Hearings on the bill were held by subcommittees of the House Committee on Education and Labor, and Post Office and Civil Services, who shared jurisdiction. These led to changes in the bill. Its title was changed to Parental and Medical Leave Act because some advocates of the handicapped objected to the use of "Disability" in the act's title. Also, coverage was restricted to businesses with more than five employees. Negotiations between the Democrats and Republicans, led by Congresswoman Marge Roukema (R, New Jersey) on the Education and Labor Committee, produced some major changes in the bill. The small-business exception was raised to fifteen or fewer employees, which meant that 22 percent of the workforce would be left uncovered. Employees had to work three months, or five hundred hours, to be eligible for leave, and the total leave taken by an employee was capped at thirty-six weeks over a two-year period. On the other hand, the right to take leave was extended to employees caring for a seriously ill family member, whether an elderly parent, a spouse, or a child. To spotlight this change, "Family" was substituted for "Parental" in the act's title.

In the Senate, Christopher J. Dodd (D, Connecticut) became the sponsor for similar legislation. However, the 99th Congress concluded with no further progress toward enactment of the Family and Medical Leave Act, although by now, it had attracted quite a bit of attention. Critics called it a yuppie bill because it provided for unpaid leave. Many Republicans opposed it as being anti-business, because it imposed a mandate on businesses, and because, they claimed, it would lead to additional mandates.

Coalitions supporting and opposing the family-leave bill formed. Among the supporters were feminist and labor groups, the U.S. Catholic Conference, and the American Association of Retired Persons. Prominent among the opposition were the National Federation of Independent Business, the Chamber of Commerce, and the National Association of Wholesale Distributors. Moreover, scores of groups opposing family leave bonded together as the Concerned Alliance of Responsible Employers (CARE).

In the 100th Congress (1987–1988), the family-leave bill again readily cleared the Education and Labor Committee, but doubts increased as to whether it had sufficient support to pass on the House floor. Consequently, negotiations were entered into with Congresswoman Roukema in an attempt to pick up some Republican votes. Most of the negotiations were handled by staff members and resulted in the exemption for small businesses being increased to fifty or fewer employees and the leave periods shortened to ten weeks for family care (over a two-year period) and fifteen weeks for employee disability (within a calendar year). Also, the top 10 percent of an employer's payroll could be exempted if leave for them would "constitute a hardship" for the business. The fifty-employee exemption meant that family leave would extend to only 39 percent of the labor force, and that business compliance costs would be much lower.

Family leave was never brought to the House floor for debate, however, because the Democratic leadership remained uncertain that it had sufficient support to pass. In the Senate, Senator Dodd was able to clear his family-leave bill through the Committee on Labor and Human Resources and bring it to the floor, where it died because of a Republican-led filibuster.

At the beginning of the 101st Congress (1989–1990), family-leave bills were again introduced in both Houses. Both specified ten weeks of leave for new parents and for people with sick children and parents. For one's own illness, the House provided for fifteen weeks leave, compared to thirteen weeks in the Senate bill. The House bill applied to all employees of more than fifty persons, with that number decreasing to thirty-five in a few years; the Senate exemption limit was twenty employees. In all, the bills were much the same as in the previous Congress because there was a desire to avoid re-fighting old legislative battles.

In an attempt to gain further support for the leave bill from Republicans and conservative Democrats, a bargain was struck with Representatives Curt Weldon (R, Pennsylvania) and Bart Gordon (D, Tennessee). A single standard of twelve weeks leave for all causes was agreed to; only one parent at a time could be on leave; and the small business exemption was set permanently at fifty employees. Representative Schroeder was nettled by this and stated, "I have trouble supporting this compromise [bill] because it has been watered down so much." The compromise, however, helped carry the family-leave bill to victory on the House floor.

In the Senate, the House bill was pushed by Senator Dodd and brought to the floor, where the Republican leader, Senator Robert Dole, agreed to its passage by a voice vote. Dole saw no need to filibuster the bill because he was expecting a presidential veto when the bill reached the White House. President George Bush defended his veto on the ground that family leave should be left to business discretion rather than being mandated by the government. The vote in the House to override was 232–195, substantially short of the required two-thirds. There was no need for the Senate to vote.

Family leave was a prominent issue once again in the 102nd Congress (1991–1992). Senator Dodd sought more support for family leave among the Republican ranks. He finally found it in Senator Christopher S. Bond (R, Missouri). The two senators brokered a compromise designed to win Bond's support and perhaps that of other senators, rather than to satisfy business groups. It was agreed that to be covered employees had to have worked 1250 hours in a year (twenty-five hours a week); that the top 10 percent of payroll could be excluded from family-leave coverage; that thirty days notice was to be given for foreseeable leave; and that lesser penalties would be imposed on employers wrongfully denying leave. The compromise had the desired effect—family leave passed the Senate by more than two-thirds. A few weeks later in November 1991, the House passed a similar bill, but by less than the two-thirds margin needed to override another promised presidential veto.

The possibility of compromise with the White House on family leave was explored, but to no avail. In August 1992 the House and Senate went to conference and quickly resolved the differences between their two bills. The Senate, for example, defined a "serious health condition" as an "illness, injury, impairment, or physical or mental condition"; the House specified that the list of conditions had to be "disabling." This was dropped from the final version. Again, the Senate defined an employee as a person who had been on the payroll for the previous twelve months and had worked at least 1250 hours. The House bill required employment for at least twelve months on other than a temporary or intermittent basis. The Senate receded from its version.

Both Houses passed the compromise bill and sent it on to the White House, where it met the expected presidential veto, but only after a hastily fashioned compromise was offered by the President. The Bush alternative plan called for a refundable tax credit for all businesses with up to five hundred employees who granted up to twelve weeks of leave. It drew little interest from the supporters of family leave. The Senate voted 68–32, with fourteen Republicans in the majority, to override President Bush's veto. In the House, however, family leave again went down to defeat, this time by 257–171, or twenty-seven votes short of the needed two-thirds.

In the fall 1992 presidential campaign, family leave became an important issue. Bill Clinton often spoke in favor of it, promising to sign it into law as soon as Congress sent it to him. Clinton's election cleared the last roadblock to the enactment of family leave legislation. Some supporters of family leave now contemplated developing a stronger bill than the 1992 version. President Clinton, however, indicated that he wanted to approve the bill that President Bush had vetoed. The Democratic majorities in Congress quickly ran a bill through the legislative process and on February 5, 1993, President Clinton signed into law the Family and Medical Leave Act. In its final form, it reflected many of the compromises that along the way were brokered to secure its passage.

The FMLA gives qualified employees up to twelve weeks of unpaid leave because of the birth or adoption of a child; the serious illness of a child, spouse, or parent; or the employee's own serious illness. To be eligible, persons must have worked for the employer for at least twelve months and at least 1250 hours during that time. Exempted from coverage are employees of a business with less than fifty employees in a seventy-five mile radius. Employers can deny leave to the highest paid 10 percent of their employees if that would cause their business "substantial and grievous economic injury." Employees taking leave must be restored to the same position held, or a comparable one, as when the leave began. Public-sector employees, including federal and congressional employees, are also covered.

As the act stands, 5 percent of the nation's employers, accounting for about 40 percent of the labor force, are covered; when originally introduced, the act had applied to all employers. At the same time that this coverage was being restricted, however, the range of matters for which an employee could take leave was expanded. Many other alterations were made to build support for the act. This case of FLMA well illustrates the blurring together of policy formulation and adoption as the legislative process unfolds.

A CONCLUDING COMMENT

Problem identification, agenda setting, and policy formulation constitute the predecision segment of the policy process in that they do not involve formal decisions on what will become public policy. They are important, however, because they help determine which issues will be considered, which will be given further examination, and which will be abandoned. Thus they involve political conflict and help set the terms for additional conflict. E. E. Schattschneider comments,

> Political conflict is not like an inter-collegiate debate in which the opponents agree in advance on the definition of the issues. As a matter of fact, the definition of the alternatives is the supreme instrument of power. . . . He who determines what politics is about runs the country, because the definition of the alternatives is the choice of conflicts, and the choice of conflicts allocates power.[66]

In actuality it is often difficult to separate policy formulation from policy adoption, the subject of Chapter 4. Analytically, they are distinct functional activities that occur in the policy process. They do not, however, "have to be performed by separate individuals at different times in different institutions."[67] Most often, as the two case studies demonstrate, those who formulate courses of action will be influenced by the need to win adoption of their proposals. Some provisions will be included, others excluded, and words and phrasing will be carefully chosen in an attempt to build support for a proposed policy. Looking further ahead, the formulators may also be influenced by what they think may happen during the administration of the policy once adopted. Possible reactions may be anticipated and taken into account in an effort to help ensure that the policy will accomplish its intended purposes. Such actions help tie together the different stages of the policy process.

Notes

1. Janet A. Weiss, "The Powers of Problem Definition: The Case of Government Paperwork," *Policy Sciences,* Vol. 22 (January 1989), pp. 99–100.
2. Ibid.
3. *A Report of the Commission on Federal Paperwork: Final Summary Report* (Washington, D.C.: Government Printing Office, October 3, 1977), p. 5.
4. House Committee on Government Operations, Hearings on *Implementation of the Paperwork Reduction Act Amendments of 1983,* 98th Cong., 2nd Sess., April 1983, pp. 27–28.
5. *Congressional Quarterly Weekly Report,* Vol. 53 (April 8, 1995), p. 1205.
6. For an extended discussion of policy problems, see David A. Rochefort and Roger W. Cobb, eds., *The Politics of Problem Definition: Shaping the Policy Agenda* (Lawrence: University Press of Kansas, 1994).
7. Aaron Wildavsky, *Speaking Truth to Power* (Boston: Little, Brown, 1979), p. 42.
8. George C. Edwards III and Ira Sharkansky, *The Policy Predicament* (San Francisco: W. H. Freeman, 1978), p. 90.
9. David G. Smith, "Pragmatism and the Group Theory of Politics," *American Political Science Review,* LVIII (September 1964), pp. 607–610.
10. See Barbara J. Nelson, *Making an Issue of Child Abuse* (Chicago: University of Chicago Press, 1984); and Elizabeth Pleck, *Domestic Tyranny* (New York: Oxford University Press, 1987).
11. Robert A. Katzmann, *Institutional Disability* (Washington: Brookings Institution, 1986).
12. General Accounting Office, *Homeless Mentally Ill: Problems and Options in Estimating Numbers and Trends* (Washington, 1988).
13. Charles S. Bullock III and Charles M. Lamb, eds., *Implementation of Civil Rights Policy* (Monterey, Calif.: Brooks/Cole, 1984), chaps. 2,3.
14. James Q. Wilson, "How to Teach Better Values in Inner Cities," *Wall Street Journal,* May 18, 1992, p. A14.
15. See John Dewey, *The Public and Its Problems* (Denver: Swallow, 1927), pp. 12, 15–16.
16. Murray Edleman, *Constructing the Political Spectacle* (Chicago: University of Chicago Press, 1988), chap. 2.
17. Cf. Layne Hoppe, "Agenda-Setting Strategies: The Case of Pollution Problems." Unpublished paper presented at the annual meeting of the American Political Science Association (September 1970).
18. Robert Eyestone, *From Social Issues to Public Policy* (New York: Wiley, 1978), p. 3.

19. Roger W. Cobb and Charles D. Elder, *Participation in American Politics: The Dynamics of Agenda-Building,* 2nd ed. (Baltimore: Johns Hopkins University Press, 1983), p. 85.

20. John W. Kingdon, *Agendas, Alternatives, and Public Policies,* 2nd ed. (New York: Harper Collins, 1995), p. 4.

21.· See Jack L. Walker, "Setting the Agenda in the United States Senate: A Theory of Problem Selection," *British Journal of Political Science,* VII (October 1977), pp. 423–446.

22. Barbara Sinclair, *The Transformation of the U.S. Senate* (Baltimore: Johns Hopkins University Press, 1989), p. 51.

23. Kingdon, op. cit., chap. 4.

24. Ibid., p. 87.

25. Ibid., p. 165.

26. For yet another view of agenda setting, see Frank R. Baumgartner and Bryan D. Jones, *Agendas and Instability in American Politics* (Chicago: University of Chicago Press, 1993).

27. David B. Truman, *The Governmental Process* (New York: Knopf, 1951), p. 30.

28. Paul Light, *The President's Agenda,* rev. ed. (Baltimore: Johns Hopkins University Press, 1991), chap. 3. The quotation is on p. 69.

29. Walker, op cit., p. 431.

30. Beth M. Hensikin and Edward I. Sidlow, "The Supreme Court and the Congressional Agenda-Setting Process." Unpublished paper presented at the annual meeting of the Midwest Political Science Association (April 1989); and Roy B. Flemming, B. Dan Wood, and John Bohte, "Policy Attention in a System of Separated Powers: An Inquiry into the Dynamics of American Agenda Setting," unpublished paper presented at the annual meeting of the Midwest Political Science Association (April 1995).

31. Cf. Cobb and Elder, op. cit., p. 25.

32. See Michael Lipsky, "Protest as a Political Resource," *American Political Science Review,* Vol. 67 (December 1968), pp. 1144–1158.

33. This subject is discussed in fascinating style in W. A. Swanberg, *Citizen Hearst* (New York: Scribner's, 1961), pp. 79–169.

34. Kingdon, op. cit., pp. 95–99.

35. Ibid., pp. 152–160. See generally James A. Stimson, *Public Opinion in America: Moods, Cycles, and Swings* (Boulder, Colo.: Westview Press, 1991).

36. Joseph A. Page and Mary Winn O'Brien, *Bitter Wages* (New York: Grossman, 1973), chap. 7.

37. Those who wish to pursue this topic further should consult the highly informative study by Cobb and Elder, op. cit.

38. Peter Bachrach and Morton S. Baratz, *Power and Poverty* (New York: Oxford University Press, 1970), p. 44. See also John Gaventa, *Powerlessness: Quiescence and Change in an Appalachian Valley* (Urbana: University of Illinois Press, 1980).

39. E. E. Schattschneider, *The Semi-Sovereign People* (New York: Holt, Rinehart and Winston, 1960), p. 71.

40. T. R. Reid, *Congressional Odyssey: The Saga of a Senate Bill* (San Francisco: W. H. Freeman, 1980).

41. Anthony Downs, "Up and Down with Ecology: The Issue-Attention Cycle," *Public Interest*, XXXII (Summer 1972), pp. 38–50.

42. William Graebner, *Coal Mining Safety in the Progressive Period* (Lexington: University of Kentucky Press, 1976).

43. Daniel J. Curran, *Dead Laws for Dead Men: The Politics of Federal Coal Mine Health and Safe Legislation* (Pittsburgh: University of Pittsburgh Press, 1993), chap. 5.

44. *The New York Times*, May 8, 1973, p. 21.

45. Laurence E. Lynn, Jr., *Managing Public Policy* (Boston: Little, Brown, 1987), pp. 254–256.

46. *The New York Times*, March 12, 1987, p. 11; *Wall Street Journal*, June 1, 1987, pp. 1, 10.

47. David Maraniss and Michael Weisskopf, "OSHA's Enemies Find Themselves in High Places," *Washington Post*, July 24, 1995, pp. A8–A9.

48. See Phillip Shabecoff, *A Fierce Green Fire: The American Environmental Movement* (New York: Harper Collins, 1993), pp. 106–111.

49. J. Clarence Davies, *The Politics of Pollution*, 2nd ed. (Indianapolis: Bobbs-Merrill, 1975), p. 7. This discussion relies considerably on Davies.

50. Ibid., pp. 8–9.

51. "Our Filthy Seas," *Time*, Vol. 132 (August 1, 1988), pp. 44–50; and "Don't Go Near the Water," *Newsweek*, Vol. 112 (August 1988), pp. 42–47.

52. Quoted in Richard E. Neustadt, *Presidential Power* (New York: Wiley, 1960), p. 102.

53. Francis E. Rourke and Paul R. Schulman, "Adhocracy in Policy Development." Unpublished paper presented at the annual meeting of the American Political Science Association (September 1988).

54. *Congressional Quarterly Weekly Report*, Vol. 46 (February 6, 1988), pp. 243–245.

55. Emmette S. Redford and Richard T. McCulley, *White House Operations: The Johnson Presidency* (Austin: University of Texas Press, 1986), chap. 5.

56. Richard E. Cohen, *Washington at Work: Backrooms and Clean Air*, 2nd ed. (Boston: Allyn and Bacon, 1995), chap. 11.

57. Gilbert Y. Steiner and Samuel K. Gove, *Legislative Politics in Illinois* (Urbana: University of Illinois Press, 1960), p. 52. Also Diane Blair, *Arkansas Politics and Government* (Lincoln: University of Nebraska Press, 1988), chap. 9.

58. This discussion draws on Julie Rovner, "Congress Feels the Pressure of Health-Care Squeeze," *Congressional Quarterly Weekly Report*, Vol. 49 (February 16, 1991), pp. 414–421.

59. Haynes Johnson and David Broder's *The System: The American Way of Politics at the Breaking Point* (Boston: Little, Brown, 1996), presents an extensive discussion of the drafting of and struggle over the Clinton health-care proposal.

60. Quoted in *The New York Times*, November 18, 1991, p. C10.

61. Note, "Why Learned Hand Would Never Consult Legislative History Today," *Harvard Law Review*, CV (April 1992), p. 1005.

62. *Congressional Quarterly Weekly Report*, Vol. 39 (July 25, 1981), p. 1323.

63. Steven R. Weisman, "Reaganomics and the President's Men," *New York Times Magazine* (October 24, 1982), p. 90.

64. John L. Palmer and Isabel V. Sawhill, eds., *The Reagan Experiment* (Washington: Urban Institute Press, 1982), pp. 111–115. For a partial summary of the 1981 act, see Joseph A. Pechman, ed., *Setting National Priorities: The 1983 Budget* (Washington: Brookings Institution, 1982), pp. 251–262. See also *Congressional Quarterly Weekly Report,* Vol. 31 (August 8, 1981), pp. 1431–1438.

65. This case study relies mostly on Ronald D. Elving, *Conflict and Compromise: How Congress Makes a Law* (New York: Simon and Schuster, 1995). Quotations are from this source. For a summary of the law, see *Congressional Quarterly Almanac, 1993,* Vol. 49 (Washington, D.C.: Congressional Quarterly, 1994), p. 390.

66. Schattschneider, op. cit., p. 68.

67. Charles O. Jones, *An Introduction to the Study of Public Policy* (Belmont, Calif.: Wadsworth, 1970), p. 53.

4

POLICY ADOPTION

President Clinton signs the family-leave bill into law. It was the first legislative triumph for his administration.

A policy decision involves action by some official person or body to adopt, modify, or reject a preferred policy alternative. In positive fashion it takes such forms as the enactment of legislation or the issuance of an executive order. It is helpful to recall the distinction made in Chapter 1 between policy decisions, which significantly affect the content of public policy, and routine decisions, which involve the day-to-day application of policy. Furthermore, a policy decision is usually the culmination of many decisions, some routine and some not so routine, made during the operation of the policy process.

What is typically involved at the policy-adoption stage is not selection from among a number of full-blown policy alternatives but rather action on a preferred policy alternative for which the proponents of action think they can win approval, even though it does not provide all they might like. As the formulation process moves toward the decision stage, some provisions will be rejected, others accepted, and still others modified; differences will be narrowed; bargains will be struck; until ultimately, in some instances, the final policy decision will be only a formality. In other instances, the question will be in doubt until the votes are counted or the decision is announced.

Although private individuals and organizations also participate in making policy decisions, the formal authority to decide rests with public officials: legislators, executives, administrators, judges. In democracies, the task of making policy decisions is most closely identified with the legislature, which is designed to represent the interests of the populace. One frequently hears that a majority of the legislature represents a majority of the people. Whatever its accuracy in describing reality, such a contention does accord with our notion that in a democracy the people should rule, at least through their representatives. Policy decisions made by the legislature are usually accepted as legitimate, as being made in the proper way and hence binding on all. Generally, decisions made by public officials are regarded as legitimate if the officials have legal authority to act and they meet accepted procedural and substantive standards in taking action.

Legitimacy is a difficult concept to define. It is not the same as legality, although legality can contribute to belief in legitimacy, which focuses people's attention on the rightness or appropriateness of government and its actions. For policymaking, legitimacy is affected both by how something is done (i.e., whether proper procedures are used) and by what is being done. Some actions of government, even when within the legal or constitutional authority of officials, may not be regarded as legitimate because they depart too far from prevailing notions of what is acceptable. Thus many Americans never accepted the legitimacy of the Vietnam War. Other people do not accept the legitimacy of a constitutional right to privacy as a barrier to some governmental actions. On the other hand, even though the legislative veto was held unconstitutional in 1983 by the Supreme Court, it continues to be regarded as a necessary and appropriate—that is, legitimate—arrangement by Congress and the executive. Legislative veto arrangements have been incorporated into legislation dozens of times since 1983.[1] Constitutionality is not always a *sine qua non* for legitimacy. Legitimacy is an important factor in developing public support and acceptance for both government and the policies that it adopts. Public officials must be cognizant of this importance. When legitimacy erodes, governments and their policies diminish in effectiveness.

Political and social scientists frequently disagree and diverge over political decision-making, including how to study it, how decisions are actually made, and what constitutes a decision. I make no attempt to resolve any of these controversies. Rather, I discuss some topics that will help the reader get a handle on decision-making, including decision theories, criteria, and styles; the process of majority building (or decision-making) in Congress; and presidential decision-making. The chapter ends with a case study of the economic regulation and deregulation of commercial passenger airlines to provide an integrated and longitudinal view of how policy is formed and changed. The case also illustrates the complex and multifaceted nature of the policy process.

THEORIES OF DECISION-MAKING

Decision-making, as stated in Chapter 1, involves making a choice from among alternatives. Many highly formal, quantitative models of decision-making exist, including linear programming, game theory, and the Monte Carlo method. These are often grouped under the rubric "decision sciences." Some very informal and nonrational ways to make decisions include palmistry, dart throwing, and reflection on one's belly button. None of these genres is reviewed here.

Three theories of decision-making that emphasize the procedure and intellectual activities involved in making a decision are presented here: the rational–comprehensive theory, the incremental theory, and multiple advocacy. To the extent that these theories may describe how decisions are actually made by individuals and groups, they are empirical. Viewed as statements of how decisions *should* be made, they become normative. It is not always easy to separate these two qualities in decision-making theories and studies, as we will discover.

The Rational–Comprehensive Theory

Perhaps the best-known theory of decision-making is the rational–comprehensive theory. It draws considerably from the economist's view of how a rational person would make decisions as well as from theories of rational decision-making developed by mathematicians, psychologists, and other social scientists. It should not be confused with rational-choice theory. Whereas rational-choice theory is used for developing deductive models of self-interested decision-makers, the rational–comprehensive theory specifies the procedures involved in making well-considered decisions that maximize the attainment of goals, whether personal or organizational.

The rational–comprehensive theory usually includes these elements:

1. The decision-maker is confronted with a problem that can be separated from other problems or at least considered meaningfully in comparison with them.
2. The goals, values, or objectives that guide the decision-maker are known and can be clarified and ranked according to their importance.
3. The various alternatives for dealing with the problem are examined.
4. The consequences (costs and benefits, advantages and disadvantages) that would follow from selecting each alternative are investigated.
5. Each alternative, and its attendant consequences, is then compared with the other alternatives.
6. The decision-maker will choose the alternative, and its consequences, that maximizes attainment of his or her goals, values, or objectives.

The result of this procedure is a rational decision—that is, one that most effectively achieves a given end. In short, it optimizes; it is the best possible decision. Rational decisions may make either large and basic or limited changes in public policies.

The rational–comprehensive theory has had substantial criticism directed at it. Professor Charles Lindblom contends that decision-makers are not faced with concrete, clearly defined problems. Rather, he says that they first have to identify and formulate the problems on which they make decisions. For example, when prices are rising rapidly and people are saying, "We must do something about the problem of inflation," what is the problem? Excessive demand? Inadequate production of goods and services? Administered prices controlled by powerful corporations and unions? Inflationary psychology? Some combination of these? One does not, willy-nilly, attack inflation. Instead, the causes of inflation must be dealt with, and these may be difficult to determine. Defining the problem is, in short, often a major problem for the decision-maker.

A second criticism holds that rational–comprehensive theory is unrealistic in the intellectual demands it makes on the decision-maker. It assumes that he or she will have enough information on the alternatives for dealing with a problem, will be able to predict their consequences with some accuracy, and will be capable of making correct cost-benefit comparisons of the alternatives. A moment's reflection on the informational and intellectual resources needed for acting rationally on the problem of inflation posed above indicates the barriers to rational action implied in these assumptions: lack of time, difficulty in collecting information and predicting the future, complexity of calculations. Even use of that modern miracle, the computer, and sophisticated economic models replete with equations cannot fully alleviate these problems, as economists continually demonstrate. There is no need to overload the arguments, as some do, by talking of the need to consider all possible alternatives. Even a rational–comprehensive decision-maker should be permitted to ignore the absurd and the far-fetched.

The value aspect of the rational–comprehensive theory also receives some knocks. Thus, it is contended that in actuality the public decision-maker is usually confronted with a situation of value conflict rather than value agreement, and that the conflicting values do not permit easy comparison or weighing. Moreover, the decision-maker might confuse personal values with those of the public. In addition, the rationalistic assumption that facts and values can be readily separated does not hold up in practice. Some may support a dam on a stream as demonstrably necessary to control flooding, and others may oppose it, preferring a free-flowing stream for aesthetic and ecological reasons. Recourse to the "facts," even lots of them, will not resolve such controversies.

Yet another problem is that of "sunk costs." Previous decisions and commitments, investments in existing policies and programs, may foreclose or severely complicate the consideration of many alternatives. The Clinton administration's formulation of a national health-care program was restricted by the nation's extensive reliance upon employer-sponsored health insurance. An airport, once constructed, cannot be easily moved to the other side of town. Even if only partially constructed, pressure will be strong to complete the project rather than "waste" the money already invested by relocating the airport. Finally, the rational–comprehensive model assumes the existence of a unitary decision-maker. This condition cannot be met by legislative bodies, plural-headed agencies, or multiple-member courts.

The Incremental Theory

The incremental theory of decision-making is presented as a decision theory that avoids many of the problems of the rational–comprehensive theory and, at the same time, is more descriptive of the way in which public officials actually make decisions.[2] Certainly there is little evidence to indicate that the members of Congress utilize anything akin to the rational–comprehensive model in enacting legislation. Incremental decisions involve limited changes or additions to existing policies, such as a small-percentage increase in an agency's budget or a modest tightening of eligibility requirements for student loans. Incrementalism (Lindblom refers to it as "disjointed incrementalism") can be summarized in the following manner:

1. The selection of goals or objectives and the empirical analysis of the action needed to attain them are closely intertwined with, rather than distinct from, one another.
2. The decision-maker considers only some of the alternatives for dealing with a problem, which will differ only incrementally (i.e., marginally) from existing policies.
3. For each alternative, only a limited number of "important" consequences are evaluated.
4. The problem confronting the decision-maker is continually redefined. Incrementalism allows for countless ends–means and means–ends adjustments that help make the problem more manageable.
5. There is no single decision or "right" solution for a problem. The test of a good decision is that various analysts find themselves directly agreeing on it, without agreeing that the decision is the most appropriate or optimum means to an agreed objective.
6. Incremental decision-making is essentially remedial and is geared more to ameliorating present, concrete social imperfections than to promoting future social goals.[3]

Lindblom contends that incrementalism is the typical decision-making procedure in pluralist societies such as the United States. Decisions and policies are the product of give and take and mutual consent among numerous participants ("partisans") in the decision process. Incrementalism is politically expedient because it is easier to reach agreement when the matters in dispute among various groups are only limited modifications of existing programs rather than policy issues of great magnitude or of an "all-or-nothing" character. Because decision-makers operate under conditions of uncertainty about the future consequences of their actions, incremental decisions reduce the risks and costs of uncertainty. Incrementalism is also realistic because it recognizes that decision-makers lack the time, intelligence, and other resources needed to engage in comprehensive analysis of all alternative solutions to existing problems. Moreover, people are essentially pragmatic, seeking not always the single best way to deal with a problem but, more modestly, "something that will work." Incrementalism, in short, utilizes limited analysis to yield limited, practical, acceptable decisions. A sequence of incremental decisions, however, may produce a fundamental change in public policy. Myriad incremental decisions have made Social Security a vastly different program from the one Congress first authorized in 1935.

Several criticisms have been directed at incrementalism. One is that it is too conservative, too focused on the current order; hence, it is a barrier to innovation, which is often necessary for effective public policies. Another is that in crisis situations (such as the Iraqi invasion of Kuwait) or when major changes are made in policy (for instance, the 1981 tax cut), incrementalism provides no guidelines for handling the tasks of decision. Third, geared as it is to past actions and existing programs, and to limited changes in them, incrementalism may discourage the search for or use of other readily available alternatives. Fourth, incrementalism does not eliminate the need for theory in decision-making, as some of its more enthusiastic advocates contend. For, unless changes in policy (increments) are to be made simply at random or arbitrarily, some theory (of causation, relationships, etc.) is needed to guide the action and to indicate the likely effects of proposed changes.[4] Notwithstanding reservations of these sorts, incrementalism has become a form of conventional wisdom. Statements to the effect that policymaking in the United States is incremental are common. National budgeting during the three decades following World War II epitomized incrementalism. (See Chapter 5).

Multiple Advocacy

Multiple advocacy has been most commonly presented as a theory to guide presidential decision-making. It rests on the premise that "a competition of ideas and viewpoints is the best method of developing policy—not unregulated entrepreneurial advocacy, but orderly, systematic, and balanced competition."[5] It accepts the fact that in large, complex organizations there will inevitably be conflicts and disagreements over policy. Consequently, the decision-making process should be structured to ensure that the president or some other decision-maker will be supplied with adequate information about all of the important viewpoints on an issue.

For multiple advocacy to work properly, there is need for an "honest broker" or custodian to manage the process. The responsibilities of the honest broker include ensuring that all interested parties are identified and represented in the deliberations and that the debate is structured, balanced, conducted fairly, and high-quality in content. It may be necessary for the honest broker to bring in persons to present unpopular perspectives or to strengthen the presentations of weaker advocates. To be effective the honest broker must be neutral, lest his role be undermined by advocacy or partisan action.

The decision-maker, according to Professor Alexander George, "should adopt the stance of a magistrate—one who listens to the arguments made, evaluates them, poses issues and asks questions, and finally, judges which action to take either from among those articulated by advocates or as formulated independently by himself after hearing them." The decision maker also should avoid conveying his or her policy preferences because this might skew the debate.[6]

There are some limitations on multiple advocacy. Advocates may differ in resources and abilities and there is no guarantee that all viable policy alternatives will be presented. Moreover, no one may challenge an agency or official who either presents biased analysis or withholds useful information. Multiple advocacy tends to emphasize differences rather than consensus. Finally, while multiple advocacy may help prevent uninformed decisions, it does not ensure that good or wise decisions will result.[7]

Examples of decision-making processes that approximate multiple advocacy can be identified in several presidential administrations. What is perhaps the most prominent example, the Economic Policy Board in the Ford administration, will be commented on here.[8] Created by an executive order, the Economic Policy Board handled both domestic and international issues. Its membership consisted of the secretaries of agriculture; commerce; health, education and welfare; housing and urban development; interior; labor; state; and treasury; the directors of the Office of Management and Budget and Council on International Economic Policy; the chair of the council of Economic Advisors; and the special assistant to the president for economic affairs. It was chaired by Treasury Secretary William Simon while William Seidman, the special assistant, was executive director in charge of its day-to-day operations. Much of EPB's work was done by a smaller executive committee which met three or four times a week, including about once a week with the president. When the president attended meetings Seidman acted as an honest broker who "called the meetings, set the agenda, and distributed the minutes as well as the papers that had been prepared by members setting out their often rival views. It was my purpose to ensure that all views on every issue were fairly presented to the president."[9] Subsequently, a report for the Clinton administration, prepared by two Washington research organizations, concluded that the Ford administration was "the best organized of all recent administrations in its ability to lay all the resources of the government before the president and ensure that his decisions were carried out. The report also concluded that good organization does not always yield good policy."[10]

DECISION CRITERIA

Decision-making can be studied either as an individual or as a collective process. In the first instance, the focus is on the criteria individuals use in making choices. In the latter, the focus is the processes by which majorities are built, or by which approval is otherwise gained, for specific decisions. Individual choices, of course, are usually made with some reference to how others involved in the decisional situation are likely to respond.

An individual may be subject to various influencing factors when deciding how to vote on or resolve a policy question. Which of these concerns is most crucial to the choice is often hard to specify. Public officials frequently make statements explaining their decisions in the *Congressional Record,* constituency newsletters, speeches, press conferences, court opinions, memoirs, and elsewhere. The reasons they give for their decisions may be those which were actually controlling, or they may be those which are thought to be acceptable to the public at large or to important constituents, while their actual bases for choice go unstated. Nonetheless, it is often possible, by careful observation and analysis, to determine which factors were operating in a situation, if not necessarily to assign them specific weights. A number of criteria that may influence policy choice are discussed here. They include values, party affiliation, constituency interests, public opinion, deference, and decision rules. The concept of the public interest is scrutinized in the following section.

Values

In considering the broader social and political forces that impinge on decision-makers, we tend to neglect their own values (or standards or preferences), which help them decide what is good or bad, desirable or undesirable. Often these may be difficult to determine and impossible to isolate. Decision-making persons, however, are not simply pieces of clay to be molded by others. Rather, their values may be important or even determinative in shaping their behavior. Some decision-makers may come under criticism if they insist too strenuously on the primacy of what they personally value. Here I comment on five categories of values that may guide the behavior of decision-makers: organizational, professional, personal, policy, and ideological.

ORGANIZATIONAL VALUES Decision-makers, especially bureaucrats, may be influenced by organizational values. Those who work for any agency for any extended period of time, whether the Tennessee Valley Authority, the Social Security Administration, or the Federal Trade Commission, are likely to become firm believers in the importance of the agency's goals and programs. Moreover, organizations may utilize a variety of rewards and sanctions to induce their members to accept and act in accordance with organizationally determined values.[11] Consequently, agency officials' decisions may reflect such considerations as a desire to see the agency survive, to increase its budget, to enhance or expand its programs or to maintain its power and prerogatives against external assaults. Career officials in the Environmental Protection Agency successfully resisted the Reagan administration's attempt to blunt the enforcement of agency programs.

Organizational values may sometimes lead to conflict among agencies with competing or overlapping jurisdictions. The Army Corps of Engineers, the Bureau of Reclamation, and the Natural Resources Conservation Services (formerly the Soil Conservation Service) have differed over water-resource policies and projects.[12] "Turf" battles of this sort are an understandable, if not laudable, manifestation of differing organizational values.

PROFESSIONAL VALUES   The professional values of agency personnel may be important. Professions tend to form distinctive preferences as to how problems should be handled. Professionally trained people carry these preferences or values with them into organizations, some of which become dominated by particular professions; two such examples are the prevalence of engineers in the National Highway Traffic Safety Administration and industrial hygienists in the Occupational Safety and Health Administration. OSHA's industrial health and safety rules reflect the industrial hygienist's preference for engineering or design standards over performance standards. Design standards specify the use of particular equipment, ventilating systems, and safety devices and are intended to eliminate hazards. Performance standards, in contrast, set health or safety goals, but leave the methods for attaining these goals to the company's discretion. Economists, preferring market solutions and efficiency, held sway in the Federal Trade Commission during the 1980s. Their influence was manifested in the agency's disinclination to challenge many large corporate mergers and unfair trade practices on the grounds that mergers contributed to efficiency and the latter were simply forms of intense competition.

PERSONAL VALUES   Decision-makers may also be guided by their personal values, or by the urge to protect or promote their own physical or financial well-being, reputation, or historical position. The politician who accepts a bribe to make a decision, such as the award of a license or contract, obviously has personal benefit in mind. On a different plane, the president who says he is not going to be "the first president to lose a war" and then acts accordingly is also manifesting the influence of personal values, such as concern for his place in history. Personal values are important, but the rational-choice theorists go much too far when they try to explain officials' behavior as totally driven by self-interest. The location of public buildings is probably better explained by self-interest than is the adoption of civil-rights policies.

POLICY VALUES   Policy values are also significant. Neither the discussion thus far nor cynicism should lead us to assume that decision-makers are influenced only by personal, professional, and organization considerations. Decision-makers may well act according to their perceptions of the public interest or their beliefs about what is proper, necessary, or morally correct public policy. Legislators may vote in favor of civil-rights legislation because they believe that it is morally correct and that equality of opportunity is a desirable policy goal, even though their vote may place them in political jeopardy. Studies of the Supreme Court also indicate that in deciding cases the justices are influenced by policy values.

IDEOLOGICAL VALUES   Finally we come to ideological values. Ideologies are sets of coherent or logically related values and beliefs that present simplified pictures of the world and serve as guides to action for believers. For Communists, Marxist–Leninist ideology has served at least partly as a set of prescriptions for social and economic change. Although the Soviets sometimes deviated from this body of beliefs, as in their use of economic incentives to increase production toward the end of the regime, Marxist–Leninist ideology still served the regime as a means for rationalizing and legitimizing policy actions. In the twentieth century, nationalism—the desire of a nation or people for autonomy and the deep regard for their own characteristics, needs, and problems—has been a major factor shaping the actions of many nations, especially developing countries in Asia, Africa, and the Middle East.

During the Reagan years, conservative ideology, and notably its intense variant known as "movement conservatism," influenced the actions of many Reagan administration members. Devout believers in individualism, minimal government, and the free market, they strongly supported deregulation, privatization, and reduced governmental spending. For movement conservatives, that ideology was both their beacon and their shepherd. For some, it was more important to be right—to be true to their ideology—than to win on some legislative issue by compromising their principles. To them, "pragmatist" was a pejorative label, the American cultural preference for practicality notwithstanding. Quite a few members of the Republican House majority elected in 1994 fell into this category.

Arrayed against conservatives are modern liberals. Their ideology calls for vigorous use of the government's powers to serve the interests of the poor, working people, minorities, and the disadvantaged generally.[13] They are defenders of civil rights and liberties, protectors of the environment, and proponents of consumer interests. "The regulatory state and the welfare state are two pillars of modern liberal ideology." On the other hand, they are skeptical about the maintenance of a large defense establishment in the post–Cold War era. Although liberals are less sure of their policy preferences than they once were, on the whole they are optimistic concerning their ability to use government to improve the human condition and promote an egalitarian society.

Political-Party Affiliation

Party loyalty is an important decision-making criterion for most members of Congress, even though it is difficult to separate that loyalty from such other influences as party leadership pressures, ideological commitments, and constituency interests. Party affiliation is the best single predictor as to how members of Congress will vote on legislative issues. If one knows a member's party affiliation and the party's position on issues, and then uses party affiliation as the basis for predicting votes, he or she will probably be correct more often than when using any other indicator. In recent years, the average legislator has voted with the majority of his or her party about three-fourths of the time.[14] Party-unity voting, in which a majority of one party opposes a majority of the other party, has also been increasing. In the 1990s party-unity votes occurred on over half of the roll-call votes in both the House and the Senate.[15]

Contributing to an increase in voting along party lines has been a decrease in the appearance of the conservative coalition, an alliance between Republicans and conservative southern Democrats that formed on social welfare, labor, and some other issues. Electoral changes in the South have led to the replacement of many conservative Democrats by Republicans. The remaining "new breed" southern Democrats are more likely to vote with their other Democratic colleagues. In Republican ranks, the number of "liberals" and moderates has been diminished.[16] The inclination of the parties in Congress to engage in party-based conflict has also increased as they have become more polarized. This was highly evident in the House in 1995–1996 under the control of the new Republican majority.

Strong-party voting, in which 90 percent or more of one party is aligned against 90 percent or more of the other party, customarily occurs on only a small percentage of roll-call votes in either the House or Senate. This type of party voting reached a peak in the nineteenth century during the McKinley era, when approximately 50 percent of the House votes met this standard.[17] The strong-party leadership and control that yielded such voting proved to be unacceptable to both members of Congress and the public, however, and were eliminated by congressional reforms early in the twentieth century.

In parliamentary systems, such as the British House of Commons, voting along strict party lines is the order of the day. In Commons most votes meet the "90 percent versus 90 percent" strong-party vote criterion. On many government proposals, formal votes (divisions) are not taken because they are unnecessary. Although dissenting votes to party positions have increased since 1970, they usually involve only a handful of a party's members and customarily do not occur on crucial issues.[18]

Party loyalties or attachments in Congress have varied in importance among issue areas. Party conflict has arisen most consistently on such topics as business regulation, labor–management relations, social welfare, taxation, and agricultural price supports. Democrats have been more inclined, for example, to support new welfare programs—such as family leave and child care—and expansion of or increased funding for existing ones—such as Medicare and food stamps—than have Republicans. Again, Democrats have been stronger supporters of air and water pollution-control regulations than have Republicans. In some issue areas, however, it is difficult to delineate distinct and persistent party differences. Public works, veterans' benefits, medical research, and international trade, are illustrative. Members of both parties have displayed a proclivity for securing pork-barrel projects (research facilities, public buildings, dams, highway "demonstration" projects), that is, those that are of particular benefit to their states and districts.

Constituency Interests

A bit of conventional wisdom in Congress holds that, when party interests and state or district constituency interests conflict on some issue, members should "vote their constituency." It is, after all, the voters at home who hold the ultimate power to hire and fire. In looking after the interests of his or her constituents, the representative may act as either a delegate, carrying out their actual or perceived instructions, or a trustee, exercising his or her best judgment in their behalf, when voting on policy questions.[19] Of course, the representative may try to combine these two styles, acting as a delegate on some issues and as a trustee on others, thus becoming a politico.

In some instances, constituents' interests will be rather clear and strongly held, and representatives will act contrary to them at their own peril. In the past, southern members of Congress were well aware of the strong opposition among their white constituents to civil-rights legislation and voted accordingly. A legislator from a strong labor district will likewise probably have little doubt about the constituents' interests on minimum-wage and right-to-work legislation. On a great many issues, however, representatives will be hard put to determine what their constituents want. Large portions of the electorate have little knowledge of most issues. How, then, do representatives measure which way the wind is blowing from their districts if no air currents are moving? Legislators must then make a decision drawing on their own values or other criteria, such as recommendations from party leaders or the chief executive. They may also solicit opinions from some of their constituents or listen to the interested few.

Nonelected public officials, such as administrators, may also act as representatives. Agencies often have well-developed relationships with interest groups and strive to represent their interests in forming and administering policy. The Department of Agriculture is especially responsive to the interests of commercial farmers, and the Federal Maritime Commission has viewed itself as the representative of international shipping interests in the national administrative system. The two agencies' decisions and actions have reflected the interests of their clienteles. Some commentators have contended that administrative agencies may in fact be more representative of particular interests in society than are elected officials.[20] Whatever the validity of this contention, it is clear that legislators are not the only officials influenced by the need or desire to act representatively in making decisions.

Public Opinion

Public opinion can be defined operationally as those public perspectives or viewpoints on policy issues that public officials consider or take into account in making decisions. Public opinion may be expressed in many ways—letters to the editor and to public officials, meetings, public demonstrations, editorials, election results, legislators meeting with constituents, plebiscites, and radio talk shows. Most commonly, however, public opinion is identified with the findings of opinion surveys that poll a representative sample of the population on political issues. Despite their increasing numbers and sophistication, opinion surveys have various limitations. Notably, they do not provide much insight into either the depth or intensity of people's opinions. Small focus groups are sometimes used to gauge the depth or intensity of feelings on some issues.

Moreover, although most people are quite willing to express their opinions to pollsters, typically it is unclear how much information or understanding underlies their perspectives. But consider this example. In 1995, a University of Maryland research organization released an opinion survey that found that 75 percent of the respondents thought the national government spent too much money on foreign-aid programs. Asked how much of the national budget went for foreign aid, the median response was 15 percent and the average response was 18 percent. In actuality, foreign aid accounted for less than one percent of the budget (about $14 billion). To questions about how much foreign spending would be "appropriate" and how much would be "too little," the median responses were 5 percent and 3 percent, respectively.[21] The lack of respondent information indicated by this poll suggests that the "don't know" should have been the standard response. This example is likely not atypical.

Public opinion is also subject to manipulation by public officials, as through the management of the news—that is, the careful control of information provided to media representatives. Reagan administration officials, for instance, used a "theme of the day" format to influence the view of the president and his policies presented through the media to the public.

Notwithstanding their limitations, opinion surveys draw much attention because of their frequency, regularity, and accessibility, and the seeming precision of the numbers they yield.

Political scientists have devoted much time and effort to studying the formation, content, and change of public opinion on political issues. The more philosophically inclined have considered the role of public opinion in the governmental process. Our subject is the effect of public opinion on the actions of policy-makers. Are the policy-makers' choices shaped or determined by public opinion? Does public opinion serve as a criterion for decision? It is advisable to proceed tentatively in answering such questions, bearing in mind Professor V. O. Key's comment that "to speak with precision of public opinion is a task not unlike coming to grips with the Holy Ghost."[22]

A useful way to approach the problem of how public opinion influences policymaking is to distinguish between decisions that shape the broad direction of policy and the day-to-day, often routine, decisions on specific aspects of policy. Public opinion is probably not a significant criterion for decisions in the second category. Drawing on Key again, "Many, if not most, policy decisions by legislatures and by other authorities exercising broad discretion are made under circumstances in which extremely small proportions of the general public have any awareness of the particular issue, much less any understanding of the consequences of the decision."[23] The legislator deciding how to vote on a specific tax amendment or a public-works bill will probably be unaffected by public opinion in any direct sense. Of course, he or she may try to anticipate the public's reaction to such votes, but this tactic will leave substantial latitude to the legislator because of the lack of public awareness mentioned above.

Nonetheless, the general boundaries and direction of public policy may be shaped by public opinion. Given public attitudes, such actions as nationalizing the airline industry, repealing the Clean Air Act, or making a major cutback in the Social Security program appear highly unlikely. Conversely, officials may come to believe that public opinion demands some kind of policy action, as with tax-reduction legislation in 1981 and welfare reform in 1995. These were generalized rather than specific demands, which left to Congress much discretion on details. In foreign policy, public opinion appears to accord wide latitude to executive officials, as the conduct of American intervention in Vietnam during the 1960s clearly indicates. Ultimately, however, growing public opposition to the Vietnam War apparently contributed to President Johnson's decision not to run for reelection in 1968 and to begin to "wind down the war and withdraw."[24] Conversely, public opinion was strongly supportive of the Bush Administration's campaign to drive the Iraqis out of Kuwait.[25]

Public opinion sometimes seems to have a permissive quality, in that action on some topic is favored but not required. For years, public-opinion polls have indicated that a majority of the American population (70 percent in 1993) supports stronger gun-control legislation, such as requiring a waiting period before the purchase of a handgun.[26] However, restrictive legislation has been scarce because of the strong, well-financed opposition of the National Rifle Association. In instances like this, an intense minority may prevail over a much larger but less committed majority.

In summary, policy-makers do not appear unaffected by public opinion in their choices. The relationship between public opinion and policy actions, however, is neither as simple nor as direct as once assumed. But elected public officials who totally ignore public opinion and do not include it among their criteria for decisions, should any be so foolish, are likely to find themselves out of luck at election time.

Deference

Officials confronted with the task of making a decision may decide how to act by deferring to the judgment of others. The "others" to whom deference is given may or may not be hierarchic superiors. Administrative officials often do make decisions in accordance with directives from department heads or chief executives. That is how we expect them to act, especially when the directives of superiors are clear in meaning, which, it must be added, they sometimes are not. Administrators may also defer to the suggestions or judgments of members of Congress, as Department of Agriculture officials did when receiving advice from Congressman Jamie Whitten (D, Mississippi), who chaired the House Agricultural Appropriations Subcommittee from 1949 to 1992 (except for 1953 to 1954, when the Republicans controlled the House) and later the full Appropriations Committee. Because of his position and strong influence on the actions of the Department of Agriculture, Whitten was sometimes referred to as the "permanent Secretary of Agriculture."[27]

Members of Congress often have to vote on issues that are of little interest to them, such as those that do not affect the members' constituents, those on which they have little information, or those that are highly complex. On such issues they may decide how to vote by seeking the advice of other legislators whose judgment they trust, whether party leaders, committee chairs, or policy experts. When members are unable to decide how to vote from their own analysis of an issue, deference to someone whose judgment they trust is a reasonably rational, low-information strategy for making decisions. Political scientist Donald R. Matthews argues that, because of the widespread practice of deference to policy experts, "few institutions provide more power to the exceptionally competent member than does the House of Representatives."[28]

Judges, too, make decisions that reflect deference. When they interpret a statute, in either applying it to a case or determining its constitutionality, they may defer to the intent of the legislature.[29] Statutory language is often ambiguous and unclear. In trying to determine what the legislature intends by phrases such as "restraint of trade" or "all lawful means," they may make use of the legislative histories of statutes. One tenet in the theory of "judicial self-restraint" holds that judges "are not free to invoke their own personal notions of right and wrong or of good and bad public policy when they examine the constitutionality of legislation."[30] To the extent that judges act accordingly in deciding cases, this course involves some deference to the judgment of legislatures.

Decision Rules

Those confronted with the task of making many decisions often devise rules of thumb, or guidelines, to focus on facts and relationships and thereby both simplify and regularize decision-making. No set of decision rules is common to all decision-makers, although some may be widely utilized. Which guidelines apply in a situation is a matter to be determined by empirical investigation. A few examples are presented here to illustrate the concept.

The rule of *stare decisis* (in effect, "let the precedents stand") is often used by the judiciary in deciding cases. According to this decision rule or principle, current cases should be decided in the same way as similar cases were decided in the past. Using precedents to guide decision-making is by no means limited to the judiciary. Executives, administrators, and legislators also frequently make decisions on the basis of precedents. They are often urged to do so by those who would be affected by their actions, particularly if this act will help maintain a desired status quo. Those adversely affected by precedents are likely to find them lacking in virtue and utility, or hopelessly out of date.

In the antitrust area, some *per se* rules have been developed. Certain economic actions, such as price fixing and market allocation, have been held to be *per se* (in effect, "as such") violations of the Sherman Act. If the prohibited action is found to exist, this finding is sufficient to prove violation, and no effort is made to inquire into the reasonableness of the prices fixed or other possible justifications for the action in question. *Per se* rules thus add simplicity and certainty to antitrust decision-making.

Professor Richard F. Fenno, Jr., in his study of a number of congressional committees, finds that each committee has some rules for decision (strategic premises) that help shape its decision-making activities. Thus, the House Appropriations Committee, seeking to maintain its independence from the executive, has a "rule" that it should reduce executive budget requests, and in fact many requests are reduced. Economic and Educational Opportunities Committee (formerly the House Education and Labor Committee) has a rule for decision, in Fenno's words, "to prosecute policy partisanship." That is, strong ideological conflict between its Republican and Democratic contingents is the expected style of committee behavior.[31] Fenno points out that every committee has decision rules, although some are easier to discover than others and they will change over time.

THE PUBLIC INTEREST

The task of government, it is often proclaimed, is to serve or promote the public interest. Statutes sometimes include the public interest as a guide for agency action, as when the Federal Communications Commission is directed to license broadcasters for the "public interest, convenience, and necessity." In this section, I discuss this rather elusive normative concept and its usefulness as a criterion for decision-making.

Most people, I am certain, if asked whether public policy should be in accord with the public interest or with private interests would opt for the former, as Professor Charles Anderson remarks: "One cannot justify a policy recommendation on the grounds that 'it would make me and my friends richer.' However refreshing the candor of such an argument might be, it does not and cannot stand as legitimate warrant for a public action."[32]

Difficulty arises, however, when one is asked to define the public interest. Is it the interest of the majority? If so, how do we determine what policy the majority really wants? Is it the interest of consumers, who are a rather large group? Is it what people would want if they "thought clearly and acted rationally"? How does one define the public interest?

Many people, including most political scientists, would say that it is not possible to provide a universally accepted or objective definition of the concept, especially in substantive terms. Some would contend that whatever results from the political struggle over policy issues is the public interest. If all groups and persons had an equal chance to engage in that struggle, which in fact they do not, this notion of the public interest might be more appealing. I, for one, do not care to define a multitude of tax loopholes or inaction that permits the wanton destruction of natural resources as in the public interest. (That statement, of course, indicates a normative bias, which will be especially disturbing to those who hold that "one person's opinion is as good as another's.") Sometimes the public interest is depicted as a myth by which policy, however particularistic, can be rationalized as in the general interest and hence made more publicly acceptable. This stratagem is attempted or performed with regularity (just as scoundrels sometimes wrap themselves in the flag or cite Scripture to justify their predations). Beyond that, however, the concept can be given enough content to render it useful as a general standard for decision-making on public policy. When evaluating policy we need to be able to state not only whether the policy is accomplishing its asserted objectives but also whether the objectives are worthy of accomplishment. For the latter question a standard of more noble quality than "it is (or is not) in my interest" seems needed.

The question now arises about how to determine what constitutes the public interest. Professor Emmette S. Redford suggests three approaches to this task.[33] One is to look at policy areas rich in conflict among group interests, as in agriculture, labor relations, energy, and transportation. In some instances the direct interests of one group or another may prevail and become accepted as the public interest. There is no reason to assume that private interests and the public interest must always be antithetical. If it is in the private interest of medical doctors to prevent the practice of medicine by various quacks, because this would give the medical profession a bad reputation, so, too, it is in the public interest not to have unqualified people practicing medicine. (It would seem difficult to argue the contrary position reasonably.) In the struggle among private group interests, however, it may become apparent that others are indirectly involved and have interests that should be considered in policymaking. These public interests, though not represented by organized groups, may be responded to by decision-makers and thus influence the outcome. In the conflict between labor and management over terms and conditions of employment, it becomes apparent that the public has an interest in maintaining industrial peace and preventing disruptions in the flow of vital goods and services. The result has been the adoption of several procedures for settling labor disputes. In a dispute such as one involving the railroad industry, a public interest may become clear along with those of the railroad companies and labor unions.

2. A second approach is to search for widely and continuously shared interests that, because of these characteristics, can be called public interests. Illustrative are the interests of people in such matters as world peace, better education, clean air, avoidance of severe inflation, and an adequate traffic-control system. Here the public interest appears as public needs. Especially in large cities there is a clear public interest in having a traffic-control system to facilitate safe, orderly, and convenient movement of pedestrians and vehicles. That various alternatives are available for meeting this need can be taken to mean that more than one way can be found to meet the public interest; that availability does not negate its existence. Nor does the concept, to be meaningful, need to be so precise as to indicate whether the traffic flow on a certain street should be one-way or two-way. A concept to be useful need not always yield an answer to the most minute questions.

There is nothing very mystical in talking about the public interest as a widely shared interest. We speak, for example, of wheat farmers' shared interest in higher wheat prices or that of sport fishermen in an adequate fish-stocking program, and attribute much reality to such interests. The public interest differs only in its wider scope. There is no way to determine precisely at what point the interest is widely enough shared as to become a public interest. Few interests, indeed, would be shared by everyone. The survival of the nation-state may be opposed by the advocate of world government; even at old-time western rustler lynchings at least one dissenter might be heard. Qualitative judgments are obviously called for in determining the existence of a public interest, as in many areas of political life and academic activity. They should be made with as much care and rigor as possible.[34]

A third approach to determining the public interest is to look at the need for organization and procedures to represent and balance interests, to resolve issues, to effect compromise in policy formation, and to carry public policy into effect. There is, in short, a public interest in fair, orderly, and effective government. The focus here is on process rather than policy content. The noted columnist Walter Lippmann wrote,

> The public is interested in law, not in the laws; in the method of law, not in the substance; in the sanctity of contract, not in a particular contract; in understanding based on custom, not in this custom or that. It is concerned in these things to the end that men in their active affairs shall find a modus vivendi; its interest is in the workable rule which will define and predict the behavior of men so that they can make their adjustments.[35]

Although the public is obviously interested in individual laws as well as the law, Lippmann states well the desire for adequate process. How things are done, moreover, often affects the public's attitude about their acceptability.

The public interest is thus diverse and somewhat fugitive, and must be searched for in various ways. Although it probably cannot be converted into a precise set of guidelines to inform the action of decision-makers, neither can it fairly be described as merely a myth. It directs attention beyond the more immediate toward broader, more universal interests. It also directs attention toward unorganized and unarticulated interests that otherwise may be ignored in both the development and evaluation of policy. It is an ideal, like justice and equality of opportunity, to which all can aspire.

STYLES OF DECISION-MAKING

Most policy decisions of any magnitude are made by coalitions, which frequently take the form of numerical majorities, whether one's attention is on Congress, the Michigan State Legislature, the Oakland City Council, or the Danish Folketing. Even when a numerical majority is not officially required, the support (or consent, which is much the same) of others is needed to ensure that the decision is implemented and compliance is achieved. The president is often vested with the final authority to make decisions, as on budget recommendations to Congress and tariff reductions. However, he will need to gain cooperation or support from other officials if his decisions are to be effective. Political scientist Richard E. Neustadt, an astute observer of the presidency, remarks, "Underneath our images of Presidents-in-boots, astride decisions, are the half-observed realities of Presidents-in-sneakers, stirrups in hand, trying to induce particular department heads, or Congressmen or

Senators, to climb aboard."[36] President John F. Kennedy sometimes told friends who offered policy suggestions or criticism, "Well I agree with you, but I'm not sure the government will."[37] These comments emphasize the coalitional form of much presidential decision-making and the president's need to induce others to go along if he is to be successful.

Although coalition building is necessary in all democratic legislative bodies, it is especially notable in multiparty legislatures. This requirement is well illustrated by the Danish Folketing, whose 179 seats are divided among nine or ten parties, none of which holds close to a majority of seats. To take office, a Danish prime minister must draw on several parties to put together a majority coalition, which takes considerable negotiation and bargaining. Once in office the prime minister, in taking policy actions, must always be alert to the need to hold the coalition together, lest he lose his majority and thus the power to govern. In India, following the 1996 elections, coalition building was more precarious than in Denmark. More than twenty political parties held seats in the 545 member Parliament.[38]

In this section the focus shifts from individual decision-making to decision-making as a social or collective process. We examine three styles of collective decision-making: bargaining, persuasion, and command. Each entails action to reach agreement and induce others to comply. Practitioners of these styles of decision-making will be motivated by the decision criteria examined in the preceding section.

Bargaining

The most common style of decision-making in the American political system is bargaining. Bargaining can be defined as a process in which two or more persons in positions of power or authority adjust their at least partially inconsistent goals in order to formulate a course of action that is acceptable but not necessarily ideal for all the participants. In short, bargaining involves negotiation, give-and-take, and compromise to reach a mutually acceptable position. In the private realm, it is epitomized in collective bargaining over the terms of work by union leaders and management officials, or by the haggling that takes place at flea markets. For bargaining to occur, the bargainers must be willing to negotiate, they must have something to negotiate about, and each must have something (i.e., resources) that others want or need.

Two factors seem especially important in making bargaining the dominant mode of decision-making in our society. One is social pluralism, or the presence of a multitude of partially autonomous groups such as labor unions, business organizations, professional associations, farm organizations, environmental groups, sportsmen's clubs, and civil-rights groups. Although partially autonomous, these groups are also interdependent and "must bargain with one another for protection and advantage."[39] The second factor is use of such constitutional practices as federalism, separation of powers, bicameral legislatures, and legislative committees, which fragment and disperse political power among many public officials and decision points. Major policy decisions at the national level often require approval by all branches of government plus acceptance by state or local governments and affected private groups. This is the case with many current federal policies on aid to public education and environmental pollution control.

Bargaining may be either explicit or implicit. When it is explicit, the bargainers (group leaders, party officials, committee chairs, department heads, executives, and so on) state their agreements (bargains) clearly to minimize the likelihood of misunderstanding. The U.S. Constitution was a product of explicit bargaining between large and small states, North and South, and other interests at the Philadelphia convention in 1787. An explicit bargain was struck by President George Bush and the Democratic Congressional leadership in 1990 when the president agreed to tax increases in return for the Democratic agreement to expenditure reductions in order to reduce the budget deficit. In international politics, treaties exemplify explicit bargains. Bargaining is widely practiced in the international arena because the idea of national interests is well accepted. In domestic politics bargaining, however necessary and prevalent, is often looked upon as incompatible with a quest for the "public interest" or, in more crude language, as a sell-out.

More frequently, however, bargaining is probably implicit. In implicit bargaining, the terms of agreement among the bargainers are often vague or ambiguous, and may be expressed in such phrases as "future support" or "favorable disposition." Such bargaining frequently occurs in Congress, where one member will agree to support another on a bill in return for "future cooperation." Understandings or "gentlemen's agreements" may be negotiated by administrators in agencies with overlapping responsibilities for administering programs so as to reduce or eliminate conflict among themselves. Sometimes implicit bargaining is so nebulous that it is unclear whether an agreement actually has been reached. In Congress, bargaining frequently occurs on procedural actions intended either to slow down or to accelerate the handling of legislation as well as on the content of legislation.

Three common forms of bargaining are logrolling, side payments, and compromise. Logrolling, a way of gaining support from those who are indifferent to or have little interest in a matter, usually encompasses a straightforward mutual exchange of support on two different topics. This is a common form of bargaining because every item on an agenda is not of interest to all decision-makers. The classic example of logrolling is an appropriations bill for rivers-and-harbors legislation, which funds various river, harbor, and flood-control projects. Members of Congress care mainly about the projects in their own districts; consequently those who want a project in their district essentially agree to support the projects for all the other members' districts. Logrolling is usually implicit.[40]

Side payments are rewards offered to prospective supporters or coalition members who are not directly related to the decision at hand, or at least to its main provisions, but are valued by them for other reasons. Legislative leaders may use committee assignments, allocation of office space, campaign assistance, and support for members' "pet" bills as means of securing their support for legislation. During consideration of the 1986 tax-reform legislation, the chairman of the House Ways and Means Committee, Dan Rostenkowski (D, Illinois) used "transition rules" to gain support for it.[41] Supposedly, these rules ease the transition between current tax law and a new tax law for various taxpayers. However, transition rules also become legislative favors that can be doled out to win or confirm votes. Because they provide millions of dollars in tax benefits to companies and others in legislators' home states or districts, they are highly valued. The chairman of the Senate Finance Committee also used this form of bargaining to elicit support for the tax-reform proposal. In all, about 340 transition rules were included in the Tax Reform Act of 1986 at an estimated total cost in lost revenue of $10.6 billion over five years.[42]

Compromise typically involves explicit bargaining, is normally centered on a single issue, and involves questions of more or less of something. Here the bargainers regard half a loaf as better than none and consequently adjust their differences, each giving up something so as to come into agreement. This tactic contrasts with logrolling, which requires no change in the bargainers' original positions. A fine historical example is the Missouri Compromise of 1820, which temporarily settled the conflict between North and South over extending slavery into the Louisiana Territory. The North wanted slavery excluded from the territory, and the South wanted no such prohibition. It was finally agreed that slavery would be prohibited in the territory except in Missouri, north of latitude 36° 30'. The Civil Rights Act of 1964 also involved many compromises between those favoring stronger legislation and those wanting weaker or no legislation, especially on the provisions pertaining to public accommodations, equal employment opportunity, and judicial enforcement. On equal employment opportunity it was provided that the federal Equal Employment Opportunity Commission (EEOC) could handle discrimination cases only after existing state equal opportunity agencies had a chance to act, and even then the EEOC could use only voluntary means to reach settlements. This limited enforcement authority was chosen in an attempt to reduce conservative opposition to the legislation. Issues involving money, such as budgets, are probably the easiest matters on which to compromise because they are readily amenable to the splitting of differences.

Persuasion

Persuasion involves the marshaling of facts, data, and information, the skillful construction of arguments, and the use of reason and logic to convince another person of the wisdom or correctness of one's own position.[43] Unlike bargainers, persuaders seek to build support for what they favor without having to modify their own positions. This task may involve striving to convince others of the merits or soundness of one's position, or the benefits that will accrue to them or their constituents if they accept it, or some combination of the two. In short, persuaders seek to induce others to go along or do it their way. Accurate information, reason and logic, and effective argument are the instruments of persuasion; manipulation, deception, and bullying and hectoring are beyond its bounds.

President Harry S. Truman once remarked, "I sit here all day trying to persuade people to do things that they ought to have sense enough to do without my persuading them. . . . That's all the powers of the President amount to."[44] Presidential meetings with congressional leaders, for example, are often sessions in which presidential programs and priorities are explained, their likely benefits for members of Congress and their constituents are outlined, and appeals are made for Congressional leaders' support. Meetings with administrative officials are used to explain presidential preferences and to win their allegiance. "A President is most persuasive when he makes his pitch personally in direct conversation with those involved."[45] Presidents, of course, also have extensive capacity to bargain and command.

The use of persuasion is widespread in the governmental process. Attorneys who argue cases before the Supreme Court not only present their side of the issue through written briefs and oral arguments but also seek to convince a majority of the justices of the correctness of their position. In this process the justices are more than inert sponges absorbing the advocacy directed at them. Their questions and comments provide positive or negative responses and guidance to the opposing attorneys. Within Congress, appeals by party leaders to the rank-and-file members to the effect that "your party needs your support on this issue, can't you go along?" are essentially persuasive in style and content. In these and many other instances, decision-makers or those wishing to influence their decisions, as the case may be, either lack the capacity to command or know that bargaining is inappropriate or of limited utility. Persuasion is then the alternative on which they must rely.

Command

Bargaining involves interaction among peers; command involves hierarchic relationships among superordinates and subordinates. Command is the ability of those in superior positions to make decisions that are binding upon those who come within their jurisdiction. They may use sanctions in the form of either rewards or penalties, although usually sanctions are thought of as penalties, to reinforce their decisions. Thus, the subordinate who faithfully accepts and carries out a superior's decision may be rewarded with favorable recognition or a promotion, and the one who refuses to comply may be fired or demoted. President Clinton's decision to issue an executive order replacing the Reagan-Bush regulatory review program with one of his own devising was essentially an act of command. The Office of Management and Budget engages in command behavior when it approves, rejects, or modifies agency requests for appropriations and proposals for legislation prior to their transmittal to Congress. On the whole, however, command is more characteristic of decision processes in dictatorial rather than democratic societies and in military rather than civilian organizations because of their greater hierarchic qualities. Command is the primary style of decision-making in many developing countries in Africa and Southeast Asia.

In practice, bargaining, persuasion, and command often become blended in decisional situations. The president, although he has authority to make many decisions unilaterally, may nonetheless also bargain with subordinates, modifying his position somewhat and accepting some of their suggestions, in order to gain more ready and enthusiastic support.[46] Within agencies, subordinates often seek to convert command relationships into bargaining relationships. A bureau that gains considerable congressional support may thus put itself into position to bargain with, rather than simply be commanded by, the department head. A pollution-control agency may have the statutory authority to set and enforce pollutant-emission standards. In the course of setting the standards it may, however, bargain with those potentially affected, hoping to gain easier and greater compliance with the standards set. Presidential and gubernatorial efforts to win support for legislative proposals also typically combine persuasion and bargaining.

In summary, then, bargaining is the most common form of decision-making in the American policy process. Persuasion and command are supplementary, being "better suited to a society marked by more universal agreements on values and a more tightly integrated system of authority."[47] Nowhere is the bargaining process better illustrated than in Congress, to which we now turn.

Majority Building in Congress

The enactment of major legislation by Congress requires development of a numerical majority or, more likely, a series of numerical majorities, which are most commonly created by bargaining. Even if a majority in Congress agrees on the need for action on an issue such as labor-union reform, they may not agree on the form it should take, thereby making bargaining essential.

A highly important characteristic of Congress that has much importance for policy formation is its decentralization of political power. Three factors contribute to this condition. First, the political parties in Congress are weak, and party leaders have only limited power to control and discipline party members. (A partial exception to these comments must be made for the House Republicans in 1995–1996.) In contrast with the strong-party leaders in the British House of Commons, who have a variety of means for ensuring support of party policy proposals by party members, congressional leaders, such as the floor leaders, have few sanctions with which to discipline or punish recalcitrant party members. The party leadership has only "bits and fragments" of power, such as desired committee assignments, office space, use of the rules, and ability to persuade, with which to influence the rank and file. The member who chooses to defy party leadership can usually do so with impunity, and, indeed, not a few people will probably applaud such independence.

Second, the system of geographic representation and decentralized elections contributes to the decentralization of power in Congress. Members of the House and Senate are nominated and elected by the voters in their constituencies and owe little or nothing for their election to the national party organizations or congressional leaders. It is their constituencies that ultimately wield the power to hire and fire them, and it is therefore to their constituencies that they must be responsive, at least on some matters, if they wish to remain in Congress. From time to time, important constituent interests in a district may be adversely affected by party programs. Conventional congressional wisdom holds that, when party and constituency interests conflict, members should vote their constituency, as their reelection may depend upon it.

A third factor contributing to the decentralization of power in Congress is the committee system. The House has nineteen standing committees and the Senate sixteen, with jurisdiction over legislation in such areas as agriculture, appropriations, energy and natural resources, international relations, and human resources. Traditionally, these committees have done most of the legislative work in Congress. Nearly all bills are referred to the appropriate standing committees for consideration before being brought to the floor of the House or Senate for debate and decision. The standing committees possess vast power to kill, alter, or report unchanged the bills sent to them; most bills sent to committees are never heard from again. Until the 1970s the committee chairs, who gained their positions by seniority, had much power over the operation of their committees. Often referred to as "barons," they selected the committee staff, scheduled and presided over meetings, set the agenda, scheduled hearings and chose witnesses, and decided when votes would be taken. Through long experience, they were often highly knowledgeable on the policy matters within their committees' jurisdiction. Because of the fairly large number of interests that came within their jurisdiction, the chairs could act as brokers to build compromises among conflicting or differing interests.

During the 1970s, reform of the committee system reduced the power of the committee chairs and altered the organization and operation of the committees. As a consequence, much of the power of many of the standing committees has shifted to their more than 150 subcommittees and the subcommittee chairs. The subcommittees, whose jurisdictions are of course more specialized or narrowly focused than the parent committees, now handle much of the legislative activity and make many of the important decisions on legislation. In the House, for example, almost all legislative hearings are currently conducted by the subcommittees. The subcommittee chairs frequently can act with substantial independence in the direction of their subcommittees. This shift to "subcommittee government" gets more members of the House and Senate involved in the policymaking process and gives them an opportunity to make policy innovations. Another consequence is that the committees have lost much of their role as arenas in which interests can be mediated and compromised. The subcommittees have become more responsive to particular interests and single-interest groups, further fragmenting the legislative process. The standing committees of course have not lost all their importance, but most of them are no longer the "feudal baronies" they were once depicted as being.

Decentralization of power in Congress, together with the complexities of its legislative procedures, usually requires the cobbling together of a series of majorities to enact important legislation. A bill must pass through a number of decision stages in becoming a law.[48] Briefly, in the House, these are subcommittee, committee, Rules Committee, and finally floor action; and in the Senate, subcommittee, committee, and floor action. Assuming that the bill is passed in different versions by the two houses, a conference committee must agree on a compromise version, which then must be approved by the two houses. If the president approves it, the bill becomes law; if he vetoes it, however, the bill becomes law only if it is passed again by a two-thirds majority in each house. Thus at ten or twelve stages a bill requires approval by some kind of majority. If it fails to win majority approval at any one of these stages, it is probably dead. Should it win approval, its enactment is not ensured; rather, its supporters face the task of building a majority at the next stage.

Extraordinary majorities are sometimes needed to get bills through some stages in the legislative process. I have referred to the two-thirds majorities needed to override a presidential veto. Only infrequently are bills able to secure these majorities. From 1954 to 1994, of the 740 bills vetoed by the presidents, only 45 were subsequently enacted into law. Congress overrode only one of George Bush's 46 vetoes.[49] In the Senate, debate on a bill can be effectively terminated only by a unanimous-consent agreement or by imposing cloture. The cloture rule provides that debate may be terminated upon a motion signed by sixteen senators that then must be approved by three-fifths of the entire membership (sixty senators). Because one senator who is so inclined can block the closing of debate by a unanimous-consent agreement, cloture is left as the only alternative for shutting down a filibuster. Because of the difficulties in obtaining cloture in times past, southern Democrats were consistently able to block enactment of major civil-rights legislation through filibusters or threats thereof until the adoption of the 1964 Civil Rights Act. Since then, resistance to cloture has weakened and the procedure has been used dozens of times to close off filibusters on numerous bills. Still, filibusters have frequently been used successfully to block legislation, such as a campaign-finance reform bill, a 1987 measure banning aid to the Nicaraguan rebels, and the Clinton administration's 1993 economic stimulus package.

Indeed, for controversial legislation, the multiplicity of stages, or decision points, in the congressional legislative process provides access for many groups and interests. Those who lack access or influence at one stage may secure it at another. It thus becomes quite unlikely that one group or interest will dominate the process. The complexity of the legislative process, however, has a conservative effect in that it gives an advantage to those seeking to block the enactment of legislation. And it is well to remember that many groups are more interested in preventing than securing enactment of legislation, or in holding change to a minimum when the adoption of legislation is inevitable. All they have to do to achieve their preference is to win support by a majority, or perhaps only a dominant legislator, at one stage in the process. Here is support for the familiar generalization that procedure is not neutral in its effects.

Much bargaining is usually necessary for the enactment of legislation by Congress. Those who control the various decision points, or whose votes are needed to construct a majority, may require the modification of a bill as a condition for their approval, or they may exact future support for some item of interest to themselves. Bargaining is facilitated not only by the many decision points but also because legislators are not intensely interested in many matters on which they must decide. It is no doubt easier for them to bargain on such issues than on issues on which they have strong feelings. It seems necessary to elaborate further here upon the ubiquity of bargaining in Congress.

PRESIDENTIAL DECISION-MAKING

Apart from an integral role in the legislative process, the president can also be viewed as a policy adopter in his own right. In foreign affairs, much policy is a product of presidential actions and decisions, based either on the president's constitutional authority or broad congressional delegations of power. Decisions to recognize foreign governments and to establish formal diplomatic relations with them, as the Nixon and Carter administrations did with the People's Republic of China, are in the president's domain. Treaties with other nations are made and entered into on behalf of the United States by the president, subject to approval by the Senate. One can cavil on whether the president is the true decision-maker here. In the instance of executive agreements, which have the same legal force as treaties, and which are used much more frequently than treaties in foreign relations, there can be no doubt: the president makes the decisions. Executive agreements have been used to end wars, establish or expand military bases in other countries, and limit possession of offensive weapons by the United States and the Soviet Union. They are also often used for such routine purposes as customs enforcement.[50]

For more than a half-century, international trade policies have been primarily a construct of presidential action, albeit based on congressional authorizations, because the Constitution delegates to Congress control of "commerce with foreign nations." Through the time of the 1930 Smoot-Hawley Tariff, by which Congress in an orgy of logrolling elevated tariffs to an all-time high, this issue area had been dominated by Congress. Change began with the New Deal and enactment of the Reciprocal Trade Agreements Act of 1935. This statute authorized the president to enter into agreements with other nations to lower tariffs and other trade barriers (e.g., import quotas). Since then, under the guidance of presidential leadership and decisions, the United States has continually advocated and moved toward free trade. All presidents since the Great Depression have been advocates of the reduction of trade barriers. By the late 1980s, United States tariffs averaged less than 5 percent of the value of imported products.

In domestic matters, Congress often delegates discretionary authority to the president or to agencies under his direction and control. Executive orders, which are not mentioned in the Constitution, but which have become an accepted presidential prerogative, are also used by presidents for making domestic policies.[51] Executive orders have been promulgated to desegregate the armed services, establish loyalty–security programs, require affirmative action by government contractors, classify and withhold government documents from the public, and provide for presidential supervision of agency rule-making. Presidents Johnson and Carter used executive orders to establish systems of voluntary wage and price controls to combat inflation. Nothing in the Constitution or laws specifically authorized them to so act. On the other hand, nothing prohibited them from so doing. Operating with a broad view of presidential power under the Constitution, they responded to necessity as they saw it.

By considering some of the factors that shape and limit presidential decision-making, we not only can gain useful insight into presidential decision-making but also discover another perspective from which to view decision-making in general. Before proceeding further, it must be stressed that presidential decision-making is an institutional process. Many executive staff agencies, White House aides, and other advisers (both official and unofficial) assist the president in the discharge of his responsibilities. But whether he simply approves a recommendation from below or makes his own independent choice, the president alone has the ultimate responsibility for decision.

Several factors help shape and limit presidential decision-making.[52] One is permissibility, an aspect of which is legality. The president is expected to act in conformity with the Constitution, statutes, and court decisions. The lack of a clear constitutional or legal basis certainly contributed to congressional criticism of the Nixon administration's Cambodian bombing policy in the summer of 1973 and to an agreement by the administration to cease bombing after August 15, 1973, in the absence of congressional authorization. Another aspect of permissibility is acceptability. Foreign-policy decisions often depend for their effectiveness upon acceptance by other nations, and domestic-policy decisions, such as that by President Reagan to recommend elimination of the Department of Energy, may depend upon their acceptance by Congress, executive-branch officials and agencies, or the public.

A second factor is available resources. The president does not have the resources to do everything he might want to do, whether by resources one means money, manpower, patronage, time, or credibility. Funds allocated to defense are not available for education or medical research. Only a limited number of appeals to the public for support for his actions can be made without the possibility of diminishing returns. Time devoted to foreign-policy problems is time not available for domestic matters. Although the president has considerable control over the use of his time—over whether he devotes more time to foreign than domestic affairs, for instance—he does not have time to involve himself with everything that he might wish.[53] Lack of credibility (or the existence of a "credibility gap") may also limit the president, as the experiences of Presidents Johnson and Nixon attest.

A third factor is available time, in the sense of timing and the need to act. A foreign-policy crisis may require a quick response, as in the Cuban missile crisis of 1962, or the Iraqi invasion of Kuwait in 1990, without all the time for deliberation and fact-gathering one might prefer.[54] Domestic-policy decisions may be "forced," as by the need to submit the annual budget to Congress in February or the constitutional requirement to act on a bill passed by Congress within ten days if the president wishes to veto it, barring the possibility of a pocket veto. (If a bill reaches the President during the last ten days of a session, or after the Congress has adjourned, and the President does not sign it, it is automatically vetoed.) Former White House aide Theodore C. Sorensen states,

> There is a time to act and a time to wait. By not acting too soon, the President may find that the problem dissolves or resolves itself, that the facts are different from what he thought, or that the state of the nation has changed. By not waiting too long, he may make the most of the mood of the moment, or retain that element of surprise which is so often essential to military and other maneuvers.[55]

President Reagan demonstrated the importance of timing when he moved quickly and decisively in the first months of his term to secure adoption of his economic program of tax cuts and reductions in domestic expenditures. By so doing he was able to capitalize on the euphoria and political support that attend the early days of a new administration. As time goes on, these conditions decline, and the president's political life becomes more difficult.

Professor Paul Light states that presidents are confronted with cycles of increasing effectiveness and decreasing influence. Presidents become more effective over the course of their terms as their information and expertness expand and their staffs become more knowledgeable and skilled in handling their duties. In short, learning occurs. At the same time, however, presidential influence diminishes. Presidents customarily suffer a midterm loss of party seats in Congress and their standing in public opinion polls declines as more people find fault with their performance. Also, time becomes too short to launch major initiatives, and staff energy and creative stamina lessen. The two cycles create a presidential dilemma. The cycle of decreasing influence encourages a president to move quickly on his agenda; the cycle of increasing effectiveness suggests restraint. "If there is any point in the presidential term when the cycles are at the best blend," Light says, "it is in the first moments of the second term."[56] But that depends on the president being lucky enough to have a second term.

Previous commitments are a fourth factor that may shape presidential decisions. These commitments may be personal, taking the form, for instance, of campaign promises or earlier decisions. Although too much emphasis can be placed on the need for consistency, the president must avoid the appearance of deception or vacillation if he is to retain his credibility and political support. Jimmy Carter suffered from a reputation (not fully deserved) for indecisiveness, as when in 1977 he proposed a tax rebate to stimulate the economy and then reversed himself a few months later. Campaigning for the presidency in 1980, Ronald Reagan pledged to eliminate the Department of Education. He neither made good on the pledge nor suffered much in reputation as a consequence. People were often more attentive to and influenced by his words than by his actions. But woe may befall the reneger. When George Bush violated his 1988 campaign pledge of "Read my lips. No new taxes" by supporting a tax increase in 1990, this greatly angered many of his supporters and caused him much political discomfort.

Commitments may also take the form of traditions and principles, such as those holding that the United States meets its treaty obligations and engages in military action only if attacked. During the Cuban missile crisis, an air strike without warning on the Soviet missile sites was rejected by the Kennedy administration as a "Pearl Harbor in reverse"; a naval blockade of Cuba was chosen instead. A "first-strike" strategy generally has been excluded from American foreign policy.

Finally, available information can be an important influence on presidential decisions. Many sources of information—official and unofficial, overt and covert—are available to the president. At times, particularly on domestic policy issues, he may be subject to drowning in a torrent of words, paper, and conflicting recommendations. Still, the president at times may be confronted by a shortage of reliable information, especially in foreign affairs, even though he has the best information that is available. Reliable information on possible national and international reactions to the possible bombing of Serbian forces in Bosnia, the resumption of nuclear testing, or a Strategic Defense Initiative ("Star Wars"), may be scarce because of the need to predict what will happen in the future. Predicting the future is an uncertain task, except perhaps for a few who claim a sixth sense or a clear crystal ball.

Domestic-policy decisions may also involve some uncertainty. This may become quite obvious when economic-stability policy is under consideration. Will a reduction in income taxes encourage higher levels of investment and economic growth? How much restraint must be imposed on the economy to break the back of the inflationary psychology contributing to inflation? When all the advice is in, the president has to make a choice—a calculated one based on limited information—that the alternative chosen will produce the desired result. Uncertainty may contribute to delay and lack of action on some matters. Amid doubts as to what needs to be done, or what effect an action may have, the decision may be to hold off, to see whether things will work themselves out or to let the situation "clarify itself " (i.e., to give oneself more time to gather information on conditions and alternatives). Sometimes doing nothing can be a good policy.

As a leader in policy formation, the president is subject to numerous political pressures and constraints, however great his legal powers may appear to be. Legal authority by itself often does not convey the capacity to act effectively. Thus the president may have to persuade because he cannot command; he may have to bargain because he cannot compel action. On many issues, once he has made a decision, he must seek the support of an often fickle public or a skeptical Washington community. "The struggling facilitator, not the dominating director, is the description that matches the process of presidential decision-making most of the time."[57]

THE DYNAMICS OF POLICY FORMULATION: THE CASE OF AIRLINE DEREGULATION

The American air-transportation industry began with the Air Mail Act of 1925, which authorized the Post Office Department to use competitive bidding to award air-mail contracts to private airlines.[58] Government payments to the airlines often exceeded the revenue produced by air mail. Nonetheless, many airlines suffered operating losses and the possibility or abandonment of services arose. New legislation increasing the level of air-mail subsidies was adopted in 1930. Because passenger service was just beginning to catch on in the 1930s, carrying the mail continued to be a major source of revenues for the airlines. As a consequence of the Great Depression, by the mid-1930s the airlines were once again in financial distress; and again there emerged a demand for favorable government action to bail them out.

It was widely agreed among industry and governmental officials that there was a need for new economic and safety regulation. Because it appeared that there were more airlines than could be supported by available revenues, it was feared that unregulated competition among the many small companies making up the industry would degenerate into "destructive competition." The airlines themselves were united in favor of restrictive legislation. Between 1934 and 1938, the enactment of legislation was delayed by problems in resolving two issues: whether regulation should be handled by the Interstate Commerce Commission, which was the position of President Franklin Roosevelt, or a new independent commission; and whether the same agency should administer both economic and safety regulation. These issues were finally resolved by the Civil Aeronautics Act of 1938, which passed Congress by substantial majorities.[59] We will trace its history here.

The Civil Aeronautics Act, as modified by a 1940 presidential executive order, established the Civil Aeronautics Board to handle economic regulation and the Civil Aeronautics Authority in the Department of Commerce to administer safety regulation, to control air traffic, and to maintain a national airway system of guidance systems, airports, and the like. In 1956 the collision of two passenger planes over the Grand Canyon led to questions about the adequacy of air-traffic control and safety regulation.[60] Consequently, Congress enacted the Federal Aviation Act of 1958, which replaced the CAA with a new independent agency, the Federal Aviation Administration, which was given a strengthened air-safety mandate. The FAA later became a unit in the Department of Transportation and continues to be responsible for air-traffic control and safety. We will not deal further with it in this case study.

The Civil Aeronautics Board, an independent regulatory commission, was headed by a five-member board serving six-year, staggered terms of office. Appointed by the president with senatorial consent, no more than a majority of the board members could come from the same political party. The CAB was authorized to regulate entry into the commercial airline industry by the issuance of certificates of "public convenience and necessity," which were also used to determine the particular routes that an air carrier could serve. The abandonment of service also required CAB approval. Airline rates had to be "just and reasonable" and could be changed by the CAB if it found them unjust or unreasonable because they were too high or too low. The CAB was also authorized to administer air-mail payments and operating subsidies. The act "grandfathered" the existing sixteen air trunklines (carriers providing service between major cities) into the business. No new trunklines were subsequently admitted to the industry by the CAB during the next forty years. This was often viewed as a shortcoming of the airline regulatory system.

The Civil Aeronautics Act's declaration of policy directed the CAB to use its authority to "foster sound economic conditions" in air transportation; to promote "adequate, economical, and efficient service by air carriers at reasonable charges"; to ensure "competition to the extent necessary to assure the development of an air-transportation system properly adapted to the needs of the foreign and domestic commerce of the United States"; and, for good measure, to be concerned with the "promotion, encouragement, and development of civil aeronautics." Essentially, the act laid out a number of desirable objectives and then left to the CAB the choice of which ones it would emphasize. The agency's multiple mandate was a frequent target of critics.

Through its regulatory authority, the CAB significantly influenced the structure of the airline industry. Several categories of carriers were developed. The trunk carriers, whose numbers, through mergers, had been diminished to eleven by 1970, provided regularly scheduled service between major cities and accounted for the lion's share of passenger service. Local-service (or regional) carriers provided short-haul service between smaller cities, and commuter airlines, operating small planes, provided service to places not reached by the larger carriers. The latter did not need prior CAB approval for their route and rate decisions. There were also all-cargo and charter airlines. A few intrastate airlines serving cities entirely within the boundaries of a single state also existed, and these were not subject to CAB regulation. The discussion here focuses on the trunk carriers.

During its forty years of existence, CAB regulatory policy fluctuated between pro- and anticompetitive tendencies, depending upon the economic situation of the airlines. When airline profits were high or "excessive," the

CAB increased competitive route awards and encouraged the companies to reduce or discount airfares. Conversely, when profits were low, the CAB adopted an anticompetitive stance on new route awards and encouraged or approved fare increases to offset lower passenger traffic. Service competition—the frequency of flights, seating arrangements, food services, and other amenities—was left alone by the CAB. Barred from rate competition, airlines occasionally featured champagne flights and gourmet meals in their efforts to attract passengers. Both the airlines and the traveling public generally found the CAB's regulatory policies to be acceptable.

In the 1970s, a recession that reduced passenger traffic, rising fuel costs caused by the energy crisis, and inflation drove down airline earnings and propelled the CAB to take a strong anticompetitive position. A moratorium was imposed on the award of new airline routes and substantial rate hikes were granted. Departing from previous policy, the agency also sought to discourage service competition. Further, a scandal erupted involving the CAB chair, who had accepted free trips and favors from the airlines.[61] Collectively, these events drew attention to the CAB; much criticism of the agency arose from both governmental and private sources. For many people it seemed clear that the CAB was the "captive" of the airlines, serving their interests rather than the public interest. The CAB, however, was not as fully under the sway of the airlines as the captive charge implied.

A number of studies conducted by economists in the 1960s and 1970s concluded that the CAB's policies protected inefficient airlines by preventing rate competition. The result was higher costs for the traveling public than would occur in a more competitive situation. This line of argument was supported, in turn, by other analyses comparing the operations of CAB-regulated interstate carriers with those of intrastate carriers in Texas and California that were not controlled by the CAB. The rates for the latter over similar routes were considerably lower.[62] Although these studies initially were generally ignored by the CAB and others, in time, they helped make deregulation a viable alternative to the CAB's regulatory regime.

In 1974 and 1975 airline regulation (and deregulation) reached the national policy agenda as a consequence of two sets of circumstances. First, in 1974 Senator Edward Kennedy (D, Massachusetts), chair of the Senate Judiciary Committee's Subcommittee on Administrative Practice and Procedure, decided to hold hearings on CAB regulation. These hearings, which actually took place in 1975, revealed much dissatisfaction with the CAB and publicized the large differential between the rates of CAB-regulated and nonregulated carriers.[63] There was no agreement on the specific direction that reform should take, however.

Second, in August 1974 Gerald Ford became president following the resignation of Richard M. Nixon. A conservative Republican, Ford took office confronted by double-digit inflation. Advised that government regulatory programs contributed to inflation by raising business costs and prices, Ford made regulatory reform part of his anti-inflation program. (This action also coincided with his dislike of big government.) Although there was not much public clamor for regulatory reform per se, inflation was an issue of high public salience. In October 1975, Ford sent an aviation regulatory reform bill to Congress that called for reduced CAB control of the airlines.

In 1977, Jimmy Carter replaced Ford as president. Although he had not said much about it while campaigning, Carter quickly made airline deregulation a high-priority item in his legislative program. Rather than introduce its own bill, however, the Carter administration chose to support legislation that was already being considered in Congress, hoping thereby to secure a quick and easy legislative victory. Carter officials also stressed the relationship between regulation and inflation. (In actuality, because they constituted such a small portion of gross domestic product, setting airfares at the zero level would have had little impact on inflation.)

In the Senate, Kennedy and Howard Cannon (D, Nevada), chair of the Subcommittee on Aviation of the Senate Commerce Committee, became the sponsors of a bill entitled the Air Transportation Regulatory Reform Act. Not initially a supporter of aviation regulatory reform, Cannon at first had been irritated by Kennedy's hearings. However, he shifted his position and became a supporter of reform rather than be left behind by the surge for reform. The Kennedy-Cannon bill provided for increased competition in the airline industry by making it easier for carriers to obtain authorization to serve new routes and giving them substantial leeway in setting fares. Other provisions authorized subsidies for small-community air service and compensation for airline employees suffering wage reductions or unemployment because of increased competition. These provisions were designed to counteract some of the opposition to regulatory reform, which we will discuss later in this section. The reform legislation under consideration in the House, where there was difficulty in getting agreement on a bill, was weaker than the Senate bill.

Supporting and opposing coalitions emerged.[64] Among the supporters of reform were several government agencies, including the Council on Wage and Price Stability, the Council of Economic Advisors, the Federal Trade Commission, and the Antitrust Division; many consumer groups; Ralph Nader; most economists; and such conservative groups as the American Farm Bureau Federation, the National Federation of Independent Business, and the National Association of Manufacturers. Also supporting reform was United Airlines, which believed that it had been unfairly treated by the CAB in its route decisions. The supporters of reform believed that greater competition would benefit both passengers and airlines. The former would get lower fares while the greater volume of passenger traffic these generated would yield larger profits for the airlines.

Opponents of reform comprised most of the larger scheduled airlines and their trade organization, the Air Transportation Association; airline employees' unions; and organizations representing the interests of airport operators and small communities. Diverse interests drew them together. The air carriers feared that major changes in CAB rate and route regulation would lead to "cutthroat competition" and instability in the industry. The unions saw deregulation as a threat to job security, wage levels, and their status as employee representatives. Some airport operators were concerned that deregulation would mean reduced business, and small communities and rural states fretted about the possible reduction or total loss of air service.

At this point we need to pick up another facet of the deregulation story. In the course of a few years in the mid-1970s the CAB was transformed into a leading proponent of deregulation. The change began with President Ford's appointment of John Robson in mid-1975 to chair the agency. Under Robson's leadership, the CAB began to review its regulatory policies and to shift to a more procompetitive position. Robson also testified before Congress concerning the need to replace the current aviation regulatory regime. This came as a surprise to many people.

The pace of change within the CAB accelerated in June 1977 when Carter appointee Alfred Kahn, a Cornell University economics professor, replaced Robson as CAB chair. He was soon joined by economist Elizabeth Bailey as a board member. Kahn moved quickly to fill key CAB staff positions with supporters of deregulation. Then, under his skillful direction, various actions were taken to substantially reduce CAB control of airline rate and route decisions so as to increase competition in the industry. For instance, it became much easier for airlines to obtain new routes and to initiate or terminate service on unprofitable routes at their own discretion. In all likelihood, some of the CAB initiatives were in violation of the Federal Aviation Act (which had replaced the Civil Aeronautics Act.)[65] Indeed, one airline sued the CAB in federal court, alleging that the agency had failed to meet its responsibilities under the act.

This administrative deregulation increased the odds in favor of the enactment of reform legislation for two reasons. First, the CAB itself was rapidly implementing many of the reforms included in the legislation being considered by Congress. Second, airline profits increased in 1977 and 1978. Whether because of the CAB's policy changes or improved economic conditions, this reduced the resistance of the airlines to regulatory reform. In fact, their opposition largely collapsed by the end of summer 1978.[66]

The Senate passed its version of airline regulatory reform in April 1978, but the House was not able to complete action on its bill until September. Included in the House bill was a provision calling for the termination of the CAB at the end of 1983. Initially included in a substitute bill by a strong advocate of "sunset review" (the periodic evaluation of agencies to determine whether they should be continued), it was incorporated in the final House bill as a concession to deregulation supporters in exchange for making milder reductions in CAB regulatory authority than in the Senate bill.[67] In the Conference Committee, however, the House yielded to most of the Senate's stronger reform provisions. The bill, now entitled the Airline Deregulation Act, was passed by both houses and signed into law by President Jimmy Carter. "For the first time in decades," he said, "we have deregulated a major industry."[68]

The Airline Deregulation Act initially made it easier for airlines to enter new routes and gave them flexibility in setting fares. It provided for continuation of "essential air transportation service" to smaller communities, with subsidies to ensure such service, for ten years. Compensation was authorized for a maximum of six years for airline employees who lost their jobs, had their pay reduced, or were forced to relocate because of competition engendered by the act. Then, what is most significant, the act set forth a deregulation schedule. Unless Congress decided otherwise, the CAB's authority over domestic routes would end on December 31, 1981; its authority over domestic rates and fares would expire on January 1, 1983; and the board itself would be abolished on January 1, 1985. Its remaining authority would then be transferred to the Departments of Transportation and Justice and the U.S. Postal Service. All of this happened on the specified dates.

The Airline Deregulation Act marked a basic change in public policy on commercial airlines, a shift from detailed administrative regulations to reliance on the market and competition to control their economic behavior. It ran directly counter to the theory of economic regulation, which holds that "regulation is acquired by the industry and is designed and operated primarily for its benefit."[69] Although that theory is a plausible, but not fully convincing, explanation for the Civil Aeronautics Act of 1938, it is simply not applicable to airline deregulation (or to trucking and railroad deregulation either, for that matter), which was strongly opposed by most of the industry until there was little doubt that strong deregulatory legislation would be adopted.

What then accounts for the Airline Deregulation Act? Martha Derthick and Paul Quirk provide a good explanation.[70] First, there was wide support for deregulation in the academic world and in the political sphere. "Procompetitive reform . . . proved to have a broad appeal, engaging liberals (led by Senator Edward M. Kennedy), who stressed the benefits of lower prices for consumers and an end to government protection of business, and conservatives (led by President Gerald R. Ford), who stressed the benefits of reducing the burdens of government regulation in private markets.[71] Second, many public officials in leadership positions—presidents, committee chairs, CAB chairs—were advocates of deregulation. Third, much deregulation would have accrued even had Congress not acted because of the CAB, which, whatever its history, demonstrated in the mid-1970s that it was not the captive of the airlines. Fourth, strong majorities in Congress, despite the opposition of most of the airlines, supported aviation regulatory reform. They acted not only in response to executive and legislative leadership, but also out of a desire to produce policy that responded to public concerns about inflation and intrusive government. Fifth, economists and other policy analysts had produced myriad studies that portrayed reliance on the market and competition as a viable alternative to economic regulation. This was in line with the old adage that "you can't beat something with nothing." Finally, the airline industry was unable to maintain a united front in opposition to major regulatory change. First United defected. Then other airlines split off, especially as the CAB's removal of controls accelerated. Finally, airline opposition collapsed, leaving the way open for Congress to enact sweeping deregulation legislation.

What has happened in the airline industry since 1978? Some developments are reported here. Whether they are all the direct consequence of deregulation is not clear.

The control of domestic air travel has become more concentrated. The eight largest air carriers controlled 81 percent of the market in 1978; in 1991 they accounted for 95 percent.[72] After deregulation, many new airlines entered the industry, but within a few years, almost all of them either had failed or had been absorbed by major airlines. In the 1990s a second wave of new carriers—e.g., Kiwi, Valuejet, and Reno—entered the industry. Each, however, accounts for only a very tiny portion of the domestic market. It now seems unlikely that a new major airline will emerge to compete with American, United, Delta, and the few other major companies. It is unlikely that this oligopolistic situation is what the proponents of deregulation had in mind back in the 1970s.

Further, the hub-and-spoke system, whereby flights from many "spoke" cities converge in a single "hub" city, has enabled one or two carriers to dominate service to and from most large cities. Thus, 88 percent of the total passenger traffic in Atlanta and 90 percent of that in Pittsburgh was controlled in 1992 by Delta and USAir, respectively. United and Continental shared 83 percent of Denver's traffic.[73]

The picture concerning airfare is cloudy. Controlling for the effects of inflation, one study found that average rates overall had declined by nearly 25 percent between 1979 and 1989.[74] Many variations are concealed by such averages, however. For instance, rates on long, highly traveled routes have declined and those on short, less-traveled routes have increased. Passengers at major airports dominated by one or two airlines pay substantially higher rates than do travelers leaving airports where more competition prevails.[75] Discount fares—such as for those who purchase tickets fourteen to thirty days in advance and stay over Saturday night—permit leisure travelers to fly much more cheaply than business and other travelers who buy tickets on short notice and do not want to spend weekends at their destinations. The conditions attached to discount fares do create some inconvenience for travelers.

Service also presents a mixed view. The number of seats and flights available to passengers has increased, but the airplanes are more crowded. Meals and other amenities are being reduced, and flight times on many routes have increased.[76] Since deregulation, and despite subsidies for service, many small cities have lost some or all of their air service, or no longer receive jet service.[77] Despite fears that unregulated competition might cause airlines to skimp on maintenance and safety considerations, the safety of air travel appears to have improved.[78]

Notes

1. Louis Fisher, *Constitutional Conflicts Between Congress and the President,* 3rd ed., revised (Lawrence: University Press of Kansas, 1991), pp. 146–152.
2. The leading proponent of incrementalism undoubtedly is Charles Lindblom. See his "The Science of Muddling Through," *Public Administration Review,* XIX (1959), pp. 79–88; *The Intelligence of Democracy* (New York: Macmillan, 1964); *The Policy-Making Process* (Englewood Cliffs, N.J.: Prentice-Hall, 1964); and, with David Braybrook, *The Strategy of Decision* (New York: Free Press, 1963).
3. This summary draws primarily on Lindblom's "The Science of Muddling Through," op. cit., and *The Intelligence of Democracy,* op cit., pp. 144–148. See also Charles E. Lindblom, "Still Muddling, Not Yet Through," *Public Administration Review,* XLIX (November–December 1979), pp. 517–526.
4. Michael T. Hayes, *Incrementalism and Public Policy* (New York: Longman, 1992), chap. 2.
5. Roger B. Porter, *Presidential Decision Making: The Economic Policy Board* (New York: Cambridge University Press, 1980), pp. 246–247.
6. Alexander L. George, *Presidential Decision Making in Foreign Policy* (Boulder, Colo.: Westview Press, 1980), p. 201.
7. Porter, op cit., pp. 246–247.
8. Its activities are fully reported in Ibid.
9. L. William Seidman, *Full Faith and Credit* (New York: Times Books, 1993), p. 26.
10. Ibid., p. 27.
11. A classic study is Herbert Kaufman, *The Forest Ranger: A Study in Administrative Behavior* (Baltimore: Johns Hopkins University Press, 1960).
12. Daniel McCool, *Command of the Waters* (Berkeley: University of California Press, 1987).
13. This paragraph draws on Charles Funderburk and Robert G. Thobaben, *Political Ideologies: Left, Center, Right,* 2nd ed. (New York: Harper Collins, 1994), chap. 5. The quotation is on p. 113.
14. Roger H. Davidson and Walter J. Oleszek, *Congress and Its Members,* 4th ed. (Washington: CQ Press, 1994), p. 365.
15. Harold W. Stanley and Richard G. Niemi, *Vital Statistics on American Politics,* 4th ed. (Washington: CQ Press, 1994), p. 200.
16. Davidson and Oleszek, op. cit., pp. 194–195.
17. David W. Brady, "Congressional Leadership and Party Voting in the McKinley

Era: A Comparison to the Modern House," *Midwest Journal of Political Science*, XVI (August 1972), pp. 439–441.

18. Richard Rose, *Do Parties Make a Difference?* 2nd ed. (Chatham, N.J.: Chatham House, 1984), pp. 74–91; and Edward Crowe, "Consensus and Structure in Legislative Norms: Party Discipline in the House of Commons," *Journal of Politics*, XLV (August 1983), pp. 907–931.

19. Discussions of the concept of representation can be found in John C. Wahlke et al., *The Legislative System* (New York: Wiley, 1962), chap. 12; and Leroy N. Reiselbach, *Congressional Politics*, 2nd ed. (Boulder, Colo.: Westview Press, 1995), chap. 17.

20. See, e.g., Peter Woll, *American Bureaucracy*, 2nd ed. (New York: Norton, 1977).

21. Michael Kinsley, "The Intellectual Free Lunch," *The New Yorker*, Vol. 71 (February 6, 1995), p. 4. See also Richard Morin, "Tuned Out, Turned Off: Millions of Americans Know Little About How Their Government Works," *Washington Post Weekly Edition*, February 5–11, 1996, pp. 6–7.

22. V. O. Key, Jr., *Public Opinion and American Democracy* (New York: Knopf, 1961), p. 14.

23. Ibid., pp. 81–90.

24. Cf. John E. Mueller, "Trends in Popular Support for the Wars in Korea and Vietnam," *American Political Science Review*, LXV (June 1971), pp. 358–375.

25. Thomas Patterson, *The American Democracy*, 3rd ed. (New York: McGraw-Hill, 1996), pp. 147–148.

26. Cf. Robert J. Spitzer, *The Politics of Gun Control* (Chatham, N.J.: Chatham House, 1995), p. 118.

27. Nick Kotz, *Let Them Eat Promises: The Politics of Hunger in America* (Englewood Cliffs, N.J.: Prentice-Hall, 1969).

28. Donald R. Matthews and James A. Stimson, "The Decision-Making Approach to the Study of Legislative Behavior." Unpublished paper presented at the annual meeting of the American Political Science Association (September 1969), p. 19.

29. Robert H. Salisbury, *Governing America: Public Choice and Political Action* (New York: Appleton-Century-Crofts, 1973), p. 237. Chapter 13 includes a very useful treatment of decison-making.

30. Robert A. Carp and Ronald Stidham, *The Federal Courts* (Washington: Congressional Quarterly Press, 1985), p. 57.

31. Richard F. Fenno, Jr., *Congressmen in Committees* (Boston: Little, Brown, 1973), pp. 48–75.

32. Charles W. Anderson, "The Place of Principles in Policy Analysis," *American Political Science Review*, LXXIII (September 1979), p. 718.

33. Emmette S. Redford, *Ideal and Practice in Public Administration* (Tuscaloosa: University of Alabama Press, 1957), chap. 5.

34. Cf. Robert E. Goodin, "Institutionalizing the Public Interest: The Defense of Deadlock and Beyond," *American Political Science Review*, Vol. 90 (June 1996), pp. 331–343.

35. Walter Lippman, *The Phantom Public* (New York: Harcourt, Brace, 1925), p. 105. Cf. Frank J. Sorauf, "The Public Interest Reconsidered," *Journal of Politics*, XIX (November 1957), pp. 616–639.

36. Richard E. Neustadt, "White House and Whitehall," *The Public Interest* (Winter 1966), pp. 55–69.

37. As quoted in Roger Hilsman, *The Politics of Policy Making in Defense and Foreign Affairs* (New York: Harper & Row, 1971), p. 1.

38. *The New York Times*, June 4, 1996, p. A6.

39. Robert A. Dahl and Charles E. Lindblom, *Politics, Economics, and Welfare* (New York: Harper & Row, 1953), p. 328. Chapters 12 and 13 present a thorough and insightful discussion of bargaining in American politics.

40. Lewis A. Froman, Jr., *People and Politics* (Englewood Cliffs, N.J.: Prentice-Hall, 1962), pp. 56–57.

41. Jeffrey H. Birnbaum and Alan S. Murray, *Showdown at Gucci Gulch* (New York: Random House, 1987), pp. 146, 240–243.

42. *The New York Times*, September 20, 1986, p. 24.

43. Peter Burnell and Andrew Reeve, "Persuasion as a Political Concept," *British Journal of Political Studies*, XIV (October 1984), pp. 393–410.

44. Quoted in Richard E. Neustadt, *Presidential Power* (New York: Wiley, 1960), pp. 9–10.

45. Morton H. Halperin, *Bureaucratic Politics and Foreign Policy* (Washington: Brookings Insitution, 1974), p. 282.

46. Neustadt, op. cit., chap. 3.

47. Dan Nimmo and Thomas D. Ungs, *American Political Patterns*, 2nd ed. (Boston: Little, Brown, 1969), p. 367.

48. A good discussion of congressional procedures can be found in Walter J. Oleszak, *Congressional Procedures and the Policy Process*, 4th ed. (Washington: Brookings Institution, 1996), chaps. 5–8.

49. *Congressional Quarterly Weekly Report*, Vol. 50 (December 19, 1992), p. 3925.

50. Norman C. Thomas, Joseph A. Pika, and Richard A. Waters, *The Politics of the Presidency*, 3rd ed. (Washington: CQ Press, 1993), pp. 258–262. See also General Accounting Office, *National Security: The Use of Presidential Directives to Make and Implement U.S. Policy* (Washington: USGAO, December 1988).

51. Cf. Ruth P. Morgan, *The Presidential and Civil Rights: Policy-Making by Executive Order* (New York: St. Martin's, 1970).

52. In this discussion I depend substantially on an insightful little book by Theodore C. Sorensen, *Decision-Making in the White House* (New York: Columbia University Press, 1963). Sorensen served as Special Counsel to President Kennedy.

53. Cf. George Reed, *The Twilight of the Presidency*, 2nd ed. (New York: New American Library, 1987).

54. See Graham Allison, *The Essence of Decision: Explaining the Cuban Missile Crisis* (Boston: Little, Brown, 1971).

55. Sorensen, op. cit., p. 29.

56. Paul C. Light, *The Presidential Agenda*, rev. ed. (Baltimore: Johns Hopkins University Press, 1991), pp. 36–38, 60.

57. George C. Edwards III and Stephen J. Wayne, *Presidential Leadership: Politics and Policy-Making* (New York: St. Martin's, 1993), p. 224.

58. Merle Fainsod, Lincoln Gordon, and Joseph C. Palamountain, Jr., *Government and the American Economy*, 3rd ed. (New York: Norton, 1959), pp. 120–121.

59. Robert E. Cushman, *The Independent Regulatory Commissions* (New York: Oxford University Press, 1941), pp. 389–416.

60. Emmette S. Redford, *Congress Passes the Federal Aviation Act of 1958,* ICP case series: no. 52 (Tuscaloosa: University of Alabama Press, 1961).

61. *The New York Times,* November 1, 1974, p. 1.

62. Anthony E. Brown, *The Politics of Airline Regulation* (Knoxville: University of Tennessee Press, 1987), pp. 133–136.

63. Bradley Behrman, "Civil Aeronautics Board," in James Q. Wilson, ed., *The Politics of Deregulation* (New York: Basic Books, 1980), pp. 99–102.

64. Brown, op. cit., pp. 104–105.

65. *Wall Street Journal,* July 3, 1978, pp. 1, 7.

66. Brown, op. cit., pp. 116–119.

67. *Congressional Quarterly Almanac 1978* (Washington: Congressional Quarterly, Inc., 1979), Vol. 34, pp. 496–504.

68. Quoted in Brown, op. cit., p. 2.

69. George J. Stigler, *The Citizen and the State* (Chicago: University of Chicago Press, 1975), p. 114.

70. Martha Derthick and Paul J. Quirk, *The Politics of Regulation* (Washington: Brookings Institution, 1985), pp. 238–245.

71. Ibid., p. 238.

72. Paul Stephen Dempsey and Andrew R. Goetz, *Airline Deregulation and Laissez-Faire Mythology* (Westport, Conn.: Quorum Books, 1992), p. 227.

73. General Accounting Office, *Airline Competition: Higher Fares and Less Competition Continues at Concentrated Airports* (Washington: USGAO, July 1993), p. 33.

74. Charles F. Bonser, Eugene B. McGregor, Jr., and Clinton V. Oster, Jr., *Policy Choices and Public Action* (Upper Saddle River, N.J.: Prentice-Hall, 1996), p. 226.

75. General Accounting Office, *Airline Competition: Higher Fares and Reduced Competition at Concentrated Airports* (Washington: USGAO, July 1990), p. 1.

76. Don Phillips, "The Crowded Skies of Sardine Airlines," *Washington Post National Weekly Edition* (June 26–July 2, 1995), p. 19.

77. Paul Stephen Dempsey, "The Dark Side of Deregulation: Its Impact on Small Communities," *Administrative Law Review,* Vol. 39 (Fall 1987), pp. 454–459.

78. Steven A. Morrison and Clifford Winston, *The Evolution of the Airline Industry* (Washington: Brookings Institution, 1995), pp. 31–33.

5

BUDGETING AND
PUBLIC POLICY

*Budget decisions produce conflicts. In 1995, some senators and senior citizens
protested proposed reductions in Medicare spending.*

177

U ntil the 1920s, national budgeting in the United States was a disjointed activity lacking central direction. On their own initiative, departments and agencies prepared their annual budget requests. These requests were then assembled by the Department of the Treasury, without alteration, in a book of estimates and transmitted to Congress for its consideration and enactment. The president typically had little to do with agency budget requests, either prior to or after their enactment. This haphazard and fragmented budgetary process was satisfactory because ample funds were available to finance the national government's limited array of activities. Indeed, in the later decades of the nineteenth century, the major financial problem confronting the government was how to spend all of the revenues produced by high protective tariffs so as to provide for their continued justification.

This rather idyllic situation evanesced after the turn of the century. The expansion of the national government's activities during the Progressive Era created strong pressures on the national revenue system. The level of government expenditures soared upward during World War I, and following the Armistice, remained above pre-war levels. These changed conditions generated pressure for budget reform. The executive budget, whereby the chief executive in a government has responsibility for budget formulation, was identified as an appropriate corrective measure. Following several years of study, reports, deliberation, and political struggle, it was instituted by the Budget and Accounting Act of 1921. Interestingly, support for the executive budget came from two disparate sources: conservatives and businessmen supported it as a means of retrenchment, or reducing governmental expenditures; liberals and reformers advocated the executive budget as a way of accomplishing more with a given level of expenditures, of making government more effective.

The Budget and Accounting Act delegated authority to the president to annually prepare a budget and submit it for Congress's approval. Agencies were prohibited from submitting funding requests directly to Congress unless specifically requested to do so. (In the 1970s, Congress adopted legislation directing several agencies to submit their budget requests concurrently to itself and the executive.)[1] The Bureau of the Budget (now the Office of Management and Budget) was created to assist the president in budget preparation, and the General Accounting Office was set up to handle the auditing of expenditures. Finally, each department and agency was directed to appoint a budget officer. Reform also had occurred in 1920 in the House of Representatives where authority to act on appropriations legislation, which previously had been scattered among several committees, was consolidated in a single appropriations committee. That had long been the practice in the Senate. Collectively, these reforms were intended to produce a centralized budgeting system.

This chapter examines the structure and operation of the national government's budgetary process and the political struggle to reduce the national budget deficit, and perhaps balance the budget. Also, the chapter will cast some light on how budgeting affects the development and implementation of public policies. Budgeting is more than a set of procedures for controlling the volume of funds flowing to agencies and programs; it is also a means and a source of opportunities for shaping the direction and intensity of public policies and the scope of governmental activities.

Few public policies can be put into effect without the expenditure of money. Many programs, such as Social Security, Medicare, Aid to Families with Dependent Children (AFDC), and unemployment compensation, primarily entail the transfer of funds from taxpayers to the government and thence to individual recipients. The effectiveness of other programs, such as those involving economic regulation, medical research, and wildlife management, is often largely determined by the amount of money available for their conduct and implementation.

At an extreme, a policy without funding will become a nullity. Thus in 1973 Congress killed the Subversive Activities Control Program, not by repealing the legislation upon which it was based, but by ceasing to appropriate money for its administration. Although the agency administering the program (the Subversive Activities Control Board) had never succeeded in registering any subversive persons or organizations (e.g., the Communist Party), the program had symbolic importance for some conservatives and was a source of employment for a few others for more than two decades.

An example of how budgetary action can cripple a policy involves noise control. In 1972 Congress passed the Noise Control Act, authorizing the Environmental Protection Agency (EPA) to issue and enforce standards reducing the noise coming from vehicles and industrial products (e.g., air compressors and air hammers) when these adversely affected human health.[2] An Office of Noise Abatement and Control (ONAC) in EPA was created to handle the Noise Act's implementation. In the next several years ONAC issued standards, coordinated noise research, and disseminated information. Late in the 1970s its efforts to reduce the noise created by garbage trucks created a major stink and focused attention on its activities. The Reagan Administration in 1981 decided to eliminate funding for ONAC, a decision acquiesced in by the EPA leadership and in turn by Congress. The ONAC, which lacked strong political allies, expired. Since then next to nothing has been done by EPA to carry out the Noise Control Act[3] because the agency is strapped for resources to carry out its many other programs.

It is also possible for a department or agency to be better funded than necessary. Thus the Reagan Administration sought and obtained increased funding for defense programs early in the 1980s. Some observers were doubtful that the Defense Department could wisely use all the additional funds, or that their outlay would strengthen defense capabilities. Stories of cost over-runs and waste were numerous, and many questions were raised about the necessity for or capabilities of various weapons systems. The Department of Defense was sometimes hard pressed to devise ways to spend all the funds bestowed on it.

THE BUDGET AND PUBLIC POLICY

The national budget has increased greatly in size and complexity in recent decades. In 1960 federal expenditures totaled $92.2 billion; by 1996 they had increased to more than $1.5 trillion. Even when inflation is taken into account, the budget has quadrupled. Many new policies and programs have been added and others have been expanded during these decades. Much of the growth in expenditure here, however, is accounted for by a few programmatic areas: national defense, social and income security, Medicare (which began operating in 1966), and interest payments on the national debt. Table 5.1 portrays expenditure patterns for several functional areas from 1950 through 1995. In addition to providing detail on the major areas of spending growth, it indicates how spending patterns vary with changing policy preferences. The jump in national-resource spending in the 1970s reflects the politics of environmental concern and the proliferation of environmental-protection policies. Again, the energy crises of the 1970s triggered greater spending on energy development programs. Then as worries about energy supplies, especially oil, faded in the 1980s, and the Reagan Administration put more reliance on the market, energy spending fell off markedly.

Until the 1960s, most governmental expenditures went to pay the direct costs of operating government agencies and programs. One's tax dollars were used mostly to pay the salaries of government employees, buy vehicles and equipment, cover rent and building-maintenance costs, and the like. Consequently, most people were at best indirectly affected by budget decisions. Whether appropriations were increased for the Department of Commerce or sharply cut for the foreign-aid program had little bearing on the lives of people in Des Moines, Detroit, Dubuque, or Dixon. No longer does government spending have this distant or abstract quality. Now a large portion of the budget goes directly to provide income support for retired persons, veterans, farmers, the needy, bondholders, and other claimants. Also, many corporations and communities have also come to rely upon defense spending (or contracting) for their continued prosperity. Projected and actual cutbacks in defense spending because of the end of the Cold War have caused consternation in many corporate boardrooms and communities around the nation.

TABLE 5.1 National Government Expenditures for Selected Functions and Selected Years, 1950–1995, in Billions of Current Dollars

	1950	1960	1970	1975	1980	1982	1984	1986	1988	1990	1991	1992	1993	1994	1995
National Defense	13.7	48.1	81.7	86.5	134.0	185.3	227.4	273.4	290.1	299.3	273.3	298.4	291.1	281.6	272.1
Income Security*	4.1	7.4	15.7	50.2	32.1	107.7	112.7	119.8	129.3	147.3	170.9	196.9	207.3	214.0	220.1
Social Security	0.8	11.6	30.3	64.7	118.6	156.0	178.2	198.8	219.4	248.6	269.0	287.6	304.6	319.6	335.9
Medicare		—	5.9	12.9	23.1	46.6	57.5	70.2	44.5	98.1	104.5	119	130.6	144.8	159.9
Agriculture	2.1	2.6	5.2	3.1	8.9	15.9	13.6	31.5	17.2	12.0	15.2	15.2	20.5	15.1	9.8
Natural Resources	1.3	1.6	3.1	7.4	13.9	13.0	12.6	13.6	14.6	17.1	18.6	20	20.2	21.1	22.1
Energy	0.3	0.5	1.0	2.9	10.2	13.5	7.1	4.7	2.3	2.4	1.7	4.5	4.3	5.2	4.9
Veterans' Benefits	8.8	5.4	8.7	16.6	21.2	24.0	25.6	26.4	29.4	29.1	31.4	34.1	35.7	37.6	37.9
Net Interest on Debt	4.8	7.0	14.4	23.3	52.6	85.1	111.1	136.1	151.9	184.2	194.5	199.4	198.8	203.0	232.2
All Others**	9.7	8.0	29.7	64.7	176.3	98.7	106.1	115.6	165.4	213.7	243.9	105.7	195.6	201.9	237.3
Total	45.6	92.2	195.7	332.3	590.9	745.8	851.9	990.1	1,064.1	1,251.8	1,323.0	1,380.8	1,408.7	1,460.9	1,519.1

*Income security includes public assistance, food stamps, railroad and federal employee retirement benefits, and unemployment compensation.
**All others includes international affairs, science, space, transportation, education, commerce, community development, justice, health, and general government.

Source: Budget of the United States Government, Fiscal Year 1997, Historical Tables (Washington: Government Printing Office, 1996), pp. 56–64.

These changes in the composition of the budget reflect changes in national policy priorities. They also have important consequences for the politics of the budgetary process. Those directly affected by governmental programs have organized to defend and increase their benefits and have become major participants in the budgetary process. This development has made budget decision-making both more political and more difficult. The American Association of Retired Persons, for instance, with its millions of members and hundreds of staff people, strongly opposes efforts to cutback Social Security and Medicare benefits. Even in an age of trillion-dollar budgets, there is not enough money to meet all demands. As elsewhere in the political process, those who are well-to-do and organized tend to fare better than the poor or unorganized.

The budget conveys a good overview of the government's total set of policies for the fiscal year it covers. In the budget one can find or extract answers to such policy issues as the balance between private and governmental (national) spending, the balance between civilian and military spending, whether medical research (including AIDS research) will be accelerated or slowed, whether welfare spending in general as well as spending for specific welfare programs will be expanded or contracted, whether more or less regulation is planned for surface or strip mining, and whether more or less emphasis will be given to environmental protection. This happens because the budgetary process, within the framework of substantive law, is a means for making choices among competing social values and allocating resources for their attainment. The budget is not simply a financial statement; it is also a statement of policy. Conflicts over money are in reality conflicts over policy.

The supporters of a policy or program cannot rest content once it has been legislatively authorized. Rather, they must now strive to ensure that it is funded, and continues to be funded, at levels adequate to ensure satisfactory attainment of its goals. Conversely, those who are opposed to it have an opportunity to reduce, cripple, or even kill it by reducing or eliminating its funding. Consequently, once substantive legislation is adopted the political struggle over a policy typically is renewed during the appropriations process.

The content and effectiveness of public policies often depend substantially upon the amount of funds provided for their enforcement or implementation. The rigorousness of antitrust enforcement, the number of children enrolled in Head Start programs, the control of illegal immigrants, the quality of national-park facilities, and the availability of housing subsidies for low-income people are among the many government programs much affected by appropriations. The Occupational Safety and Health Administration (OSHA) has a legislative mandate to ensure that workplaces, which number in the hundreds of thousands, are safe and healthful. However, it has funding to hire only enough inspectors to permit inspection of workplaces on the average of once every ten years. Twenty-five workers were killed in 1991 by a fire in a North Carolina food-processing plant. The building had no sprinklers and the fire doors could not be opened from the inside. It had never been inspected by OSHA.

In addition to being used to finance the government's activities and policies, the budget can also be used as an instrument to stabilize the economy, to help prevent inflation or recession. Fiscal policy involves the deliberate use of the government's taxing and spending powers to stimulate or restrain the economy by incurring budget deficits or surpluses, respectively. Briefly stated, according to Keynesian economic theory, a budget deficit, or a larger budget deficit, by putting more money into the hands of people and businesses, adds to the total demand for goods and services in the economy, thereby stimulating the economy. Conversely, a budget surplus, or a smaller budget deficit, will extract money from the economy and reduce the total demand for goods and services, thereby imposing restraint on the economy. Fiscal policy was heavily relied upon by presidential administrations in the 1960s and 1970s in their efforts to stabilize the economy. The large annual budget deficits incurred by the government since the early 1980s can be viewed as either "neutralizing" fiscal policy, because they foreclosed most major alterations in taxing and spending rates, or as providing a continual stimulus to the economy. Regardless of the interpretation, the budgetary situation meant that the task of stabilizing the economy fell mostly upon the Federal Reserve Board and its use of monetary policy (which involves controlling the interest rate and money supply). The FRB has accepted the challenge and has acted to hold down the level of inflation.

Finally, the budgetary process provides the president and Congress with an opportunity to review periodically the various policies and programs of the government, to assess their effectiveness, and to inquire into the manner of their administration. Every policy and program will not be examined in detail every year, but over a few years most if not all will come under scrutiny. Thus the budgetary process provides a continuing opportunity for exerting presidential and congressional influence and control over implementation of policies. Favored agencies and programs are likely to prosper; those under attack, whether for wasting money, harassing citizens, or misconstruing policies, may suffer cutbacks and restraints. Thus in 1989 congressional conservatives levied an attack on the appropriation for the National Endowment for the Arts because they considered pornographic a couple of art exhibitions sponsored by an organization that the agency had funded. Subsequently they took the position that support of the arts was not an appropriate national activity. Although many of the budget decisions made in a given year are marginal, involving limited increases or decreases in agency funds, this constraint does not diminish their importance.

THE NATIONAL BUDGETARY PROCESS

The budget that the president submits to Congress each February runs for a single fiscal year, which extends from October 1 in one calendar year through September 30 in the following year. It takes its name from the calendar year in which it ends. Thus the period from October 1, 1993, through September 30, 1994, is designated fiscal year (FY) 1994.

The national budgetary process, like state and local budgetary processes, can be divided into four fairly distinct stages: preparation, authorization, execution, and audit. Auditing, which involves checking on expenditures to determine whether illegality, waste, or extravagance occurred, is not discussed here.

Executive Preparation

The executive budget system set in place by the Budget and Accounting Act of 1921 required agencies (Congress and the Supreme Court are exempted) to transmit their budget requests to the president for approval before they were sent to Congress in a single, comprehensive budget document. The Bureau of the Budget was delegated authority to "assemble, correlate, revise, reduce, or increase the estimates." In its early years, BOB acted on the assumption that its major task was to hold down agency spending and ensure efficiency and economy in the operation of the government. This orientation continues to motivate the Office of Management and Budget.

Preparation of the national budget within the executive branch begins nine months or so before it is sent to Congress in February. Most of the day-to-day work in developing the budget is handled by the Office of Management and Budget and the executive departments and agencies. Acting on the basis of presidential directives, the OMB provides instructions, policy guidance, and tentative budget ceilings to help the departments and agencies assemble their budget requests. The latter, who are directly and specifically affected by budget decisions, and who are normally believers in the value and necessity of their programs, are expected to act as the advocates of increased spending (appropriations). What they request is subject to review and revision, upward or downward, by OMB in accordance with the policies and programs of the president. Because the "policies and programs" of the president are not subject to precise definition, OMB has latitude in determining what is consistent with them. Agencies sufficiently aggrieved by OMB decisions may try to appeal them to the president, who more often than not will uphold the OMB. Some presidents (Richard M. Nixon, for one) have discouraged the appeal of OMB decisions, however, thereby letting OMB make the final decisions on agency appropriations requests.

During the early years of the Reagan administration a "top-down" budgetary process overlaid the traditional ("bottom-up") budgetary pattern, except for the Department of Defense. Basic budget decisions were made at the presidential level by the OMB director and others and, in effect, imposed on the departments and agencies. This sequence meant that departments and agencies had less budgetary influence and discretion than under the former bottom-up procedure. As time went on, however, the centralization of executive authority and ideological unity necessary to make top-down budgeting workable and acceptable waned within the administration. The budgetary process then inched back toward the traditional bottom-up pattern, where the agencies have more influences on the size and content of their budget requests. Whether subsequent presidential administrations will be able to duplicate the early Reagan administration's budgetary control is problematical.[4]

The budget sent to Congress reflects the president's decisions and priorities on such matters as its overall size, its possible effects on the economy, its major directions in public policy, and its allocation of funds among the major agencies and programs. Lyndon Johnson in 1967 wanted both "guns and butter"—increased spending for both the Vietnam War and the social-welfare programs for his Great Society. Ronald Reagan in the 1980s, on the other hand, wanted less spending for various welfare and domestic programs and more spending for national defense. President George Bush's budget priorities in his first year in office were unclear. Campaigning for the presidency, he had advocated a "flexible freeze" on spending, no new taxes, and a reduction in the budget deficit. Although these goals were perhaps sufficient for campaign purposes, they did not amount to a real set of priorities. Once in office he did little to clarify them.

The discretion of the president and Congress in making budget decisions is constrained by the fact that about two-thirds of national expenditures are "uncontrollable," at least in the short run, as a consequence of political consideration and legal commitments. Beneficiaries of programs in the uncontrollable category strongly resist changes in authorizing statutes that will reduce their benefits. Based on existing law, uncontrollable expenditures represent continuing obligations and commitments that can be modified or eliminated only if the statutes authorizing them are changed. Examples include entitlement programs, such as Social Security, Medicare, Medicaid, food stamps, federal retirement, veterans' pensions, Guaranteed Student Loans, and agricultural price-support payments; grant-in-aid payments to the states; and interest on the national debt. Entitlement payments are so called because everyone who meets the eligibility criteria is legally entitled to benefits on the basis of a formula spelled out in the law. Appropriations for entitlements are typically open-ended—that is, the payment of benefits is authorized to all who apply, whatever the ultimate total may amount to. (Surprisingly, for instance, some people eligible for Medicaid benefits do not apply for them.) Much of the spending that is controllable (or discretionary) falls within the national security area, which, as a practical matter, is not subject to extensive alteration.[5] Department of Defense officials and their congressional and corporate allies successfully argue that reduction in military personnel and weapons procurement would adversely affect defense preparedness and the ability of the armed forces to simultaneously conduct two major military operations. There is also concern that military cutbacks will adversely affect the economic well-being of localities that are home to defense contractors and military installations. The Clinton administration proposed limited reductions in defense expenditures during its first term, only some of which were accepted by Congress.

Many of the entitlement programs are indexed to the consumer price index in order to maintain the real purchasing power of recipients. Consequently, expenditures for these programs automatically rise during inflationary periods. Much of the indexing was put in place during the early 1970s when inflation was low and consequently automatic increases were low. As inflation became stronger, the increases became larger and contributed to rising entitlement expenditure levels. Sometimes referred to as "automatic government," at the time it was instituted indexation was a technique that policy-makers also could use to avoid being blamed for potentially unpopular decisions.[6] Entitlement-program beneficiaries have been able to mobilize strong political support for the retention of indexation. Thus indexation stands as another practice that inhibits the ability of the president and Congress to control expenditures or to alter budget priorities.

Congressional Authorization

The Constitution provides in Article I that "no money shall be drawn from the treasury, but in consequence of appropriations made by law," which means appropriations legislation enacted by Congress. To begin, it should be noted that two distinct steps are usually involved in the funding of public policies and programs. First, substantive legislation has to be enacted establishing a policy or program (e.g., the Clean Water Act) and authorizing the expenditure of money in its support. Second, money actually has to be made available for the policy or program by the adoption of appropriations legislation. The House has had a rule since 1833 stating that "no appropriation shall be reported in any general appropriations bill, or be in order as an amendment thereto, for any expenditure not previously authorized by law." (This rule, like other congressional rules, is occasionally waived.) Authorization legislation is handled by the substantive or legislative committees (such as Agriculture,

Commerce, and Armed Services), and appropriations legislation is the domain of the House and Senate Appropriations Committees. Programs for which funding is authorized sometimes either go unfunded or are funded at levels lower than those authorized. The foreign-aid program has frequently been funded below its authorized level. Different committees, members, and processes in Congress can produce different policy results.

The legislative committees have sometimes circumvented the appropriations committees and the obstacles they represent by resorting to "backdoor spending," which takes a number of forms. Backdoor spending may involve authorizing an agency to borrow money from the Treasury, which the agency can then spend. Or it may involve authorizing an agency to contract for purchasing goods and services. Subsequently, funds will have to be appropriated to cover the borrowing or contracts. The alternative would be for the government to renege on its commitments, which is highly unlikely. Entitlement spending also falls within the backdoor category. The House Appropriations Committee has been especially opposed to backdoor practices because they effectively diminish the committee's authority over agency spending.

For purposes of legislative enactment, the president's budget, which comes to Congress as a document of several hundred pages, is divided into thirteen appropriations bills (e.g., for defense, energy and water development, interior and related agencies, and foreign operations). These are then referred to the House Appropriations Committee, which by long custom acts first on the budget. Its thirteen subcommittees (one for each appropriations bill) hold hearings, at which agency officials and others testify in explanation and defense of their budget requests, and otherwise do most of the detailed legislative work on the budget. In reviewing agencies and their programs, the members of Congress may seek information on topics such as these:[7]

1. Existence: Is the agency or program necessary? Should it be retained?
2. Objectives: What are the goals of the agency or program? Are they the correct ones?
3. Results: What is the program accomplishing? Can the agency demonstrate benefits? Why are there complaints about the agency or the program?
4. Line-item changes: Why does the agency need more money for personnel, equipment, or other matters? Why does it cost so much to run the program? What will a new program cost? What will be accomplished if more money is provided to the agency?

Hearings often focus on the fourth item, which involves changes in the level of an agency's program funding. This is both easier and more determinate than is deciding whether a program is necessary or what a program has accomplished or might accomplish. Members appear more comfortable in dealing with the financial aspects of agency operations. They are also much interested in how an agency's activities and expenditures will affect their constituents.

The subcommittees' recommendations are usually accepted with only minimal change by the full Appropriations Committee. In turn, its recommendations are customarily approved by the House with few changes. As a consequence of this pattern, detailed decision-making on appropriations is handled by small groups of House members with a strong interest in the programs with which they deal.

The Senate Appropriations Committee, to which appropriations bills passed by the House are sent, does not examine budget requests as intensively as does the House. Rather, the Senate Appropriations Committee tends to focus on "items in dispute," and serves as an appellate body to which agencies that have had their budget requests reduced in the House can appeal for restoration of at least a portion of the cuts. The Senate frequently responds positively to such pleas.

Conference committees drawn from the members of the relevant subcommittees are used to resolve the differences between the House and Senate versions of appropriations bills. Conflict resolution here often involves "splitting the difference" between the two bills. Compromises are considerably easier to reach on money matters than on social issues such as abortion, school prayer, or gun control. The latter involve "moral" choices on which it is hard to compromise or divide up the difference. Because its members are more specialized and better informed, and have more time and determination, the House usually does better than the Senate in appropriations conferences.[8]

BUDGETARY DECISION-MAKING   From the 1950s on into the 1970s, national budgeting was commonly described as incremental.[9] Economic growth made more revenue available to the government each year; consequently most agencies requested, and the president typically recommended, increased funding for their programs for the next year. In incremental budgeting, an agency's budget for the current year became its "base"; the additional funds sought for the next year were an "increment," which were to be used to improve or expand its activities and which represented its "fair share" of the government's additional revenues. Congressional examination of agency budget requests centered on the increments; the frequent result was a congressional decision to provide an agency with more funds than it had in the current year but less than the president's recommendation for the next. This permitted members of Congress to claim that they were holding down or cutting spending at the same time they were increasing funding for public programs.

Incremental budgeting was depicted by its proponents as a good budgeting process because it lessened conflict over budgetary issues, simplified budgetary decision-making by reducing the need for information and planning, and contributed to stability and predictability in budgeting. Critics contended that incrementalism was a barrier to rational decision-making and change, that it assumed a situation involving only public officials, and that it did not adequately acknowledge differences among budgetary actors in power and influence.[10]

Although some vestiges of incrementalism linger on, for the most part it has been done in by the growth of entitlements, top-down budgeting, and the pressures for and reality of budgetary cutbacks in a time of revenue shortfalls. Budgeting for agency and program funding reductions, or what Allen Schick calls decrementalism, is quite productive of conflict because of its redistributive nature.[11] More for one agency often means less for another. Agency officials now are often pleased to be able to hold cutbacks to modest proportions.

Baseline budgeting, though by no means comparable to incrementalism, has become an important aspect of budgetary decision-making. Essentially, baseline budgeting involves the estimation of the future budget implications of current policies, taking into account inflation and uncontrollable changes such as population growth, unemployment rates, and the extent to which people eligible for program benefits will seek them.[12] Changes in expenditures caused by new legislation or presidential actions are omitted from baseline projections. What the baseline projection does, in short, is estimate, on the basis of a number of assumptions, such as the expected inflation rate and growth in target population, the real future costs of current policies. This can be done for next year, the next five years, or some other time period. It yields what are essentially imaginary numbers.

Baseline budgeting also involves making estimates of the future revenues that will be generated by existing tax programs. These estimates will depend upon the assumptions made about the rate of economic growth, employment levels, and other economic variables. As with spending projections, revenue projections will be as sound and accurate as the assumptions on which they are based. By manipulating assumptions, officials can increase or decrease projected future revenue and spending levels.

Although appropriate as a way for policy-makers to estimate future revenue and spending levels and the impact that policy changes will have on them, baseline budgeting also can be used for less laudable purposes. It can be used, for instance, to make a particular budget decision appear as a reduction or an increase, depending on one's preference. Take the case of the Reagan administration's famous fiscal 1982 baseline budget reduction of $35 billion. On a current law projection, which does not figure in inflation, the amount was estimated at $10 billion, a less impressive sum. Allen Schick provides an explanation for the choice of the larger figure.

> Why did the Republicans, who only a few years earlier lambasted the current policy [baseline] concept as biased and expansionary, embrace it in 1981, and

why did the congressional Democrats go along with this method of measuring cutbacks? The simple but sufficient answer is that the Republicans wanted to magnify the reported savings, and the Democrats wanted the actual cuts to be less than they appeared to be. The . . . baseline allowed the Republicans to claim more savings and the Democrats to save more programs, a happy combination for politicians facing difficult choices.[13]

PRESIDENTIAL ACTION   Following the completion of congressional action, appropriations bills are transmitted to the president for approval. Once described as "veto-proof" because the continued operation of the government depends on the spending they authorize, recent presidents have invalidated this bit of conventional wisdom. A number of appropriations bills viewed as budget-busting or inflationary, or including funding for purposes not favored, have been turned down by the executive. Congress must then either rework the appropriations bill to meet presidential objections or seek to override the veto. Three of four appropriations bills vetoed by President Gerald R. Ford as inflationary were enacted into law by the democratically controlled Congress by overriding the vetoes.

Presidents may also use their veto power more positively by threatening to wield it on an appropriations bill under congressional consideration. This threat may induce Congress to tailor the bill to fit presidential objectives and avoid the veto, especially if congressional leaders think the votes are not available for an override. This is really a form of strategic bargaining, in which the possibility of future action is used in an effort to influence current action.

Most of the nation's governors long have had item-veto authority, which enables them to reject, or perhaps reduce, particular items in spending bills while approving most of the bill. This enhances their power vis-à-vis the legislature on appropriations. In comparison, the president has had to accept or reject a budget bill in its entirety. Consequently, provisions for pork-barrel projects or other matters objectionable to the president could get past him if incorporated in general appropriations bills that he felt compelled to approve.

Many presidents recommended that they be given the item veto. President Ronald Reagan, for example, frequently proclaimed that if Congress gave him item-veto authority, he would act to balance the budget. The Democratic majorities in Congress had little interest in so doing. In 1996, however, the Republican majorities in Congress were joined by many Democrats in enacting the Line-Item Veto Act. Apparently, they viewed this as a means of helping to bring government spending under control and balance the budget, matters which had much public support.[14] The Line-Item Veto Act, taking effect in 1997 and extending through 2004, authorizes presidential cancellation of particular discretionary spending items, including items in lump-sum categories, that are described in the manager's statements, or committee reports, accompanying spending bills; authorizations of new or expanded entitlement programs; and tax provisions of benefit to one hundred or fewer beneficiaries.

Such items that are specified by the president in a "special message" to Congress will be automatically vetoed unless both houses of Congress pass a "disapproval bill" reversing the president's cancellations. This bill is subject to a presidential veto, which in turn can be overridden by a two-thirds vote of each house.

Historically, Congress has jealously guarded its power of the purse; the adoption of the Line-Item Veto Act represents a significant departure from this stance. Potentially, the law could produce a major shift in budgetary power from Congress to the president. Whether this happens will depend upon how presidents choose to wield this authority. Will they decide to use it simply to strike down "wasteful" pork-barrel spending? Or will it become a form of leverage that presidents can employ to pressure members of Congress into accepting their budget priorities? A president, for instance, could engage in horse trading with members, offering to withhold his veto of their pet projects in return for support of some of his policy preferences.[15]

Considerable doubt has been expressed concerning the constitutionality of the legislated version of the line-item veto. For instance, the Judicial Conference of the United States, an organization representing federal judges, feared that the line-item veto could upset the separation of powers and permit the president to interfere with the independence of the judiciary.[16] No sooner had President Clinton signed the line-item veto bill into law than a public employee's union filed suit in federal court challenging its constitutionality. Other challenges were also likely. There matters stood in summer 1996.

The total amount of funds appropriated by Congress for a fiscal year usually does not deviate significantly from the figure recommended in the president's budget. A change of 3 or 4 percent, up or down, would be exceptional. For fiscal year 1995, for example, President Clinton asked for a total of $1,537 billion in new spending authority; Congress authorized $1,540.7 billion. For some agencies and programs, however, congressional action may diverge substantially from what the president recommends. As shown in Table 5.2, Congress appropriated more for the Department of Transportation than President Clinton sought, most notably for the Federal Highway Administration. Although the president requested nothing, Congress added $350 million here for highway demonstration projects, which are often derided as a species of pork-barrel spending. Funds were reduced for mass transit and the Federal Aviation Administration. (The appropriation does not list about $22 billion from the airport and highway trust funds, which are accounted for separately.)

Action on all the appropriations bills, including presidential approval, is supposed to be completed before the beginning of the fiscal year on October 1. It is quite common, however, for some or all of the bills to be pending on that date. When this delay occurs, a continuing resolution, which enables the affected agencies to continue operating on the basis of last year's budget or on some other agreed-on level, will be adopted. In 1987, none of the

TABLE 5.2 Department of Transportation Appropriation, Fiscal Year 1995, in Thousands of Dollars

	President's Request	House Bill	Senate Bill	Enacted
Office of the Secretary	$ 224,336	$ 231,116	$ 223,161	$ 218,766
Coast Guard	3,742,632	3,661,095	3,667,276	3,657,326
Federal Aviation Administration	7,116,948	7,015,700	6,942,969	6,942,223
Federal Highway Administration		299,862	352,055	352,055
National Highway Traffic Safety Administration	125,835	121,349	128,887	126,553
Federal Railroad Administration	1,191,870	1,051,562	1,164,485	1,135,319
Federal Transit Administration	2,110,890	1,745,390	1,729,840	1,739,340
Other Transportation Department	−577,354	207,141	250,706	243,415
	$13,710,821	$14,102,099	$14,236,218	$14,196,231

Source: Congressional Quarterly Weekly Report, Vol. 52 (October 1, 1994), p. 2775.

appropriations bills for fiscal year 1988 had been enacted when it began. Agencies operated with continuing resolutions for nearly three months before the budget was finally adopted in the form of an omnibus continuing resolution, which incorporated all the appropriations bills.

A matter of terminology now needs to be handled. Appropriations acts create budget authority, which permits agencies to obligate themselves for the expenditure or loan of money. When the money is actually paid out or expended, it is called an outlay. An agency must have budget authority before it can make an outlay. When Congress considers and acts on presidential budget requests, the focus is on budget authority (or appropriations). Discussions of budget deficits and surpluses, however, focus on outlays (or expenditures). Money that an agency obligates itself to spend in a given fiscal year, however, may not actually be paid out until a subsequent year, as with many Defense Department purchases of weapons systems. Also, sometimes budget authority may be made available for a multi-year or indefinite period of time. Thus outlays or expenditures for a given fiscal year must be estimated; they cannot be precisely known until after the year is over.

The relationship between appropriations and outlays is illustrated in Figure 5.1. In a given year, fiscal 1997 for instance, the money spent (outlays)

FIGURE 5.1 Relationship of Budget Authority to Outlays for FY 1997, in Billions of Dollars

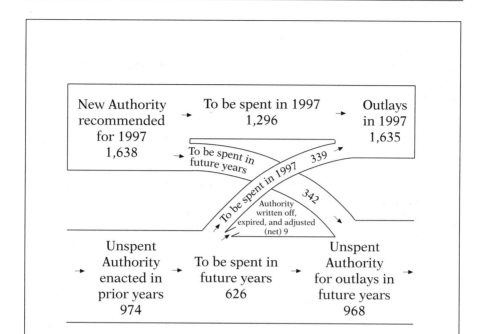

Source: Budget of the United States Government, Fiscal Year 1997, Analytical Perspectives (Washington: Government Printing Office, 1996).

will come from both that year's budget and previous budgets (in the form of unspent authority). Also, some of the funds appropriated for fiscal 1997 will actually be paid out in later years. Once money gets into the pipeline—that is, once expenditures are authorized—tremendous pressure grows to spend the money. If one wants to choke off government spending, the best time to act is at the appropriations (or authorization) stage in the budgetary process, before money enters the spending pipeline, but even then it is politically difficult.

THE CONGRESSIONAL BUDGET PROCESS   In the decades immediately after World War II, the budgetary process again became somewhat disjointed and chaotic. Appropriations and revenues were considered separately by different committees and processes. The budget surplus or deficit for a fiscal year was an "accidental figure," determined only when all the appropriations bills, considered separately, were enacted, totaled, and compared with available revenue. Dissatisfaction with this situation, concern about the rapid growth of governmental spending and continued budget deficits, and a desire for greater congressional attention to the fiscal-policy implications of the budget, contributed to adoption of the Congressional Budget and Impoundment Control Act of 1974.[17] The budgetary reform provisions of the act provide for a congressional budget process to coordinate the decentralized process by which budget decisions in Congress had been made. This procedure involves setting overall levels of revenues and expenditures and establishing priorities (and spending limits) among functional areas (such as agriculture, international relations, and transportation) included in the budget. New budget committees were created in the House and Senate to handle these tasks, subject to approval by the full houses. To assist the budget committees in their work, and to provide Congress with its own source of budgeting data and studies, a Congressional Budget Office (CBO) was established. The CBO has typically been more accurate than OMB in making budgetary estimations and economic forecasts.

Based on their review of the president's budget proposal, and on information from CBO and other congressional committees, the budget committees produce a concurrent budget resolution that sets overall levels of budget authority, outlays, revenues, and the budget surplus or deficit.[18] The budget resolution, which in effect is Congress's own budget, also specifies spending ceilings for each of the functional areas. It is supposed to be passed by April 15, although this is rarely achieved, and it does not require presidential approval. The appropriations committees are then expected to perform their scrutiny and evaluation of agency budget requests within the policy framework provided by the budget resolution. (See Figure 5.2.)

Reconciliation legislation is subsequently adopted in most years to ensure that the revenue goals and spending limits in the budget resolution are actually met. In the reconciliation process, the taxation and the legislative committees propose changes in *existing* tax laws and entitlement programs (usually to increase revenues or cut spending by specified amounts). These proposed changes are packaged by the budget committees into a single omnibus reconciliation bill which must be adopted by both houses and, unlike the budget resolution, signed into law by the president. Reconciliation, which makes permanent changes in the affected policies and programs, has been used to cut entitlement spending, increase taxes, modify discretionary programs, and sell government assets.[19]

Reconciliation was first used in 1980 under the Carter administration to make a modest reduction in the budget deficit for fiscal year 1981. The next year the Reagan administration and the Republican leadership in Congress employed reconciliation to impose a $35 billion cutback in baseline spending. This constitutes the most sweeping use of reconciliation to the present time.

Observers seem to agree that the new budgetary process has improved the quality of congressional decision-making on the budget. More and better budgetary information is available to Congress. Budget decisions are more

FIGURE 5.2 The Congressional Budget Process

February	Presidential budget is sent to Congress on the first Monday of the month
March 15	Standing committees send their budget estimates to the House and Senate budget committees
April 1	Budget committees report budget resolutions to House and Senate
April 15	Congress adopts a concurrent resolution setting targets for revenues, budget authorities, and outlays
May–July	House completes action on appropriations bills
July–Sept	Senate acts on appropriations bills; conference committees resolve differences; appropriations are enacted
September	Reconciliation legislation enacted if needed
October 1	Fiscal year begins; continuing resolutions are passed if all appropriations have not been enacted.

fully considered and debated, and members of Congress are compelled to address the overall dimensions of the budget. The budget decision-making process has been made more complex by the new procedures and participation by the budget committees. Conflict sometimes occurs between the budget committees and the appropriations and tax committees. The House Appropriations Committee, once famed for its role as "guardian of the Treasury," and its subcommittees have consequently become more protective of their members' favorite agencies and programs. This change in committee behavior illustrates one of the propositions of systems theory, namely, that change in one part of a system will produce changes elsewhere in the system.

Budget Execution

The obligation and actual expenditure (or outlay) of funds, once appropriated, rest with the various departments and agencies. To begin spending, however, they must first secure an apportionment from the OMB, which is authorized by the Antideficiency Act of 1905, as amended. An apportionment distributes "appropriations and other budgetary resources" (e.g., the authority to borrow money) to an agency "by time periods [usually quarterly] and by activities in order to ensure the effective use of available resources and to preclude the need for additional appropriations."[20] The OMB may also direct agencies to set aside funds for contingencies or not to spend funds when greater efficiency in operations or altered needs permit savings to be achieved without restricting accomplishment of agency goals.

The amount of discretion that the president and agency officials have in spending funds and achieving objectives is significantly affected by the language of the appropriations laws. Executive officials would prefer to have broad discretion in deciding whether to spend funds or to shift funds among programs. Congress, however, often includes considerable substantive detail in appropriations legislation to reduce agency discretion and compel adherence to congressional preferences. Specific restrictions or instructions may be included—as when an amendment to an appropriations bill required the Occupational Health and Safety Administration to get rid of "nuisance" standards—or else an agency may be prohibited from using its funds for specified purposes. On the other hand, Congress may sometimes provide agencies with "lump-sum" or very broad appropriations that confer much spending discretion, albeit within boundaries provided by substantive legislation pertaining to agency action. Figure 5.3 illustrates the inclusion of directions, limitations, and provisions for specific projects ("pork") in appropriations legislation for the National Park Service.

The committee and subcommittee reports accompanying appropriations bills are commonly used to specify how funds should be spent and to help shape policy. The example presented below comes from the House Appropriations Committee's report on the annual appropriation for Food Safety and Inspection Service, located in the Department of Agriculture. FSIS has responsibility for regulating the meat and poultry industries to ensure that meat and poultry products are safe, wholesome, and accurately labeled.

> The Committee believes a HACCP regulatory reform process is needed to maintain the production of a clean, safe, quality meat product that ensures consumer confidence. The Committee believes its objective of timely implementation of regulations that make the strongest practicable improvement in food safety is dependent upon the development of workable, scientifically sound rules. Therefore, the Committee has included language directing the Department to convert the rulemaking on Pathogen Reduction, Hazard Analysis and Critical Control Point (HACCP) Systems, the so-called "Mega-Reg," to a negotiated rulemaking procedure. The Committee expects that the Department will be able to develop more effective food safety rules due to the quality of input this procedure will permit regarding issues addressed in this rulemaking and related regulatory requirements. Further, the Committee directs the Department to proceed expeditiously with this rulemaking to avoid significant delay in the promulgation of modernized meat and poultry regulations. Specifically, the Department is expected to act promptly to initi-

FIGURE 5.3 The First Page of the Appropriations Act for the National Park Service for Fiscal Year 1994

PUBLIC LAW 103–138—NOV. 11, 1993   107 STAT. 1385

NATIONAL PARK SERVICE

OPERATION OF THE NATIONAL PARK SYSTEM

For expenses necessary for the management, operation, and maintenance of areas and facilities administered by the National Park Service (including special road maintenance service to trucking permittees on a reimbursable basis), and for the general administration of the National Park Service, including not to exceed $1,599,000 for the Volunteers-in-Parks program, $38,400 for a lump-sum payment to Marlene Anita Hudson of Washington, District of Columbia, which payment shall be in addition to any other amount that is otherwise payable under any other provision of law based on the death of James A. Hudson, and not less than $1,000,000 for high priority projects within the scope of the approved budget which shall be carried out by the Youth Conservation Corps as authorized by the Act of August 13, 1970, as amended by Public Law 93–408, $1,061,823,000, without regard to the Act of August 24, 1912, as amended (16 U.S.C. 451), of which not to exceed $78,559,000 to remain available until expended is to be derived from the special fee account established pursuant to title V, section 5201, of Public Law 100–203.

Marlene Anita Hudson

NATIONAL RECREATION AND PRESERVATION

For expenses necessary to carry out recreation programs, natural programs, cultural programs, environmental compliance and review, international park affairs, statutory or contractual aid for other activities, and grant administration, not otherwise provided for, $42,585,000.

HISTORIC PRESERVATION FUND

For expenses necessary in carrying out the provisions of the Historic Preservation Act of 1966 (80 Stat. 915), as amended (16 U.S.C. 470), $40,000,000 to be derived from the Historic Preservation Fund, established by section 108 of that Act, as amended, to remain available for obligation until September 30, 1995.

CONSTRUCTION

For construction, improvements, repair or replacement of physical facilities, $201,724,000, to remain available until expended, $4,377,000 to be derived from amounts made available under this head in Public Law 101–512 as a grant for the restoration of the Keith Albee Theatre in Huntington, West Virginia, and $1,844,000 to be derived from amounts made available under this head in Public Law 102–381 for a pedestrian walkway and interpretive park (A Walk on the Mountain): *Provided,* That $2,000,000 for the Boston Public Library and $500,000 for the Penn Center shall be derived from the Historic Preservation Fund pursuant to 16 U.S.C. 470a: *Provided further,* That of the funds provided under this heading, not to exceed $350,000 shall be made available to the City of Hot Springs, Arkansas, to be used as part of the non-Federal share of a cost-shared feasibility study of flood protection for the downtown area which contains a significant amount of National Park Service property and improvements: *Provided further,* That notwithstanding any other provision of law a single procurement for the construction of the Franklin Delano Roosevelt ate a negotiated rulemaking and to require a report from the negotiated rulemaking committee within nine months of its establishment.[21]

The negotiated rule-making specified by the Committee in its convoluted language was intended to afford meat-industry groups greater opportunity to help shape the content of new meat and poultry regulations. Designed to reduce bacterial contamination, the new rules did not bear down as hard on the meat-packing industry as consumer groups had hoped.

The funding of pork-barrel projects that benefit particular localities or groups, such as a railroad museum, a blueberry research program, or a highway interchange, is also frequently provided for in committee reports. There it may be stated that the Committee hopes, expects, or directs that funding will be used for specified purposes. Even if the president had an item veto on appropriations legislation it might not reach such projects. Although committee and subcommittee reports are not legally binding on agencies, it is impolitic for officials to ignore them. Members of Congress may subsequently call to account those who disregard committee instructions.

The practice of presidential impoundment of funds frequently stirred controversy with Congress.[22] Beginning with Thomas Jefferson, who withheld funds for a couple of gunboats to operate on the Mississippi River, presidents claimed and exercised authority to prevent expenditure of funds for purposes they disagreed with on budgetary or policy grounds. Presidents Truman and Eisenhower refused to spend funds for military programs that they had not requested. President Lyndon Johnson impounded billions of dollars to combat inflation, although much of what he held back was subsequently released. Until the 1970s impoundment was usually done on a selective and limited basis and, although some dissatisfaction was created and voiced in Congress, major confrontations were avoided.

President Nixon, however, precipitated an intense political conflict over impoundment that made it a high-priority item on the national policy agenda. Following his reelection in 1972, he decided to use an administrative strategy to "take on the bureaucracy and take over the government." One facet of this strategy entailed extensive impoundment of appropriations for water-pollution controls, mass transit, food stamps, medical research, urban renewal, agricultural programs, and highway construction. These impoundments "were unprecedented in their scope and severity."[23] Numerous rationales were provided, including the need to prevent the inflationary effects of "reckless" spending and the existence of inherent and implied executive power under the Constitution to take such action. In various instances, however, it was apparent that presidential impoundment was simply being used to reduce or eliminate congressionally authorized programs of which the administration disapproved. Nearly all the impoundments were challenged by adversely affected parties and were held to be illegal by the federal courts.[24]

Congress also was provoked into action by the Nixon impoundments and included some controls on impoundment in the 1974 budget law. Under the act a deferral of expenditures, in which the executive seeks to delay or stretch out spending until a time in the fiscal year when it is needed, could be done unless or until either house of Congress voted to disapprove. In contrast, an executive rescission of funds, which cancels budget authority and thus stops the expenditure of funds, becomes effective only if, within forty-five days of notification, both houses pass a rescission bill. In actuality it is not always easy to distinguish deferrals from rescissions. Overall, the new impoundment procedures gave Congress more (and the executive less) authority over spending and made appropriations legislation more of a mandate for agencies to spend allocated funds.

In *Immigration and Naturalization Service v. Chadha* of 1983,[25] a case involving a minor immigration matter, the Supreme Court declared unconstitutional the use of the legislative veto. The legislative veto was held to permit Congress or its committee to disapprove rules or actions of executive agencies and officials, such as deferral of spending, in violation of the Constitution's presentment clause, which requires that bills must be presented to the president for approval or veto before they become law. Did this ruling mean, then, that the president could still engage in deferral of spending although Congress, if it so desired, could not veto the actions? This issue came to a head in 1986, when President Reagan moved to defer expenditure of $5.1 billion for housing and related aid to low-income people. This action was quickly contested in the courts. In May 1986, a federal district court, later upheld by an appeals court, ruled that the president no longer had deferral authority under the 1974 budget law. Both courts took the view that Congress would not have given deferral authority to the president without retaining a legislative veto for itself. Hence, when the legislative veto perished, so too did deferral authority.

The problem pointed up in the controversy over deferral applies to the budgetary process generally: What is the appropriate balance between presidential discretion and congressional control in spending? In cases of conflict, whose judgment should prevail? It would be much easier to answer these questions if only managerial matters were at stake. As we have seen, though, the budget is a policy document that reflects major policy values and priorities, a characteristic that makes budgetary decision-making much more contentious.

FIGHTING BUDGET DEFICITS

The United States national debt rapidly increased during the late 1970s and 1980s because of rising expenditures for entitlement programs and national defense and declining revenues stemming from the 1981 tax cut and the recession in the early 1980s. Annual budget deficits reached proportions that many considered alarming; some said the budget was hemorrhaging. The deficit for fiscal year 1986 reached minus $220.1 billion. The national debt skyrocketed between 1980 and 1995 (see Table 5.3). In this section we treat some efforts to fashion and implement policy for bringing the budget deficit under control.[26]

Congress adopted the Balanced Budget and Emergency Deficit Control Act (better known as the Gramm-Rudman-Hollings Act) in December 1985. Public and congressional concern over the large budget deficits in the early 1980s provided the context and motivation for its enactment. Efforts to reduce the deficit by conventional budgetary procedures had been unsuccessful because of strong partisan differences between members of Congress (especially the Democrats) and the Reagan administration on military and social-welfare spending as well as tax increases.

The Gramm-Rudman-Hollings proposal was introduced in the Senate in late September 1985 as an amendment to a bill authorizing an increase in the national debt, which was required to enable the government to continue borrowing money to meet its spending obligations. The amendment never received committee hearings or consideration in either house, however, although these are customary for legislation of such importance. The proposal required the president and Congress to eliminate the budget deficit within five years, either by regular budget procedures or, if these were unavailing, with automatic, uniform, across-the-board budget cuts implemented by the CBO and the OMB. Described by Senator Warren Rudman (R, New Hampshire) as "a bad idea whose time had come," within a couple of weeks the Republican-led Senate had passed the measure by a 75-to-24 vote. This indicates how strongly the Senate felt compelled to do something about the deficit, even if its action was only symbolic.

The House, controlled by the Democrats, now faced the need to deal with the Gramm-Rudman-Hollings proposal.[27] Essentially, the House had three alternatives: ignore the proposal, explicitly reject it, or seek to modify it to make it more palatable. The Democratic leadership opted to modify the proposal as the only politically viable alternative, given the public dismay over the budget deficit. Negotiations to resolve differences with the Senate were entered into through the use of bipartisan conference task forces rather than a regular conference committee. A compromise version of the Gramm-Rudman-Hollings bill was passed by the House, only to be rejected by a 24-to-74 vote when it was sent back to the Senate. The Senate then approved a version of the bill that was much the same as the one it had originally passed. This bill in turn was quickly rejected by the House by a 117-to-239 party-line vote, the Democrats being in the majority. Momentarily, stalemate loomed.

Important issues in dispute between the two houses (and the political parties) included the timetable for deficit reduction, the number and kind of programs to be exempted from automatic budget cuts, and the procedure to

TABLE 5.3 Budget Receipts, Outlays, Surplus or Deficit, and Total National Debt for Selected Years from 1940 to 1995, in Billions of Dollars

Year	Receipts	Outlays	Surplus or Deficit	National Debt
1940	6.5	9.5	−2.9	50.7
1945	45.2	92.7	−47.6	260.1
1950	39.4	42.6	−3.1	256.8
1955	65.5	68.4	−4.1	274.4
1960	92.5	92.3	0.3	290.5
1965	116.8	118.2	−1.4	322.3
1970	186.9	183.6	3.2	380.9
1975	279.1	332.3	−2.8	541.9
1980	517.1	590.9	−53.2	909.1
1985	734.1	946.3	−212.3	1,817.5
1988	908.9	1,064.0	−155.1	2,601.3
1990	1,031.3	1,251.8	−220.5	3,206.6
1991	1,054.3	1,323.4	−269.2	3,598.5
1992	1,090.5	1,380.9	−290.4	4,002.1
1993	1,153.5	1,408.7	−255.1	4,351.4
1994	1,257.7	1,460.9	−203.2	4,643.7
1995*	1,350.6	1,514.4	−163.8	4,921.0

*Estimated.

Source: Annual Report of the Council of Economic Advisers, 1996 (Washington: U.S. Government Printing Office, 1996), p. 367.

be used in making the automatic cuts. Questions were also raised about the constitutionality of the legislation. Negotiations between the House and the Senate were resumed, now handled by a small group of leaders meeting in private sessions rather than the conference committee. They succeeded in hammering out an agreement that was adopted by both houses in mid-December 1985 and signed into law by the president.

As originally enacted, the Gramm-Rudman-Hollings Act required that federal budget deficits be reduced to $171.9 billion in fiscal year 1986, $144 billion in 1987, $108 billion in 1988, $72 billion in 1989, $36 billion in 1990, and zero in 1991. At the insistence of the Democrats, a number of programs were exempted from the automatic budget cuts, including Social Security, veterans' pensions, Medicaid, food stamps, Aid to Families with Dependent Children (AFDC), child nutrition, and interest on the national debt. Cuts were limited in amount for five health programs, including Medicare. These exemptions were an indication of congressional priorities on spending. If regular budget and appropriations action failed to reach the deficit targets, then uniform and across-the-board reductions, divided equally in amount between non-exempt domestic programs and defense programs, would be made. Thus across-the-board cuts would hit hard on nonexempt programs, because a large portion of the budget was immune to automatic reduction.

The amount of any automatic reductions required, called a sequester, was to be jointly determined by the CBO, OMB, and General Accounting Office (GAO), with the final decision resting with the GAO, a congressional agency headed by the comptroller general, who can be removed from office only by Congress. Although budget reduction action would be initiated by a presidential sequestration order, an overall effect of the act was to give the president little or no discretion in imposing the automatic budget cuts. Some doubted the constitutionality of the act because of the GAO's involvement in making the automatic budget cuts. Consequently, the act provided that if the courts struck down the procedure for making automatic cuts, the reductions would have to be approved by both houses of Congress and the president, meaning that they were no longer automatic.

Several members of Congress immediately brought suit challenging the act's constitutionality because of the role assigned to the GAO and the comptroller general. The Reagan administration also questioned its constitutionality. In July 1986 the United States Supreme Court, by a 7-to-2 vote, determined that the automatic procedure for spending reduction was unconstitutional but left the remainder of the law intact. The majority held that by giving final responsibility to the comptroller general, "who is subject to removal only by itself, Congress in effect has retained control over the execution of the act and has intruded into the executive function. The Constitution does not permit such intrusion."[28] The minority thought that this opinion took too narrow a view of what was permissible under the separation-of-powers principle. The Court's decision removed from the statute its vital, action-forcing core.

Efforts to restore the act's vitality were quickly begun but initially came to naught. Late in summer 1986, however, the CBO and OMB issued a report stating that $45.4 billion in budget cuts were needed to meet the Gramm-Rudman-Hollings Act's target for fiscal year 1988. Cuts of this magnitude were unacceptable to most members of Congress, and also to the Reagan administration because of the large reduction in defense spending that would be entailed. Consequently, pressure intensified to amend the act to alter the schedule for reducing the debt and to provide again for an automatic budget-reduction mechanism. Legislation for this purpose was adopted late in September 1987 and included these provisions:

1. The CBO and OMB were both directed to issue reports on the estimated budget deficit and the uniform percentage that program accounts must be reduced to meet the deficit-reduction targets. The OMB was further

directed to "give due regard" to the CBO report in deciding how much spending had to be cut.

2. New budget-deficit targets were set: $144 billion for fiscal year 1988, $136 billion for 1989, $100 billion for 1990, $64 billion for 1991, $28 billion for 1992, and zero for 1993.
3. A spending reduction of $23 billion was provided for 1988. (This figure was less than the original act required.)
4. The manner of calculating the spending total used in estimating the deficit from which cuts were to be made was revised. This revision eased the effect of cuts by expanding the base to which they would be applied.
5. The president was given some discretion to deviate from uniform reductions in military spending accounts.
6. No change was made in the programs protected against automatic reductions by the original act.

From a congressional perspective, the legislation was intended to push the president into negotiations on tax increases, defense-spending restraints, and domestic-spending cuts as part of a budget-deficit reduction plan. Otherwise, the president would have to accept the consequences of the automatic, across-the-board cuts called for by the amended Gramm-Rudman-Hollings Act. Because Congress was slow in taking action, however, in October 1987 the president moved to put into effect the $23 billion in across-the-board cuts the act specified for fiscal year 1988. This ploy was intended to put pressure on Congress to reduce spending through regular budget procedures.

A few days later, on October 19, the New York stock market collapsed and the Dow Jones Industrial Average, a leading stock-market indicator, fell by 508 points. Many wondered whether this was the precursor of a stock-market crash like that in 1929. Some observers attributed the collapse, at least in part, to worry in the financial communities, both in the United States and abroad, about the size of the budget deficit and the government's ability to control its finances. This fear created a crisis atmosphere that quickly produced negotiations among Democratic and Republican leaders in Congress, the secretary of the Treasury, and other high-level Reagan administration officials to reduce the budget deficit.

A few weeks of closed-door meetings resulted in a Bipartisan Budget Agreement calling for budget-deficit reductions of $30 billion in 1988 and $46 billion in 1989. Included in the package were $9 billion in new tax revenues for 1988 and another $14 billion for 1989. These taxes represented concessions by both House Democrats, who had advocated twice as much in increased taxes, and by President Reagan, who had opposed any new taxes. Defense spending was increased somewhat, but not as much as the president wanted, and some entitlements were to be reduced. Legislative action was required to put the Bipartisan Budget Agreement into effect. Strong pressure from congressional leaders of both parties was necessary to get the balky members of Congress to approve an omnibus appropriations resolution (which incorporated all thirteen annual appropriations bills) and a reconciliation bill providing for tax increases and expenditure reductions to implement the bipartisan agreement. Their enactment was marked by long bargaining sessions, partisan conflicts, and disagreement over what had been agreed to in the Bipartisan Budget Agreement, because no records had been kept and the participants had different recollections about what they had agreed to. Many rank-and-file members of Congress were dissatisfied with the entire process and felt excluded from real involvement. "That feeling of disfranchisement was aggravated by the way those two decisions were enacted: in two massive omnibus bills, each beyond the comprehension of any single member."[29]

As a consequence of the Bipartisan Budget Agreement and the implementing legislation, the automatic spending cuts initiated in October under the Gramm-Rudman-Hollings Act were rescinded. Regular budgetary procedures had proved sufficient. In the crisis-like conditions under which they were exercised, however, one hesitates to designate them "normal."

Another chapter was added to the saga of budget-deficit reduction in 1990.[30] When President Bush sent his proposed budget for fiscal year 1991 to Congress early in 1990, it appeared that the reductions needed to meet the 1991 GRH target ($64 billion) would be politically acceptable. As the months passed, though, the budgetary situation increasingly worsened, fueled in part by the recession afflicting the economy. By September the picture was indeed ominous; predictions about the 1991 budget deficit ranged as high as $170 billion. Budget cutbacks to meet the GRH target were now too drastic to seriously contemplate.

During spring and summer, desultory budget negotiations between the White House and Congress had been unproductive. President Bush continued for a time to assert his 1988 campaign pledge of "Read my lips. No new taxes." In June, under pressure from Democratic congressional leaders, he backed away from his "no new taxes" position: everything was put on the table. As the beginning of the 1991 fiscal year neared, bargaining became more intense and, finally, an agreement on a package of tax increases and spending cutbacks was reached at the end of September. Dissatisfaction about this agreement was rife and it was rejected in the House by an "unholy" alliance of liberal Democrats and conservative Republicans. The latter, led by Representative Newt Gingrich (R, Georgia), were outraged by the president's violation of his "no new taxes" vow.

Negotiations between the White House and Congress resumed in the context of recriminations from both sides. At the end of October, agreement finally was reached on a new combination of tax increases, spending reductions, and budget procedures. With approval by both houses of Congress and the President, it became law as part of the Omnibus Budget Reconciliation Act (OBRA). Called the Budget Enforcement Act, its provisions are briefly summarized here.

For 1991 to 1993, the Budget Enforcement Act established separate limits for three areas of discretionary spending: domestic, international, and defense. If spending exceeded the limits in an area, automatic cutbacks would be levied on all programs in that area. For 1994 and 1995, OBRA provided only a total discretionary-spending cap. In the mandatory spending area, a pay-as-you-go rule applied; spending increases or tax decreases were permitted only if offset by other spending decreases or tax increases. Second, the act provided for various tax increases, including five cents a gallon on gasoline and a new 31 percent income-tax bracket. Third, new budget-deficit targets were specified (see Table 5.4), which could be adjusted (in all likelihood, upward) when economic conditions changed. The president and Congress could also designate "emergency spending" that was exempt from spending limitations. In all, it was predicted that the budget agreement would reduce projected budget deficits by $496 billion over the 1991 to 1995 period. The Clinton administration extended the Budget Enforcement Act's rules through 1997.

Assessing the influence of the Gramm-Rudman-Hollings Act and the 1990 Omnibus Budget Reconciliation Act on budget-deficit reduction is a puzzling task. An easy answer is not possible given the complexity of budgetary policy and politics and their economic context. In Table 5.4, the budget-deficit goals set by the various actions are compared with actual budget deficits. It does not portray success, although one could argue that the deficits would have been larger had it not been for the deficit-reduction policies. The 1992 budget deficit was under the target figure only because Congress chose not to

TABLE 5.4 The Gramm-Rudman-Hollings Act Budget Deficit Goals and Actual Deficits, in Billions of Dollars

Year	1985 Deficit Goals	1987 Revision of Deficit Goals	1990 Revision of Deficit Goals	Actual Deficits
1986	171.9			221.3
1987	144			149.8
1988	108	144		155.2
1989	72	136		152.5
1990	36	100		220.5
1991	0	64	327	269.2
1992		28	317	290.4
1993		0	236	255.1
1994			102	203.2
1995			83	163.8*

*Estimated.

appropriate tens of billions of dollars needed for the savings-and-loan-association bailout. That was delayed until a future year, when the costs of the bailout had become much greater.

The budget deficit and what to do about it was a major issue in the 1992 presidential campaign. Billionaire and independent candidate Ross Perot constantly harped about the need to eliminate the deficit. Democratic candidate Bill Clinton pledged to cut the deficit in half by the end of his first term. Once in office, however, he found this to be a daunting task, more so because he wanted to increase government spending for a number of purposes. Early in 1993 the Clinton administration devised a budget plan combining tax increases (for instance, an energy tax based on the heat content of fuels and hikes in personal and corporate income taxes) and spending cutbacks in both discretionary and entitlement programs. The administration estimated that this plan would reduce the deficit by a total of $447 billion over a five-year period, thereby lowering the deficit in 1997 to around $200 billion. Democrats in Congress were generally supportive of the proposal, but Republicans sharply criticized it for including too many tax increases and insufficient spending decreases, and for not reducing the deficit enough.

Over the next several months a titanic partisan political struggle took place in Congress, first over the adoption of a congressional budget resolution in line with the president's proposal and then over the enactment of reconciliation legislation needed to implement the budget resolution. The budget resolution passed by votes of 240–184 in the House and 55–45 in the Senate. No Republicans voted in favor of the resolution and only a few conservative Democrats voted against it. The budget resolution called for $246 billion in tax increases and $247 billion in spending cutbacks. The amount of spending cutbacks had been enlarged in the House to mollify conservative Democrats.[31]

Reconciliation legislation was required to implement the tax increases and entitlement spending reductions (about two-thirds of the $493 billion total). The remainder of the spending cutbacks (those in discretionary spending) were left to the appropriations committees. Partisan and interest-group conflict intensified over reconciliation because of its binding character. Clinton administration officials, including the president and vice president, had to do much persuading and bargaining in order to secure Democratic majorities sufficient for its enactment, there being little hope of picking up Republican votes.

Especially productive of conflict was the proposal for a broad-based energy tax. Although it did win approval in the House, sufficient votes to pass it could not be found in the Senate. Hundreds of businesses and business organizations banded together as the American Energy Alliance and fought unrelentingly against the energy tax.[32] In the face of imminent defeat because of the defection of several conservative Democratic senators, the Clinton Administration agreed to replace the energy tax with a tax on gasoline only, which eventually was set at 4.3 cents per gallon.

The Omnibus Budget Reconciliation Act of 1993 was adopted by votes of 218–216 in the House and 51–50 in the Senate. Forty-one conservative House Democrats voted against it. In the Senate, Vice President Al Gore cast the tie-breaking vote as five Democratic senators joined the opposition. In addition to the gasoline tax, the reconciliation act increased corporate income taxes, added personal income-tax brackets of 36 percent and 39.6 percent, which hit higher-income individuals, and raised many user fees. Cuts were made in many spending programs, most notably defense and Medicare. In all, the act made several hundreds of changes in existing laws and programs.[33]

Although Republicans and conservative Democrats in 1994 called for additional spending cutbacks, the Clinton administration, preoccupied with such matters as reform of the nation's medical system that year, chose not to renew the deficit reduction struggle.

The Republican majorities swept into Congress by the 1994 congressional elections made not merely deficit reduction but also balancing the budget top agenda items. They launched a two-pronged attack on the deficit. First, they sought to propose a constitutional amendment requiring an annually balanced budget, as was called for by the House Republicans' "Contract with America." Readily winning approval in the House, the amendment fell one vote short of the two-thirds approval needed in the Senate. Proponents of the amendment contended that it was needed to provide officials with sufficient motivation (or backbone) to balance the budget. Opponents questioned whether this would happen. Further, they argued that the annually balanced budget requirement would handcuff the government in dealing with economic fluctuations, especially recessions.

Dismayed, but undaunted by the failure to pass the balanced budget amendment, the Republicans now trained their guns directly on the budget. In June, once again sharply split along party lines, Congress passed a budget resolution calling for a balanced budget by the year 2002. To achieve this goal, over a seven-year period, spending was to be reduced by a total of $984 billion while taxes were to be cut by $245 billion. This arrangement represented a compromise between the tax-cutting and deficit-hawk segments of the congressional Republicans.[34] (The Clinton administration's proposed budget was ignored.) The Republican plan called for extensive cutbacks in Medicare, Medicaid, and other entitlement programs, and in discretionary spending, along with an increase in defense spending.

The Republicans' attention then turned to the complex task of drafting reconciliation legislation to put their plan into law. Work on the reconciliation bill was not completed until late in November. In final form, it specified, over a seven-year span, reduction of $270 billion in Medicare, $163 billion in Medicaid, $114 billion in entitlement programs for the poor, and a multitude of other cutbacks. The $245 billion in tax cuts included a $500 per-child tax credit for families with incomes under $110,000 and reductions in the capital gains tax and various business taxes.[35] When the reconciliation bill reached

President Clinton it received the expected veto. Denouncing the bill as extreme and wrongheaded, the president said he would present a more acceptable proposal for balancing the budget by 2002. Indeed, negotiations on an alternative had been underway prior to his veto.[36]

To back up for a bit, when fiscal year 1996 got underway on October 1, none of the appropriations bills had been enacted into law. Consequently, a continuing resolution providing for partial and temporary funding was enacted to permit the government to continue operating. When that resolution expired in November, a partial, four-day shutdown of the government occurred. In the parlance of budgetary negotiations, this was a "train wreck." Subsequently, another continuing resolution was passed to permit the government to resume full operations. Also, by this time (late November) a half-dozen appropriations bills had been enacted into law.

Following President Clinton's veto of the reconciliation bill, protracted negotiations over balancing the budget occurred between executive officials, including the president, and congressional leaders from both parties; these negotiations were not concluded until near the end of April 1996. During this time span the president vetoed three appropriations bills, another partial government shutdown lasting twenty-one days occurred, and a dozen temporary continuing resolutions were adopted. Much acrimony, wheeling and dealing, dissembling, and bargaining accompanied the negotiations.[37]

In April, with half of the 1996 fiscal year gone, five appropriations bills not enacted, and the likelihood of an agreement on a balanced budget a poor bet, the White House and the Republicans reached agreement to pass an omnibus appropriations bill to fund much of the government for the remainder of the fiscal year.[38] Both sides could claim some success. The Republicans succeeded in reducing discretionary spending by $20 billion below its 1995 level, in the process cutting funding for many agencies and programs and eliminating a substantial number of small programs. They also got President Clinton to agree to their goal of balancing the budget in 2002 and to using the more cautious CBO figures in making budget estimates. For his part, President Clinton had been able to protect his priorities on education, job training, and the environment. For example, EPA's budget was cut by about 10 percent, but that was less than half of the cut that was initially sought by the House Republicans. Also, almost all of the restrictive riders added by House Republicans to reorient regulatory policies were deleted. Except for agriculture, where the Federal Agricultural Improvement and Reform Act (FAIR) removed production controls as a condition for receiving income supports for most farmers, no major changes were made in entitlement programs.

When President Clinton sent his proposed budget for fiscal year 1997 to Congress, he called for the national budget to be balanced by 2002. Because neither side wanted to renew the intense political struggle that had revolved around the 1996 budget, however, the action to achieve balance was restrained. For example, the Republicans decided to try to hold discretionary spending at its 1996 level rather than work for another round of substantial reductions, and plans for major changes in entitlement spending and for tax reductions were deferred until after the 1996 elections.

CONCLUDING REMARKS

Congressional legislation on deficit reduction represents an attempt to use procedural rules to solve a substantive problem. The large budget deficits that occurred in the 1980s reflected important differences between President Reagan and the congressional Democrats on taxing and spending issues. President Reagan favored increased defense spending and lower domestic spending, and was adamantly opposed to increasing taxes, especially in the later years of his administration. The Democrats, who controlled the House of Representatives throughout his term and the Senate for his final two years, advocated more domestic spending and less defense spending, and contended that a major tax increase was needed to help balance the budget. The consequence was a stand-off. In this sort of situation, adopting new rules to govern the budgetary process is not likely to be very effective, especially when many of the players don't like the rules.

Moreover, rules made by Congress can be altered by Congress when they become inconvenient, as is demonstrated by the differences between the 1985 and 1987 versions of the Gramm-Rudman-Hollings Act. Rules may also be designed to permit their manipulation and avoidance, as was done with the act in 1986 and subsequent years. To illustrate, whether the GRH deficit target was met at the onset of a fiscal year involved estimating revenues and expenditures (outlays) for the year. These estimates, in turn, depended upon a forecast of economic conditions, such as the rates of inflation, employment, and economic growth, which affect future revenue and spending levels. Congress, primarily on the basis of an overly optimistic economic forecast, declared that it had met the deficit target for fiscal year 1987 and that no sequestration resolution was required. In actuality, that proved wrong.

Rules, Professor Aaron Wildavsky suggests, "might help enforce a political consensus on the budget if there was one."[39] This consensus, however, was lacking in the Reagan years. Large budget deficits were the consequence. It is unlikely that the important policy disagreements involved in the budget-deficit struggle can be solved by procedural tinkering. The 1990 budget agreement between the executive and Congress did ease worries about the deficit and, for a brief time, deficit reduction ceased to be a high-priority item on the national policy agenda.

For public officials really wanting to balance the budget and to move beyond the realm of symbolic action, there are only a couple of options. One is to make major reductions in government spending, especially for entitlement programs because of the large share of the budget that they constitute. The other option is a major increase in tax revenues. Of course, some combination of the two is also possible. Neither has enjoyed strong public support, notwithstanding much public distress about the budget deficits. The Republicans in 1995 took a clear stand in favor of balancing the budget through draconian spending cutbacks. It was a "riverboat gamble" that did not pay out. Supporters and beneficiaries of the programs targeted for cutbacks (even if only in projected or baseline spending) were able to ward off most of the proposed reductions. Budgets are not balanced in the abstract. When budget balancing involves major changes in the scope of government and the reorientation of public policy, as it did in 1995, much resistance is predictable.

Notes

1. Louis Fisher, *The Politics of Shared Power: Congress and the Executive,* 3rd ed. (Washington: CQ Press, 1993), p. 133.
2. Gordon McKay Stevenson, Jr., *The Politics of Airport Noise* (Belmont, Calif.: Duxbury Press, 1972).
3. Sidney A. Shapiro, "Lessons from a Public Policy Failure: EPA and Noise Abatement," *Ecology Law Quarterly,* Vol. 19, no. 1 (1992), p. 1062.
4. Hugh Heclo, "Executive Budget Making," in Gregory B. Mills and John L. Palmer, eds., *Federal Budget Policy in the 1980s* (Washington: Urban Institute Press, 1984), pp. 255–291.
5. Cf. James L. True, "Is the National Budget Controllable?" *Public Budgeting and Finance,* Vol. 15 (Summer 1995), pp. 18–32.
6. R. Kent Weaver, *Automatic Government: The Politics of Indexation* (Washington: Brookings Institution, 1988).
7. Lance L. LeLoup, *Budgetary Politics,* 2nd ed. (Brunswick, Ohio: King's Court Communications, 1980), p. 200.
8. Howard E. Shuman, *Politics and the Budget,* 2nd ed. (Englewood Cliffs, N.J.: Prentice-Hall, 1988), p. 79.
9. The classic statement of incremental budgeting is Aaron Wildavsky, *The Politics of the Budgetary Process* (Boston: Little, Brown, 1964).
10. Irene S. Rubin, *The Politics of Public Budgeting,* 2nd ed. (Chatham, N.J.: Chatham House, 1993), pp. 113–114.
11. Allen Schick, "Incremental Budgeting in a Decremental Age," in Albert C. Hyde, ed., *Government Budgeting: Theory, Process, Politics* (Pacific Grove, Calif.: Brooks/Cole, 1992), pp. 410–425.
12. This discussion draws on Allen Schick, *The Federal Budget: Politics, Policy, Process* (Washington: Brookings Institution, 1995), pp. 20–24.

13. Allen Schick, *The Capacity to Budget* (Washington: Urban Institute Press, 1990), p. 99.
14. Andrew Taylor, "Congress Hands President a Budgetary Scalpel," *Congressional Quarterly Weekly Report*, Vol. 56 (March 30, 1996), pp. 864–867.
15. R. W. Apple, Jr., "Line-Item Veto Is a Great Unknown," *The New York Times*, March 27, 1996, p. 1.
16. *The New York Times*, March 27, 1996, p. 1.
17. John W. Ellwood and James A. Thurber, "The Politics of the Congressional Budget Process Re-Examined," in Lawrence C. Dodd and Bruce I. Oppenheimer, eds., *Congress Reconsidered*, 2nd ed. (Washington: Congressional Quarterly Press, 1981), pp. 247–251.
18. John Cranford, *Budgeting for America*, 2nd ed. (Washington: Congressional Quarterly Press, 1989), pp. 197–198.
19. Ibid., p. 200.
20. *Budget of the United States Government*, Fiscal Year 1989 (Washington: U.S. Government Printing Office, 1988), p. 6e.
21. Committee on Appropriations, "Agriculture, Rural Development, Food and Drug Administration, and Related Agencies Appropriations Bill, 1996," House Report 172, 104th Cong., 1st Sess., 1995, p. 39.
22. For fuller discussions, see Louis Fisher, *Presidential Spending Power* (Princeton: Princeton University Press, 1975), chaps. 7–8; and James P. Pfiffner, *The President, the Budget, and Congress: Impoundment and the 1974 Budget Act* (Boulder, Colo.: Westview Press, 1979).
23. Fisher, op. cit., p. 176.
24. Louis Fisher, *Constitutional Conflicts Between Congress and the President*, 3rd ed., rev. (Lawrence: University Press of Kansas, 1991), pp. 196–198.
25. *Immigration and Naturalization Service* v. *Chadha*, 462 U.S. 919 (1983).
26. James A. Thurber, ed., *Rivals of Power: Presidential–Congressional Relations* (Washington: CQ Press, 1996), chap. 10.
27. Darrell M. West, *Congress and Economic Policymaking* (Pittsburgh: University of Pittsburgh Press, 1987), chap. 7.
28. *Bowsher* v. *Synar* (1986). Reported in *Congressional Quarterly Weekly Report*, Vol. 44 (July 12, 1986), p. 1582.
29. *Congressional Quarterly Weekly Report*, Vol. 45 (December 26, 1987), p. 3184.
30. The following account draws on Daniel P. Franklin, *Making Ends Meet: Congressional Budgeting in the Age of Deficits* (Washington: Congressional Quarterly Press, 1993); and *Congressional Quarterly Almanac 1990* (Washington: Congressional Quarterly Press, 1991), Vol. 46, pp. 111–178.
31. *Congressional Quarterly Weekly Report*, Vol. 51 (February 20, 1993), pp. 355–359.
32. *The New York Times*, June 5, 1993, p. 17; June 14, 1993, p. A1.
33. *Congressional Quarterly Almanac 1993* (Washington, D.C.: Congressional Quarterly Press, 1994), Vol. 49, pp. 107–124.
34. *Congressional Quarterly Weekly Report*, June 24, 1995, p. 1814.
35. *The New York Times*, November 17, 1995, p. A14.
36. *The New York Times*, December 7, 1995, pp. 1, A14.
37. For accounts of some of the negotiations, see Elizabeth Drew, *Showdown: The Struggle Between the Gingrich Congress and the Clinton White House* (New

York: Simon & Schuster, 1996), chaps. 16–24; and Michael Weisskopf and David Maraniss, "Behind the Stage: Common Problems," *Washington Post National Weekly Edition*, February 5–11, 1996, pp. 9–13.

38. *Congressional Quarterly Weekly Report*, Vol. 54 (April 27, 1996), pp. 1155-1162.

39. Aaron Wildavsky, *The New Politics of the Budgetary Process* (Glenview, Ill.: Scott, Foresman, 1988), p. 253.

6

POLICY
IMPLEMENTATION

*Policy implementation at the grass-roots level: Customs Service agents seize a
shipment of illegal drugs.*

W hen the adoption phase of the policy process has been completed and, for instance, a bill has been enacted into law by a legislature, we can begin to refer to something called public policy. Policymaking is not concluded, however, once a policy decision has been expressed in statutory or other official form. The policies that are embodied in statutes, for example, often are rudimentary and require much additional development. Thus, the Americans with Disabilities Act of 1990, which prohibited discrimination against the 43 million Americans with disabilities, required extensive rulemaking to spell out its requirements by the Equal Employment Opportunity Commission, the Department of Transportation, the Department of Education, the Federal Communications Commission, and other agencies. Subsequently, they produced hundreds of pages of detailed rules in the *Federal Register*.[1]

With this qualification in mind, our attention now can turn to policy implementation (or administration), which can succinctly be defined as "what happens after a bill becomes law." It consists of those players, organizations, procedures, techniques, and target groups (for example, beneficiaries or regulated firms) that are involved in carrying policies, whether of legislative, executive, or judicial origin, into effect in an endeavor to accomplish their goals.[2] The uncertainty that typically prevails concerning what a policy will accomplish and the consequences that it will have for society makes the study of policy implementation both interesting and worthwhile from a policy-studies perspective. Policy implementation is neither a routine nor a highly predictable process.

In actuality it is frequently difficult, sometimes impossible, to neatly separate a policy's adoption from its implementation. Here again we may find that the line between functional activities is smudgy. Statutes sometimes do not do much beyond setting some policy goals and creating a framework of guidelines and restrictions for their realization. Congress usually does not attempt to define fully the intended impact of a law nor try to anticipate all of the problems and situations that may be encountered in its implementation.[3] Even the goals of a statute may not be clearly or consistently specified, as we saw in Chapter 4 in the case of the Civil Aeronautics Act.

Administrative agencies are often assigned much discretion or latitude to issue rules and directives that will fill in the details of policy and make it more specific. The Occupational Safety and Health Act of 1970 exemplifies this pattern. Although the right of workers to a safe and healthful workplace is generally guaranteed, the statute itself does not contain substantive health and safety standards. Rather, the Occupational Safety and Health Administration (OSHA), a bureau in the Department of Labor, is authorized to promulgate rules creating specific health and safety standards. Only as this occurs do we have meaningful and enforceable standards that can be applied to protect workers' health and safety. In effect, within the framework provided by Congress, OSHA both makes and implements policy on industrial health and safety. Different units within OSHA handle the tasks of rulemaking and enforcement.

Much that occurs during policy implementation may appear to be routine, tedious, or mundane, and may be performed with limited awareness of it by the public. Nonetheless, the consequences of implementation for the substance or content of policy may be every bit as important as what happens at the adoption stage. Moreover, closer examination reveals that strong, and sometimes bitter, political struggles attend the implementation of many policies, such as those pertaining to environmental protection, equal employment opportunity, and the management of the nation's public lands and forests. Groups that suffer losses in the legislature, for example, may seek to recoup some of their losses by influencing or disrupting the administration of a policy. Thus were automobile manufacturers able to delay for decades the National Highway Traffic Safety Administration's air-bag requirement.

A few policy decisions are essentially self-executing, such as the national government's refusal to extend formal recognition to the government of a foreign country, presidential decisions to veto legislation passed by Congress (especially when it involves a pocket veto), and the National Parks Service's decision in the early 1970s not to fight fires caused by lightning in the national parks. Such decisions, entailing clear-cut, one-time actions are relatively few, however. Those who study public policy, consequently, can ill afford to neglect the implementation stage of the policy process.

Until the great expansion of social-welfare programs during the Johnson years focused their attention on implementation (the term began to gain currency in the 1960s), it had not been of much interest to most political and social scientists.[4] The study of implementation was made salient for political scientists by Professors Jeffrey L. Pressman and Aaron Wildavsky's *Implementation,* a case study of the failure in the early 1970s of a federal jobs-creation project undertaken by the Economic Development Administration in Oakland, California.[5] Since that seminal event, political scientists have expended much effort researching the implementation of public policies, debating whether policies can be successfully implemented (or administered), and, finally, striving to build systematic theories that will rigorously explain why some policies are likely to be more successfully implemented than others. They have yet to strike theoretical pay dirt, such as identifying the variables critical to successful implementation. Their labors, however, have produced a mound of implementation literature and increased our understanding of the implementation process.[6]

Most of the implementation studies take either a "top-down" or "bottom-up" approach.[7] Top-downers focus on the actions of top-level officials, the factors affecting their behavior, whether policy goals are attained, and whether policy was reformulated on the basis of experience. Bottom-uppers contend that this approach gives too much attention to top-level officials and either ignores or underestimates the efforts of lower-level (or "street-level") officials to either avoid policy or divert it to their own purposes. Implementation studies, they argue, should focus on lower-level officials and how they interact with their clients. State and local economic conditions, the attitudes of local officials, and the actions of clients are among the factors affecting implementation. As one would expect, there have also been efforts to combine these two approaches. Agreement has not been reached, however, on what is the best way to study implementation.

In this chapter, though I draw generally on this implementation literature, I have decided to take a more traditional tack in discussing policy implementation. The chapter opens with a survey of some of the players in policy implementation. Then the focus narrows to administrative agencies. Administrative structures, politics, policymaking patterns, and implementation techniques are taken up in that order. These can be viewed as independent variables that condition and affect the outcomes and success of implementation. The concluding section on compliance with policy is concerned with the responses of those who are benefited or regulated by agencies' programs. The goal of this chapter is to provide the reader with a working knowledge of the politics and processes of policy implementation, and some tools for their analysis.

WHO IMPLEMENTS POLICY?

In the United States, as in other modern political systems, policy implementation is formally the province of a complex array of administrative agencies, now often referred to as bureaucracies, a term that carries both descriptive and pejorative connotations.[8] Administrative agencies collect taxes; operate the postal system, prisons, and schools; regulate banks, utility companies, and agricultural production; construct and maintain streets and highways; inspect food, meat, water, and drugs to ensure their safety; provide medical benefits and services; and perform many other tasks of modern governments. Because they perform most of the day-to-day work of government, their actions affect citizens more regularly and directly than those of other governmental bodies. Nevertheless, policy students would not need to spend much time fretting about implementation except that agencies usually have much discretion (that is, leeway or the opportunity to choose among alternatives) in carrying out policies under their jurisdiction. Although at one time it was widely believed that agencies automatically applied policies adopted by legislatures and executives, this is not generally the case, except in such matters as the sale of postage stamps and the printing of money.

A classic feature of the traditional literature of public administration was the notion that politics and administration were separate and distinct spheres of activity. Politics, wrote Professor Frank Goodnow in 1900, dealt with formulating the will of the state, with making value judgments, and with determining what government should or should not do. It was to be handled by the "political" branches of government—that is, the legislature and the executive.[9] Administration, on the other hand, was concerned with implementing the will of the state, with carrying into effect the decisions of the political branches. Administration dealt with questions of fact, with what is rather than what should be, and consequently could focus on identifying the most efficient means (or "one best way") of implementing policy. Were this viewpoint indeed accurate, policy analysts could end their inquiry with the adoption of policy.

Administrative agencies often are provided with broad and ambiguous statutory mandates that leave them with much discretion to decide what should or should not be done on some matter. Thus, the National Labor Relations Board is directed to ensure that labor and management bargain in "good faith"; the Federal Communications Commission, to license television broadcasters for the "public interest, convenience and necessity"; the Forest Service, to follow a "multiple-use" policy in managing the national forests that balances the interests of lumber companies, sportsmen and sportswomen, livestock grazers, and other users; the Consumer Product Safety Commission, to ban products that present an "unreasonable hazard"; and the Environmental Protection Agency (EPA), to ensure that the "best available technology economically achievable" is used to control water pollution. Such statutory mandates are essentially directives to the agencies involved to go out and make some policy. Moreover, because they possess discretion, they become the political targets of pressure groups and others seeking to influence their decisions. Consequently, agencies become embroiled in politics.

Frequently those who participate in the legislative process are unable or unwilling to arrive at precise settlements of the conflicting interests on many issues. Only by leaving some matters nebulous and unsettled can agreement on legislation be reached. Lack of time, interest, information, and expertness as well as the need for flexibility in implementation may also help explain the delegation of broad authority to agencies. The product of these factors is a statute couched in general language, such as that mentioned above, which shifts to agencies the tasks of filling in the details, making policy more precise and concrete, and trying to make more definitive adjustments among conflicting interests. Under these conditions, the administrative process becomes an extension of the legislative process.

Although legislatures have delegated much policymaking authority to administrative agencies, especially in the twentieth century, it should not be assumed that legislatures cannot act with specificity. An illustration is Social Security legislation, which sets forth in explicit terms the standards for eligibility, the levels of benefits, the amount of additional earnings permitted, and other considerations for old-age and survivors' benefits. Most administrative decisions on application for these benefits simply involve applying the legislatively set standards to the facts of the case at hand, and deciding whether an applicant is entitled to retirement benefits, and, if so, what the level of benefits should be. Under such circumstances, administrative decision-making becomes mostly routine and is therefore unlikely to produce controversy. In comparison, the disability standard under the Social Security program has produced considerable controversy. Disability is loosely defined as the inability to engage in any substantial gainful activity by reason of a medically determinable physical or mental impairment expected to result in death or to last at least twelve months. This definition leaves much room for interpretation, conjecture, and disagreement.[10] Thousands of cases involving the denial of disability benefits have been litigated in the federal courts.

Although administrative agencies are the primary implementers of public policy, many other players may also be involved and contribute in various ways to the execution of policies. Those examined here include the legislature, the courts, pressure groups, and community organizations. These may be directly involved in policy implementation or act to influence administrative agencies, or both. By no means are agencies fully in control of the implementation process. Here again, we find the sharing of power in the American political system.

The Legislature

Legislative bodies display much interest in the implementation of policies and use several techniques to influence administrative action. Indeed, Professor Theodore Lowi argues that "the major problem and major focus of Congress is no longer simply that of prescribing the behavior of citizens but more often that of affecting the behavior of administrators."[11] Here I will note some of the techniques that are available to Congress.

One such control device is the specificity of legislation. The more detailed the legislation that Congress passes, the less discretion agencies usually will have. Specific limitations on the use of funds may be written into statutes, or deadlines may be specified for some actions, as has been done in some environmental-protection laws; "hammers," or stringent rules or requirements, may be incorporated in a law, to go into effect if an agency does not act with alacrity or effectiveness; or specific standards may be set, as in minimum-wage legislation. The committee reports that accompany many bills often include suggestions or statements explaining how legislation should be implemented or specifying projects that money should go for. These reports do not have the force of law but are ignored by administrators only at their own peril.

Senatorial approval, which is required for many top-level executive appointments, provides senators with a lever that can be used to influence policy. Commitments on policy matters may be extracted by senators from nominees during hearings on their appointment. Or a nominee for a position may be rejected because some senators find objectionable his or her policy views or actions. In 1993 President Bill Clinton nominated law professor Lani Guinier to head the Justice Department Civil Rights Division. Drawing on statements made in her legal writings, Senate conservatives attacked Guinier as being radical and extremist in some of her views on civil-rights issues. She suggested, for example, that cumulative voting (which had been used for several decades in the state of Illinois) might be used to increase black representation in legislative bodies and that legislative procedures might be modified to enhance minority impacts on decisions. When moderate Democrats also began to express doubts about the viability of Guinier's nomination, it was withdrawn by President Clinton, to the dismay of many liberals and civil-rights groups.[12] Thus the Senate can help determine who occupies leadership positions in the implementation process.

The legislative veto is an arrangement under which either congressional approval has to be secured before an administrative action can be taken or a specific action can be subsequently rejected by Congress or its committees; the veto originated in 1932. President Herbert Hoover wanted authority to reorganize the national administrative system but Congress was reluctant to grant it. A deal was made. The president was authorized to reorganize the system, but Congress gave itself the right to disapprove his actions if it deemed them objectionable. Since then, and especially in the 1960s and 1970s, provisions for legislative-veto arrangements were included in over two hundred laws. The legislative veto gives administrative agencies the desired flexibility in the implementation of legislation while permitting Congress, if it so chooses, to exercise control over what is done. It also enables Congress to become involved in the details of administration.[13]

As reported in Chapter 5, the Supreme Court declared the legislative veto unconstitutional in 1983. Nonetheless, between then and the end of 1991, more than two hundred new legislative-veto provisions were included in laws. Others have been put in place by informal agreements between Congress and the executive.[14] An agreement on aid to the Nicaraguan "Contras" (rebels) negotiated by Bush administration officials and congressional leaders gave each of four congressional committees a veto over the program. Had this not been done, Congress might not have passed legislation authorizing the program. The legislative veto persists because both the executive and legislative branches find that it serves their interests.

Finally, much of the time of many members of Congress and their staffs, and some of the time of all members, is devoted to "casework."[15] Typically, casework involves handling problems that constituents have with administrative agencies, such as delayed Social Security or veterans' benefits, difficulty in getting action on a license request, or uncertainty about how to apply for a grant. The constituents, of course, want their representatives to secure favorable action for them. Members of Congress engage in casework because it is thought helpful to their chances of reelection and because it contributes to their oversight of agencies. Beyond that, the practice helps "humanize" administration by making it more responsive to individual needs and problems. As for agency officials, responsiveness to congressional inquiries is seen both as appropriate and as a means of building or maintaining political support.

The Courts

Some legislation is enforced primarily through judicial action. Laws dealing with crimes are the most obvious example. Some economic regulatory statutes, such as the Sherman Act, are enforced by lawsuits brought in the federal district courts, some of which are eventually appealed to the Supreme Court. Because of this tactic and the act's general language, the meaning of antitrust policy depends greatly upon judicial interpretation and application of the statute. In the nineteenth century, it was quite common for legislatures to enact laws requiring or prohibiting some action and then to leave it to the citizens to protect their rights under the law through proceedings brought in the courts. Generally, administrative regulation, in which primary responsibility is assigned to an agency for the enforcement of a statute, is now much more common than judicial regulation in the American political system.

In some instances, the courts may be directly involved in the administration of policy. Naturalization proceedings for aliens are really administrative in form, but they are handled by the federal district courts. Bankruptcy proceedings are another illustration. A complex system of trustees, receivers, appraisers, accountants, auctioneers, and others is supervised by federal bankruptcy courts. In all, it is "a large scale example of routine administrative machinery."[16] Many divorce and domestic-relations cases handled by state courts also appear essentially administrative, involving matters of guidance and management rather than disputed law or facts. There is no reason to assume that persons appointed or elected to judgeships are distinctly qualified to act in these matters.

The courts' most important influence on administration, however, flows from their interpretation of statutes and administrative rules and regulations, and their review of administrative decisions in cases brought before them. Courts can facilitate, hinder, or largely nullify implementation of a policy through their decisions. The story of how the Supreme Court destroyed the effectiveness of early national railroad regulation under the Interstate Commerce Act of 1887 by unfavorable rulings on the ICC's authority to regulate rates is well-recorded history. In recent years the Supreme Court's rulings have complicated and restricted the enforcement of equal-opportunity and affirmative-action programs. For instance, in 1995 the Court ruled that to be constitutional, an affirmative action program had to be "narrowly tailored" to meet "a compelling government interest." A Colorado program providing for the award of a portion of highway construction projects to minority contractors was struck down because it failed to square with this standard.[17]

Pressure Groups

Because of the discretion often vested in agencies by legislation, once an act is adopted the group struggle shifts from the legislative to the administrative arena. Given the operating discretion of many agencies, a group that can successfully influence agency action may have a substantial effect on the course and impact of public policies. Sometimes relationships between a group and an agency may become so close as to lead to the allegation that the group has "captured" the agency. In the past it was frequently stated that the ICC was the captive of the railroads,[18] and it is not uncommon now to hear comments to the effect that the Federal Maritime Commission is unduly influenced by the shipping companies and that the Forest Service is too responsive to the interests of commercial timber companies. Also, groups may complain to Congress or the executive if they believe a statute is not being implemented in accordance with the intent of Congress (as they interpret it).

Groups also directly participate in administration, as when the representation of particular interests is specified for the boards of plural-headed agencies. A common illustration is state occupational licensing boards, whose governing statutes frequently provide that some or all of the board members must come from the licensed profession. Occupational licensing (and regulatory) programs are usually controlled by the dominant elements within the licensed groups. Consequently, such programs may do more to protect the interests of the licensed group than those of the general public.

Advisory bodies, such as the Advisory Committee on Vocational Education, the Advisory Committee on Hog Cholera Eradication, and the Advisory

Committee on Reactor Safeguards, are another means by which groups may become participants in policy administration. Currently around a thousand advisory groups serve national administrative agencies.[19] Some simply provide needed advice to agencies and their officials, as their name implies; others become more directly involved in program administration. Membership in advisory bodies may give group representatives privileged or special access to governmental agencies. Thus many large defense contractors are represented on advisory committees for the Department of Defense. When advisory groups have a role in agency decision-making, they add legitimacy to the policies that they have helped to develop.[20]

Some advisory committees may have direct control over program administration. Each of the eleven institutes within the National Institutes of Health (NIH) has a twelve-member advisory council. Committee members must be leaders in science, medicine, and public affairs, including six who are specialists in the field covered by a particular institute (e.g., cancer, aging, or allergy and infectious diseases). Research grants to medical schools, universities, and others, which total around $6 billion annually, can be made only after review and approval by each institute's advisory council. This is intended to ensure that grants meet both scientific norms and public-policy criteria.[21]

Community Organizations

At the local level, community and other organizations occasionally have been used in the administration of national policies. Examples include farmer committees under the price-support and soil-conservation programs of the Department of Agriculture; advisory boards for the Bureau of Land Management; and representatives of the poor for Community Action agencies. Participatory democracy of this sort may give those involved considerable influence over application of programs at the grass-roots level and also build program support. Local draft boards ("little groups of neighbors," as they were sometimes called) had a vital role during the Vietnam War years in determining, when only a portion of eligible males were required to meet military needs, who got drafted and who did not.[22] Many losers in the draft wound up in Vietnam. The compulsory draft and draft boards were later eliminated, although eligible males are still required to register with the Selective Service System.

In sum, a variety of participants may have a hand in administration of a given policy. In addition to those discussed above, political-party officials, the communications media (by reporting, publicizing, or criticizing an agency's actions), and executive-staff agencies may also get involved. Certainly this is true of the Office of Management and Budget (OMB), whose involvement extends much beyond funding. Since 1981, for example, the OMB has had authority to supervise the issuance of economic rules and regulations by executive-branch regulatory agencies. (More will be said on this subject in Chapter 7.) The number and variety of participants in implementation will vary from one policy area to another, depending upon the policy's salience and the extent of its impact.

ADMINISTRATIVE ORGANIZATION

One could say that one administrative agency looks pretty much like another or, if you have seen one agency, you have seen them all. Such a notion, however, is badly mistaken. Agencies in fact do differ greatly in structure, operating style, political support, expertness, and policy orientation. Those who want to influence the nature of public policy often are much interested in the agency or type of agency that will administer a policy. Conflict over questions of administrative organization can be every bit as sharp as conflict over substantive policies. Forming administrative organizations is a political as well as a technical task. As a longtime observer of administration has remarked:

> Organizational arrangements are not neutral. We do not organize in a vacuum. Organization is one way of expressing national commitments, influencing program direction, and ordering priorities. Organizational arrangements tend to give some interests and perspectives more effective access to those with decision-making authority, whether they be in the Congress or in the executive branch.[23]

The national executive branch comprises approximately seventy-five separate administrative entities and three million civilian employees, most of whom are covered by merit systems. Basically, there are four kinds of agencies: executive departments, independent regulatory commissions, government corporations, and independent agencies. They are listed in the historical order in which they appeared in the national administrative system.

The fourteen executive departments—State, Defense, Commerce, Health and Human Services, to name a few—constitute the core of the executive branch. At the helm of an executive department is a presidentially appointed secretary who has cabinet rank and who is assisted in running it by various under-, deputy, and assistant secretaries. These are also political appointees, whose number has expanded in recent decades.[24] Most of the work of the departments in implementing programs and policies is handled by major administrative units that can generally be designated as "bureaus." Thus, in the Department of Justice, one finds bureaus such as the Federal Bureau of

Investigation, the Bureau of Prisons, the Drug Enforcement Administration, the Civil Rights Division, the Antitrust Division, and the Immigration and Naturalization Service. Because of their typically short tenure in office and lack of technical knowledge, the political appointees at the top levels of a department are often hard pressed to exercise effective control and direction of its bureaus.

Independent regulatory commissions are plural-headed agencies that engage in the regulation of private economic activities, such as stock markets, banks, or labor–management relations. Examples include the Securities and Exchange Commission, the Federal Reserve Board, the National Labor Relations Board, and the Nuclear Regulatory Commission. Appointed by the president for fixed, staggered terms of office, only a majority of a commission can come from the same political party. Unlike department secretaries, who serve for "the time being" and can be fired by the president whenever he chooses, regulatory commissioners can be removed only for such specified causes as malfeasance, inefficiency, and neglect of duties. Thus, as a practical matter, the independent regulatory commissions, which handle a significant share of the government's regulatory programs, are somewhat free from presidential control and direction. This is one reason why Congress has created them. On the other hand, the President can bring the commissions under his sway by appointing commissioners who share his policy preferences.

Government corporations, which first became a part of the executive branch during the World War I era, are sometimes set up to handle business-like or commercial activities for the government. Prominent examples are the United States Postal Service, the Tennessee Valley Authority, and the Federal Deposit Insurance Corporation. Wholly owned by the government, they look pretty much like other government agencies, but they have greater operating flexibility in financial and personnel matters. Typically, they impose fees or charges for the goods or services that they provide.

Independent agencies number in the forties and, like independent and regulatory commissions and government corporations, are located outside of the executive departments. Some are large, well known, and important, such as the National Aeronautics and Space Administration, the Environmental Protection Agency, and the Central Intelligence Agency; others are smaller and somewhat obscure, such as the National Mediation and Conciliation Service, the Railroad Retirement Board, and the National Credit Union Administration. A variety of factors has contributed to their establishment. Some would not fit well into the executive departments (such as NASA and EPA); others have watchdog or review duties (such as the Occupational Safety and Health Review Commission); still others provide services to a variety of agencies (such as the Office of Personnel Management); and some provide special notice for programs (such the Peace Corps and the Commission on Civil Rights). Although all are subject to presidential control, much of what many of them do is not of presidential interest.

Responsibility for implementing public policies is now usually assigned to existing agencies. Occasionally, however, a new agency is created for this purpose, usually by legislative action. In other instances, new agencies have been created by the executive under administrative reorganization authority, which permitted the president to propose reorganization plans that went into effect automatically unless disapproved by either house of Congress. The EPA, which was established by a Nixon administration proposal for reorganization in 1970, now handles environmental protection activities formerly scattered among a number of agencies. The effect has given sharper focus to the administration of antipollution policies. A few other agencies—such as ACTION, which administers some volunteer-service programs, and the Health Care Financing Administration in the Department of Health and Human Services—have been set up through the use of broad substantive authority delegated by Congress to executive officials.

The policy implications of administrative organization are the main focus of this section. Several propositions will be presented and illustrated to indicate how organizational considerations affect policy implementation, and thus why they should receive attention from policy analysts.

1. When a new program is adopted, the contending interests may seek to have its administration awarded to an agency they think will be more favorable to their interests. A major controversy during the enactment of the Occupational Safety and Health Act, the first major general industrial safety law passed by Congress, focused on the question of who should administer it. Organized labor and most liberal Democrats favored locating all standard-setting and enforcement activity in the Department of Labor, which they regarded as sympathetic toward labor. Many Republicans, the Nixon administration, and business groups wanted an independent board (or boards) to make and enforce standards, to avoid Labor Department control of the program. The result was a compromise. The Department of Labor was given authority to set standards, to enforce them, and to assess penalties. Within the department these tasks are handled by OSHA. An independent three-member, quasi-judicial Occupational Safety and Health Review Commission was created to hear appeals from Labor Department enforcement actions. The National Institute for Occupational Safety and Health was established within the Department of Health, Education, and Welfare (now Health and Human Services) to conduct research and create an information base for health standards. Both organized labor and business expressed satisfaction with this administrative arrangement. Soon OSHA became a highly controversial agency because of some of its rule-making and enforcement actions. The penalties it has imposed frequently have been reduced when appealed to the review commission.

In 1953, an independent Small Business Administration (SBA) was set up to handle assistance programs for small business, after the Eisenhower administration dismantled the Reconstruction Finance Corporation. Some argued that control of such programs rested properly with the Department of

Commerce, but small-business interests and their congressional supporters contended that the Department of Commerce was too heavily oriented toward big business to satisfactorily administer small-business programs. Although the Reagan administration several times called for the abolition of SBA, small-business groups and their congressional allies successfully fended off these assaults. The Office of Economic Opportunity (OEO) was likewise given primary control of administering the War on Poverty, partly because it was thought that old-line agencies like the Departments of Labor and Health, Education, and Welfare would not be sufficiently sympathetic and vigorous. "The best way to kill a new idea," President Lyndon Johnson remarked, "is to put it in an old-line agency."[25] OEO was later abolished because of extensive criticism of its activities. Several of its programs still exist and are administered by other agencies.

2. Administrative organization may also be used to emphasize the need for action or to facilitate action on particular policy problems. The Kennedy administration established the Arms Control and Disarmament Agency to handle the topics named in its title and to symbolize the abandonment of the visionary goal of total disarmament.[26] The agency, however, has never been the lead player in developing arms-control policy because of competition from the Departments of State and Defense as well as national security advisers to the President.

To coordinate national drug policy, Congress established in 1989 the Office of National Drug Control Policy in the Executive Office of the President. Various duties were assigned to the agency, including development of an annual national drug-control strategy. Early in his administration, President Bush appointed William Bennett, a formerly controversial secretary of education, to lead the drug agency. Bennett was quickly designated "Drug Czar," although he did not have directive power over agencies enforcing the laws against drug trafficking.[27] The effectiveness of the new agency, whatever its symbolic value, has been problematical. It was much reduced in size by the Clinton Administration.

Some of the congressional supporters of the conversion of the Veterans Administration, an independent agency, into the cabinet-level Department of Veterans Affairs, with a revamped internal structure, hoped that this would result in improved implementation of veterans benefits programs. The veterans lobby, in contrast, viewed departmental status for "their agency" as an appropriate way to acknowledge veterans' contributions to the nation's security and well-being.[28]

3. The internal structure of an agency may be contrived to help secure desired action. Take the case of the National Institutes of Health, which were set up within the Department of Health, Education, and Welfare in the 1950s. It would have been quite logical to have named the various institutes according to the kind of research they would support, such as pathology, microbiology, biochemistry, and genetics; that is how university research centers are

usually organized. Instead, among the institutes established were the National Cancer Institute, the National Heart and Lung Institute, and the National Institute of Arthritis and Metabolic Diseases. The reasoning was that, although it might be easy for members of Congress to vote against an appropriation for microbiology, they would be highly reluctant to vote against funds for cancer or heart research. This strategy has proved effective, for Congress consistently provides more funds for the NIH than are requested by executive budget officials. When new institutes are set up, they too focus on particular health problems or ailments.

Another example is the 1985 legislation that Congress adopted reorganizing the Department of Defense because of congressional beliefs that the parochial perspectives of the various armed services impeded interservice coordination and prevented the president from getting coherent military advice. Consequently, the chairman of the Joint Chiefs of Staff was named as the principal military adviser to the president, whereas previously this responsibility was held collectively by the Joint Chiefs. The chairman was also given control over the Joint Staff. Another significant change gave the seven commanders-in-chief, who were responsible for directing multiservice operations in many geographic areas, more authority over their units. The intent was to lessen control by the individual services over units assigned to the area commanders-in-chief. In all, the 1985 law was designed to strengthen the "joint" side of the Pentagon.[29]

4. Congress has established independent regulatory commissions, such as the ICC, the Federal Reserve Board, and the Commodity Futures Trading Commission, in order to reduce presidential control of the implementation of some regulatory programs. Ten regulatory commissions now reside in the national administrative system. The ICC was abolished in 1995 and its remaining duties were assigned to a new Surface Transportation Board in the Department of Transportation.

Progressive Era political theory held that the independent-commission device was a way of taking regulation "out of politics" and handling it in a scientific manner (that is, expert, informed, and impartial). Other factors have since gained more weight in congressional decisions to set up commissions—namely, institutional rivalry between president and Congress, partisan differences between the two branches, and a desire to disrupt clientele ties between executive departmental bureaus and interest groups.[30] It is not fully clear, however, why Congress sometimes sets up independent regulatory commissions and at other times relies on bureaus in executive departments to implement regulatory programs.

5. Once a group has developed a satisfactory, if not ideal, relationship with an agency or a program, it will resist changes in the agency's organizational location that might disrupt the relationship or weaken the program. Thus, banking groups have opposed consolidating the regulatory functions of the Office of the Controller of the Currency, the Federal Reserve Board, and

the Federal Deposit Insurance Corporation in a single banking regulatory agency, believing that the current fragmented implementation structure works to their advantage.

Under the Carter administration's plan for the new Department of Education, the Indian education program was to be transferred to it from the Bureau of Indian Affairs (BIA) in the Department of the Interior. Various Indian groups, although not fully satisfied with the operation of the BIA, feared that the transfer would contribute to the breakup of the BIA. They worried also that Indian education might become a minor program in the new department. Motivated by these concerns, they succeeded in blocking the transfer.[31]

Such opposition to program relocation does not always succeed, however. Scientific and higher-education organizations opposed a proposal to shift most funding for science education from the National Science Foundation (NSF) to the Department of Education. They were afraid that their interests, well represented in the NSF, would be swamped in the new department because of its many programs. They did not prevail.[32]

As a corollary to the fifth point, congressional committees typically oppose shifts that will remove an agency or program from a committee's jurisdiction and thus reduce its power. The Agriculture Committees have fended off efforts to move the multibillion-dollar food-stamp program, which is clearly a social-welfare program, from the Department of Agriculture to the Department of Health and Human Services, which would provide a more logical home for it. Control of the program is important because of the large amount of money involved. It is also quite useful to the Agriculture Committees for bargaining and coalition building with urban interests for support of general farm legislation.[33] Such committee and subcommittee preferences for continued influence over "their" agencies thus lends some rigidity to national administrative organization.

7. Those who support a program may seek to have it moved to another department or agency to avoid hostile or unfavorable handling of it. Conversely, opponents of a current program may seek to lessen its influence, or even kill it, by getting it reassigned to a hostile agency. A classic illustration of the first possibility is the Forest Service, transferred early in this century from the Department of the Interior to the Department of Agriculture at the insistence of conservationists. According to Gifford Pinchot, "The national forest idea ran counter to the whole tradition of the Interior Department. Bred into its marrow, bone, and fiber, was the idea of disposing of the public lands to private owners."[34] In Chapter 3 we saw, too, how supporters of mine safety regulation have tried to get better enforcement by moving the program to a new agency in the Department of the Interior and then later to another new agency in the Department of Labor.

Viewed as a course of action, the substance of policy is affected by how it is implemented. How it is implemented, in turn, is thought to depend upon which agency implements it. Determining which agency should implement a program, or where the agency should be located, is more than a technical matter; it is also a political issue.

ADMINISTRATIVE POLITICS

A statute confers upon an agency only the legal authority to take action to implement policy on some topic. How effectively the agency carries out its legal mandate and what it actually does or does not accomplish will be substantially affected by the amount of cooperation and political support it gets, and, conversely, the political opposition it runs into. To put it differently, an agency dwells and acts in a political milieu that affects how it exercises its discretion and carries out its programs.

The environments of some agencies are more political, more volatile, and more tumultuous than those of others. The Bureau of Engraving and Printing and the U.S. Geological Survey lead much more serene political lives than do the Federal Reserve Board and the Consumer Product Safety Commission. But whatever the conditions, the environment in which an agency exists may contain many forces that may, at one time or another, impinge on it and help give direction to its actions in multitudinous ways.[35] These forces may arise out of the following sources.

THE "BASIC RULES OF THE GAME"   Included here are the relevant laws, rules, and regulations, accepted modes of procedure, and concepts of fair play that help form and guide official behavior and to which officials are expected to conform. Public opinion and group pressures may focus adversely on officials who violate the rules of the game, as by appearing or proposing not to enforce a statutory provision or by enticing persons to violate a law so that they can be prosecuted. Officials who are overly zealous in enforcing laws, who cite companies for too many minor violations of health or safety standards, may be seen as unreasonable zealots. Adverse executive or legislative action may stem from such criticism.

THE CHIEF EXECUTIVE   Most administrative agencies are located within the presidential chain of command or are otherwise subject to presidential control and direction in such matters as personnel appointments, budget recommendations, expenditure controls, and policy directives. The presidential chain of command includes agencies and officials in the Executive Office of the President and top-level political appointees (e.g., secretaries and assistant secretaries) in the departments and agencies. Control and direction are more likely to emanate from those who work for the president than from the president himself. Those who act for the president may or may not always act according to his preferences. There is sometimes suspicion, for example, that White House aides "go into business for themselves."

THE CONGRESSIONAL SYSTEM OF SUPERVISION   This supervisory system includes the standing committees and subcommittees, their chairs, committee staffs, and influential members of Congress. Congressional concern and influence is fragmented and sporadic rather than monolithic and continuous. It flows from parts of Congress, rarely from Congress as a whole, and focuses mostly on specific issues or controversies. Professional staff members handle much of the day-to-day congressional communication with agencies and may develop close working relationships with agency officials.

THE COURTS   Agencies may be strongly affected by the judiciary's use of its powers of judicial review and statutory interpretation. Agencies may have their statutory authority expanded or contracted by judicial interpretation, or their decisions may be overruled because improper procedures were employed in making them. OSHA and the Federal Trade Commission (FTC) have often had their actions challenged in the courts. Other agencies, such as the Federal Reserve Board and the Bureau of the Mint, have little contact with the courts because their operations do not give rise to issues of the sort normally handled by the judiciary.

OTHER ADMINISTRATIVE AGENCIES   Agencies with competing or overlapping jurisdictions may affect one another's operations. In drug-law enforcement, the Drug Enforcement Administration, the U.S. Coast Guard, the Customs Service, and other agencies engage in turf battles and compete for recognition and credit in making drug busts, sometimes appearing to lose sight of their main task.[36] Water agencies such as the Army Corps of Engineers and the Bureau of Reclamation have also been rivals for the right to control and construct water projects. Occasionally an agency may aspire to take over a program of another agency, and may succeed. Thus the Department of Labor acquired the Job Corps program, which was initially run by the Office of Economic Opportunity. Agency imperialism, however, is not as rampant as some commentators imply.[37] Some agencies may indeed form cooperative relationships, as have the FTC and the Antitrust Division of the Department of Justice in antitrust enforcement. An agency may even refuse to take a program from another agency. Stuart Udall, Secretary of the Interior during the Johnson administration, relates that he offered to give the Bureau of Indian Affairs Indian-education program to the Department of Health, Education, and Welfare so that its secretary, John Gardner, would have his own school system to run. Gardner refused the offer.[38]

OTHER GOVERNMENTS   State, municipal, and county governments, school districts, and associations of state and local officials (such as the National League of Cities) may attempt to influence a national agency's decisions. Associations of state highway officials are much interested in the activities of the Federal Highway Administration. The EPA encounters quite a lot of pressure, criticism, and resistance from state and local governments and environmental agencies in developing and implementing standards for pollution control. The effectiveness of many national programs depends upon how they are implemented by state and local agencies, which provides such governments with some leverage over their conduct.

INTEREST GROUPS The group context differs considerably from one agency to another. Some agencies, such as the Forest Service and the Food and Drug Administration (FDA), attract the attention of many groups, some supportive and others hostile. Buffeted by opposition, such agencies may move more cautiously than one that deals primarily with one group, such as the Department of Veterans Affairs. No matter what the FDA's decision is on an important issue, some groups probably will be sufficiently offended as to launch a judicial or legislative challenge. Other agencies, such as the Administrative Conference of the United States and the Railroad Retirement Board, experience few, if any, group pressures.

Agencies often actively seek group support (or consent) to increase the size, ease, or effectiveness of their operations. Advisory groups may be created, presentations made at group meetings by agency officials, and program modifications initiated in the quest for support.

POLITICAL PARTIES The role of the party organizations has declined in recent decades with the extension of the merit system of hiring to most agency personnel. Appointments to top-level agency positions, however, still may be influenced by considerations of party welfare and policy orientation. Because only a majority of the members of an independent regulatory commission can belong to the same political party, party affiliation is an explicit consideration in these appointments. Some agency actions may be influenced by an urge to enhance party success at the polls, as when the Reagan administration expanded the availability of agricultural loans in the months prior to the 1986 congressional elections.

COMMUNICATIONS MEDIA Beyond their use as forums for pressure groups, political parties, and others trying to influence an agency's action, the mass-communications media have an independent role. The media may play an important part in shaping public opinion toward an agency by revealing and publicizing its actions, favorably or unfavorably. For decades the Federal Bureau of Investigation was quite well treated by the press, although its problems in recent years have caused some decline in its support. In contrast, the political lives of OSHA and the Bureau of Alcohol, Tobacco, and Firearms have been made more difficult by the batterings they have received in the media. Also, it should be noted that agencies scrutinize the media in order to acquire information about the public and its preferences.

Specialized media too, mostly journals, newspapers, and newsletters, inform their clients and other interested persons about the operations of agencies or programs. These are increasingly more important for many agencies than are the more general media. This would be true of the Agricultural Marketing Service and the U.S. Fish and Wildlife Service. *Field and Stream* and *Outdoor Life* provide their readers with a particular slant on the U.S. Fish and Wildlife Service.

Each of the forces sketched above is multiple rather than monolithic. Conflicting viewpoints may be held by members in the same category as well as by those in different ones. Thus a number of political forces may impinge on an agency, pushing and pulling against each other with varying intensity, and growing and ebbing. Agencies of course are not simply sitting ducks but rather will try to shape, influence, and mollify the forces in their environment. Pressure relationships between an agency and those who seek to influence it are therefore usually reciprocal.

The field of forces surrounding an agency (as shown in Figure 6.1) will be drawn from the above categories and will form the constituency of the agency, that is, "any group, body, or interest to which [an administrator] looks for aid or guidance, or which seeks to establish itself as so important [in his judgment] that he 'had better' take account of its preferences even if he finds himself averse to those preferences."[39] Note that the concept of constituency is broader than that of clientele, which comprises the reasonably distinct set of individuals and groups directly served or regulated by an agency. Thus savings and loan associations are the clientele of the Office of Thrift Supervision; its constituency comprises a broader set of forces or stakeholders concerned with its operations.

The constituency of an agency is dynamic rather than static. Some constituents will be concerned with the agency only as certain issues arise or are settled; others will be more or less continually involved and will compose the stable core of the agency's constituency. The stable core of the Food Safety and Inspection Service (FSIS) in the Department of Agriculture includes commercial meat- and poultry-processing companies, the congressional Agriculture Committees, and the relevant appropriations subcommittees. The chief executive, the Food and Drug Administration, the communications media, and consumer groups are intermittently involved with the FSIS. All other things being equal, the constituents who continually interact with an agency are likely to have the most success in influencing the agency's action.

The character of an agency's constituency will affect its power relations and capacity to make policy decisions and carry those decisions into effect. The relationship of an agency to one part of its constituency will partially depend on the kinds of relationships it has with other parts. For example, an agency with strong presidential support can afford to be less responsive to pressure groups than an agency without such support. On the other hand, strong congressional and group support may lessen presidential influence, as with the Army Corps of Engineers.[40] An agency encountering criticism from

FIGURE 6.1 The Political Environment of an Agency

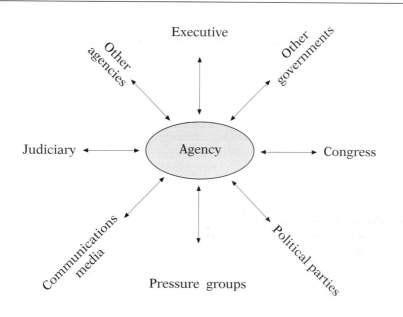

*Note: The two-headed arrows indicate that influence relationships may run in both directions.

state and local government officials may find that its congressional support also wanes as a consequence. In general, it can be said that an agency's policymaking and implementation activities will reflect the interests supported by the dominant elements within its constituency, whether they are hostile or supportive.

An agency's clientele is an important component of its constituency. Some agencies benefit from large, active clienteles, such as the Social Security Administration, the Small Business Administration, and the Department of Agriculture. But size alone is not enough. Consumers are a vast group, but because they tend to be poorly organized and lack self-consciousness as a group, they provide little support to consumer agencies such as the FDA and the Consumer Product Safety Commission. If the FDA has been unduly responsive to food and drug manufacturers, it is partly because it lacks consumer support and partly because the agency both needs the manufacturers' cooperation in the administration of its programs and encounters organized pressure from them. Some agencies have underprivileged or disadvantaged clienteles, such as the Legal Services Corporation, most welfare agencies, and the Federal Bureau of Prisons. The OEO was hindered in its efforts to administer the War on Poverty because its clientele, the poor and especially the black poor, were not a strong source of political support. An agency with a two-party constituency, such as the National Labor Relations Board, whose clientele includes labor union and management groups, may be able to maintain its independence by playing off one against the other.

Agencies providing services usually elicit more support from their clientele than do regulatory agencies. Most people obviously prefer receiving benefits to being restricted or controlled. An agency with a foreign clientele, such as the Agency for International Development, can draw little usable political support from its clientele. The lack of an internal clientele has clearly been disadvantageous for the foreign-aid program. Examining an agency's constituency and clientele can provide insight into, and explanation of, why an agency acts as it does. It should not, however, be assumed that an agency is an inert force at the mercy of its constituency or the dominant elements therein. Because of their expertise, organizational spirit, or administrative statecraft, agencies can exert some independent control over events and help determine the scope of their power.[41]

Any bureaucratic agency has some expertise in the performance of its assigned tasks, whether these entail garbage collection or the conduct of foreign policy. All bureaucratic skills, however, do not receive equal deference from society. Agencies whose expertise derives from the natural and physical ("hard") sciences will receive more deference than those drawing from the social sciences, which are less highly regarded in society. Compare, for example, the situations of the National Aeronautics and Space Administration and the National Cancer Institute with the Census Bureau and the Office of Family Assistance (Department of Health and Human Services). Considerable deference is shown to the military as "specialists in violence," and Congress often defers to the judgment of the Department of Defense and the Joint Chiefs of Staff in military and defense policy. Professional diplomats ("cookie pushers in striped pants"), on the other hand, no longer receive the deference in foreign policy that they once did. Power based on expertise may fluctuate as conditions and attitudes change.

Some agencies are more capable than others of generating interest in, and enthusiasm and commitment for, their programs from both their own members and the public. This condition is designated organizational esprit. Its existence depends upon an agency's capacity to develop "an appropriate ideology or sense of mission, both as a method of binding outsiders to the agency and as a technique for intensifying its employees' loyalty to its purposes."[42] The Marine Corps, Peace Corps, Forest Service, and EPA are served with considerable fervor and commitment by their members. Other agencies have displayed much zeal in their early years, only to ease into bureaucratic routines and stodginess as the years slip by. This decline has weakened some of the national independent regulatory commissions.

Leadership, or the ability Professor Francis E. Rourke calls "administrative statecraft,"[43] can also enhance an agency's power and effectiveness. A government agency's leadership, like that in all organizations, is situational, being shaped significantly by factors in the environment other than the leaders themselves. Nevertheless, leadership can still significantly influence the agency's operation and success. Some agency leaders are more effective than others in dealing with outside interest groups, cultivating congressional committees, opening the organization to new ideas, and communicating a sense of purpose to its personnel. The mid-1980s revitalization of the EPA following its decline in the early years of the Reagan administration was aided by the able leadership of William Ruckelshaus and Lee Thomas as successive administrators. James A. Baker, III, was a capable and vigorous secretary of the Treasury during Reagan's second term. Under Baker's skilled leadership the department had a major role in developing both domestic and international economic policy. President Reagan generally deferred to Baker's leadership, as on the 1985 decision to weaken the dollar and encourage exports, reduce imports, and lessen the balance-of-payments deficit. In the Bush administration, Baker won approval for his performance as Secretary of State.

ADMINISTRATIVE POLICYMAKING

As we saw in Chapter 3, administrative agencies frequently participate in policymaking at the legislative stage. Here our analytical lens shifts to the administrative arena, where administrative officials have the capacity to make decisions that shape policy, and are subject to influences radiating from their clienteles and constituencies. Something of a role reversal occurs for legislators who now act not as decision-makers, but as potential influencers of decisions. Agency policy-makers—political appointees and upper-level civil servants—occupy positions that convey discretion to them in the direction of the agency and its programs. Tension often exists between the civil servants—possessed by long service and experience in agency affairs—and political appointees who represent the victorious political party and sometimes manifest a desire to make substantial alterations in agency activities. Both differ greatly from the lower-level agency personnel a citizen is most likely to encounter—those selling stamps, guiding tours at national parks, handling customs matters at international airports, or processing Social Security documents. Not usually policy-makers, for them the line between politics and administration remains pretty distinct.

In this section, two aspects of agency policymaking are examined: the characteristics of agency decision-making and the processes by which an agency can develop policy. It is well to keep in mind here the distinction between a decision and a policy.

Decision-Making

Hierarchy is of central importance in agency decision-making. Although in legislatures each member has an equal vote, if not equal influence, within agencies those at upper levels have more authority over final decisions than the occupants of lower levels. To be sure, factors such as decentralization of authority, responsiveness of subunits to outside forces (such as pressure groups), and participation by professionals in administrative activity work against hierarchical authority, but hierarchy should nonetheless not be under-estimated. Complexity, size, and the desire for economical operation and more control over the bureaucratic apparatus all contribute to the develop-ment of hierarchical authority. Also, compliance with hierarchial authority is one of the rules of the game that organization members generally accept.

As for its consequences for decision-making, hierarchy provides a means by which discrete decisions can be coordinated and conflicts among officials at lower levels in the agency can be resolved. Hierarchy also means that those at upper levels have a larger voice in agency decisions because of their higher status, even though lower-level officials may have more substantive qualifi-cations and information. A separation of power and knowledge may thus threaten the rationality of administrative decisions.[44] Hierarchy can also ad-versely affect the free flow of ideas and information in an organization; subordinates may hesitate to advance proposals they think might run counter to "official" policy or antagonize their superiors. Few want to carry the message that causes the messenger to be shot.

Secrecy also is an important feature of administrative decision-making. Compared with that of legislatures, administrative decision-making is a rela-tively invisible part of government. Agencies may hold public hearings, issue press releases, and the like, but they exercise much control over the informa-tion that becomes available about their internal deliberations and decisions. Much of what they do is little noticed by the public or reported by the media. This secrecy or invisibility can contribute to the effectiveness of decisions by providing a congenial environment for presenting and discussing policy pro-posals that might otherwise be avoided as publicly unpopular. Deliberations by Kennedy administration officials during the Cuban missile crisis were more effective because they were private, or closed.[45] Additionally, secrecy may facilitate the bargaining and compromise often necessary to reach deci-sions and take action, because officials find it easier to move away from privately stated than publicly stated positions. On the other hand, privacy in administrative deliberation could mean that some pertinent facts are not considered and that significant interests are not consulted. Though secrecy contributed to the effectiveness of the Cuban missile crisis decisions, it had the opposite effect with regard to the Bay of Pigs invasion debacle in the previous year.

Secrecy is, on the whole, more a part of administrative deliberations in foreign and defense policy than in domestic matters.[46] In the latter area, secrecy has been reduced by legislation expected to open the administrative process to greater public participation and scrutiny. The Freedom of Information Act provides a procedure for extracting documents and records from agencies, and the Government in the Sunshine Act requires most plural-headed agencies to open their decision-making sessions to the public.

Administrative agencies constitute "a governmental habitat in which expertise finds a wealth of opportunity to exert itself and to influence policy."[47] Agencies clearly are affected by political considerations, including the wish to protect their own power, in making decisions. Thus the Department of Commerce is unlikely to make policy decisions that sharply conflict with important business interests. Nor is the Tennessee Valley Authority inclined to ignore major economic interests in its region. Agencies nonetheless do provide a context within which experts and professionals, official and private, can work on policy problems.

Scientific and technical considerations and professional advice are important factors in most administrative decision-making. Whether it is the Federal Aviation Agency considering the adoption of a rule on aircraft safety, the FDA acting on the safety of implanted medical devices, or the secretary of labor confronting a major choice on job-training programs, each needs good information on the technical feasibility of proposed alternatives. Decisions that are made without adequate consideration of their technical aspects or that conflict with strong professional advice may turn out to be faulty on both technical and political grounds.

Professional and scientific advice is not always sound, however. In 1976, following the identification of a few cases of influenza at Fort Dix, New Jersey, public-health officials decided that the nation was confronted with the possibility of a swine-flu epidemic, similar to one that had killed 500,000 people in 1918. Acting on their advice, the Ford administration decided to initiate a nationwide immunization campaign. The flu epidemic never came, however, and the entire venture became a policy fiasco.[48]

Finally, administrative decision-making is very frequently characterized by bargaining. Experts and facts are important in administrative decision-making, but so also are accommodation and compromise. Some agencies may be less apt to engage in bargaining than others. Decisions from the National Institute of Standards and Technology and the Patent Office are primarily expert findings based on factual records. Economic regulatory agencies, such as the Securities and Exchange Commission and the EPA, often find it necessary to bargain with those whom they regulate. In setting emission standards, the EPA has had to bargain with both polluters and state and local officials to reach tolerable decisions and help secure compliance. Another notable example of bargaining involves the consent decrees used by the Antitrust Division of the Department of Justice to close most civil antitrust cases. Negotiated beyond public view by representatives of the division and the alleged offender, the consent decree states that the division will drop its formal proceedings in turn for the alleged offender's agreement to stop practices such as price-fixing or acquisition of a competitor. Negotiations with other countries for tariff reductions also illustrate bargaining, in this instance with foreign administrators.[49]

Patterns of Policymaking

Administrative agencies engage in a wide range of activities and make multitudes of decisions as they administer the laws within their jurisdiction. (Some of these activities or techniques are discussed in the next section.) Out of this welter of activity, four patterns can be identified and designated as policymaking because of the ways in which they help define the content and thrust of public policies. These patterns are rule-making, adjudication, law-enforcement practices, and program operations.

RULE-MAKING   The Administrative Procedure Act defines a rule as "an agency statement of general or particular applicability and future effect designed to implement, interpret, or prescribe law or policy or describing the organization, procedure, or practice requirements of an agency." Substantive rules fill in the details of general statutory provisions and have the force and effect of law. Interpretive rules indicate how an agency views or interprets the laws that it enforces and the meaning it gives to statutory terms such as "discriminate," "small business," or "an appropriate education." Procedural rules describe an agency's organization and how it will conduct its various activities. In practice, it is not always easy to distinguish these types of rules, or to separate them from informal statements of agency policy or practice.[50]

Congress has delegated rule-making authority to a large number of administrative agencies. Thus the Securities and Exchange Commission is authorized to make rules governing the stock exchanges "as it seems necessary in the public interest or for the protection of investors." OSHA is empowered to make rules setting health and safety standards for work places. In the case of toxic substances, OSHA is directed to set the standard "which most adequately assures, to the extent feasible, on the basis of the best available evidence, that no worker suffers material impairment of health," even when exposed to a toxic substance over the course of a working career. The conditions embedded in this delegation reflect compromises made during the legislative process. They leave the meaning of the law vague and the agency uncertain as to what is required to meet the standard.

Rule-making, which is one of the primary instruments of government in the United States, is the part of the administrative process that most resembles the legislative process.[51] Most frequently it takes the form of informal, or notice and comment, rule-making. Several procedural requirements governing informal rule-making are set forth by the Administrative Procedure Act (Section 553):

1. A notice of a proposed rule-making (NPRM) must be published in the *Federal Register* that specifies the legal authority for the rule, the terms or substance of the proposed rule, and the time, place, and nature of the public rule-making proceeding.
2. An opportunity must be provided for interested persons to participate in the rule-making, through either oral or written comments. For controversial rules, agencies will often choose to hold hearings. Although a hearing rarely changes anyone's mind on a proposed rule, it serves to educate the public and permits a more extensive record of public participation to be compiled. This can help the agency if the rule is challenged in the courts.[52]
3. A concise statement of the rule's "basis and purpose" must be included with the final rule. In the preamble to a rule, the agency indicates the information, data, and analyses that it relied on in developing the rule. Also, the number and nature of public comments, the issues that they raised, and actions taken (or not taken) by the agency in response may be detailed. The preambles to rules often exceed the actual rules in length.[53]
4. The final rule must be published at least thirty days before it becomes effective.

These requirements are intended to provide for fairness in rule-making, which includes furnishing those interested in or affected by a rule with an opportunity to participate in its development and perhaps influence its content. (In actuality, most final rules differ little from their proposed form.) In some instances, agencies are required by statutes to follow more detailed and stringent procedures in rule-making actions. Thus, if a statute specifies that rules must be based on a formal record, then an agency, in making a rule, must hold a trial-type hearing, follow rigorous procedures, and base its rule on "substantial evidence in the record." The comparable standard for rules emanating from informal proceedings is that they must not constitute an "arbitrary or capricious abuse of discretion." This is yet another of the mushy standards that one encounters in the policy world.

In the exercise of their rule-making authority, agencies may have much discretion or latitude in fashioning the substance of rules because of the vague or general wording of the legislation under which they operate. Customarily, though, agencies can exercise their authority only in well-bounded areas. Thus the Food Safety and Inspection Service is restricted to meat and poultry processors, the Comptroller of the Currency to national banks, and the Bureau of Land Management to public-owned grazing lands. Few agencies can rival the jurisdiction of the Consumer Product Safety Commission, whose legal domain includes several thousand consumer products. One of its problems has been the identification of appropriate targets for rule-making and other actions.

In addition to the Administrative Procedure Act, some other statutes impose limitations on rule-making agencies. If a rule has a significant impact on the environment, the National Environmental Policy Act requires the agency to prepare an environmental impact statement. Should small businesses be disproportionately affected, the Regulatory Flexibility Act requires the agency to take steps to reduce a rule's impact on them. If a rule necessitates the collection of information from the public, then the Paperwork Reduction Act applies. Office of Management and Budget approval is needed to ensure that the information collection does not impose an unnecessary burden on the public. These various requirements complicate and slow the rule-making process. And, as law-school dean Cornelius Kerwin notes:

> Our legislators enact programs of regulation on social welfare but then encumber them with procedural requirements that will almost certainly stall their implementation. This simply confirms that political decision making is multidimensional. The combination of an aggressive and ambitious substantive mission combined with a cautious and painstaking process of implementation can satisfy different sets of constituents.[54]

National administrative agencies issue thousands of rules annually. These range from those that are of small moment and short duration—such as some Agricultural Marketing Service rules on fruits and vegetables—to those that impose major costs and affect large numbers of people—such as Environmental Protection Agency rules on air quality and hazardous-waste disposal. Collectively, these rules, which daily are reported in the *Federal Register,* are much larger in volume than the legislation enacted by Congress. Agency rules are codified in the *Code of Federal Regulations.*

ADJUDICATION   Agencies can make policy when they apply existing laws or rules to particular situations by case-to-case decision-making. In so doing, they act in much the same manner as courts, just as they act in legislative fashion when engaged in rule-making. In the past, the Federal Trade Commission made policy by applying the legislative prohibition of unfair methods of competition to specific cases. These cases gradually marked out public policy and by induction indicated the kinds of practices banned by the general prohibition. Again, an agency may make policy when it gives an interpretation to a statutory provision in applying it in a case. Thus, the National Labor Relations Board (NLRB), which administers labor–management relations legislation, makes and announces statutory interpretations in deciding unfair-practice cases, which then inform its action in future cases. In such instances

NLRB opinions become policy statements of much importance to union and company officials.

Agencies frequently choose to make policy by adjudication, even though they have rule-making authority. This is true for the NLRB, for instance. (They may be authorized, but not required, to engage in rule-making.) An agency may find it no easier than a legislature to reach a decision on the content of general policy, especially in a novel or highly controversial situation. Consequently, it may choose to proceed in a more piecemeal or incremental manner. Those affected by agency action, however, may be left in the dark as to what policy is supposed to be when it is made case by case. And indeed, agencies often have been criticized for relying too much on adjudication and too little on rule-making as they develop policy.[55]

Much of the adjudication that administrative agencies engage in is routine, such as the hundreds of thousands of decisions made annually by the Department of Veterans Affairs and the Social Security Administration on applications for benefits. Still, within the framework of statutory language, seemingly routine decisions may shift the direction or skew the effect of policy. A noteworthy example is the operation of the Internal Revenue Service (IRS), which routinely closes most cases of disputed income-tax returns by informal adjudication (and bargaining). The IRS statistics for fiscal year 1972, which were obtained under a Freedom of Information Act proceeding, showed that in cases that did not end up in the courts (and most do not) the agency settled for 67 percent of the amounts owed in the $1 to $999 range, and for an average of 34 percent when $1 million or more was allegedly owed. Moreover, settlements varied widely from district to district, ranging from 12 percent of the amount alleged by the IRS in the St. Paul district to 76 percent in Pittsburgh.[56] Obviously such actions significantly affect the content and impact of policy.

LAW ENFORCEMENT   Agencies may also mold policy through their various law-enforcement actions. A statute may be enforced vigorously or even rigidly, in a lax manner, or not at all; it may be applied in some situations and not in others, or to some persons or companies and not to others. Everyone is familiar with the discretion exercised by the police officer on the beat or, what is more likely, in the patrol car. A ticket may be given to a speeder, or only a warning may be issued. If no drivers are ticketed unless they exceed posted speed limits by a specific rate, this choice amounts to an amendment of public policy. Even when statutory provisions are quite precise, thus seeming to eliminate discretion in their interpretation, enforcement officers still have some discretion with respect to the manner in which they will be enforced.

Policy may be shaped by administrative inaction or apathy as well as by an agency's positive action and zeal. Inaction often adversely affects only the inarticulate or inattentive general public and consequently may pass unnoticed. In 1936, Congress enacted the Robinson-Patman Act to protect small retailers against price discrimination by large competitors such as chain stores and discount houses. Economists have long criticized the law as a barrier to price competition. During the last decade or two, both the Federal Trade Commission and the Antitrust Division of the Department of Justice, under whose jurisdiction the Robinson-Patman Act falls, have ceased to enforce it. Some question exists as to whether agencies should be able to ignore a law in this manner.

A second example involves the Reclamation Act of 1902, which authorized a massive irrigation program to encourage agricultural development in the western states. The land that a farmer could irrigate with low-cost water from federally constructed reservoirs was limited to 160 acres, or 320 acres for a farmer and his or her spouse. Further, they were required to live on or near their land. For many decades these restrictions, which were clearly spelled out in the law, were not enforced by the Bureau of Reclamation. As a consequence, much of the below-market-cost water from federal reclamation projects was provided to large farms, often owned by corporations, encompassing thousands of acres. Many were (and are) located in California's Central Valley. These large landholders were strong supporters of BOR's reinterpretation of the law.[57]

Pressure by environmentalists and organizations representing small farmers finally induced Congress in 1982 to pass the Reclamation Reform Act. The irrigation limit was increased to 960 acres and the residency requirement was repealed. Still intransigent, the Bureau of Reclamation has acquiesced in the evasion by large landholders of the 960 acre limit.[58] In this instance, as well as that of the Robinson-Patman Act, one encounters agency nullification of legislative policy.

In addition to the attitudes and motives of its officials, external pressures, and financial resources, an agency's capacity to carry out policies will be significantly affected by the enforcement authority and techniques available to it. Opponents unable to block legislative enactment of a law may seek to blunt its impact by handicapping its enforcement. Take the equal employment opportunity provisions in Title 7 of the Civil Rights Act of 1964, which prohibit firms or unions representing twenty-five or more employees from discriminating against individuals because of their race, color, religion, national origin, or sex. Along with the other titles in the act, these provisions were adopted over strong conservative opposition. The Equal Employment Opportunity Commission (EEOC) was authorized to enforce the law through investigations, conferences, and conciliation, which means essentially voluntary action. If these methods failed, the EEOC could recommend civil action in the federal courts, which required cooperation by the Department of Justice to prosecute cases. Moreover, the law provided that the EEOC could not act on complaints from states that had an anti-discrimination law and an agency to enforce it, unless the state agency was unable to complete action within sixty days. Complaints had to be filed "in writing under oath," which is an unusual requirement for a law-violation complaint. This stipulation undoubtedly had a chilling effect on many southern blacks and others. Whatever the intent behind these provisions, they clearly limited the law's effectiveness by making the successful completion of cases a slow, tedious process.

After 1964, the EEOC and many supporters of stronger enforcement advocated giving the agency authority to issue cease-and-desist orders[59] in discrimination cases and then to seek, on its own initiative, their enforcement in the federal courts. Opposition to this proposed change was particularly strong from conservatives and southerners. In 1972, the EEOC was finally empowered to bring court action on its own initiative but not to issue cease-and-desist orders when the conciliation of complaints was not successful. Though perhaps not as much as hoped, this new authority did help strengthen the enforcement and effectiveness of the anti-job discrimination policy.

PROGRAM OPERATIONS   Many agencies administer loan, grant, benefit, insurance, and service policies and programs, or engage in the management of public properties, such as forests, parks, and hydroelectric plants. Although these activities are not usually thought of as law enforcement because they are not designed directly to regulate or shape people's behavior, they are often of much importance to many people. How such programs are implemented helps determine policy both directly and indirectly. Some examples will provide clarification.

Fire was once anathema to both the U.S. Forest Service and the National Park Service (NPS) in their management of national forest and park lands.[60] In 1971, however, using scientific findings concerning the role of fire in the natural regeneration of forests, the NPS decided that it would allow most naturally caused fires (i.e., those touched off by lightning strikes) in national parks to burn themselves out. Such fires were a part of the normal life cycle of forests. (The Forest Service continued to fight all fires, however caused). The NPS policy on fires came under severe challenge in the summer of 1988, when the buildup of flammable materials on the ground because of the previous policy of putting out fires, plus an exceptionally dry summer, contributed to severe forest fires in Yellowstone National Park. A substantial portion of the park land was burned, leading many public officials to call for changes in the NPS policy. Assessments of the fires' effects revealed that it had not been as disastrous as originally thought. The natural, or "let-it-burn," regulation was not repealed but, on the other hand, all national park fires were fought in 1989.[61] During the next several years, a fire plan evolved for most parks that called for suppression of all fires in areas where necessary to protect lives and property while permitting most naturally caused fires to burn on other park lands.[62]

A second example involves the Federal Housing Administration (FHA) of the Department of Housing and Urban Development. Since the 1930s, FHA has administered a mortgage-insurance program under which the risks of nonpayment and foreclosure are assumed by the government rather than by private lenders. Until 1967, a regulation provided that, to be FHA-insured, housing loans had to meet a standard of "economic soundness." Consequently, many low-income people in slum or deteriorating areas could not obtain FHA-insured loans because of "excessive risk." When loans were available, the interest costs were high relative to the incomes of the poor. Because of these operating requirements the mortgage insurance was much more beneficial for high- and middle-income persons than for the poor. Only a tiny fraction of FHA-insured home loans went to the poor.[63]

In 1968 Congress enacted legislation to reorder FHA priorities and to make public policy more responsive to the needs of low-income people. This change lessened but did not eliminate discrimination against low-income borrowers. Also, over the years the FHA has become less important because private loan-guarantee companies have offered borrowers more flexible insurance.

The Elementary and Secondary Education Act (ESEA) of 1965, which under its Title I provides federal financial aid for educating disadvantaged children in urban and rural poor areas, is another good example. The social-reform advocates among its supporters thought that this policy was intended to reduce poverty by improving the educational facilities and opportunities that state and local governments made available to the educationally disadvantaged children of low-income families. As initially administered by the Office of Education (now the Department of Education), however, it was unclear to what extent the funds were actually expended on poor children, and whether they bought services beyond the level of those provided for other children in the districts aided. Many cases of the misuse of funds were also reported.[64]

A number of factors contributed to this situation. Although the ESEA clearly specified that disadvantaged children were its focus, its legislative history provided "the semblance if not the reality of general aid." This ambiguity, together with the reality that reformers supporting the legislation did not themselves get much involved in implementation, meant that officials in the then Office of Education were given leeway to interpret the legislation in accord with accepted modes of operation. The traditional task of the Office of Education had long been to provide assistance and advice to state and local school agencies. It was not inclined to regulate or police their activities and consequently acted with little vigor to ensure that Title I funds were expended as intended. Further, state and local agencies had historically dominated public education, and they enjoyed strong political support for their hegemony. This meant that it would have been difficult for national officials, even if they were so inclined, to impose directives that did not mesh with local priorities.

By the end of the 1970s, however, the administration of the ESEA's Title I had changed markedly. New staff members in the Office of Education had succeeded in securing much tighter supervision of spending under the program. Interest groups, such as the National Welfare Rights Organization and the National Advisory Council for Education of Disadvantaged Children, helped keep the program centered on the disadvantaged. Offices dealing with compensatory education were established in most state departments of education, and they developed a stake in ensuring that funds were used for the disadvantaged. Such developments made the effort to target Title I funds on the disadvantaged much more successful. Studies indicated that Title I funds had strengthened the educational performance of the students affected.

The change in administration of the Title I program brought it more closely into line with the expectations of its originators—that is, to provide benefits to the disadvantaged. In 1981 it was maintained as a separate program, although over twenty other education programs were consolidated in an education block grant by the Education Consolidation and Improvement Act, a Reagan administration initiative. In the 1990s, the appropriation for Title I annually was $6 billion to $7 billion. Funds were allocated on the basis of a formula based on the number of low-income children in a county and average spending per pupil and went to most of the nation's fifteen thousand school districts. An effort by the Clinton administration to direct more money to districts with large numbers of low-income students was unsuccessful.[65]

TECHNIQUES OF CONTROL

Whether labeled promotional, regulatory, prohibitive, redistributive, or whatever, all policies incorporate an element of control. That is, by one means or another, overtly or subtly, they are designed to cause people to do things, refrain from doing things, or continue doing things that they otherwise would not do. This holds true whether reference is to tax provisions intended to encourage industrial-plant modernization or charitable giving, the provision of information and financial assistance to expand international trade, or a prohibition of an activity such as price-fixing with penalties for violators. Even Smokey Bear's admonition that "only you can prevent forest fires" embodies a control element.[66]

The control techniques authorized for their implementation are an important component of public policies. Decisions on these matters, like those on the substance of policy itself, can be highly productive of controversy during the policy adoption process. The control techniques that an agency is permitted to use may in practice have important consequences for the content and impact of policy, for policy as an "operational reality" that affects human behavior. Those who oppose a policy, for example, may attempt to lessen or even negate its effects by restricting the administering agency's powers of enforcement or implementation. Two examples illustrate this point. In 1912,

Massachusetts became the first state to enact a minimum-wage law. While strongly supported by organized labor, it met with vigorous opposition from manufacturers. The result was compromise legislation that provided for enforcement only by the publication in newspapers of the names of companies not complying with the wage standard. As one might guess, the Massachusetts law was not overly effective.

In the 1970s a wave of corporate mergers led to efforts to strengthen antimerger law. After much struggle, including a Senate filibuster by opponents, legislation was enacted providing that the Antitrust Division of the Department of Justice had to be given advance notice of proposed large corporate mergers. Proponents believed that this requirement would increase the effectiveness of antitrust enforcement by enabling the government to block mergers before they were completed and the companies involved lost their separate identities. Opponents, notably investment bankers, who put together mergers, and others in conservative and business ranks, apparently shared this view. Otherwise, there would have been no controversy.

Control techniques may be based on a number of behavioral assumptions.[67] Economic incentives such as subsidies, tax credits, and loans are based on the assumption that people are utility maximizers. Incentives to act in their own interest will cause them to comply with policies. Capacity-enhancing techniques, such as job training, information, and counseling programs, rely on the notion that people have the desire or motivation to do what is required but lack the capacity to act accordingly. Hortatory techniques—declarations of policy, appeals for voluntary cooperation, warnings against littering or drunk driving—assume that people act on the basis of their beliefs and values and will likely do what is right if they know about it. Authoritative techniques rest on the premise that requirements and restrictions, backed up by sanctions, are necessary to prevent people from engaging in undesirable, evil, immoral, or unfair behavior. Many government agencies, consequently, have authority to set and enforce standards on environmental pollution, consumer safety, financial transactions, and other topics.

In sum, for a policy to be effective, more is needed than substantive authority and sufficient funding to cover the financial costs for implementation. Adequate and suitable techniques of control and implementation must be authorized for the responsible agency. In this section a variety of control techniques are examined, but the list is not exhaustive.

Noncoercive Forms of Action

Many of the methods used to implement policies to bring about compliance are noncoercive. Here "noncoercive" means that they do not involve the imposition of legal sanctions or penalties, rewards, or deprivations. The effectiveness of these forms depends mostly upon voluntary collaboration or acceptance by the affected parties, although social and economic pressures arising out of society may lend them an element of compulsion. The following are examples of noncoercive forms of action.

Declarations of policy by themselves may cause people to comply, "to go along." This result seems reasonable, especially if the declarations are made by respected or high-status officials. Presidential appeals to labor and management to avoid making inflationary wage contracts or price increases, for example, may themselves have a restraining effect, as may mayoral appeals to citizens to conserve water by not watering their lawns during periods of drought.

Voluntary standards may be established by official action. The National Institute of Standards and Technology has developed commercial standards, such as uniform weights, measures, and grades of products and materials, which are not mandatory. They are widely adhered to because their use facilitates or promotes business and economic activity. While the use of most of the standard grades—such as prime, choice, and select for beef—established by the U.S. Department of Agriculture for agricultural commodities is permissive (some are mandatory for interstate commerce), they are widely followed in practice.

Mediation and conciliation are noncoercive measures often used in efforts to settle labor–management disputes, as by the Federal Mediation and Conciliation Service. The mediator works to bring the parties together, to clarify the facts in the disputes and the points at issue, and to offer advice and suggestions to promote settlement. The mediator, however, has no formal powers of decision or sanction. Many labor–management disputes are successfully resolved by these procedures.

The use of publicity to bring the social and economic effects of adverse public opinion to bear on violators may induce compliance with policy. Much stress was placed on "pitiless publicity" during the Progressive Era as a way of preventing monopoly. Although labor and business organizations today exhibit much awareness about their public image, it is impossible to measure how effective publicity is as a control device. Still, the revelation of "poor" working conditions or "undesirable" business practices by congressional or agency investigations may produce some correction or improvement.

Educational and demonstration programs are widely used by agencies in securing compliance with policy. Much effort is expended to inform people about their rights under Social Security and veterans' benefits programs, for example. Employers are informed through publications and conferences about the meaning and requirements of wage and hours legislation. The demonstration technique is especially used in agriculture. Preferred practices in soil conservation and crop production are shown and explained to farmers with the hope that their demonstrated superiority will lead to widespread acceptance and use.

Inspection

Inspection is the examination of some matter (such as premises, products, or records) to determine whether it conforms to officially prescribed standards. The inspection may be either continuous, as in the inspection of meat in packing plants, or periodic, as in the inspection of banks and food-processing establishments. Whichever form it takes, inspection is intended to reveal compliance or noncompliance by those involved in an activity, with the objective of preventing or correcting undesirable or dangerous conditions. Typically an effort is first made to persuade violators to conform with the law; imposing sanctions or penalties is a last recourse. Indeed, the ultimate purpose of inspection is to help gain the cooperation of the regulated. Inspection is the most commonly used form of regulatory action. Examples of its use at the national level include the inspection of locomotives and railroad safety devices by the Federal Railroad Administration, sanitary conditions in food- and drug-manufacturing establishments by the FDA, income-tax returns by the IRS, and national banks by the Comptroller of the Currency.

Licensing

Licensing, or enabling action, as it is sometimes called, involves government authorization to engage in a business or profession or to do something otherwise forbidden. An extensively used form of action, licensing is known by various names. Licenses are required to engage in many professions and occupations and to do such things as operate motor vehicles and radio stations. In addition, the term "certificate of public convenience and necessity" is used in the public-utility field. "Permits" may be necessary to drill oil wells; the "corporate charter" constitutes authorization to use a form of business organization; and "franchises" are granted to utilities to use city streets for their pipe and wire lines.

Licensing is a form of advance check in which a person who wishes to engage in a particular activity (such as driving a car) must demonstrate certain qualifications or meet specified standards or requirements. The burden of proof in securing a license rests with the applicant rather than the granting official. The use of licensing ordinarily goes beyond the initial authorization or denial to do something. It may also include: "(1) imposition of conditions as part of the authorization; (2) modification of the terms or conditions at the discretion of the granting authority; (3) renewal or denial of the authorization at periodic intervals; (4) revocation of the authorization." When these are included, licensing becomes a form of continuing control.[68] Radio and television broadcasters, for example, must periodically renew their licenses with the FCC and may have them revoked under specified circumstances. Only rarely, however, is an applicant's request for a broadcast license renewal denied.[69]

Loans, Subsidies, and Benefits

Loans, subsidies, and benefits are means by which public purposes are advanced through aid, in the form of money or other resources, to companies, farmers, students, home buyers, and others. Under the Local Service Program, cash operating subsidies are granted to some commuter airlines to maintain an adequate system of air transport. Operating subsidies are used to promote the American merchant marine. It also benefits from the Jones Act, which provides that ocean commerce among United States ports can be carried only in ships built and registered in the U.S. Commodity loans and payments are made to farmers to support farm prices and income. Small businesses are assisted by loans from the Small Business Administration. Also related is the guarantee of loans by the government to expand the volume of private lending, as with the guarantee of home mortgages by the FHA and bank loans to college students.

In addition to their broad control quality, loans, subsidies, and benefit programs may include explicit regulatory features. Under the agricultural price-support programs, commodity loans and payments are available only to those who comply with production and marketing controls. Farmers Home Administration loans for purchasing farms are made under conditions designed to ensure good farm management. In effect, the government is using the loan and benefit operations to purchase consent to policies. The effectiveness of such programs depends considerably upon the need or desire for the assistance offered.

Contracts

Many governmental programs are carried out in substantial part through contracts with private companies. At the national level, the defense, nuclear weapons, and space programs are well-known examples. State and local governments contract with private companies for the construction of highways and streets and, in some instances, the management of public schools. Many private companies looking for profits want to do business with the government, and some, as in the aerospace industry, depend heavily upon government contracts for their very existence. The power to grant or deny contracts includes an obvious element of control.

Every presidential administration since Dwight Eisenhower's has encouraged agencies to contract out commercial activities. The Office of Management and Budget, pursuant to its Circular A-76, directs them to contract for goods and services when these can be obtained at lower cost from the private sector. Implementation of A-76, however, has varied widely among federal agencies and its cost savings are difficult to measure.[70]

Contracts sometimes serve as the basis for specific economic controls. Under the Walsh-Healey Act, companies wanting to sell goods or services to the national government must pay prevailing wages and comply with other standards on the hours and conditions of work. Executive Order 11246, issued by President Lyndon Johnson in 1965, prohibits discrimination in employment by federal contracts. The Office of Federal Contract Compliance programs, which administers the order, requires that contracts also have affirmative action programs.[71] Violators of these requirements can be denied present or future government contracts.

General Expenditures

Apart from their use in connection with the loan, subsidy, and benefit operations, governmental expenditures for purchasing goods and services can be used by agency officials to attain various policy goals. Administrative agencies often have considerable discretion in spending funds appropriated by Congress. Expenditures of funds for goods and services can be used to foster favored domestic or local industries, or to increase economic activity in depressed areas. Competition may be promoted by purchasing from smaller rather than larger businesses so as to strengthen their economic position. The rate and timing of expenditures may be geared to counteract inflationary or deflationary trends in the economy. In order to reduce inflationary pressures, for instance, spending can be deferred or cut back for some programs.

Market and Proprietary Operations

When government enters the market to buy, sell, or provide goods and services, its actions often have control effects. Thus the purchase and sale of government securities in the market (that is, open-market operations) is a potent tool used by the Federal Reserve Board to expand or contract the money supply in the economy. When the FRB buys government securities this increases bank reserves and their lending capacity; the opposite occurs when the FRB sells securities. The prices of some agricultural commodities, such as milk, have been supported by direct Department of Agriculture purchases in the market. The Johnson administration sold some of the government's previously acquired stockpiles of aluminum and copper in its efforts to prevent price increases in those industries in the mid-1960s.

Government enterprises also may have a control effect, as when they compete with private enterprises. Thus the sale of electric power at "reasonable" rates by the Tennessee Valley Authority led to rate reductions by private companies operating in the region. This is sometimes referred to as "yardstick regulation" in that the reasonableness of private utility rates can be measured by the public rates. Governmental competition has not been used extensively as a control device, although it remains a possibility. Some states use state-owned liquor stores rather than regulation of privately owned stores as a means for controlling liquor traffic.[72]

Taxation

Taxes are important policy instruments "because they not only provide revenue but also serve to sanction or encourage certain types of behavior."[73] The power to tax has occasionally been wielded for regulatory purposes. A 10 percent annual tax on state bank notes levied by Congress in 1865 drove them out of existence. For several decades high taxes were levied on colored oleomargarine to discourage its use in preference to butter. The Carter administration proposed increasing the federal tax on gasoline as a means of discouraging its consumption and promoting energy conservation. Congress refused to act on the recommendation, however, because of strong public opposition. This is a policy idea that will not die, however. In 1993, a gasoline-tax increase was adopted instead of the Clinton administration's proposal for an energy tax.

In recent years, some have advocated more positive use of taxation. Thus it has been contended that environmental pollution could be better reduced by levying a tax on effluents rather than relying on the system of standard-setting and enforcement.[74] The tax would provide businesses with an economic incentive to reduce discharges while permitting them to determine the most efficient manner to do this. Resistance to the use of taxation in this fashion has been based on various premises: taxes should be used only to raise revenue; the present pattern of regulation is adequate; and the tax device would be difficult to administer in practice. As a consequence, little use has been made of taxation as a more positive regulatory technique.

Exemptions from existing taxes have now become a widely used promotional device and are often referred to as "tax expenditures."[75] A variety of deductions, exclusions from income, preferential rates, and the like permit individuals and corporations who engage in favored activities, such as capital investment, purchase of homes, or charitable giving, to retain funds that would otherwise be paid in taxes. The effect is the same as if the government had made a direct payment to the favored party, but it is less open and obvious. The use of tax expenditures has become widespread and, in 1988, it was estimated that on a combined basis they amounted to $79.8 billion for corporations and $281.2 billion for individuals.[76] This technique capitalizes on the general aversion to paying taxes that seems characteristic of Americans, and it makes the subsidization of private activity less visible. The administrative costs of tax expenditures are negligible because people and corporations claim their benefits when they file their income-tax forms.

Directive Power

Many agencies have authority, through the use of adjudicatory proceedings, to issue orders or directives that are binding on private parties. (In the preceding section, we discussed the general nature of administrative adjudication and its use in developing policy.) Agencies may issue orders to settle disputes between private parties, as when a mover claims that a moving company damaged or lost some of his or her furniture; to resolve complaints, as when a company is charged with false or misleading advertising; and to approve or deny applications, as for a license for a nuclear power project or a Social Security benefit. Congressional standards governing administrative adjudication are usually more specific for benefit programs, such as Social Security and veterans benefits, than for regulatory programs, perhaps because political conflict is often less intense over the passage of benefit legislation than regulatory legislation.[77] Consequently, Congress is less inclined to pass the buck to agencies through the guise of general legislation on benefit programs.

Services

Many public policies, mostly of the distributive variety, involve the provision of services such as information, advice, legal counsel, medical treatment, and psychiatric services. Thus, the Small Business Administration, in addition to making loans, administers a variety of informational and technical services for the operators of small businesses. The National Weather Service's forecasts are useful to groups such as farmers, commercial fishermen, and airline companies, as well as to weekend weather-watchers generally. The Department of Veterans Affairs provides many medical, psychiatric, and counseling services to veterans, often at no cost. Service programs variously provide benefits to recipients or users, help enhance the personal or material well-being of many people, and support the more efficient operation of markets (as in job-training and the provision of foreign-trade data).

Informal Procedures

Much of the work done by agencies in settling questions involving private rights, privileges, and interests is accomplished by informal procedures—that is, without formal action and adversary hearings. Most disputes arising out of income-tax returns are settled by consultation and correspondence between the IRS and the private parties involved. Claims for retirement benefits under the Social Security program are mostly settled by administrative officials using work records, personal interviews, and eligibility rules. A large portion of the complaint cases alleging unfair labor or management practices initiated with the NLRB are also informally disposed of in conferences between agency field examiners and the parties in dispute.

Informal procedures have been referred to as "the lifeblood of the administrative process" because of their contributions to its efficiency and success. Certainly they are an important facet of policy implementation. Many decisions affecting private rights and interests are reached by such means as negotiation, bargaining and compromise, consultation, conference, correspondence, reference to technical data, and examination of material. Extensive use is made of such methods because of the large number of cases coming before agencies, the need or desire for quick action, agencies' wish to avoid becoming embroiled in formal proceedings, and private parties' desires to avoid the courthouse and unfavorable publicity.

Sanctions

Sanctions are the means, penalties, and rewards that agencies use to encourage or compel compliance with their decisions.[78] Sanctions put some sting into administrative action. In some instances, sanctions are built into control techniques. Thus, when an agency decides to grant or deny a conditional benefit, the sanction rests in this action. Other sanctions that may be applied by agencies include the threat of prosecution, monetary penalties, favorable or unfavorable publicity, modification or revocation of licenses, seizure or destruction of goods, award of damages, and issuance of injunctions. Agencies may also seek to impose criminal penalties (fines and jail sentences), but this requires action through the courts. Further, those who deal with agencies often seek to maintain their good will and hence may be reluctant to challenge agency actions.

Concluding Comment

There appears to be general agreement that policies should be implemented in such manner as to cause the least possible material and psychological disturbance to the persons affected. (This generalization may not hold for some criminal laws.) Within this constraint, the most technically or economically efficient method of enforcement may not be the most acceptable politically. This consideration will influence both the legislature in authorizing control techniques for an agency and the agency in using its techniques and sanctions. Another consideration in choosing control techniques stems from the general objective of public policy, which is to control behavior (or secure compliance) and not to punish violators, except as a last resort. Consequently, the usual preference will be for less harsh or coercive techniques. Some sanctions may be considered so harsh that they are rarely used, as with jail sentences for business executives who violate the antitrust laws. Government tends to follow the rule of parsimony in employing legal restraint and compulsion in policy implementation, except for some types of criminal conduct.

A Controversy: Standards or Incentives?

Traditionally, economic regulatory programs have relied heavily upon such administrative practices as setting standards, inspection to determine compliance, and imposing sanctions upon violators. Following the lead of economist Charles Schultze, however, many now designate and stigmatize this pattern of regulation as "command-and-control" regulation. (In reality, of course, a great deal of education, persuasion, negotiation, bargaining, and compromise goes on in the regulatory process.) Opponents object to use of the "command-and-control" approach because, they say, it dictates behavior, discourages private initiative and innovation in attaining policy goals, and causes waste or misuse of societal resources. In its stead they prefer economic incentives in the form of rewards or penalties, which they see as utilizing individual self-interest to achieve public purposes. The incentive system, it is said, "lets individuals make their own decisions, thus enhancing freedom and voluntarism, and yet (under the right circumstances) achieves desired goals at the lowest possible cost to society.[79]

Let us take the question of how to control environmental pollution as an illustration of the incentive system, because it is here that the incentive approach has been most widely proposed. The system apparently would work like this: First it would be determined how much reduction in a pollutant would be necessary to meet a policy goal. A tax or fee would then be imposed on each unit (perhaps a ton) of the pollutant (perhaps sulfur dioxide) discharged sufficient to achieve the goal. Those discharging the pollutant could then choose to pay the tax or lower their discharges. Ideally, they would choose the latter, reducing their discharges, by whatever means chosen, as much as economically practicable, or to the extent that it costs less to reduce pollution than to pay the tax. Economists Allen Kneese and Charles Schultze explain the consequences of a selected level of taxes:

> Firms with low costs of control would remove a larger percentage [of a pollutant] than would firms with higher costs, precisely the situation needed to achieve a least-cost approach to reducing pollution for the economy as a whole. Firms would tend to choose the least expensive methods of control, whether treatment of wastes, modification in production processes, or substitution of raw materials that had less serious polluting consequences. Further, the kinds of products whose manufacture entailed a lot of pollution would become more expensive and could carry higher prices than those that generated less, so consumers would be induced to buy more of the latter.[80]

The incentive system, its supporters believe, would be easy to administer. Once the level of taxes appropriate for achieving a policy goal was determined, it would then be a simple matter to monitor discharges and collect the taxes due. Large bureaucracies would be unnecessary, and political struggles would be avoided. Governmental coercion to cause compliance with standards, with all the balkiness that it creates, would give way to choice driven by self-interest.

In practice, however, the incentive system would be unlikely to eliminate the need for either politics or administrative agencies. Determining how much reduction of pollution was necessary (or conversely, how clean the air should be) and what level of taxes would be needed to achieve this goal would be open to much disagreement, conflict, and struggle; in short, such decisions would be highly political. Businesses would want to hold down the taxes, environmentalists would opt for higher taxes, small businesses would seek preferential treatment because it would cost them more to reduce discharges, and so on. Administrative structures would be needed to develop studies and information for making these decisions. Moreover, once goals and taxes were set, an agency would be needed to monitor the discharge of pollutants (unless one was willing to trust polluters to monitor themselves) and to collect the taxes due. The more complex and finely calibrated the structure of pollution taxes, the more complex the monitoring program would have to be. Professor Deborah A. Stone remarks, "Where a standard and penalty system might levy a single fee for all discharges in excess of the standard, an incentive system would vary the taxes according to the amount of the discharges, and thus its information needs are greater than those of a standard system.[81]

Nor would the incentive system eliminate government coercion, because it consists of a control system contrived and imposed by government on economic behavior. Companies do have a choice between cleaning up or paying up, or some combination of the two. Their real preference, however, might be to do nothing; they are left to select from among governmentally mandated alternatives.

A couple of other objections to the incentive system should be noted. One is that it leaves decisions on how much to pollute to the judgment of private parties, dictated by self-interest, and fails to stigmatize pollution as "morally wrong."[82] A second objection is based on equity. Because of their stronger economic position, some will be better able to pay the emission taxes and avoid restriction. In other words, the law will bear down more heavily on some than on others.

An emissions-trading system was authorized by the Clean Air Act Amendments (CAAA) of 1990 as part of a strategy to combat acid rain. Each of 110 electric power plants named in the act was issued a specified number of allowables. An allowable permits a utility to discharge annually a ton of sulfur dioxide, beginning either in 1995, when the program became effective, or in the year 2000, when more stringent controls take effect. Companies reducing discharges below their specified levels by energy conservation programs, the burning of low-sulfur fuels, or the installation of smokestack scrubbers, can sell or "bank" excess allowables. Companies that exceed their specified levels of sulfur dioxide, and that do not buy additional allowables, will be subject to heavy fines.

The Chicago Board of Trade, a large commodity exchange, was authorized to establish a market for the purchase and sale of allowables. The first auction of allowables was held in March 1993. All of the allowables put on the market by EPA were bought but only a few privately offered allowables changed hands. The prices paid were only a fraction of the estimated costs of meeting pollution-reduction requirements by the use of scrubbers. Utility companies appeared wary of involvement in this new market.[83] The volume of allowables changing hands increased at the 1994 and 1995 auctions and prices rose a bit. One study concluded that "though the auction market has been sluggish and prices have fallen short of expectations, it appears that the intent of CAAA '90 is working."[84]

The hope for the emissions trading system is that it will both reduce air pollution and help minimize the costs of so doing. It will also provide an empirical test of the feasibility of using economic incentives to regulate economic activity.

COMPLIANCE

All public policies are intended to influence or control human behavior in some way and to induce people to act in accordance with government-prescribed rules or goals, whether reference is to policy on such diverse matters as interest rates, nighttime burglary, patents and copyrights, open housing, agricultural production, or military recruitment. If compliance with policy is not achieved, if people continue to act in undesired ways, if they do not take desired actions, or if they cease doing what is desired, to that extent policy becomes ineffective or, at the extreme, a nullity. (Foreign policy also depends for its effectiveness on compliance by the affected foreign countries and their officials.) To make consideration of this problem more manageable, we focus primarily but not exclusively on compliance with domestic economic policies.

Except perhaps for crime policies, social scientists have not given much attention to the problem of compliance.[85] This neglect may be caused partly by our traditional legalistic approach to government, with the assumption that people have an absolute duty to obey the law. Too, those whose aim is securing governmental action on public problems often lose interest therein or shift their attention elsewhere once they secure the enactment of legislation. So it was with the Elementary and Secondary Education Act of 1965, referred to above. Political scientists have certainly been far more interested in the legislative and executive formulation and adoption of policy than in its administration, which is where compliance comes into the picture. A complete study of policymaking must cover not only the events leading up to a decision on policy but also what is done to implement it and, ultimately, whether people comply with it.

In this section we examine some of the conditions affecting compliance and noncompliance with policy, along with the role of administrative agencies in securing compliance.[86] Because empirical data are not plentiful, the discussion must be somewhat speculative.

Causes of Compliance

Respect for authority, including authority as expressed in decisions by governmental agencies, is substantial in our society. Statements that Americans are a lawless people are exaggerations and should not be permitted to obscure the favorable disposition of most people toward compliance with public policies. Respect for and deference to authority are built into our psychological makeup by the process of socialization. Most of us are taught from birth to respect the authority of parents, knowledge, status, the law, and governmental officials, especially if these forms of authority are considered reasonable. Consequently, we grow up generally believing it to be morally right and proper to obey the law. Disobeying the law may produce feelings of guilt or shame. Prior conditioning and force of habit thus contribute to policy compliance.

Compliance with policy may also be based on some form of reasoned, conscious acceptance. Even some whose immediate self-interest conflicts with a policy may be convinced that it is reasonable, necessary, or just. Most people undoubtedly would rather not pay taxes, and many do try to avoid or evade their payment. But when people believe that tax laws are reasonable and just, or perhaps that taxation is necessary to provide needed governmental services, such beliefs will in all likelihood contribute to compliance with tax policy. Factors such as this and respect for authority clearly seem to contribute to the high degree of compliance with the national income tax in the United States.

Another possible cause of compliance is the belief that a governmental decision or policy should be obeyed because it is legitimate, in the sense that it is constitutional, or was made by officials with proper authority to act, or that correct procedures were followed in its development. People would be less inclined to accept judicial decisions as legitimate if the courts utilized decision-making procedures akin to those of legislatures. Courts gain legitimacy and acceptance for their decisions by acting as courts are supposed to act. Some people in the South were willing to comply with the Supreme Court's 1954 school desegregation decision because they considered it legitimate and within the Court's competence, even though they disagreed with its substance.

Self-interest is often an important consideration in compliance. Individuals and groups may directly benefit from accepting policy norms and standards. Thus farmers for decades complied with production limitations in the form of acreage allotments, marketing quotas, and set-asides in order to qualify for price supports and deficiency payments. Securities regulation is accepted by responsible members of the securities business as a way of protecting themselves and the reputation of their business against unethical practices by some wayward dealers. Businesses engage in industrial-plant modernization in order to receive investment tax credits. Milk price-control laws have long been supported and complied with by dairy interests as a way of improving their economic well-being. Compliance thus results because private interests and policy prescriptions are harmonious, a fact sometimes ignored. That is, compliance may yield monetary rewards. This arrangement, though, is not likely to occur outside the economic-policy area.

Any piece of legislation, such as a minimum-wage law or a Sunday-closing law, has more than simply supporters and opponents. Rather, many points of view will surround it, ranging from strong support through indifference to intense opposition. A sizable proportion of the population will often be indifferent or neutral toward the legislation, if indeed they feel affected by it at all. This group, given the general predisposition toward obedience, would seem especially subject to the authority of the law. Here in effect the law becomes a "self-fulfilling prophecy"; by its very existence it operates to create a climate of opinion conducive to compliance.

The possibility of punishment in the form of fines, jail sentences, and other penalties many also contribute to compliance. "Classical deterrence theory assumes that individuals respond to the severity, certainty, and celerity [speed] of punishment," state political scientists Anne Schneider and Helen Ingram, "and in this respect it implies that individuals are utility maximizers."[87] The threat or imposition of sanctions alone, however, is not always sufficient, even though the likelihood of their use is overestimated. "The strong disposition in this country to believe that any behavior can be controlled by threatening punishment has filled American statute books with hundreds of unenforced and unenforceable laws."[88] Experience with national prohibition, World War II price and rationing controls, many Sunday "blue laws," highway speed limits, and penalties for using marijuana show that the threat of punishment is not always sufficient to induce general compliance with policies.

Although many people may comply with policies because they fear punishment, the main function of sanctions is to reinforce and supplement other causes of compliance. Policies depend greatly for their effectiveness upon voluntary or noncoerced compliance, because those responsible for implementation cannot effectively handle and apply sanctions in large numbers of cases. The IRS, for example, would find itself at an impasse if several million people decided not to file returns. If those who would normally comply with policies see others benefiting from noncompliance, they too may become violators. Here the application of sanctions to some violators may be an effective promoter of compliance. Thus the IRS does prosecute flagrant and prominent tax evaders to prove by example that punishment awaits the tax evader.

In many instances, sanctions are effective more because people desire to avoid being stigmatized as lawbreakers than because they fear the possible penalties. In criminal proceedings for antitrust violations, the fines levied usually have been quite nominal, considering the violators' economic resources. Not until 1961 did a businessman actually spend time in jail for an antitrust violation, although this punishment had been possible since the Sherman Act was adopted in 1890. The real deterrent in these cases is probably the adverse publicity that flows from the proceedings. In recent years, Antitrust Division officials have been successfully advocating harsher penalties for antitrust violators, especially jail sentences, to encourage compliance. Legislators and judges, however, remain somewhat reluctant to create or impose jail sentences and other severe penalties on business people because of their social status and because of the often diffuse and complex nature of such law violations as embezzlement and the misuse of "insider information" in stock deals. In other situations, sanctions may be more severe and certain and have a more powerful deterrent effect.

Finally, acceptance of most policies seems to increase with the length of time they are in effect. As time passes (and it always does) a once-controversial policy becomes more familiar, part of the accepted state of things, a condition of doing business. Further, more and more persons come under the policy who have no experience with the prepolicy situation. Because "freedom is (in part) a state of mind, such men feel the restrictions to rest more lightly upon them."[89] Although at one time business interests found the Wagner Act of 1935 highly objectionable, and the Taft-Hartley Act of 1947 was bitterly opposed by labor unions, today these statutes have lost much of their controversial quality. They have become a fixed part of the environment of labor–management relations, and businesses and labor unions have "learned to live with them." Predictably, environmental pollution-control policies will seem less restrictive or intrusive in a decade or two than they do at present.

Causes of Noncompliance

Even to the most casual observer it is readily apparent that not all persons affected by public policies comply with them. Statistical information on reported violations is readily obtainable, as in the Federal Bureau of Investigation's Uniform Crime Reports. In addition, a lot of law violations go undetected or unreported. Why do some people, or in some situations many people, deviate from officially prescribed norms of behavior? As the obverse of compliance, noncompliance may result when laws conflict too sharply with the prevailing values, mores, and beliefs of the people generally or of particular groups. Much of the extensive violations of national prohibition and wartime price and rationing controls can be attributed in considerable measure to this cause, as may much of the noncompliance in the South with the Supreme Court's school desegregation decisions and related policies. In such instances, the general predisposition to obey the law is outweighed by strong attachment to strongly held values and established practices.

It is not very useful, however, to ascribe noncompliance to a broad conflict between law and morality. Those who proclaim that "you can't legislate morality" not only oversimplify the situation but also ignore the fact that morality is frequently legislated with considerable success. (Those who make this contention often cite national prohibition in its support). Failure to comply results when a law or set of laws conflicts with values or beliefs in a particular time and situation. This law–value conflict must be stated with fair precision if it is to have operational value in explaining noncompliance.

Thus quite a bit of noncompliance has confronted the Supreme Court's 1962 decision in *Engel* v. *Vitale* that using officially required prayers, even those that were thought nondenominational, in the public schools violated the First and Fourteenth Amendments' prohibition of the establishment of religion.[90] All efforts to legally circumvent this decision have failed.[91] The Supreme Court stirred the fire again in 1989 when, in a Georgia case, it let stand an appeals-court ruling that banned religious invocations at public high-school football games.[92] In a very different area of human activity, opinion surveys indicate that tax evasion is commonest among persons who do not believe that the federal tax system is fair in its effect.[93]

The concept of selective disobedience of the law is closely related to the law–value conflict.[94] Some laws are thought to be less binding than others on the individual. Those who strongly support and obey the statutes ordinarily labeled criminal laws sometimes have a more relaxed or permissive attitude toward economic regulatory legislation and laws on the conduct of public officials. Here one can aptly reflect on the behavior of Vice President Spiro T. Agnew, a staunch advocate of "law and order," who resigned his position after pleading *nolo contendere* (following plea bargaining) to a charge of federal income-tax evasion. Likewise, many business people apparently believe that laws relating to banking operations, insider stock trading, competitive trade practices, and environmental pollution are not as compelling for individuals as laws prohibiting robbery, burglary, and embezzlement. This attitude may be common partly because legislation controlling economic activity developed later than criminal laws and has yet to gain the same moral force. Moreover, much economic legislation runs counter to the ideological belief in limited nonintervention by government in the economy held by many people in business. They regard it as "bad law." Also, the same degree of social stigma usually is not attached to violations of economic policies as to criminal law offenses. Sociologist Marshall B. Clinard writes, "This selection of obedience to law rests upon the principle that what the person may be doing is illegal, perhaps even unethical, but certainly not criminal."[95]

One's associates and group memberships may also contribute to noncompliance (or, under other conditions, to compliance). Association with persons who hold ideas disrespectful of law and government, who justify or rationalize violation of the law, or who openly violate the law, may cause people to acquire deviant norms and values that dispose them to noncompliance. In a study of labor-relations policy, Professor Robert E. Lane found that the rate of law violations varied with the community in which the firms studied were located. It was "fairly conclusive" that one reason for these patterns of difference was the "difference in attitude toward the law, the government, and the morality of illegality. Plant managers stated that they followed community patterns of behavior in their labor-relations activities."[96] Similarly, attorneys for some of the defendant executives in the great electrical-industry price-fixing conspiracy late in the 1950s, which involved dozens of companies, including some of the largest in the industry, attempted to explain and justify their actions, hoping to lessen their punishment, as being in accord with the "corporate way of life."[97] The scandals that occurred in the savings and loan business in the 1980s and early 1990s indicate that such attitudes persist.

The desire to make a fast buck, or something akin thereto, is often proposed as a cause of noncompliance. This claim certainly seems applicable to many instances of fraud and misrepresentation, such as short-weighting and passing one product off for another in retail sales, promotion of shady land sales and investment schemes, failure to comply with minimum wage laws,[98] and price-fixing agreements. (Price-fixing continues to be the most obvious and the commonest violation of the Sherman Act.) It is really not possible, however, to determine how widespread greed is as a motive for noncompliance. By itself it often seems insufficient as an explanation. If two companies have equal opportunities to profit by violating the law, and one violates the law but the other does not, what is the explanation? One answer may be that companies that are less profitable or in danger of failure are more likely to violate in an effort to survive than are more financially secure firms.[99] One should be careful, however, in attributing noncompliance to pecuniary motives. Many violations of labor–management relations policy stem from a desire to protect management's prerogatives, and noncompliance with some industrial health and safety standards may rest on the conviction that they are unnecessary or unworkable.

Noncompliance may also stem from such factors as ambiguity in the law, lack of clarity, conflicting policy standards, or failure to adequately transmit policies to those affected by them. Income-tax violations often arise from the ambiguity or complexity of provisions of the Internal Revenue Code, which someone once described as a "sustained essay in obscurity." In other instances, persons or companies may believe that a practice is not prohibited by law, only to find upon prosecution that it is. The explanation may be that the frames of reference of business people and public officials are different, thus each interprets the law differently. Violations may also result from difficulty in complying with the law, even when its meaning is understood. Insufficient time may be allowed for filing complicated forms or for making required changes in patterns of action, as in installing pollution-control devices. Sheer ignorance of laws or rules regulating conduct also cannot be discounted as a cause of noncompliance. Though ignorance of the law may be no excuse, it often does account for violations. In sum, noncompliance may stem from structural defects in the law and its administration, and from ignorance and lack of understanding of the law, as well as from behavior that is more consciously or deliberately deviant.

Administration and Compliance

The burden of securing compliance with public policies rests primarily with administrative agencies; the courts play a lesser role. The broad purpose of many administrative enforcement activities, such as conferences, persuasion, inspection, and prosecution, is to secure compliance with policies rather than merely to punish violators.

Conscious human behavior involves making choices among alternatives, deciding to do some things and not others. For purposes of discussion, we can assume that there are essentially three ways in which administrative agencies, or other governmental bodies that engage in implementing public policy, can influence people to act in the desired ways, selecting behavioral alternatives that result in compliance with policy. First, to achieve a desired result, agencies can strive to shape, alter, or utilize the values people employ in making choices. Educational and persuasional activities illustrate this type of activity. Second, agencies can seek to limit the acceptable choices available to people, as by attaching penalties to undesired alternatives and rewards or benefits to desired alternatives. Third, agencies can try to interpret and administer policies in ways designed to facilitate compliance with their requirements. Thus time limits for compliance may be extended to give automobile manufacturers more time to meet tailpipe emission standards. More than one of these alternatives are normally used in seeking compliance with a policy.

Administrative agencies engage in many educational and persuasional activities intended to convince those directly affected, and the public generally, that designated public policies are reasonable, necessary, socially beneficial, or legitimate, in addition to informing them of the existence and meaning of those policies. The effectiveness of public policies depends considerably on the ability of agencies to promote understanding and consent, thereby reducing violations and minimizing use of sanctions. This approach is in keeping with my earlier comment on the importance of voluntary compliance. When changes are made in the coverage and level of the federal minimum-wage law, the Department of Labor seeks to acquaint the public, and especially employers and employees, about them and their implications by distributing explanatory bulletins, reference guides, and posters; announcements through the news media; meetings with affected groups; appearances at conventions; direct mailings; telephone calls; and the like. After the changes become effective, press releases and mailed materials provide information on enforcement activities and agency interpretations of the law. The Federal Deposit Insurance Corporation likewise relies heavily on advice and warnings to banks, based on inspections, to get them to bring their operations into accord with banking regulations. Formal proceedings are initiated only when persuasion appears ineffective. The Nuclear Regulatory Commission typically compiles a technical-assistance manual to assist the operators of nuclear power plants in complying with new regulations.[100]

Agencies may also use propaganda appeals in support of compliance. ("Propaganda" is used here not in a pejorative sense but rather to denote efforts to gain acceptance of policies by identifying them with widely held values and beliefs.) Appeals to patriotism were used to win support and acceptance of the military draft. Agricultural programs have been depicted as necessary to ensure equality for agriculture and to help preserve the family farm as a way of life. Antitrust programs have been described as necessary to maintain our system of free competitive enterprise. The Forest Service utilizes Smokey Bear to tell us that "only you can prevent forest fires." Propaganda appeals are more emotional than rational. They can be viewed as attempts either to reduce the moral cost of adapting to a policy or to make compliance desirable by attaching positive values to policies.[101]

In administering policies, agencies may make modifications in policies or adopt practices that will contribute to compliance. Revealed inequities in the law may be reduced or eliminated, conflicts in policy standards may be resolved, or simplified procedures for compliance may be developed, such as simplified federal income-tax forms for lower-income earners. Administrative personnel may develop knowledge and skill in enforcing policy that enables them to reduce misunderstanding and antagonism. Consultation and advice may be used to help those affected by laws come into compliance without issuing citations. Laws may be interpreted or applied to make them more compatible with the interests of those affected. The administration of policy on oil-import controls by the Oil Import Administration "was almost wholly in the interests of the petroleum industry."[102] They had little cause for complaint. Several hundred of the health and safety "consensus" standards initially issued by OSHA were later rescinded because of widespread complaints that they were outmoded, trivial, or of little use in protecting against health and safety hazards.[103] OSHA hoped thereby to reduce the antagonism of the business community toward itself by eliminating those standards.

Agencies will resort to sanctions when the sociological and psychological factors supporting obedience and other available methods fail to produce compliance. Sanctions are penalties or deprivations imposed on those who violate policy norms and are intended to make undesired behavior patterns unattractive. They directly punish violators and serve to deter others who might not comply if they saw violators go unpunished.

Sanctions can be imposed by either administrative agencies or the courts. Common forms of judicial sanctions are fines, jail sentences, award of damages, and injunctions. However, in most areas of public policy (crime policy is a major exception), administrative sanctions are used much more frequently because of their greater immediacy, variety, and flexibility. Among the sanctions that agencies may impose are threat of prosecution; imposition of fines or pecuniary penalties that have the effect of fines, as by OSHA; unfavorable publicity; revocation, annulment, modification, or suspension of, or refusal to renew, licenses; summary seizure and destruction of goods; award of damages; issuance of cease-and-desist orders; and denial of services or benefits. To be most effective, the severity of sanctions must be geared to the violations against which they are directed. If they are too severe, the agency may be reluctant to use them; if they are too mild, they may have inadequate deterrent effect, as seems to be the case with fines imposed by national and state agencies for pollution violations. In many instances, when fines were assessed, they were less than the economic benefits realized by the violators.[104] The Office of Education was thus handicapped in its early administration of Title I of the Elementary and Secondary Education Act because the only sanction it had for state and local violations was totally to cut off funds.

Because of the adverse reaction this penalty would have caused, the agency was politically reluctant to impose the penalty and chose not to do so. Agencies clearly need appropriate and effective sanctions to help ensure compliance with policy.

Agencies may also seek to induce compliance by conferring positive benefits on compliers and thereby bringing self-interest into support for compliance. This method can be referred to as the purchase of consent. Benefits may take such forms as favorable publicity and recognition for nondiscrimination in hiring, price-support payments for compliance with limitations on agricultural production, tax credits for industrial-plant modernization, and federal grants-in-aid for the support of state programs of medical aid to the indigent that meet federal standards. It is often difficult, however, to distinguish rewards from sanctions. Does an individual comply with a policy to secure a benefit or to avoid losing it? Whatever the motives of persons seeking benefits, the government does use rewards extensively to gain compliance with policy. In many situations they are much more acceptable politically than would be a clear-cut prohibition or requirement of some action with penalties for noncompliance. Imagine the reaction if, rather than using tax credits, businesses were required to modernize their plants or else be subject to fines and other penalties.

Clearly, then, compliance—or noncompliance—with public policies is a function of many factors. It is a complex topic that needs more explicit attention from policy analysts because of its importance for the implementation and effectiveness of public policies.

Notes

1. Peter C. Bishop and Augustus J. Jones, Jr., "Implementing the Americans with Disabilities Act of 1990: Assessing the Variables of Success," *Public Administration Review*, Vol. 53 (March–April 1993), pp. 121–128.
2. Cf. Randall B. Ripley and Grace A. Franklin, *Policy Implementation and Bureaucracy*, 2nd ed. (Chicago: Dorsey, 1986), pp. 4–5.
3. Charles S. Bullock III, and Charles M. Lamb, eds., *Implementation of Civil Rights* (Monterey, Calif.: Brooks/Cole, 1984), p. 5.
4. Those political scientists interested in the government regulation of business had long been concerned with implementation because of its policy consequences. See Emmette S. Redford, *The Administration of National Economic Control* (New York: Macmillan, 1952); and Marver H. Bernstein, *Regulatory Business by Independent Commission* (Princeton, N.J.: Princeton University Press, 1955).
5. Jeffrey L. Pressman and Aaron Wildavsky, *Implementation* (Berkeley: University of California Press, 1973). The book's subtitle is: "How Great Expecta-

tions in Washington are Dashed in Oakland: Or, Why It Is Amazing that Federal Programs Work at All, This Being a Saga of the Economic Development Administration as Told by Two Sympathetic Observers Who Seek to Build Morals on a Foundation of Ruined Hopes."

6. Representative studies of implementation include Eugene Bardach, *The Implementation Game: What Happens After a Bill Becomes Law?* (Cambridge, Mass.: MIT Press, 1977); David A. Mazmanian and Paul A. Sabatier, *Implementation and Public Policy* (Chicago: Scott, Foresman, 1983); and Malcolm L. Goggin, *Policy Design and the Politics of Implementation* (Knoxville: University of Tennessee Press, 1987).

7. Here I draw on James P. Lester and Joseph Stewart, Jr., *Public Policy: An Evolutionary Approach* (Minneapolis: West, 1996), chap. 7.

8. Charles T. Goodsell, *The Case for Bureaucracy*, 3rd ed. (Chatham, N.J.: Chatham House, 1994), chap. 1.

9. Frank Goodnow, *Politics and Administration* (New York: Russell and Russell, 1900).

10. Martha Derthick, *Agency Under Stress: The Social Security Administration in American Government* (Washington: Brookings Institution, 1990); and Susan Gluck Mezey, "Policy-making by the Federal Judiciary: The Effects of Judicial Review on the Social Security Disability Program," *Policy Studies Journal*, Vol. 14 (March 1986), pp. 343–355.

11. Theodore J. Lowi, *Legislative Politics, U.S.A.*, 2nd ed. (Boston: Little, Brown, 1965), p. xvi. His italics.

12 *Congressional Quarterly Weekly Report*, Vol. 51 (June 5, 1993), pp. 1425–1427.

13. *The New York Times*, March 31, 1989, p. 8.

14. Louis Fisher, *The Politics of Shared Power: Congress and the Executive*, 3rd ed. (Washington: Congressional Quarterly Press, 1993), pp. 73–84.

15. Leroy N. Reiselbach, *Congressional Politics: The Evolving Legislative System*, 2nd ed. (Boulder, Colo.: Westview, 1995), pp. 400–405.

16. David T. Stanley and Marjorie Girth, *Bankruptcy: Problems, Process, Reform* (Washington: Brookings Institution, 1971), p. 172.

17. *Adarand Constructors* v. *Pena* (1995). Reported in *The New York Times*, June 13, 1995, p. A8.

18. See Samuel P. Huntington, "The Marasmus of the ICC: The Commission, the Railroads, and the Public Interest," *Yale Law Journal*, LXI (1952), pp. 470–509.

19. This discussion draws on Harold Seidman and Robert Gilmour, *Politics, Position, and Power*, 4th ed. (New York: Oxford University Press, 1986), pp. 276, 293–300. See also General Accounting Office, *Federal Advisory Committee Act* (Washington: USGAO, October 1988).

20. Kay Lehman Scholzman and John T. Tierney, *Organized Interests and American Democracy* (New York: Harper & Row, 1986), p. 334.

21. Sheila Jasanoff, *The Fifth Branch: Science Advisers as Policy-makers* (Cambridge, Mass.: Harvard University Press, 1990), pp. 65–66.

22. James W. Davis, Jr., and Kenneth M. Dolbeare, *Little Groups of Neighbors: The Selective Service System* (Chicago: Markham, 1968).

23. Seidman and Gilmour, op. cit., p. 15.

24. Paul C. Light, *Thickening Government* (Washington: Brookings Institution, 1995).
25. Rowland Evans and Robert Novak, *Lyndon B. Johnson: The Exercise of Power* (New York: New American Library, 1966), p. 430.
26. *The New York Times*, November 27, 1986, p. 4.
27. *Congressional Quarterly Weekly Report*, Vol. 46 (October 29, 1988), pp. 3145–3146; *Newsweek*, Vol. 113 (April 10, 1989), pp. 20–24.
28. Paul C. Light, *Forging Legislation* (New York: Norton, 1992) tells the story of the department's creation.
29. *Congressional Quarterly Weekly Report*, Vol. 44 (September 20, 1986), pp. 2207–2208.
30. Patty D. Renfrow, "The Politics of Organizational Structure." Unpublished paper presented at the annual meeting of the American Political Science Association (September 14, 1983).
31. *Congressional Quarterly Weekly Report*, Vol. 40 (September 16, 1978), pp. 2485–2486; and Vol. 40 (October 7, 1978), pp. 2752–2753. For a full-scale treatment of the establishment of the Department of Education, see Beryl A. Radin and Willis D. Hawley, *The Politics of Federal Reorganization: Creating the U.S. Department of Education* (New York: Pergamon Press, 1988).
32. *Congressional Quarterly Weekly Report*, Vol. 40 (October 7, 1978), p. 2753.
33. John A. Ferejohn, "Logrolling in an Institutional Context: A Case Study of Food Stamps Legislation." Working Paper No. P85–5, Hoover Institution, Stanford University (October 1985).
34. Quoted in V. O. Key, Jr., *Politics, Parties, and Pressure Groups*, 4th ed. (New York: Crowell, 1958), p. 743.
35. This discussion draws some ideas from my *Politics and the Economy* (Boston: Little, Brown, 1966), pp. 86–90.
36. *Wall Street Journal*, August 10, 1989, p. 1; and *The New York Times*, August 13, 1993, p. 1.
37. Cf. Matthew Holden, Jr., "'Imperialism' in Bureaucracy," *American Political Science Review*, LX (December 1966), pp. 943–951.
38. Interview with the author.
39. Holden, op. cit., p. 944.
40. Daniel McCool, *Command of the Waters* (Berkeley: University of California Press, 1987), chap. 2.
41. This discussion, and that in the first part of the next section, draws on Francis E. Rourke, *Bureaucracy, Politics and Public Policy*, 3rd. ed. (Boston: Little, Brown, 1984), chaps. 4–5.
42. Ibid., pp. 106–107.
43. Ibid., p. 108.
44. On the separation of the ability to decide from the authority to decide in organizations, see Victor Thompson, *Modern Organizations* (New York: Knopf, 1961). See also James G. March, *A Primer of Decision Making* (New York: Free Press, 1994).
45. Theodore C. Sorensen, *Kennedy* (New York: Harper & Row, 1965), chap. 25. On secrecy in administration generally, see Harold L. Wilensky, *Organizational Intelligence* (New York: Basic Books, 1967), chaps. 3 and 7; and

Symposium on "The Freedom of Information Act," *Public Administration Review*, XXXIX (July–August 1979), pp. 310–332.

46. See James A. Nathan and James K. Oliver, *Foreign Policy Making and the American Political System*, 3rd ed. (Baltimore: John Hopkins University Press, 1994).

47. Rourke, op. cit., p. 108.

48. This story is told well by Richard E. Neustadt and Harvey V. Finebert, *The Swine Flu Affair* (Washington: U.S. Department of Health, Education, and Welfare, 1978).

49. Stephanie Ann Lenway, *The Politics of U.S. International Trade* (Marshfield, Mass.: Pitman, 1985).

50. Florence Heffron, with Neil McFreely, *The Administrative Regulatory Process* (New York: Longman, 1983), pp. 226–235.

51. Cornelius M. Kerwin, *Rule-Making: How Government Agencies Write Law and Make Policy* (Washington: CQ Press, 1994), pp. 89–90.

52. Heffron, op. cit., p. 239.

53. Kerwin, op. cit., pp. 63–67.

54. Ibid., p. 111.

55. Heffron, op. cit., pp. 227–230.

56. *Wall Street Journal*, February 5, 1973, p. 1.

57. Clayton R. Koppes, "Public Water, Private Land: Origins of the Acreage Limitation Controversy," *Pacific Historical Review*, Vol. 47 (November 1978), pp. 607–636.

58. Hamilton Condee, "The Broken Promise of Reclamation Reform," *Hasting Law Journal*, XL (March 1989), pp. 657–685; *Wall Street Journal*, May 30, 1991, p. 1; and General Accounting Office, *Water Subsidies* (Washington: USGAO, October, 1989).

59. A cease-and-desist order is an agency's civil directive to stop engaging in a practice held to be in violation of the law. Agencies such as the Federal Trade Commission and the NLRB are authorized to issue such orders.

60. Ashley Schiff, *Fire and Water: Scientific Heresy in the Forest Service* (Cambridge: Harvard University Press, 1962).

61. Thomas Hackett, "A Reporter at Large (Yellowstone)," *The New Yorker*, Vol. 65, (October 2, 1989), pp. 50–73.

62. George Wuerthner, "Fire Power," *National Parks*, Vol. 69 (May–June 1995), pp. 33–36; and *Federal Register*, Vol. 60 (June 22, 1995), pp. 32485–32503.

63. Harold Wolman, *Politics of Federal Housing*, 20 (New York: Dodd, Mead, 1971), pp. 26–28.

64. This account relies on Michael Kirst and Richard Jong, "The Utility of a Longitudinal Approach in Assessing Implementation: A Thirteen-Year View of Title I, ESEA," in Walter K. Williams, et al., *Studying Implementation* (Chatham, N.J.: Chatham House, 1982), chap. 6; and June A. O'Neil and Margaret C. Simms, "Education," in John L. Palmer and Isabel C. Sawhill, eds., *The Reagan Experiment* (Washington: Urban Institute, 1982), chap. 11.

65. *Congressional Quarterly Weekly Report*, Vol. 52 (October 8, 1994), pp. 2885–2886.

66. "Smokey Bear at 50: Still Going Strong," *National Woodlands*, Vol. 17 (April 1994), pp. 16–19.

67. This paragraph draws on Ann Schneider and Helen Ingram, "Behavioral Assumptions of Policy Tools," *Journal of Politics,* Vol. 52 (May 1990), pp. 510–529.

68. Emmette A. Redford, *The Administration of National Economic Control* (New York: Macmillan, 1952), p. 104.

69. Stephen Breyer, *Regulation and Its Reform* (Cambridge, Mass.: Harvard University Press, 1982), pp. 90–95.

70. Donald K. Kettle, *Sharing Power: Governance and Private Markets* (Washington: Brookings Institution, 1993), chap. 3.

71. John David Skrentny, *The Ironies of Affirmative Action: Politics, Culture, and Justice in America* (Chicago: University of Chicago Press, 1996), pp. 133–134.

72. Kenneth J. Meier, *The Politics of Sin: Drugs, Alcohol, and Public Policy* (Armonk, N.Y.: M.E. Sharpe, 1994), chap. 5.

73. Daniel P. Franklin, *Making Ends Meet: Congress Budgeting in the Age of Deficits* (Washington: Congressional Quarterly Press, 1993), p. 23.

74. Charles Schultze, *The Public Use of Private Interests* (Washington: Brookings Institution, 1977).

75. Paul R. McDaniel, "Tax Expenditures as Tools of Government Action," in Lester M. Salamon, ed., *Beyond Privatization: The Tools of Government Action* (Washington: Urban Institute, 1989), chap. 6; and Christopher Howard, "Testing the Tools Approach: Tax Expenditures v. Direct Expenditures," *Public Administration Review,* Vol. 55 (September–October 1995), pp. 439–447.

76. Joseph A. Pechman, *Federal Tax Policy,* 5th ed. (Washington: Brookings Institution, 1987), pp. 355–362.

77. Peter Woll, *American Bureaucracy,* 2nd ed. (New York: Norton, 1977), p. 95.

78. Martin C. Schnitzer, *Contemporary Government and Business Relations,* 4th ed. (Boston: Houghton Mifflin, 1990), p. 242.

79. This discussion draws on Deborah A. Stone, *Policy Paradox and Political Reason* (Glenview, Ill.: Scott, Foresman, 1988), p. 225; and Schultze, op. cit.

80. Allen Kneese and Charles Schultze, *Pollution Prices and Public Policy* (Washington: Brookings Institution, 1975), p. 89.

81. Stone, op. cit., p. 228.

82. Michael D. Reagan, *Regulation: The Politics of Policy* (Boston: Little, Brown, 1987), p. 142. See also Steven Kelman, *What Price Incentives? Economists and the Environment* (Boston: Auburn House, 1981), pp. 27–28.

83. *The New York Times,* April 8, 1993, p. C2; and *Illinois Agri-News,* April 9, 1993, p. C7.

84. "Project: Regulatory Reform: A Survey of the Impact of Reregulation and Deregulation on Selected Industries and Sectors," *Administrative Law Review,* Vol. 47 (Fall 1995), p. 476.

85. A notable exception is Kenneth J. Meier and David R. Morgan, "Citizen Compliance with Public Policy: The National Maximum Speed Law," *Western Political Quarterly,* XXXV (June 1982), pp. 258–273.

86. This discussion depends heavily on my "Public Economic Policy and the Problems of Compliance: Notes for Research," *Houston Law Review,* IV (Spring–Summer 1966), pp. 62–72.

87. Anne Schneider and Helen Ingram, "Behavioral Theories in Policy Designs." Unpublished paper presented at the Midwest Political Association meeting (1989).

88. Herbert A. Simon, Donald Smithburg, and Victor Thompson, *Public Administration* (New York: Knopf, 1950), p. 479.

89. Robert Lane, *The Regulation of Businessmen* (New Haven: Yale University Press, 1954), pp. 69–70.

90. 370 U.S. 421 (1962).

91. See John A. Murley, "School Prayer: Free Exercise of Religion or Establishment of Religion," in Raymond Tatalovich and Byron W. Daynes, eds., *Social Regulatory Policy* (Boulder, Colo.: Westview Press, 1989), chap. 1.

92. *Houston Post,* May 31, 1989, pp. 1, 6.

93. Timothy B. Clark, "Honesty May Become the Best Tax Policy If Tax Compliance Bill Becomes Law," *National Journal,* Vol. 14 (July 24, 1982), pp. 1292–1296.

94. Marshall B. Clinard, *Sociology of Deviant Behavior* (New York: Holt, Rinehart and Winston, 1957), pp. 168–171.

95. Ibid.

96. Robert E. Lane, "Why Business Men Violate the Law," *Journal of Criminal Law, Criminology, and Police Science,* XLIV (1953), pp. 151, 154–160.

97. John G. Fuller, *The Gentlemen Conspirators: The Story of the Price-Fixers in the Electrical Industry* (New York: Grove Press, 1962), pp. 88, 109–110.

98. G. Pascal Zachary, "The Minimum Wage Law Is Frequently Ignored in Some Industries," *Wall Street Journal,* May 20, 1996, p. 1. See also idem., "Many Firms Refuse to Pay Overtime, Employees Complain," *Wall Street Journal,* June 24, 1996, p. 1.

99. Lane, op. cit., chap. 5.

100. Kerwin, op. cit., p. 81.

101. Simon, Smithburg, and Thompson, op. cit., p. 457.

102. Roger G. Noll, *Reforming Regulation* (Washington: Brookings Institution, 1971), p. 65.

103. *Wall Street Journal,* May 19, 1977, p. 40; and Timothy B. Clark, "What's All the Uproar Over OSHA's Nit-Picking Rules?" *National Journal,* Vol. 10 (October 7, 1978), pp. 1594–1596.

104. General Accounting Office, *Environmental Enforcement: Penalties May Not Recover Economic Benefits Gained by Violators* (Washington: USGAO, June 1991), pp. 5–10.

7

POLICY IMPACT, EVALUATION, AND CHANGE

House Speaker Newt Gingrich and Senate Majority Leader Bob Dole prepare to respond to a presidential statement. Policy and partisan differences often intermingle.

W hen the policy process is viewed as a sequential pattern of activities, its final stage is policy evaluation. More of an art than a science, policy evaluation encompasses the estimation, assessment, or appraisal of a policy, including its content, implementation, goal attainment, and other effects. Evaluation may also try to identify factors that contribute to the success or failure of a policy.

As a functional activity, policy evaluation can occur throughout the policy process, not simply after a period of policy implementation. Attempts are frequently made to determine prospectively—that is, to estimate—the likely effects of various policy alternatives for dealing with a problem prior to the adoption of one of them. In this chapter we focus primarily, but not exclusively, on policy evaluation connected with efforts to implement or carry out policies. As we shall see, evaluation may identify problems or shortcomings that cause the policy process to recycle (problem definition, formulation, adoption, and so on) in order to continue, modify, strengthen, or terminate a policy.

Policy evaluation, as a functional activity, is as old as policy itself. Legislators, administrators, judges, pressure-group officials, media commentators, and citizens have always made judgments about the worth or effects of particular policies, programs, and projects. The Boston Tea Party, for instance, was a consequence of an unfavorable evaluation of one of King George's tax policies for the colonies. Many of these judgments have been of an impressionistic or intuitive variety, based at best on anecdotal or fragmentary evidence, and strongly influenced by ideological, partisan, or idiosyncratic valuational criteria. Thus staunch conservatives may regard public housing programs as socialistic and in need of repeal, regardless of their causes or consequences; or Democrats may support higher taxes on corporations and the rich because they believe this will enhance their electoral opportunities. Unemployment compensation may be deemed a "bad" program because the evaluator claims to know "a lot of people" who improperly receive benefits. Stories about "welfare queens" who drive Cadillacs to collect their welfare checks are commonplace among welfare critics. Most of us are familiar with this style of policy evaluation and have perhaps enjoyed doing a bit of it ourselves. Much conflict results from this sort of evaluation, however, because different evaluators, depending upon the values or criteria they employ, may reach sharply divergent conclusions on the merits of the same policy.

Another form of policy evaluation centers on process, on the operation or administration of a policy or program.[1] (A program can be defined as a set of rules, routines, and resources created to implement a policy or portion thereof. The Department of Transportation's Essential Air Service program subsidizes commercial air service to small cities to help ensure its continuation.) Questions asked about how a program is being run may include: What are its financial costs? Who receives benefits (payments or services) and in what amounts? Is there unnecessary overlap with or duplication of other programs? Are legislatively prescribed standards and procedures being followed? Is the program honestly administered? This kind of evaluation, which may involve much monitoring of agencies and their officials, will tell us something about whether there is honesty or efficiency in the conduct of a program, but, like the first kind of evaluation, it will probably yield little or nothing in the way of hard information concerning the societal effects (outcomes) of a program. On the other hand, process evaluation is often helpful to program managers wanting to improve the administration of their programs and reduce their potential for political criticism.

A third, comparatively new type of policy evaluation, which has been getting increasing attention in the national government in recent decades, is the systematic and intendedly objective evaluation of programs. This form of evaluation, which I will refer to as systematic evaluation, employs social science methodology to measure the societal effects of policies or programs and the extent to which they are achieving their goals or objectives.

The Departments of Labor, Health and Human Services, and Energy, for instance, have assistant secretaries whose responsibilities include program evaluation. Bureaus within these and other departments often include policy- and program-evaluation staffs. Moreover, they enter into many contracts with private research organizations, university scholars, and others for the performance of evaluation studies. More attention appears to be given to evaluating social programs (welfare, education, health, and nutrition) than most other areas of governmental activity. This preference probably arises from the proliferation of social programs in recent decades, their substantial financial costs, and the controversies that swirl around them.

Systematic evaluation seeks information on the effects of a policy or program on the public need or problem at which it is directed. Utilizing particularly the talents of social scientists (economists, political scientists, psychologists, and sociologists), it involves the specification of goals or objectives; the collection of information and data on program inputs, outputs, and consequences; and their rigorous analysis, preferably through the use of quantitative or statistical techniques. Evaluation researchers employ a number of evaluation designs, three of which are discussed here: the experimental design, the quasi-experimental design, and the before-and-after study.[2]

The *experimental design* is the classic method for evaluating a policy or program. Two comparable groups—an experimental, or treatment, group and a control group—are randomly selected from the target population. The experimental group receives treatment through a policy or program; the control group does not. Pretests and posttests of the two groups are used to determine whether changes, such as improved reading scores or lower incidences of a disease, have occurred in the two groups. If the performance of the experimental group is significantly better than that of the control, the program is held to be effective. A high level of validity and generalizability is accorded the results of experiments. An example is in order.

In the 1980s the Delaware Department of Labor conducted a field experiment[3] to assess the effectiveness of various activities in helping "dislocated workers"—"persons who have lost long-term, stable jobs due to an increased international competition and/or changing technology."[4] The goals of the program for dislocated workers, which was funded through the Job Partnership Training Act discussed in Chapter 1, were to help increase workers' earnings and reduce their need for unemployment compensation benefits. A coterie of 175 workers with comparable characteristics was identified; 65 were randomly assigned to the treatment group, with the other 110 becoming the control group. Members of the treatment group were provided counseling on job-search activities, assistance in locating openings, retraining, and other services. Both groups were monitored for a year. Comparison of their performance revealed that the control group did better than the treatment group in meeting the program's goals. It was concluded that "the program did not appear to improve participants' job prospects."[5]

Use of the experimental design may not be possible because of costs, time, and ethical or other considerations. The *quasi-experiment* then may be a useful alternative. The process of random selection is not used. Rather, the treatment group is compared with another group (a "comparison group") that is similar in many respects. Consequently, in the quasi-experiment there is greater likelihood that the performances of the two groups could be influenced by their internal characteristics rather than the program treatment. Quasi-experiments nonetheless are still seen as quite useful for many purposes.

A well-known quasi-experiment involves the Connecticut highway speed-control program. Following a record number of highway traffic fatalities, the state initiated a crackdown on speeding. Initial data indicated that the enforcement program had significantly reduced fatalities. It was possible, however, that this resulted from other factors, such as differences in the weather or more safe cars in operation. To control for such possibilities, the Connecticut highway fatality rate per 100,000 people was compared with that of neighboring states where there had been no enhanced enforcement program. This showed that Connecticut's fatality rate was lower than the other states', thus supporting the inference that the Connecticut crackdown had a positive effect in reducing traffic deaths.

The *before-and-after study* of a program compares the results of a program after a period of implementation with the conditions existing prior to its inception. Thus one might compare the quality of water in a river before and after a pollution-control program was put into effect. Before-and-after studies often have low costs and take less time to conduct. A major drawback, however, is that the changes that occur are open to rival explanations. Improved water quality in our imaginary river could be due to increased flow, voluntary action by polluters, or economic recession having caused reduced industrial activity. On the other hand, if a before-and-after study finds little change in the desired direction, then it is likely that the program is not having much effect.[7] Given all of this, it is still possible for before-and-after studies to produce much information about a program that otherwise would be unavailable.

As this discussion indicates, systematic evaluation draws on experience in assessing the effects a policy or program has on the public need or problem at which it is directed. It permits at least tentative, informed responses to such questions as: Is this policy achieving its stated objectives? What are its costs and benefits? Who are its beneficiaries? What happened as a consequence of the policy that would not have happened in its absence? Consequently, systematic evaluation gives policy-makers and the general public, if they are interested, some notion about the actual impact of policy and provides discussions of policy with some grounding in reality. Evaluation findings can be used to modify current policies and programs and to help design others for the future.

Of course, evaluation studies can also be used for less laudable purposes. Professor Carol Weiss comments, "Program decision-makers may turn to evaluation to delay a decision; to justify and legitimate a decision already made; to extricate themselves from controversy about future directions by passing the buck; to vindicate the program in the eyes of its constituents, its funders, or the public; to satisfy conditions of a government or foundation grant through the ritual of evaluation."[8] In short, evaluators may be motivated by self-service as well as public service and by a desire to use analysis as ammunition for partisan or personal political purposes. Thus, the staff of the Federal Paperwork Commission was interested only in evaluations supportive of their goal of eliminating as much governmental regulation of business as possible, albeit under the guise of paperwork reduction.[9]

POLICY IMPACT

To begin, there is need to draw a distinct line between policy outputs and policy outcomes. Policy outputs are the things actually done by agencies in pursuance of policy decisions and statements. The concept of outputs focuses one's attention on such matters as amounts of taxes collected, miles of highways built, welfare benefits paid, price-fixing agreements prosecuted, traffic fines collected, or foreign-aid projects undertaken. Outputs usually can be readily counted, totaled, and statistically analyzed. Examining outputs may indicate, or seem to indicate, that a lot is being done to implement a policy. Such activity, however, sometimes amounts to nothing more than what Professor William T. Gormley, Jr., calls "bean counting." Agencies, under pressure from legislators, interest groups, and others to demonstrate results, "may focus on outputs, not outcomes, in order to generate statistics that create the illusion of progress."[10] If the percentage of students graduating from universities in a state increases, does this tell us anything about the quality of education that they are receiving?

Policy outcomes, in contrast, are the consequences for society, intended and unintended, that stem from deliberate governmental action or inaction. Social-welfare policies can be used to illustrate this concept. It is fairly easy to measure welfare-policy outputs such as amounts of benefits paid, average level of benefits, and number of people assisted. But what are the outcomes, or societal consequences, of these actions? Do they increase personal security and contentment? Do they reduce individual initiative? Does Aid to Families with Dependent Children (AFDC) have the effect of encouraging promiscuity and illegitimacy, or teenage pregnancies, as some allege? Do welfare programs help keep the poor quiescent, as others contend?[11] Questions such as these, which are tough to answer, direct our attention to the societal effects of policies. Among other things, as policy students we want to know whether policies are accomplishing their intended purposes, whether society is changing as a consequence of policy actions and not because of other factors such as private economic decisions, and whether it is changing as intended or in other ways. Policy impacts are an amalgam of outputs and outcomes.

The impact of a policy may have several dimensions, all of which should be taken into account either in the conduct of a formal evaluation or in the course of an informal appraisal of the policy.[12] They include the following:

1. Policies affect the public problem at which they are directed and the people involved. Those whom the policy is intended to affect must be defined, whether they are the poor, small-business people, disadvantaged schoolchildren, petroleum producers, or whoever. The intended effect of the policy must then be determined. If it is an antipoverty program, is its purpose to raise the income of the poor, to increase their opportunities for employment, or to change their attitudes and behavior? If some combination of such purposes is intended, analysis becomes more complicated because priorities should be assigned to the various intended effects. Typically, policies accomplish at least a portion of their goals or objectives.

Further, a policy may have either intended or unintended (unforeseen or unplanned) consequences, or even both. A welfare program, for example, may improve the income situation of the benefited groups, as intended by its proponents, but what impact does it have on their initiative to seek employment? Does it decrease this initiative, as some have contended? A public-housing program may improve the housing situation of urban blacks, but it may also be so administered as to contribute to racial segregation in housing. An agricultural price-support program, intended to improve farmers' incomes, also may lead to overproduction of the supported commodities, to higher food prices for consumers, or to an increase in land values.

A good illustration of a policy with unintended consequences is the 1970 legislation prohibiting the broadcasting of cigarette advertising on radio and television. This ad ban was widely viewed as a legislative victory for the antismoking forces. However, the ban also eliminated the need for broadcasters, under the Federal Communications Commission's fairness doctrine (which was repealed in the mid-1980s), to donate airtime to antismoking groups on the controversial issue of smoking. Research indicates that the antismoking messages prepared by these groups, which contained grim or unappealing portrayals of smoking, had a substantial deterrent effect upon cigarette consumption. The antismoking ad campaign, however, depended heavily upon donated time. As a consequence, after the ban on cigarette ads went into effect, most of the antismoking ads were also eliminated. The short-term effect was clearly a significant increase in smoking, obviously not what the proponents of the ban had intended. Although the long-run effects are less clear, "the weight of the evidence seems to favor the conclusion that the ad ban was myopic policy."[13]

2. Policies may affect situations or groups other than those at which they are directed. These are variously called third-party effects, spillover effects, or externalities.[14] The construction of urban interstate highways are of much benefit to motorists and trucking companies. However, they also cause inconvenience, disruption, and social discretion for the neighborhoods through which they run. Clear-cutting in national forests, which is of benefit to timber companies and in line with the perspective of those who view forests as tree farms, is profoundly disturbing to environmentalists, nature lovers, and many sportsmen, because it results in the destruction of wildlife habitat, the loss of aesthetic value, and the siltation of trout streams.

These two examples portray negative externalities, but externalities may also be positive. Public-education programs not only educate students, they also provide employers with a more capable work force and the community with better-informed citizens. Those who contend that only those who have children in public schools should contribute toward their support ignore such positive externalities. Although pollution-control programs impose costs on many industries, they are a boon to the manufacturers of pollution-control equipment. Many of the outcomes of public policies can be most meaningfully understood as externalities that impose costs or provide benefits for third parties.

3. Policies have consequences for future as well as current conditions; for some policies most of their benefits or some of their costs may occur in the far future. Was the Head Start program—a preschool education program for the

poor—supposed to improve participating children's short-term cognitive abilities or their long-range development and earning capacity? Did regulation of the field price of natural gas, a policy initiated in the 1950s and extending into the 1980s, really produce a shortage of gas in the 1970s, as some contended (notably petroleum-industry officials and their supporters, who had long been critics of price regulation)?

The future effects of some policies may be very diffuse or uncertain. Assuming that patent and copyright policies do indeed stimulate invention and creativity, and that these activities in turn enhance economic growth and societal development, how does one measure their benefits, either qualitatively or quantitatively? Again, how does one appraise (with reasonable objectivity) the effects of the National Foundation on the Arts and Humanities' support for literacy, artistic, and museum activities? Would the elimination of such policies as these have deleterious consequences for American society?

4. Just as policies have positive effects or benefits, they also entail costs. Economists seem never to tire of telling us that there is no such thing as a free lunch. Costs come in different forms. First, there are the direct costs for the governmental implementation of a policy or program. These are usually fairly easy to calculate, whether stated as the actual amount of money spent on the program, its share of total governmental expenditures, or the proportion of the gross domestic product devoted to it. Budgeting documents will yield such figures. If, however, a governmental expenditure serves multiple purposes, such as operating the space program and developing new technology, the allocation of costs becomes more perplexing.

Direct costs also include private expenditures that are necessary in order to comply with public policies, such as those on industrial health and safety and environmental pollution control. These may be more difficult to discover or calculate. Moreover, it is possible that some companies would have installed protective devices in the absence of policy. Should their costs then be assigned to the policy? In the absence of governmental subsidies, the costs of complying with regulatory policies initially fall primarily on the regulated, who have an ideological incentive to inflate claimed costs, deliberately making the policies appear more burdensome. Ultimately, of course, such compliance costs are likely to be shifted to consumers in the form of higher prices for goods and services.

This brings us to the matter of indirect costs. Public policies may cause reduced production, higher prices, or mental anguish or distress. Expenditures to meet coal-mine safety requirements may cause a reduction in mine output. People called for jury services typically receive compensation that does no more than cover commuting costs. The consequence is lost wages, or lost production, or both. Many public policies have indirect or social costs of these sorts. Mental anguish may occur when one's home town is flooded by a new impoundment. Financial compensation may be paid for one's childhood home, but what of the loss that occurs because, being under forty feet of water, it can no longer be visited? The concept of indirect cost often calls for putting a price tag on intangibles. They tend to defy measurement.

Finally, there are opportunity costs, a concept that rests upon the facts that we cannot do everything at once, and that resources used for one purpose (e.g., flood control) cannot be used for another purpose (e.g., public housing). "Opportunity cost is a decision making rather than an accounting concept."[15] It focuses attention on what one has to give up (or, alternatively, what one will gain) if resources are used for one purpose rather than another. Thus economists argue that the United States' all-volunteer army will not attract needed recruits if the opportunity costs of military service are kept below those of civilian life. When the ranks of the military were largely filled by draftees, less concern had to be given to opportunity costs and the compensation of service personnel.[16]

5. The effects of policies and programs may be either material (tangible) or symbolic (intangible). The consequences of symbols are both important and hard to measure. Symbolic outputs, according to political scientists Gabriel A. Almond and G. Bingham Powell, "include affirmations of values by elites; displays of flags, troops, and military ceremony; visits by royalty or high officials; and statements of policy or intent by political leaders." Consequently, they "are highly dependent on tapping popular beliefs, attitudes, and aspirations for their effectiveness."[17] Symbolic policy outputs produce no readily discernible changes in societal conditions. No one eats better because of a Memorial Day parade or a stirring speech by a high public official on the virtues of free enterprise, however ideologically or emotionally satisfying such actions may be for many people. More to the point, however, policy actions ostensibly directed toward meeting material wants or needs may turn out in practice to be more symbolic than material in their effect.

This shift in policy tone is well illustrated by the Fair Housing Act of 1968. Enacted by Congress in part because of pressure created by the assassination of Dr. Martin Luther King, Jr., the 1968 law prohibited discrimination in the rental or sale of housing because of race, color, religion, sex, or national origin. However, the Department of Housing and Urban Development (HUD), which was assigned primary responsibility for its enforcement, could only seek to mediate disputes between a person who thought he or she had been discriminated against and the renter or seller. The Justice Department in turn could not act unless it found a "pattern or practice" of discrimination. As a consequence of these weak enforcement provisions, the Fair Housing Act in practice did not live up to its promise. The act, which one member of Congress called a "toothless tiger," was of little use in preventing discrimination in housing.

The Congress in 1988 reached a compromise agreement on legislation to strengthen enforcement of the Fair Housing Act. Now a person who believes he or she has been discriminated against can file a complaint with HUD, which, if it cannot settle the dispute, can issue a charge of housing discrimination. At this point either party to the dispute can choose to have it decided by either a federal district court or an administrative hearing. If either party chooses to go to the federal court, that choice prevails. It was expected that this procedure would put some real "teeth" into the enforcement of the act and give it material rather than merely symbolic effect.

Other public policies that appear to promise more symbolically than their implementation yields in material benefits include antitrust activity, public-utility rate regulation, and equal employment opportunity. Even though the actual effect of a policy may be considerably less than is intended or desired, it nonetheless may have significant consequences for society. An antipoverty program that falls short of its mark may provide some assurance to people that the government cares about poor people and wants to reduce poverty. Legislation on equal employment opportunity informs people that their government, officially at least, does not condone discrimination in hiring on the basis of race, sex, or nationality. Apart from the effects such policies have on societal conditions, they may contribute to the maintenance of social order, support for government, and personal self-esteem, which are not inconsequential considerations.

The analysis and evaluation of public policy is usually focused upon what governments actually do, why, and with what material effects. We should not, however, neglect the symbolic aspects of government, despite their intangible and nebulous nature. The rhetoric of government—what governments say, or appear to say—is clearly a necessary and proper subject for the policy analyst.

We now turn to some of the ways in which policy evaluation is handled in the national government.

POLICY EVALUATION PROCESSES

Much policy evaluation is performed by nongovernmental actors. The communications media; university scholars and research centers; private research organizations such as the Brookings Institution, the Urban Institute, and the American Enterprise Institute; pressure groups; and public-interest organizations such as Common Cause, the Audubon Society, and Ralph Nader and his "raiders" (a collection of public-interest activists) all make evaluations of public policies and programs that have greater or lesser effects on public officials. They also provide the general public with information, publicize policy success and failure, sometimes act as advocates for unpopular causes, and occasionally provide representation for those unrepresented in the policy process, such as the aged confined to negligently run nursing homes or exploited migratory farm workers.

Private actors may engage in policy evaluation on their own initiative or under contracts with government agencies, who annually spend many millions of dollars on policy evaluations. Some private organizations, such as the nonprofit Manpower Development Research Corporation, exist solely for the purpose of performing evaluation studies. Many academic social scientists have departed, some permanently, others temporarily, from the ivory tower to engage in policy evaluation. Collectively, this aggregation of private policy evaluators has been designated by Richard Hofferbert as the "policy evaluation industry."[18]

Within the boundaries of the national government, policy evaluation is undertaken in numerous ways by a variety of officials and organizations. Sometimes this evaluation is highly rigorous and systematic; at other times it is rather haphazard or sporadic. In some instances policy evaluation has become institutionalized; in others it is essentially informal and unstructured. In this section we take a short look at a few forms of official policy evaluation, including congressional oversight, studies by the General Accounting Office (GAO), the activities of presidential commissions, and "in-house" evaluations by agencies themselves.[19]

Congressional Oversight

Although it is not specified in the Constitution, one of the primary functions of Congress is the supervision and evaluation of the administration and execution of laws and policies, which is commonly referred to as congressional oversight. Some, agreeing with the English political theorist John Stuart Mill, think that this is the most important function a legislature performs.[20] Oversight, however, is not a separable, distinct activity; rather, it is an integral part of almost everything that members of Congress do, including gathering information, legislating, authorizing appropriations, and being of service to constituents. It may be intended either to control the actions of agencies, as when they sometimes are required to clear actions in advance with particular committees, or to evaluate agency actions, as when individual members or committees seek to determine whether administrators are complying with program objectives established by Congress. It is the evaluative aspect of oversight that is pertinent here.

Oversight may be performed by a number of techniques, including: (1) casework, that is, intercession with agencies as a consequence of constituents' demands and requests; (2) committee hearings and investigations; (3) the appropriations process; (4) approval of presidential appointments; and (5) committee staff studies.[21] In the course of these activities, members of Congress reach conclusions about the efficiency, effectiveness, and impact of policies and programs—conclusions that can have profound consequences for the policy process. Congressional oversight is in essence more fragmented and disjointed than continuous and systematic. Bits and pieces of information, impressionistic judgments, and the members' intuition and values are blended to yield evaluation of policies and those who administer them. On the whole, however, members of Congress are more likely to be involved with initiation and adoption of policy than with evaluation, at least in any systematic sense.

General Accounting Office

The GAO, usually regarded as an arm of Congress, has broad statutory authority to audit the operations and financial activities of federal agencies, to evaluate their programs, and to report its findings to Congress.[22] The agency, which has several thousand employees, has become increasingly involved with the evaluation of programs since the early 1970s and now gives only a minor portion of its attention to financial auditing.

The Legislative Reorganization Act of 1970, which revamped the congressional committee system, also directed the GAO to "review and analyze the results of government programs and activities carried on under existing law, including the making of cost-benefit studies," and to make personnel available to assist congressional committees in handling similar activities. A subsequent statute authorized GAO to establish an Office of Program Review and Evaluation. Because of its expanded evaluation activities, the agency hires many more people trained in the social sciences than it once did.

Evaluation activities may be undertaken by the GAO on its own initiative, because of directives in legislation, at the request of congressional committees, or sometimes at the behest of individual members of Congress. In the course of a year, the GAO will produce several hundred evaluation studies, varying in length from several pages to a few hundred. Three important studies in 1995 bore titles that indicate both their subject and intent: "EPA and the States: Environmental Challenges Require a Better Working Relationship," "Job Corps: High Costs and Mixed Results Raise Questions About Program's Effectiveness," and "Economic Statistics: Measurement Problems Can Affect the Budget and Economic Policy-making." GAO officials also frequently testify before congressional committees.[23]

Copies of GAO studies are sent to members of Congress and the affected agencies. The agencies are required by law to report to Congress and the

Office of Management and Budget on actions taken in response to GAO's recommendations or on why they did not act.

A short case study will help convey an understanding of the GAO evaluation process. Food safety continues to be a problem in the United States. The Federal Centers for Disease Control estimate that 9,000 people die in the U.S. each year from food-borne illnesses; millions more suffer from food-related illnesses. In 1992 at the request of the chair of the Subcommittee on Oversight and Investigations of the House Committee on Energy and Commerce, the GAO undertook an evaluation of the consistency, effectiveness, and coordination of the federal food-safety inspection system.[24] Data and information for the study were acquired by interviewing officials of food-inspection agencies; analyzing agencies' inspection procedures, policies, and records; and meeting with representatives of industry and consumer groups.

The five primary federal food-inspection agencies are the Food and Drug Administration (FDA) in the Department of Health and Human Services; the Food Safety and Inspection Service (FSIS), Agricultural Marketing Service (AMS), and Grain Inspection and Packers and Stockyards Administration (GIPSA) in the U.S. Department of Agriculture; and the National Marine Fisheries Service (NMFS) in the Department of Commerce. (Seven other agencies also have some food-safety responsibilities.) The FDA regulates some 53,000 food-processing establishments and sets standards of identity and quality for food products. The FSIS supervises approximately 6,100 plants engaged in slaughtering and processing meat and poultry products, and AMS has jurisdiction over hundreds of egg and egg-product facilities. The NMFS conducts a voluntary, fee-based program of grading and inspection services for seafood products.

From its study, the GAO reached several negative conclusions about the system for inspecting food safety. The agencies' effectiveness was limited by inconsistencies and illogical differences, based on statutory authority and funding, in their approaches to food safety. Thus, plants processing meat and poultry were inspected daily by FSIS, but food-processing plants under FDA jurisdiction were inspected once every three to five years. Moreover, the agencies drew some narrow jurisdictional lines. For one, FSIS handled inspection of open-faced meat sandwiches made with one slice of bread whereas the traditional sandwich with two slices of bread was the FDA's responsibility. Although meat and poultry plants were required to register for inspection with FSIS before they could sell products, food-processing plants were under no such requirement and had to be tracked down by the FDA. The GAO found that food products presenting similar health risks were treated differently by the agencies, that duplicative inspections occurred, and that coordination among the agencies was inadequate.

To correct these and other problems, GAO opined that the best alternative would be a single food-safety agency, but they realized this was not a good political possibility. A "more realistic" approach to change would be to create a panel of experts to develop an inspection model based on public-health risks and adequate enforcement powers. This model would provide a rational basis for needed changes in the food-safety system. In 1996 the food-safety system remained unreformed.

Presidential Commissions

Earlier we examined the presidential commissions' role in formulating policy. Now we will see that they can also be used as an instrument of policy evaluation. Whether set up specifically to evaluate policy or governmental management in some area or for other purposes such as fact finding, making policy recommendations, or simply creating the appearance of presidential concern, most commissions involve themselves in policy evaluation to some degree.

In November 1986 it was disclosed that the United States government, under the leadership of National Security Council (NSC) officials, had sold arms to the Iranian government and diverted some of the profits to the Nicaraguan rebels. This news touched off a major political controversy. To inquire into this matter and to make recommendations for correction, President Reagan appointed the President's Special Review Board. Better known as the Tower Commission, it was composed of former Republican senator John Tower (from Texas) as chair, Edmund Muskie, former Democratic senator from Maine and secretary of state, and Brent Scowcroft, former national security adviser to President Gerald Ford (and later to President George Bush).

In its report issued early in 1987, the Tower Commission sharply criticized President Reagan and his administration for their conduct in the Iran–Contra affair. The NSC was depicted as carrying on operations outside its advisory realm, deceiving Congress, paying little heed to the law, and avoiding any effective oversight. The president himself was viewed as uninformed, detached, and not in control of NSC action, which ran counter to his administration's own policy of no arms sales to the Iranians. The commission's report made specific recommendations for bringing the NSC system under more effective presidential control and direction.[25] President Reagan accepted the commission's report and instituted some changes designed to prevent recurrence of such problems.[26]

A more "traditional" presidential commission was the Commission on Aviation Safety, established in 1986 to appraise the adequacy of governmental efforts to ensure safety in commercial airline operations. It concluded that the Federal Aviation Agency (FAA), which has primary responsibility for commercial air safety, was hampered by its location in and subordination to the

Department of Transportation. The commission, to the distress of the secretary of transportation, recommended that the FAA be converted into an independent agency and given more operating freedom.

It appears that the policy evaluations and recommendations made by presidential commissions often have little immediate influence on policymaking. For whatever effect they do have, the important variables are probably not the quality and soundness of their findings. Charles Jones concludes that an evaluation commission is likely to have the greatest effect when its report coincides with other supporting events and accords with the president's policy preferences, when it includes some members who hold important governmental positions and are committed to its recommendations, and when commission staff personnel return to governmental positions in which they can influence acceptance of its recommendations.[27] These conditions, however, are often not present.

Administrative Agencies

Many evaluations of policies and programs are produced within the administering agencies, either on their own initiative or at the direction of Congress or the executive. Agencies usually want to get some notion of how their programs are working and what can be done to improve them. Educational program evaluations are often labeled either formative or summative. Formative evaluations (also known as program monitoring) are designed to assist officials in making mid-course corrections or adjustments in programs to improve their operation. Summative evaluations are broader and more thorough in scope and are used to inform upper-level policy-makers of the overall effects of important policies and programs. They may lead to major program changes. There is not much reason to expect, however, that such evaluations will cause agency officials to recommend terminating favored policies or programs.

In the 1960s and 1970s the Johnson, Nixon, and Carter administrations tried to build policy analysis and evaluation into the national budgetary process.[28] The Johnson administration instituted the Planning-Programming-Budgeting System (PPBS), which required agencies to search for the most effective and efficient (least-cost) means to achieve their goals. The Nixon administration replaced PPBS with Management by Objectives (MBO), a more modest effort requiring agencies to specify goals and measure progress toward achieving them. By the time the Carter administration came to town and installed Zero-Base Budgeting (ZBB), MBO had evaporated. This new system required agencies to specify different levels of funding and accomplishment for programs, including the "zero" base (defined not as nothing but rather as the funding level below which the program would have no real worth). By so doing, agencies would assess the worth of programs and indicate where spending would do the most good. ZBB did not survive the Carter administration.

These efforts at reform failed for a number of reasons. They were instituted on a governmentwide basis without much planning or testing; they conflicted with existing budgetary practices and habits; they were difficult and time-consuming to use; they were viewed as efforts to shift power to higher executive levels; and they lacked continuing presidential interest and support. They were not, however, without effect, for they left behind in the agencies a residue of interest and support for more systematic analysis and evaluation of agencies' activities. It has now become fairly standard practice for Congress to specifically direct agencies to undertake program and policy evaluations.

During its initial year in office especially, the Clinton administration gave much attention to improving the operation of the executive branch. Much was said about the need to "reinvent government" and to move from red tape to results to create a government "that works better and costs less."[29] Under the direction of Vice President Al Gore the National Performance Review identified hundreds of ways by which the operation of the departments and agencies could be made more effective and economical. Overall, it was claimed, the recommendations of the National Performance Review would eliminate a quarter of a million government jobs and save $108 billion over five years.[30] In all, the NPR can be regarded as a sweeping, but not overly rigorous, evaluation of the executive branch. Early appraisals of the NPR were mixed. One held that it had "accomplished in its first year, far more than anyone thought possible."[31] Another said that "the Gore effort bodes to become not the fundamental transformation that the 'reinventing' tag promises, but a modest move toward better public management, based on some welcome applications of common sense."[32]

The Government Performance and Results Act (GPRA) of 1993 is more specifically concerned with agency program management.[33] Supported by the Clinton administration and adopted by Congress with little public notice or controversy, the act's intent is to shift the focus of agencies from inputs and processes to outputs, or results. To this end it directs agencies to prepare five-year strategic plans in which they identify the goals of their programs and describe the resources needed to achieve these goals. External factors that could affect their success in meeting their goals are also to be identified. These agency plans are to be updated every three years. Annually, agencies are directed to submit performance plans to the Office of Management and Budget, which are to include indicators for measuring success or failure in achieving their goals. Subsequently, agencies are to report on their success or failure in goal attainment. The requirements of GPRA take effect in fiscal year

1997. During fiscal years 1994 through 1996, OMB was directed to conduct pilot programs in at least ten agencies to test the act's effectiveness.

According to the Senate Committee on Government Affairs, GPRA "will provide the information necessary to strengthen program management, to make objective evaluations of program management, and to set realistic, measurable goals for future performance. . . . "[34] Given the act's apparently greater emphasis on program outputs than on program goals, these may be reasonable aspirations. It seems doubtful, however, that GPRA will do much to expand our knowledge of program or policy outcomes. It may turn out to be just another symbolic congressional product.

PROBLEMS IN POLICY EVALUATION

The most useful form of policy evaluation for policy-makers and administrators, and for policy critics who want a factual basis for their positions, is a systematic evaluation that tries to determine cause-and-effect relationships and rigorously measures the results of policy. It is of course often impossible to measure quantitatively the effect of public policies, especially social policies, with any real precision. In this context, then, to "measure rigorously" is to seek to assess policy impacts as carefully and objectively as possible, using the best information available and making careful judgments. There is no reason to assume that "if it cannot be counted, it does not count."

Determining whether a policy or program is doing what it is supposed to do, or doing something else, is not an easy, straightforward task, as some appear to assume. Snap judgments are easy to make but lack definitiveness. A variety of conditions raise obstacles or create problems for the effective accomplishment of policy evaluation. These include uncertainty over policy goals, difficulty in determining causality, diffuse policy impacts, and others, all of which are reviewed in this section.

Uncertainty over Policy Goals

When the goals of a policy are unclear, diffuse, or diverse, as they frequently are, determining the extent to which they have been attained becomes a difficult and frustrating task.[35] This situation is often a product of the policy adoption process. Because the support of a majority coalition is needed to secure adoption of a policy, it is usually necessary to appeal to persons and groups possessing differing interests and diverse values. To win their votes, commitments to the preferred policy goals of these various groups may be included in the legislation. The Model Cities Act, which was a major attempt to deal with urban problems, reflected this technique. Its goals included rebuilding slum and blighted areas; improving housing, income, and cultural opportunities; reducing crime and delinquency; lessening dependency on welfare; and maintaining historic landmarks. No priorities were assigned to the various goals, nor were their dimensions well specified. Model Cities evaluation research had to try to come to grips with the extent to which these diverse goals were being accomplished.

It may be no easy task to determine the real goals of a program. Officials in different positions in the policy system, such as legislators and administrators, or national and state officials, may define them differently, act accordingly, and reach differing conclusions about a program's accomplishments. Later in the chapter we will see how the multiple goals of the Head Start program have complicated its evaluation.

Difficulty in Determining Causality

Systematic evaluation requires that societal changes must be demonstrably caused by policy actions. The mere fact that when action A is taken condition B develops does not necessarily mean the presence of a cause-and-effect relationship. Other actions (or variables) may have been the actual causes of condition B. As we know, many common colds are "cured," not by ingesting medicines, applying ointments, or using nasal sprays, but by the human body's natural recuperative power.

Consider this example. Many states require periodic automobile safety inspections, in an attempt to reduce highway traffic accidents and fatalities. Research indicates that states with mandatory inspection laws do tend to have fewer traffic fatalities than do other states. Other factors, however, such as population density, weather conditions, and percentage of young drivers might in fact have more power in explaining the difference. Only if such conditions are controlled in the analysis, and if differences remain between states with and without inspections, can it be accurately stated that a policy of periodic automobile inspections reduces traffic deaths. In actuality, such laws do seem to have a modest beneficial effect.[36]

To further illustrate the problem of determining causality, let us take the case of crime-control policies. The purpose, or at least one of the purposes, of these policies is deterring crime. Deterrence may be defined as the prevention of an action that can be said to have had a "realistic potential of actualization," that is, one that really could have happened.[37] (This assumption is required to avoid the kind of analysis that holds, for example, that consumption of alcoholic beverages prevents stomach worms, since no one has ever been afflicted with them after starting to drink.) The problem here is that not doing something is a sort of nonevent, or intangible act. Does a person's not committing burglary mean that he or she has been effectively deterred by policy from so acting? The answer, of course, first depends upon whether he or she was inclined to engage in burglary. If so, then was the person deterred by the possibility of detection and punishment, by other factors such as family influence, or by lack of opportunity? As this example indicates, the determination of causality between actions, especially in complex social and economic matters, frequently is a daunting task.

Diffuse Policy Impacts

Policy actions may affect groups other than those at whom they are specifically directed. A welfare program may affect not only the poor but also others such as taxpayers, public officials, and low-income people who are not receiving welfare benefits. The effects on these groups may be either symbolic or material. Taxpayers may grumble that their "hard-earned dollars are going to support those too lazy to work." Some low-income working people may indeed decide to go on welfare rather than continue working at grubby, unpleasant jobs for low wages. So far as the poor who receive material benefits are concerned, how do benefits affect their initiative and self-reliance, family solidarity, or maintenance of social order? We should bear in mind that policies may have unstated intentions. Thus, an antipoverty program might have been covertly intended to help defuse the demands of black activists; or a program to control importing of beef may be intended to appease cattle growers politically, but not really do much to limit foreign competition.

The effects of some programs may be very broad and long-range in nature. Antitrust policy is an example. Originally intended to help maintain competition and prevent monopoly in the economy, how does one now evaluate its effectiveness? We can look at current enforcement activity and find that some mergers have been prevented and many price-fixing conspiracies have been prosecuted, but this record will tell us little about the extent of competition and monopoly in the economy generally. It would be pleasing to be able to determine that the economy is n percent more competitive than it would have been without antitrust policy. Because its goals are general and because measuring competition and monopoly is difficult, this determination just is not possible. Interestingly, after a century of antitrust action, we are still without agreed-upon definitions of monopoly and competition to guide policy action and evaluation. No wonder those assessing the effectiveness of antitrust policy sometimes come to sharply different conclusions.[38]

Difficulties in Data Acquisition

As implied in some previous comments, a shortage of accurate and relevant statistical data and other information may handicap the policy evaluator, particularly when one's concern is with policy outcomes. Thus an econometric model may predict how a tax cut will affect economic activity, but suitable data to indicate its actual impacts on the economy are hard to come by. Again, think of the problems in securing the data needed to determine the effect on criminal law enforcement of a Supreme Court decision such as *Miranda* v. *Arizona*,[39] which held that a confession obtained when a suspect had not been informed of his or her rights when taken into custody was inherently invalid. The members of the President's Crime Commission in 1967 disagreed about its effect, the majority saying it was too early to determine that. A minority, however, held that, if fully implemented, "it could mean the virtual elimination of pretrial interrogation of suspects. . . . Few can doubt the adverse effect of Miranda upon the law enforcement process."[40] Absence of data does not necessarily hinder all evaluators.

The use of "Miranda cards" to inform suspects of their rights now has become standard police practice. A consensus exists among criminal-justice scholars and law-enforcement officers to the effect that this reform has had little adverse effect on law enforcement. Various field and quantitative studies support this view. Moreover, it is suggested that the Miranda rule has helped improve professionalism among the police.[41]

For many social and economic programs, a question that typically arises is, "Did those who participated in programs subsequently fare better than comparable persons who did not?" Providing an answer preferably involves an experimental evaluation design utilizing a control group. The difficulty in devising a control (or comparison) group for a manpower program is summed up in this passage:

> A strict comparison group in the laboratory sense of the physical sciences is virtually impossible, primarily because the behavior patterns of people are affected by so many external social, economic, and political factors. In fact, sometimes the legislation itself prevents a proper comparison group from being established. For example, the Work Incentive Program legislation of 1967 required that all fathers must be enrolled in the WIN program within 30 days after receipt of aid for their children. Therefore, a comparison group of fathers with comparable attributes to those fathers enrolled in the program could not be established. Even if all the external factors of the economy could be controlled, it would still be impossible to replicate the social and political environment affecting any experimental or demonstration program. Thus, it is easy for a decision maker to discount the results of almost any evaluation study on the basis that it lacks the precision control group.[42]

Because of problems such as those mentioned in the quotation, experimental designs frequently cannot be used. (This reason is apart from their often high dollar cost.) Second-best alternatives must then be utilized, such as a quasi-experimental design using a nonequivalent control group.[43]

Official Resistance

Evaluating policy, whether it be called policy analysis, measurement of policy impact, or something else, involves reporting findings making judgments on the merits of policy. This is true even if the evaluator is a university researcher who thinks that he or she is objectively pursuing knowledge. Agency and program officials will be alert to the possible political consequences of evaluation. If the results do not come out "right" from their perspective, or worse, if the results are negative and come to the attention of decision-makers, their program, influence, or careers may be thrown in jeopardy. Consequently, program officials may discourage or disparage evaluation studies, refuse access to data, or keep incomplete records. Within agencies, evaluation studies are likely to be most strongly supported by higher-level officials, who must make decisions about the allocation of resources among programs and the continuation of given programs. They may, however, be reluctant to require evaluations, especially if their results may have a divisive effect within the agencies. Finally, we should note that organizations tend to resist change, and evaluation implies change. Organizational inertia may thus be an obstacle to evaluation, along with more overt forms of resistance.

A Limited Time Perspective

The time horizon of legislators and other elected officials often extends only as far as the next election. Consequently, they, and others who think like them, often expect quick results from governmental programs, even social and educational programs whose effects may take many years to fully appear. This being the case, short-run evaluations of program accomplishments may be unfavorable. A good example is the New Deal's resettlement program, which provided opportunities for land ownership to thousands of black sharecroppers in the South during the late 1930s and early 1940s. It was judged as a failure and just another New Deal boondoggle by contemporary critics. A decades-later evaluation of the program by policy analyst Lester Salamon concluded, however, that it had significant, positive, long-term effects, although not as an agricultural policy.[44] At modest cost, it did transform "a group of landless black tenants into a permanent landed middle class that ultimately emerged in the 1960s as the backbone of the civil rights movement in the rural South." If the time dimension is ignored in evaluation studies, the results may be flawed and neglect important long-term effects. The pressure for rapid feedback concerning a policy can then create a dilemma for the evaluator.

Evaluation Lacks Influence

Once completed, an evaluation of a program may be ignored or attacked as inconclusive or unsound on various grounds. It may be alleged that the evaluation was poorly designed, the data used were inadequate, or the findings are inconclusive. Those strongly interested in a program, however, whether as administrators or beneficiaries, are unlikely to lose their affection for it merely because an evaluation study concluded that its costs are greater than its benefits. Moreover, there is also the possibility that the evaluation is flawed.

I am unable to think of a governmental program that has been terminated solely as a consequence of an unfavorable systematic evaluation. Of course, evaluations frequently lead to incremental changes or improvements in the design and administration of programs. That is the intent of many program evaluations done by the General Accounting Office, for instance, which, perhaps, is all that should be asked or expected of most evaluations.

POLICY EVALUATION: THE USE AND MISUSE OF COST-BENEFIT ANALYSIS

Cost-benefit analysis is a formal, quantitative evaluation technique that requires identifying the costs and benefits of either a proposed or actual policy and translating them into monetary values for purposes of comparison. It assumes that society will be made better off only by policies (or projects, or programs) whose benefits exceed their costs. Cost-benefit analysis has been most frequently used to evaluate proposed policies. Sometimes, though, it is employed to appraise existing policies. Thus economist A. Myrick Freeman III used it to evaluate national air- and water-pollution–control policies. He found that the control of air pollution from stationary sources yielded benefits that were much greater than control costs. On the other hand, the costs of controlling industrial and municipal sources of water pollution were greater than the benefits realized.[45] In the following discussion, the focus will be on cost-benefit analysis primarily as a prospective evaluation technique.

The major steps in performing a cost-benefit analysis can readily be summarized.[46] First, one identifies all of the effects or consequences of a policy and categorizes them as costs or benefits for various groups. (Note that this requires establishing which groups are entitled to be considered in determining costs and benefits.) Both direct and indirect effects should be analyzed. Second, dollar values are placed on the various costs and benefits. This will be relatively easy for items that are customarily bought and sold in markets. For such matters as good health, the prolongation of human life, or scenic vistas, it will be much more difficult. Third, because some of the consequences of a policy will be current or short-term but others will occur many years hence, a discount rate is needed to equate the value of present and future effects. The basic assumption underlying the discount rate is that a dollar today is worth more than a dollar a decade or two from now. Inflation, for instance, may diminish the dollar's value, or purchasing power. Fourth, the costs and benefits, direct and indirect, current and future, of the policy are compared. If benefits exceed costs, the policy is acceptable; conversely, if costs exceed benefits, it should be rejected, or a better way of doing it should be found.

So presented, cost-benefit analysis appears as a reasonably clear-cut method for appraising policies. In actuality, however, there are significant problems involved in its application, a few of which are examined here.

Good data on the costs and benefits of a policy are frequently difficult to come by. For example, some of the problems encountered in identifying and valuing the benefits of an improved water-quality standard are explained by an Environmental Protection Agency official:

> Take one of our water pollution effluent guidelines. . . . It will be set at, say, 10 micrograms per gram of water. So you would have an immediate measurement possible—the number of tons of pollution you will avoid putting in the water and a percentage reduction from the previous level.
>
> But that's not very meaningful, in terms of measuring benefits. So you try to convert that into the standard's effect on water quality. Using models of a streams' rate of flow, you can tell when you have done enough to make the ambient water quality good, but, of course, the quality will vary from the Mississippi to some small river. It costs a bundle to develop models, and often we just don't have data on individual streams.
>
> But if you can reach the judgment that a stream's water quality now will be improved enough to sustain fish life and to permit industrial use of the water without further treatment, so that a brewery might possibly locate there, you have now characterized the uses of the water and you have started to characterize the actual benefits.
>
> If you want to quantify the benefits, you must assign a dollar value to swimming or fishing. You must estimate the number of recreational visits

there will be and how much they are worth. You must calculate the number of adverse health effects avoided and assign a dollar value to them.

Each step is very uncertain. The water quality models are uncertain. The projections of how many fishing trips and illnesses there will be are uncertain. The range of error is larger and larger. Is it really worth the large expense entailed going to the end of the chain?[47]

As this statement illustrates, the data and the dollar values on which a cost-benefit analysis is based can be of a tenuous and arguable nature.

It is, further, no easy task to identify the appropriate discount rate. It can be based on such criteria as the interest rate, the rate of inflation, or the opportunity costs of capital—that is, the rate of return that money would earn if devoted to private investment rather than public purposes. Despite its importance, there is no scientific way to decide on a discount rate. A low discount rate preserves the value of future benefits, whereas a high discount rate can sharply reduce their value. During the Reagan years, the Office of Management and Budget advocated a discount rate of 10 percent. This discount rate meant that the value of future benefits, such as lives prolonged two or three decades hence by reducing the incidence of cancer, would have very low value. This in turn increased the likelihood that a cost-benefit ratio would be unfavorable.

Cost-benefit analysis is based on the premise that efficiency is the primary, if not the only, value to be realized. Actions are evaluated on the basis of whether resources are used to improve the aggregate public good.[48] Little attention is accorded alternative or competing values—equity, human dignity, personal freedom, and equality, to name some. These are important to most people. The American system of criminal justice, for instance, is not very efficient because of our concern with equity and due process.

Finally, let us note that cost-benefit analysis emphasizes the consequences for society as a whole. As we know, however, public policies distribute advantages and disadvantages, or costs and benefits. Those who pay the costs of policies often do not benefit from them, and vice versa. Put differently, policies have distributive consequences that are of importance. People may appropriately be more concerned with who benefits from industrial safety policies than whether their total costs exceed their benefits.

Problems such as those sketched here have not prevented cost-benefit analysis from being used as a tool in governmental decision-making for several decades. The Flood Control Act of 1936 specified that flood-control projects could be undertaken by the Army Corps of Engineers only "if the benefits to whomsoever they may accrue are in excess of the estimated costs." This standard must also be used for water projects handled by the Soil Conservation Service and has been voluntarily employed by the Bureau of Reclamation. In the 1960s cost-benefit analysis was first used in evaluating defense programs and then domestic programs as part of PPBS.

In the 1970s Presidents Ford and Carter directed executive-branch regulatory agencies to prepare "inflation impact statements" and "regulatory analyses," respectively, in developing some proposed regulations. These statements involved analyzing their expected economic consequences. The Carter administration made it clear, however, that although regulatory agencies should consider the burdens and gains of proposed regulations, a cost-benefit test was not to be used in appraising them.[49]

A goal of the Reagan administration when it took office was to substantially reduce governmental regulation of private economic activity. People who were critical of the programs under their jurisdiction were appointed to regulatory positions. A second action involved issuing Executive Order 12291 in February 1981,[50] which drew heavily upon the Carter administration's experience. The order required that proposed major regulations issued by executive-branch agencies (the independent regulatory commissions were exempt) must be accompanied by regulatory impact analyses assessing the potential benefits, costs, and net benefits of the regulations, including effects that could not be quantified in monetary terms, unless such calculations were prohibited by law. Some statutes ban use of cost-benefit analysis for the programs they establish.

Major regulations were defined as those likely to have an annual impact on the economy of $100 million or more, to lead to major cost or price increases, or to have "significant adverse effects on competition, employment, investment, productivity, innovation, or the ability of U.S.-based enterprises to compete with foreign-based enterprises in domestic or export markets." The OMB was authorized to make the final determination of what was a major rule, to supervise the evaluation process, and to delay the issuance of proposed or final rules if it found the regulatory analyses were unsatisfactory.

Rules could be issued only if their estimated benefits exceeded their estimated costs. If a choice was available, the less costly alternative was to be selected. The burden of proof that this standard was met rested with the agency. An action by the OMB holding up a rule could be appealed to the President's Task Force on Regulatory Relief, which was staffed by the OMB and comprised several executive officials under the leadership of Vice President George Bush. (The word "relief" in the task force's title indicates its orientation.) Although the task force was phased out in 1983, all of this planning was intended to ensure, among other things, that "Regulatory Action shall not be undertaken unless the potential benefits to society for the regulation outweigh the potential costs to society." Thus cost-benefit analysis was to be more than an analytical technique; it became a decision rule with a conservative bias.

In the first two years (1981–1982) of the review program established by Executive Order 12291, proposed and final rules totaling 5,436 were submitted by the agencies to OMB for review. Most were of limited import and were approved without change.[51] Only 89 of the rules were classified as

"major" and thus requiring regulatory impact analyses. Some major rules were not analyzed, however, as a consequence of the OMB's use of its authority under the executive order to exempt rules from cost-benefit analysis which "relax or defer regulatory requirements, or which delegate regulatory authority to the states." During the 1985–1986 period, 4,216 proposed and final rules, including 131 major rules, were sent to the OMB. Again most were approved without change. Whatever the specific explanation—OMB review, appointment of agency officials less inclined to be vigorous regulators, or other factors—the data indicate that a significant decline in rule-making activity occurred.

The Reagan regulatory analysis program was the center of a lot of controversy. Critics contended that it was used improperly to reduce the extent of regulation and to delay the issuance of rules rather than to improve the quality of regulations by encouraging better analysis. The OMB was also accused of improperly interfering in the regulatory process by usurping authority vested in the regulatory agencies. The administration denied such accusations. In practice, though, administration officials demonstrated much more vigilance about the costs than the benefits of regulation in trying to reduce the burden of regulatory activity on businesses.

The Bush administration continued the regulatory-analysis program and in time created the Council on Competitiveness, an interagency committee chaired by Vice President Dan Quayle, to work with the OMB in perpetuating the use of cost-benefit analysis.[52] In the final two years of the Bush administration, the Council on Competitiveness acted vigorously to represent the business community in the regulatory process and to reduce the number and strength of new regulations.[53] For the most part, it avoided publicity and sought to leave few "fingerprints."

Soon after taking office, the Clinton administration abolished the Council on Competitiveness. Then in October 1993, President Bill Clinton killed Executive Order 12291 and replaced it with Executive Order 12866, entitled "Regulatory Planning and Review." The Clinton regulatory review programs continued the use of cost-benefit analysis for major rules. The review process under Executive Order 12866 has been more open to public scrutiny and less intrusive than that under the Reagan and Bush administrations. It appears that presidential review and the use of cost-benefit analysis to evaluate proposed regulations have become a regularized feature of the regulatory process.

Properly used, cost-benefit analysis can contribute to the rationality of the decision-making process by aiding in the identification and appraisal of alternatives, and by developing information and insights that will help persons make well-considered decisions. A systematic appraisal of the likely costs and benefits of a proposed action, and of those upon whom they will fall, is certainly useful, regardless of whether all are converted into dollar figures. Cost-benefit analysis, however, is open to manipulation to support preferences

and values. In the instance of Executive Order 12291, because of the antiregulation orientation of those administering the program, their emphasis upon the costs of regulation, and their insufficient attention to its benefits, cost-benefit analysis became a form of partisan political analysis in the guise of regulatory rationality.[54] It is doubtful that the Corps of Engineers has ever been unable to undertake a project that it really wanted to construct because it could not contrive a favorable cost-benefit analysis.

Policy evaluation, as our discussion indicates, is more than a technical or objective analytical process; it is also a political process. In the next section, a case study of the Head Start program illustrates how political factors can affect the conduct and results of an evaluation of a social program. The case also demonstrates that such evaluations, even when intended to be neutral or objective in form, become political because they can affect allocation of resources.

THE POLITICS OF EVALUATION: THE CASE OF HEAD START

In January 1965, President Lyndon Johnson announced that a preschool program named Head Start would be initiated as part of the Community Action Program (CAP) authorized by the Economic Opportunity Act of 1964. The Head Start program, which was designed to help overcome the effects of poverty on the educational achievement of poor children, included early classroom education, nutritional benefits, parent counseling, and health services.

Initially, $17 million in CAP funds was earmarked for summer 1965 to enable 100,000 children to participate in Head Start. The announcement of the program, however, produced requests for a much larger volume of funds from many localities. Officials in the Office of Economic Opportunity (OEO), who had jurisdiction over the program, decided to meet this demand. Ultimately, $103 million was committed to provide places for 560,000 children. To say the least, the Head Start program was highly popular, undoubtedly because it directed attention to poor preschool children, who readily aroused the public's sympathy, and to the goal of equal opportunity.

Late in the summer of 1965, Head Start became a permanent part of the antipoverty program. According to President Johnson, Head Start had been "battle-tested" and "proven worthy." It was expanded to a full-year program. In fiscal year 1968, $330 million was allocated to provide places for 473,000 children in summer programs and another 218,000 in full-year programs, making Head Start the largest component of the CAP. Essentially, Head Start was a multifaceted program for meeting the needs of poor children. More than a traditional nursery school or kindergarten program, it was designed also to provide poor children with physical and mental health services and nutritious meals to improve their diet. Further, an effort was made to involve members of the local community in the operation of the program.

With this background, let us turn to evaluation of the program.[55] The OEO was among the agency leaders in efforts to evaluate social programs because of statutory requirements. Within the agency the task of evaluating its programs for overall effectiveness was assigned to the Office of Research, Plans, Programs and Evaluations (RPP&E). Some early efforts had been made to evaluate the effectiveness of Head Start, mostly by Head Start officials and involving particular projects, but, by mid-1967, no solid evidence was available on overall program effectiveness. This lack was beginning to trouble OEO officials, the Bureau of the Budget, and some members of Congress. Consequently, the Evaluation Division of RPP&E, as part of a series of national evaluations of OEO programs, proposed an ex post facto study design for Head Start in which former Head Start children currently in the first, second, and third grades of school would be given a series of cognitive and affective tests. Their test scores would then be compared with those of a control group who had not been in the Head Start program. The Evaluation Division believed such a design would yield results more quickly than a longitudinal study that, although more desirable, would take longer to complete. (A longitudinal study examines the effect over a period of time of a program on a given group.)

Within OEO, Head Start officials opposed the proposed study on various grounds, including its design, the test instruments to be used, and the focus on only the educational aspect of the program to the neglect of its other goals—health, nutrition, and community involvement. The RPP&E evaluators acknowledged the multiplicity of Head Start goals but contended that cognitive improvement was its primary goal. They agreed with Head Start officials that there were risks in making a limited study, such as possibly misleading negative results, but insisted that the need for evaluative data necessitated taking the risks. In the wake of much internal debate, the OEO director decided the study should be made, and in June 1968, a contract was entered into with the Westinghouse Learning Corporation and Ohio University. The study was conducted in relative quiet, but hints of its negative findings began to surface as it neared completion.

Early in 1969, a White House staff official became aware of the Westinghouse study and requested information on it because the president was preparing an address on the Economic Opportunity Act that would include a discussion of Head Start. In response to the request, OEO officials reported the preliminary negative findings of the study. In his message to Congress on economic opportunity on February 19, 1969, President Nixon referred to the study, commenting that "the preliminary reports . . . confirm what many have feared: the long term effect of Head Start appears to be extremely weak." He went on to say that "this must not discourage us" and spoke well of the program. Nonetheless, his speech raised substantial doubts about Head Start among many observers in the public arena.

The president's speech also touched off considerable pressure for release of the study's findings. The OEO officials were reluctant to do this because what had been delivered to them by Westinghouse was a preliminary draft, which was intended for use in deciding such matters as what additional statistical tests were needed and what data required reanalysis. From Congress, where hearings were being held on OEO legislation, claims were made that the study was being held back to protect Head Start and that the report was going to be rewritten. The pressure on the White House became sufficiently great that it directed OEO to make the study public by April 14. A major conclusion of the report was that the full-year Head Start program produced a statistically significant but absolutely slight improvement in participant children.

The release of the report set off a flood of criticism from Head Start proponents, including many academicians, directed at the methodological and conceptual validity of the report. A sympathetic article on the front page of *The New York Times* bore the headline "HEAD START REPORT HELD 'FULL OF HOLES.'" Much of the ensuing controversy focused on the statistical methods used in the study and involved a broad range of claims, charges, rebuttals, and denials. The proponents of Head Start seemed to fear that their program was being victimized by devious intent. This fear had several facets. One was that persons within OEO who favored Community Action over Head Start wanted a study that would spotlight Head Start's deficiencies. Another was that the administration was going to use the findings to justify a major cutback in Head Start. Finally, there was the fear that "enemies of the program" in Congress would use the negative results as an excuse for attacking it. Although there later appeared to have been little factual basis for these fears, they were real to the proponents of Head Start and contributed to the intensity of their assault on the evaluation study.

The methodological conflict which arose over the study focused on such standard items as sample size, validity of the control group, and appropriateness of the tests given the children. An examination of these matters would be too lengthy and too technical to include here. An assessment of the study by economist Walter Williams, however, provides a balanced view of the controversy:

> In terms of its methodological and conceptual base, the study is a relatively good one. This in no way denies that many of the criticisms made of the study are valid. However, for the most part, they are the kinds of criticisms that can be made of most pieces of social science research conducted outside the laboratory, in a real-world setting, with all of the logistical and measurement

problems that such studies entail. And these methodological flaws open the door to the more political issues. Thus, one needs not only to examine the methodological substance of the criticisms which have been made of the study, but also to understand the social concern which lies behind them as well. Head Start has elicited national sympathy and has had the support and involvement of the educational profession. It is understandable that so many should rush to the defense of such a popular and humane program. But how many of the concerns over the size of the sample, control-group equivalency, and the appropriateness of covariance analysis, for example, would have been registered if the study had found positive differences in favor of Head Start? We imagine that this type of positive, but qualified assessment will fit any relatively good evaluation for some time to come. We have never seen a field evaluation of a social action program that could not be faulted legitimately by good methodologists, and we may never see one.[56]

Interestingly, the findings of the Westinghouse study were as favorable to Head Start as were the earlier evaluations of specific projects made by Head Start officials. These, too, showed that the program had limited lasting effects on the children. What the Westinghouse study, and the controversy over it, did was to inject these findings into the public arena and expand the scope of the conflict over them.

Despite the essentially negative evaluations of its accomplishments, the Westinghouse report recommended that Head Start be preserved and improved, at least partly on the ground that "something must be tried here and now to help the many children of poverty who may never be helped again." Head Start was, and is, a politically popular program. Congress and the executive have generally been favorably disposed toward the program, and it has suffered little of the criticism directed at other aspects of the antipoverty program. Children are a potent symbol in policy conflicts.

Ten years after the Westinghouse study was made public, the findings of another group of researchers on the long-term effects of Head Start were published by the Department of Health, Education, and Welfare. Based on a series of longitudinal studies, this study concluded that Head Start had significant, long-lasting social and educational benefits for its participants. Thus children who had been in the program had much less need for remedial classes, were less likely to be retained in grade, and were half as likely to drop out of high school as were adolescents of comparable age who had not been in the program.[57] As a consequence, Head Start was now hailed as a success by the communications media. Why the substantial difference in findings by the two evaluations? The explanation rests primarily with the different methodological approaches. The Westinghouse study, using an experimental design, focused on short-run effects, especially as measured by intelligence-test scores. The second study focused on long-range effects.

In 1981, Head Start was designated part of President Reagan's "social safety net," which provided assistance to the "truly needy," and thus was not tagged for cutbacks in funding, as were several other programs that provided aid to poor people. In 1988 approximately 450,000 children were enrolled in Head Start, which now operated year-round, at a cost of $1.2 billion. Only about a quarter of the eligible children were actually enrolled in the program, however. Head Start continued to expand under the Bush and Clinton administrations. The program's appropriation for fiscal year 1995 was $3.5 billion, which provided funding for more than 700,000 enrollees.[58]

Research studies on the benefits of Head Start and early childhood education have continued to yield inconclusive findings. Children who go through Head Start are found to have improved cognitive abilities, greater self-esteem, and improved social skills. On the other hand, various studies report that gains in academic achievement are not lasting. After a few years, when Head Start children are compared with non–Head Start children, the educational gains fade away.[59]

A major evaluation of Head Start published in the American Economic Review in 1995 illustrates these mixed findings.[60] Using longitudinal data for a sample of nearly five thousand children, the evaluators examined the impact of Head Start on cognitive achievement, school performance (whether a child repeated one or more grades), utilization of preventive medical care, and health and nutritional status. Children who had been enrolled in Head Start were compared with their siblings who either had been enrolled in other preschool programs or had had no preschool experiences. The evaluation found that Head Start had positive and persistent effects on the cognitive achievement and school performance of white children. In contrast, although there were positive effects on the cognitive achievement of African-American children, these effects soon disappeared. No positive effects were found on the school performance of African-American children. For both white and African-American children, Head Start had a positive effect on preventive health care, as measured by measles immunization rates. For neither did it have an impact on health and nutritional status, as measured by conformity with national height-for-age norms.

Whatever the results of the evaluation studies, Head Start has been a politically popular program, usually drawing bipartisan support from Congress and the executive. It appears to be a way to provide assistance to those who really need it, although funding levels are sufficient to cover only a third of those eligible. Perhaps, too, as many believe, it will lead to future reduced expenditures for other programs, such as welfare, juvenile delinquency, and criminal justice.

THE RESPONSE TO POLICY

In this chapter, quite a bit has been said about the systematic evaluation of policy. It has clearly become a widespread and potentially significant part of the policy process. Up to the present, however, as various observers have remarked, systematic evaluation does not appear to have had a really significant impact upon policy decision-making. As with Head Start, an essentially unfavorable early evaluation of its accomplishments did not lead to its abandonment nor, we might add, to major change in its substantive form. This result should not be taken to mean, however, that systematic evaluation is either useless or unlikely ever to have much influence on policymaking. It is an activity that encounters many problems, as we have seen, but as time goes on, and as evaluation techniques and designs become more effective, its effectiveness will undoubtedly increase. After all, few would contend that intelligence does not provide a sounder basis than intuition for making decisions on public policy. (In 1995, however, House Speaker Newt Gingrich stated that intuition was the basis for deciding that the national budget should be balanced in seven years.)

People and groups, citizens and officials alike, do of course make many judgments about the effect and desirability of policies and, on this basis, react to them with support, opposition, or indifference. Much evaluatory activity of the first two kinds is discussed at the beginning of this chapter. Political decision-makers may frequently temper their evaluations of the substantive content or effectiveness of policies with responsiveness to political factors such as partisan pressures, emotional appeals, or reelection considerations. Professor Ralph K. Huitt writes that "political feasibility" is a consideration entering into the selection of policy priorities and the programs designed to meet them by decision-makers, who ask questions such as, "Will it 'go' on the Hill? Will the public buy it? Does it have political 'sex appeal'? What 'can't be done' is likely to get low priority."[61] Political feasibility, however, is not unchanging. A policy proposal that at one point is thought unfeasible may later become feasible because of changes in its content or political conditions.

While it seems obvious that technical soundness should characterize proposed public policies, proposals that do not also have extensive public support are not likely to win adoption in a democratic political system.[62] Here we can usefully bring the concept of feedback into the discussion. This concept, which was briefly touched upon in the treatment of systems theory in Chapter 1, holds that past policy decisions and impacts can generate demands for their change or retention. Thus the enactment and administration of the National Environmental Policy Act of 1969 have created problems for some agencies and groups, and have given rise to various demands for its repeal, modification, and continuation. Its use to prevent construction of the Alaskan oil pipeline finally resulted in legislation exempting that project from NEPA requirements. The Soil Conservation Act of 1935 and its administering agency, the Soil Conservation Service (now the Natural Resource Conservation Service), gave rise to a pressure group, the National Association of Soil Conservation Districts, which has strongly supported their continuation. As a consequence of feedback to decision-makers, a variety of actions sub-sequently can be taken on policy, including continuation; legislative amend-ment to strengthen or weaken the policy; adjustments in its administration, such as strong or lax enforcement of given provisions; increasing, decreasing, or restricting funds to support its administration; challenges to its meaning or constitutionality in the courts (this action is more likely to be done by private interested parties than by officials); and repealing the statute (or permitting it to expire if a time limit is included among its provisions).

As for major policies and programs, they are unlikely to be repealed or terminated, even when much controversy and even bitterness attend their adoption. They soon come to be taken for granted as part of the political environment, and debate over their propriety, if not their details or impact, soon quiets down. This has been the pattern for the Social Security Act of 1935, the Taft-Hartley Act of 1947, the Civil Rights Act of 1964, the Elemen-tary and Secondary Education Act of 1965, and even the Occupational Safety and Health Act, among others. Few statutes have stirred as much controversy as the Economic Opportunity Act, and yet, although it has been variously amended and control of the programs it created has been transferred from the now-defunct OEO to other agencies, the act remains in existence. As a general proposition, it can be suggested that the longer the policy, program, or agency stays alive, the less likely it is to be terminated. In time, accommodations are made and support is gathered that enable it to survive. Exceptions include policies, programs, or agencies established to deal with emergency problems such as relief during the Great Depression (e.g., Works Progress Administra-tion and Civilian Conservation Corps) and price controls and rationing as well as allocation of production during World War II (e.g., Office of Price Admin-istration and War Production Board).

The revision, or demands for revision, of policies will depend upon such factors as the extent to which they are held to "solve" the problem at which they are directed or their perceived effect, the skill with which they are administered, the defects or shortcomings that may be revealed during imple-mentation, and the political power and awareness of interested or affected groups. In addition, the manner in which the costs and benefits of a policy are distributed will have significant consequences for its future.

The costs and benefits of public policies may be either broadly or nar-rowly distributed. For Social Security, both benefits and costs are broadly distributed, whereas a statute regulating relationships between automobile manufacturers and dealers involves narrow distribution of costs and benefits. Narrow costs–broad benefits and broad costs–narrow benefits are other pos-sible patterns. Recall that the costs and benefits of policies can be either material or symbolic. The proposition here advanced is that the response to policies, and demands for changes therein, will be affected by the way in which their benefits and costs are distributed, or are perceived to be distributed.[63]

Broad Benefits and Broad Costs

Policies that involve broad distribution of costs and benefits, such as Social Security, highway construction, police and fire protection, public education, and national defense, tend to be readily accepted, institutionalized, and beyond major challenge. Controversy may focus on such features as location of highways, whether to provide sex education in the public schools, or acquisition of a particular weapons system, but the continuation of the programs as a whole is not seriously in question. It has been easy to propose and difficult to resist increases in the benefits of a program like Social Security because of its many millions of beneficiaries and the activities of supporting groups like the American Association of Retired Persons. National defense also provides a collective good (all benefit from it, although the amount of benefit cannot be precisely measured or defined) related to the important value of national security and survival. (Note the defensive position you tend to find yourself in when you argue that something proposed is not really necessary for national defense, even in a time when the cold war is over.) Radical changes in most policies in this category are unlikely.

Some policies that fit in this category, however, may never gain wide and continued acceptance, as occurred with the War on Poverty. It had many potential beneficiaries, but most of them were poor, and the poor in our society have long lacked substantial political power and consequently effective ability to secure and support policies benefiting them. Many changes have been made in the poverty programs since 1964, although most of them remain in being. The OEO was finally abolished, however, because it had become a strong negative symbol and the focus of controversy.

Broad Benefits and Narrow Costs

Some policies seem to provide benefits for large numbers of people, but their costs at least initially fall primarily upon fairly distinct, identifiable groups in society. Among these are the control of environmental pollution, automobile safety, inspection of food products and meat, regulation of public utilities, and safety policies for industry and coal mines. Coal-mine companies have felt that they are being asked to bear the burden of safety regulation and that many specific requirements are unnecessary. They have complained that the regulatory program is unfair and have sought both legislative and administrative amelioration of its effect upon them. Just so, many industries have protested against having to meet the costs and inconveniences of pollution-control programs. Of course, they may be able to pass the financial costs on to consumers as part of the final price of their products, but this does not eliminate the initial aggravation such programs cause. Small-business groups have been especially shrill in criticizing the National Occupational Safety and Health Act, even though undoubtedly a great many small-business people have never seen an OSHA inspector and are not reached by many of its regulations.

The enactment of policies falling within this category is usually achieved through the actions of a loose coalition of interests, perhaps in response to a crisis of some sort. Once legislation is enacted, the supporting coalition tends to lose interest in the matter, assuming that with enactment the problem is adequately cared for. The groups who oppose the law and perceive themselves as bearing the brunt of it remain concerned and active, however, as did automobile manufacturers with motor-vehicle safety legislation and, earlier, railroads with rate regulation. Much more is heard from them by the enforcing agencies and the legislature about the undesirable effects of the legislation. The result may be administrative action and legislative changes tempering the original legislation.

Conversely, it may become very difficult for supporters of the original legislation to get together again to secure amendments to strengthen the law. Early in the 1920s a loophole was created in the antimerger provision for the Clayton Act of 1914 by judicial interpretation. The Supreme Court held that mergers by asset acquisition rather than stock purchase were not banned by the act. Not until the Celler Antimerger Act of 1950 were the supporters of antitrust able to secure corrective legislation.

Narrow Benefits and Broad Costs

Some policies and programs benefit readily identifiable interest groups, though the burden of their costs falls upon taxpayers generally. Veterans' benefits, agricultural subsidies, hospital-construction grants, rivers and harbors projects, and special tax provisions (such as accelerated depreciation for machinery) fall within this category. Those who benefit from these policies have a clear incentive to organize and act to maintain them. James Q. Wilson writes that policies of this variety encourage the formation of pressure groups to support their continuation, often in close relationship with the administering agency.[64] Good examples are the National Rivers and Harbors Congress and the Army Corps of Engineers, the National Rural Electrification Cooperative Association and the Rural Electrification Administration, and veterans groups and the Department of Veterans Affairs.

Those who are critical of such policies find it difficult to mobilize sufficient interest and political support to bring about changes. Presidents Johnson and Nixon both urged Congress to reduce greatly the funds for the Rural Environmental Assistance Program, which provides financial grants to farmers for soil-conserving activities, such as applying limestone to the soil and constructing erosion-control terraces, on the grounds that such costs can and should properly be borne by farmers. They did not have much success because those who benefit from the program work actively for its continuation at existing support levels, and Congress has been responsive to them. The cost is paid by the fabled John and Mary Q. Taxpayer, who as usual are little aware of either the program or the way in which it affects their tax bill.

Sometimes, though, policies in this category may arouse sufficient opposition, among both citizens and officials, to lead to their alteration. One example is the oil depletion allowance, enacted in the 1920s, which became a symbol of privilege for the oil industry. In 1969, after years of criticism by liberals, it was reduced from 27.5 percent to 22 percent. The energy crisis of the early 1970s helped bring it under further attack, and in 1975 the depletion allowance was repealed for all but small producers. The deregulation movement, which began in the mid-1970s, similarly provided the political impetus needed to enact the Airline Deregulation Act in 1978, which eliminated economic regulation of commercial airlines and the Civil Aeronautics Board. The CAB regulation, as we saw in an earlier chapter, had long been criticized on the grounds that by restricting competition it imposed costs on many travelers in order to benefit a few airlines. The deregulation movement expanded the conflict over the program by focusing public attention on it and by increasing the forces in favor of change.[65] Expansion of the conflict contributed to policy change.

Narrow Benefits and Narrow Costs

Policies that provide benefits to a well-defined group but at the cost of another distinct group tend to produce continuing organized conflict among the groups and their partisans. Among these are the conflicts between organized labor and management over the Taft-Hartley Act and the Wagner Act, commercial banks and savings and loan associations over banking policies, and coal-mine workers and mine operators over mining safety policies. Conflict repeatedly and continually erupts over amendments to and interpretations of the original policy. Efforts may also be made to secure its repeal. Top-level appointments to the administering agency are another item of contention. The National Labor Relations Board has alternated between prolabor and promanagement treatments of the labor laws, as Democratic administrations have appointed prolabor people to the board and Republican administrations have reciprocated with promanagement people when the opportunity has arisen.[66] Where the costs and benefits of policy are concentrated on active, organized groups, major policy changes tend to result either from shifts in the balance of power among them, such as that which led to the Taft-Hartley Act, or from negotiated settlements, such as that between business and environ-mental groups, which produced an extension of pesticide-control legislation in the 1980s.

These four policy categories based on the allocation of costs and benefits are only approximate. All policies will not fit neatly and exclusively into one or another of them. The categories have been put into play here because they are useful in gaining insight into why responses to policies vary and in estimating what the feedback responses will be to particular policy actions. Moreover, the categories should also be helpful in analyzing the struggles that attend adop-tion of policy, because to some extent the kind of policy proposed will help shape the enactment process. Keep in mind, however, that the response of most people to policies will be affected by more than the distribution of costs and benefits.

POLICY TERMINATION

As noted in the preceding section, the evaluation and appraisal of a policy, dissatisfaction with its costs and consequences, and the development and expansion of political opposition may produce a variety of responses to it, including termination. Policies are only one set of targets for termination. Others are programs (e.g., the rural abandoned-mine program), projects (e.g., the cross-Florida barge canal), and organizations. More than half of the states, for example, have enacted sunset laws, which require the legislature to renew periodically the authorization for administrative agencies. If this is not done, agencies are automatically abolished.

In this section the focus is on policies. Most of us can readily identify a number of government policies that we regard as wasteful, unnecessary, or inappropriate because they offend our ideological inclinations. Others, how-ever, may not share our beliefs and instead may view these same policies as necessary and desirable, perhaps needing some change or improvement, but on the whole worth keeping. Perhaps these people directly benefit from the policies. Or their ideology may inform them that such policies are laudable uses of governmental power. Just as most policies arise out of conflict, so too there will be disagreement over their worth and retention.

If criticism of and opposition to a policy become sufficiently strong that the policy-makers feel impelled to take action, a policy is more likely to be altered than terminated. An effort may be made to strengthen the policy to make it more effective, or portions of it that appear especially ineffective or offensive may be pruned away. This sort of adjustment is illustrated by the conversion of the Comprehensive Employment and Training Act of 1973 into the Job Partnership Training Act of 1982, as discussed in Chapter 1.

Alterations were made in the administration of job training and the public-employment program was jettisoned. Several years ago the tobacco price-support program was separated from the general farm bill and much of its cost was shifted to the private sector in order to save it.

Policy termination is difficult to accomplish for a number of reasons. Policies come into being because they have political support and they typically retain some or all of that support. Though they may be few, the supporters of a policy or program probably will be strongly committed to it, and may intensely resist change and ignore contrary evidence. The U.S. Army did not eliminate the horse cavalry until World War II, even though the cavalry had been obsolete for years because of military reliance on weapons such as the machine gun and rapid-fire artillery.[67] Some army officials could not comprehend an effective fighting force without the horse cavalry, reality to the contrary. The Tea Board consisted of three tea-tasters whose task was to ensure the quality of imported tea. Since its establishment late in the nineteenth century, it survived several efforts to abolish it, finally succumbing in 1996, after a U.S. senator from Nevada made its termination a personal cause, thereby saving the government $200,000 a year.[68]

The critics and opponents of a policy may be less intense in their feelings and may be both somewhat disorganized and diverse in their interests as well. It may also be quite difficult to weld together a coalition of sufficient strength to repeal a policy. Some potential opponents of a policy may be most interested in preserving their own favored policies, and thus an attitude of "live and let live" may prevail. An intense minority often prevails over an indifferent majority in the democratic political process.

Within Congress, with its fragmented and dispersed power structures, those with jurisdiction over a policy are more likely than not to be its friends and supporters. They can then use their committee or subcommittee positions to protect the policy against attack, to fend off or stifle unwanted changes, and to block its termination, should that be proposed. Governmental structure favors those seeking to retain policies, just as it once favored those opposing their enactment. There is perhaps a rough equity in this arrangement.

Termination, moreover, is a severe action with unpleasant and negative connotations.[69] It has an undertone of admitting failure. Unpleasant consequences may ensue when a policy is terminated: people may suffer lost income and jobs, prices for services or products may increase, and communities may decline. Ill will and other political costs may be entailed. Most public officials thus prefer to be involved in creating new or better policies rather than terminating the old.

Although these factors may make policy termination controversial and difficult, successful termination does occasionally happen. Here are some terminated policies and their dates of demise.

Fair-trade legislation (1975). This legislation, adopted during the 1930s, permitted manufacturers of trademarked or brand-named products to set mandatory minimum resale prices for their products. Over the years fair trade had become a tired, worn-out policy whose time had passed. Little support for it remained, and it was easily repealed.

Commercial airline regulation (1978). Almost all economic (but not safety) regulation was eliminated by the Airline Deregulation Act, the first major victory of the deregulation movement that began in the 1970s. Many policymakers became convinced, partly as a consequence of a multitude of policy studies, that market forces would more effectively control the airlines and protect the interests of users than would regulation.

Regulation of petroleum prices (1980). This policy, which always had much opposition, came into being as a consequence of the energy crisis in the 1970s. Difficult to administer, it was intended to prevent domestic oil companies from unduly profiting from high world oil prices. Its elimination in preference for market prices was coupled with a windfall-profits tax (see below).

Synthetic-fuels research (1985). This policy was another product of the energy crisis. A costly program intended to develop commercial synthetic fuels as a substitute for fossil fuels, it had accomplished little by the time of its elimination, partly because of the length of time needed to get complex developmental projects under way. By 1985 the energy crisis and memories of it had ebbed, and the Reagan administration wanted more reliance on the market.

Revenue sharing (1986). Adopted during the Nixon administration, revenue sharing channeled billions of dollars annually to state and local governments, with few strings attached, partly to encourage them to be more creative in dealing with public problems. Large federal budget deficits were the ultimate reason for its termination, although congressional opposition to revenue sharing was always considerable.

Crude-Oil Windfall Profits Tax Act (1986). Enacted in 1980, COWPTA was the price the petroleum industry reluctantly paid for oil-price deregulation, which permitted domestic oil prices to rise. From 30 to 70 percent of the windfall, the difference between the selling (or market) price of oil and a specified base price, was taxed away. A phaseout of the tax was to begin in January 1988, if $227 billion in revenue had been collected, or within one month following the collection of that amount, but in any event no later than January 1991.

The price of oil, however, fell in the mid-1980s, and the tax ceased to produce revenue. An industry-supported effort to repeal the act failed in 1986. Success finally came in 1988, when a repeal provision was included in the Omnibus Trade and Competitiveness Act to pick up or solidify votes for that legislation. Time and events had thus made the windfall tax symbolic and readily expendable.

As these examples indicate, a number of factors may contribute to the termination of policies. A short list includes ideology, the urge to economize, altered political conditions, and clear policy failure. Systematic evaluation played a major role only in airline deregulation. Evaluators (mostly economists) over time were able to gather substantial evidence on the shortcomings of airline rate and route regulation and to effectively portray market regulation as an effective and satisfactory alternative. Most commonly, however, systematic evaluation has not been a critical element in policy termination.

Indeed, to emphasize a point made earlier, evaluation is more likely to reinitiate the policy sequence. Problems that emerge or become more intense during the implementation of a policy may be identified, alternatives for change or improvement may be formulated and debated, and so on, until perhaps the policy is modified in some fashion. It is also possible, of course, that those responsible for implementing a policy will act to make it more acceptable to complaining groups, as by speeding up the issuance of licenses or cracking down on certain kinds of law violations. Policy change, whether legislative or administrative in origin, is more likely to occur than policy termination.

Notes

1. David Nachmias, *Public Policy Evaluation: Approaches and Methods* (New York: St. Martin's, 1979), p. 5.
2. The following discussion relies on Allen D. Putt and J. Fred Springer, *Policy Research: Concepts, Methods, and Applications* (Englewood Cliffs, N.J.: Prentice-Hall, 1989), chap. 11; and Carol H. Weiss, *Evaluation Research: Methods for Assessing Program Effectiveness* (Englewood Cliffs, N.J.: Prentice-Hall, 1972), chap. 4.
3. Laboratory experiments, which are also possible, are of a more artificial and contrived nature.
4. Howard S. Bloom, "Lessons from the Delaware Dislocated Worker Pilot Program," *Evaluation Review,* Vol. II (1987), pp. 157–177. The quotation is on p. 157.
5. Ibid., p. 166.
6. Donald T. Campbell, "Reforms as Experiments," *American Psychologist,* Vol. 24 (April 1969), pp. 409–429. Although this study used time-series analysis, I focus here on its comparative component.
7. Weiss, op. cit., p. 74.
8. Ibid., p. 14.
9. Stuart S. Nagel, *Public Policy: Goals, Means, and Concepts* (New York: St. Martin's, 1984), p. 414.
10. William T. Gormley, Jr., *Taming the Bureaucracy* (Princeton, N.J.: Princeton University Press, 1989), p. 5.

11. See Frances Fox Piven and Richard A. Cloward, *Regulating the Poor* (New York: Pantheon, 1971). Also Michael B. Katz, *The Undeserving Poor* (New York: Pantheon, 1989); and Paul Pierson, *Dismantling the Welfare State* (New York: Cambridge University Press, 1994).

12. Thomas R. Dye, *Understanding Public Policy,* 7th ed. (Englewood Cliffs, N.J.: Prentice-Hall, 1992), pp. 354–358.

13. Kenneth E. Warner, "Cleaning the Airwaves: The Cigarette Ad Ban Revisited," *Policy Analysis* (Fall 1979), pp. 235–250.

14. A discussion of externalities in public policy can be found in Randall G. Holcombe, *Public Sector Economics* (Belmont, Calif.: Wadsworth, 1988), chap. 3.

15. Edith Stokey and Ricard Zeckhauser, *A Primer for Policy Analysis* (New York: Norton, 1978), p. 152.

16. Roy J. Ruffin and Paul R. Gregory, *Principles of Economics,* 2nd ed. (Glenview, Ill.: Scott Foresman, 1986), p. 734.

17. Gabriel A. Almond and G. Bingham Powell, *Comparative Politics: A Developmental Approach* (Boston: Little, Brown, 1969), p. 199.

18. Richard I. Hofferbert, *The Reach and Grasp of Policy Analysis* (Tuscaloosa: University of Alabama Press, 1990), p. 4.

19. Those who want to explore the activities of private evaluators, as well as the conduct of evaluation studies, will find useful Richard P. Nathan, *Social Science in Government: Uses and Misuses* (New York: Basic Books, 1988).

20. John Stuart Mill, *Considerations on Representative Government* (New York: Liberal Arts Press, 1958). First published in 1861.

21. Leading studies of congressional oversight include Joel D. Aberbach, *Keeping a Watchful Eye* (Washington: Brookings Institution, 1990); and Christopher J. Foreman, Jr., *Signals from the Hill* (New Haven: Yale University Press, 1988).

22. This discussion draws on Elmer B. Staats, "General Accounting Office Support of Committee Oversight," in Committee Organization in the House (panel discussion before the House Select Committee on Committees), 93rd Cong., 1st Sess. (1973), II, pp. 692–700. Staats was head of the GAO. See also Frederick C. Mosher, *A Tale of Two Agencies* (Baton Rouge: Louisiana State University Press, 1984), chap. 5.

23. Recent activities of the GAO are summarized in congressional testimony by Comptroller General Charles A. Bowsher, *Congressional Oversight* (Washington, D.C., April 1996).

24. General Accounting Office, *Food Safety and Quality: Uniform Risk-based Inspection Systems Needed to Ensure Safe Food Supply* (Washington: USGAO, June 1992).

25. *The Tower Commission Report* (New York: Bantam Books, 1987).

26. George C. Edwards and Stephen J. Wayne, *Presidential Leadership: Politics and Policy-Making,* 3rd ed. (New York: St. Martin's, 1994), p. 441.

27. Charles O. Jones, *An Introduction to the Study of Public Policy* (Belmont, Calif.: Wadsworth, 1970), p. 118. Insight into the operation of a commission set up to appraise legislation regulating the political activities of public

employees can be gained from Charles O. Jones, "Reevaluating the Hatch Act: A Report on the Commission on Political Activity of Government Employees," *Public Administration Review*, XXIX (May–June 1969), pp. 249–254.

28. Donald Axelrod, *Budgeting for Modern Government*, 2nd ed. (New York: St. Martin's, 1988), chap. 10, provides a succinct review of this reform effort.

29. *The Gore Report on Reinventing Government* (New York: Times Books, 1993), p. i. (This is a reprint of the report of the National Performance Review entitled "From Red Tape to Results: Creating a Government That Works Better and Costs Less."

30. Ibid., p. iii.

31. Donald F. Kettl, "Building Lasting Reform: Enduring Questions, Missing Answers," in Donald F. Kettl and John J. DiIulio, Jr., eds., *Inside the Reinvention Machine* (Washington: Brookings Institution, 1995), p. 83.

32. Gerald Garvey, "False Promises: The NPR in Historical Perspective," in ibid, p. 106.

33. Public Law 103–62, 107 U.S. Statutes at Large 285 (1993).

34. Senate Committee on Government Affairs, *Government Performance and Results Act of 1993*, S. Rept. 103–58, 103rd Cong., 1st Sess., 1993, p. 3.

35. Carol H. Weiss, "The Politics of Impact Measurement," *Policy Studies Journal*, Vol. 1 (Spring 1973), pp. 180–181.

36. Edward R. Tufte, *Data Analysis for Politics and Policy* (Englewood Cliffs, N.J.: Prentice-Hall, 1974), chap. 1.

37. Charles F. Bonser, Eugene B. McGregor, and Clinton V. Oster, Jr., *Policy Choices and Public Action* (Upper Saddle River, N.J.: Prentice-Hall, 1995), chap. 12.

38. See Kenneth J. Meier and E. Thomas Garman, *Regulation and Consumer Protection*, 2nd ed. (Houston: Dame Publications, 1995), chap. 4.

39. 384 U.S. 436 (1966).

40. President's Commission on Law Enforcement and the Administration of Justice, *The Challenge of Crime in a Free Society* (Washington: U.S. Government Printing Office, 1967), p. 305.

41. *Time*, Vol. 112 (July 18, 1988), p. 53.

42. Jeremy A. Lifsey, "Politics, Evaluations and Manpower Programs." Unpublished paper presented at the annual meeting of the American Political Science Association (1973).

43. Carl V. Patton and David D. Sawicki, *Basic Methods of Policy Analysis and Planning*, 2nd ed. (Englewood Cliffs, N.J.: Prentice-Hall, 1993), pp. 379–385.

44. Lester M. Salamon, "The Time Dimension in Policy Evaluation: The Case of the New Deal Land-Reform Experiments," *Public Policy*, XXVII (Spring 1979), pp. 129–184.

45. A. Myrick Freeman III, *Air and Water Pollution Control: A Benefit-Cost Assessment* (New York: Wiley, 1982).

46. For more extensive discussions of cost-benefit analysis, see Stokey and Zeckhauser, op. cit., chap. 9; and David L. Weimer and Aidan R. Vining, *Policy Analysis: Concepts and Practice* (Englewood Cliffs, N.J.: Prentice-Hall, 1989), chap. 7.

47. Quoted in Timothy B. Clark, "Do the Benefits Justify the Costs? Prove It, Says the Administration," *National Journal*, Vol. 13 (August 1, 1981), p. 1385.
48. Weimer and Vining, op. cit., p. 15.
49. See Thomas O. McGarity, *Reinventing Rationality: The Role of Regulatory Analysis in the Federal Bureaucracy* (New York: Cambridge University Press, 1991); and George Eads and Michael Fix, *Relief or Reform? Reagan's Regulatory Dilemma* (Washington: Urban Institute Press, 1984).
50. *Federal Register*, Vol. 46 (February 19, 1981), pp. 13193–13198.
51. President's Task Force on Regulatory Relief, *Reagan Administration Regulatory Achievements* (Washington: U.S. Government Printing Office, 1983), pp. 59–61.
52. Kirk Victor, "Quayle's Quiet Coup," *National Journal*, Vol. 23 (July 6, 1991), pp. 1676–1680.
53. Barry D. Friedman, *Regulation in the Reagan-Bush Era* (Pittsburgh: University of Pittsburgh Press, 1995), pp. 164–165.
54. On partisan political analysis, see Charles E. Lindblom, *The Policy-Making Process*, 2nd ed. (Englewood Cliffs, N.J.: Prentice-Hall, 1980), chap. 4.
55. This account draws upon Walter Williams, *Social Policy Research and Analysis* (New York: American Elsevier, 1971); and Walter Williams and John W. Evan, "The Politics of Evaluation: The Case of Head Start," *Annals of the American Academy of Political and Social Sciences*, CCCLXXXV (September 1969), pp. 118–132.
56. Ibid.
57. See Department of Health and Human Services, *The Impact of Head Start on Children, Families, and Communities: Head Start Synthesis Project* (Washington: U.S. Government Printing Office, 1985).
58. *Congressional Quarterly Weekly Report*, Vol. 53 (July 15, 1995), p. 2071.
59. *The New York Times*, February 14, 1990, p. 1; March 4, 1992, p. B9. *Washington Post National Weekly Edition*, May 4–10, 1992, p. 31.
60. Janet Currie and Duncan Thomas, "Does Head Start Make a Difference?" *American Economic Review*, Vol. 85 (June 1995), pp. 341–364.
61. Ralph K. Huitt, "Political Feasibility," in Austin Ranney, ed., *Political Science and Public Policy* (Chicago: Markham, 1968), p. 266.
62. David J. Webber, "Analyzing Political Feasibility: Political Scientists' Unique Contribution to Policy Analysis," *Policy Studies Journal*, XIV (June 1986), pp. 545–553.
63. This discussion leans heavily upon James Q. Wilson, *Political Organizations*, 2nd ed. (New York: Basic Books, 1995), chap. 16.
64. Wilson, op. cit., chap. 16.
65. See Martha Derthick and Paul J. Quirk, *The Politics of Deregulation* (Washington: Brookings Institution, 1985).
66. Cf. Seymour Scher, "Regulatory Agency Control Through Appointment: The Case of the Eisenhower Administration and the NLRB," *Journal of Politics*, XXIII (November 1961), pp. 667–688; and Terry M. Moe, "Control and Feedback in Economic Regulation: The Case of the NLRB," *American Political Science Review*, LXXIX (December 1985), pp. 1094–1116.
67. Edward L. Katzenbach, Jr., "The Horse Cavalry in the Twentieth Century: A

Study in Policy Response," in Carl J. Friedrich and Seymour E. Harris, eds., *Public Policy,* Vol. 8 (Cambridge: Harvard University Press, 1958), pp. 120–149.

68. *Wall Street Journal,* March 27, 1996, p. A20.
69. Garry D. Brewer and Peter deLeon, *The Foundation of Policy Analysis* (Homewood, Ill.: Dorsey Press, 1983), chap. 13.

8

Concluding Comments

Several billion banknotes are produced annually by the national government. Here, bills are tested for durability.

T he preceding chapters have laid out a general framework (or model) as well as a variety of concepts and ideas for the study and analysis of the complex process of public policymaking. The framework, which depicts the policymaking process as a sequence of functional activities (problem definition, agenda setting, policy formulation, and so on) is intended as neither a general nor a causal theory of the policy process.[1] Rather, it is a way of dividing the policy process into manageable segments and of organizing and guiding one's examination of that process. Various theories purporting to explain who makes or controls policy, some of which are discussed in Chapter 1, can be accommodated to this model. Also, I want to emphasize once again that the various segments or stages of the framework are interrelated and sometimes smudged together. What happens at one stage of the policy process has consequences for action at later stages. And stages, such as policy adoption and implementation, may blend together. Still, analytical distinctions can be made.

It would seem that the best advice for those hoping for the emergence of a general theory of policymaking is to be very patient. Not too long ago, political scientists spoke and wrote about the need to develop a general theory of politics.[2] Research projects were often justified in part as contributing to the development of a general theory. Politics and policymaking, however, are too complex to be explained satisfactorily by one grand theory, and so the quest for a general theory has been consigned to the disciplinary dustbin. These remarks are intended neither to disparage nor discourage theory development (or "building") in favor of descriptive or "factual" studies. Theory is needed to help separate more important or relevant variables and facts from those less so in describing and explaining events. In building theories it seems advisable to focus on more manageable tasks, such as explaining why some policies are more successfully implemented than others, or why only some distressful conditions out of all those existing in society become defined as public problems and reach policy agendas. These are challenging, worthy, and manageable tasks.

In the remainder of these concluding remarks I will present some general conclusions about the policymaking process, along with some of the changes that have occurred in the process since the first edition of this book was published in the early 1970s.

First, once the formation of policy on most public problems—certainly those of any magnitude—gets underway, it tends to be continuous, although fluctuations may occur in the scope and intensity of activity. It has been said that policymaking has "no beginning and no end."[3] This is an overstatement. For most purposes, the beginning of the policymaking process can be effectively marked with the emergence or identification of a problem and, at least when a policy such as commercial airline regulation is terminated, one can identify its end. Within these bounds the process is continuous—something is always happening, or perhaps not happening, that has meaning for the content and impact of policy.

As the policy process unfolds, a problem is recognized, defined, and placed on one or more governmental agendas; alternatives are developed, presented, and debated; one alternative (the policy) is officially adopted; implementation begins; experience may reveal shortcomings, loopholes, or other defects in the policy, or some sort of formal evaluation and feedback may occur; legislative or administrative adjustments may be made in the policy; more implementation follows; evaluation and feedback again happen; infrequently a policy may be terminated; and so on.

Somewhere along the way, because of changes in the policy environment, the problem at which a policy is targeted may be redefined. In the 1970s the "farm problem" shifted from too much production to too little production, with farmers being urged to plant "from fencerow to fencerow," and then back to surplus production. Then in the mid-1990s, governmental restrictions on farmers became the problem and many of these restrictions were removed by the 1996 farm legislation. A problem may also seem to disappear, at least for a time. An example is the energy problem. During the 1970s the Nixon, Ford, and Carter administrations struggled to develop governmental solutions for the perceived shortage of fuels. The Reagan administration, however, contended that there was no scarcity of energy. When actions like these occur, the consequences may be substantial changes in the direction and content of some policies. Whereas the energy policy of the Carter administration stressed governmental action, conservation, and the development of new energy sources, Reagan administration policy called for less governmental action and more reliance on the market. This course of action on energy continues to prevail, as the emergence of larger motor vehicles and higher speed limits attests.

Policies in many areas often become settled and handled for the most part by routine administrative processes. Often they will be dominated by subsystems and be characterized by low public visibility, only to be disturbed by some action that leads to identification of a new problem and that restarts the policy process. It may be a change in socioeconomic conditions, as when the aging of the population creates a "crisis" in Social Security financing. The AIDS crisis similarly created demands for change in medical-research policy, and the animal-rights movement threatens to do the same. In 1995 an outbreak of food poisoning in the Pacific Northwest called into question the adequacy of the U.S. Department of Agriculture's meat-inspection program. The result was the adoption of new rules intended to prevent bacterial contamination.[4] In all, the policy process is best thought of as cyclical rather than linear, as something that recycles as new problems emerge, as continuous rather than finite in duration.

Second, in a large, modern, pluralistic society and political system, public policymaking is likely to be complex, untidy, and perhaps a bit unruly.

Whether regularly or occasionally, many players, official and unofficial, participate, and many factors that help shape policy process are thus not sharply demarcated. Political authority and power are fragmented and dispersed by governmental structure, and by the social, economic, and ideological diversity of American society. In the early 1970s, power in Congress was further dispersed by being shifted from committees to subcommittees. Also, interest groups proliferated in number and variety. The consequence has been increased factionalism in policymaking. Factionalism, Professor Hugh Heclo says, is an old label but one that serves well to describe the current situation. The primary difference between the factionalism that James Madison wrote about in *The Federalist*, No. 10, and the present factionalism is that "our factionalism has shaped itself around a governmental presence that is doing so much more in so many different areas of life."[5] As a consequence, government often seems too responsive to narrow group, sectoral, or regional interests and insufficiently concerned with searching out and caring for the public interest.

Decision-making in the policymaking process, because of the fragmentation of power, is characterized by logrolling and alliance building, negotiation and bargaining, and compromise. Delay in decision-making and moderation in action flow from these aspects of its style. Action may be delayed on pressing problems, such as child care and the "greenhouse effect," because the necessary consensus cannot be achieved. On the other hand, sometimes the system acts quickly, as in the summer of 1993, when legislation providing financial aid to flood-stricken residents of the Midwest was quickly approved by Congress. Problems for which solutions are apparent and more readily agreed to are likely to be acted on more quickly.

In 1995 it appeared for a time that a fundamental change might be occurring in the policymaking process. For the first time in forty years, the Republicans took control of both houses of Congress. In the House, under the leadership of Speaker Newt Gingrich, a disciplined Republican majority, claiming a mandate from the voters, rammed through within a hundred days nearly all of the components of their radical "Contract with America." (The only exception was a proposed constitutional amendment providing for term limits.) The House bills, however, encountered opposition in the more moderate Senate and from the White House. By year's end, most of the Contract with America remained unenacted. Moreover, the Congressional Republicans and the President, who had the support of most Democrats in Congress, were stalemated over the issue of balancing the budget within a seven-year time frame. Once again, the separation and dispersion of power in the American political system has complicated and tempered policy change.[6]

In all, the policymaking process in the United States is not easy to comprehend, describe, or explain. Those who offer quick, certain, or pat explanations as to why policies were rejected or adopted, or later proved unsuccessful, often oversimplify and at best provide partial explanations.

Some historians assert that the Sherman Act of 1890 was adopted as a "sop to public opinion," an attempt to quell the public clamor for legislation against the trusts. Such explanations usually have within them a kernel of accuracy. Careful examination of the history of the Sherman Act, however, indicates far more than the "sop factor." There were real concerns about the effects of the trusts on the economy, society, and polity, and real differences in views about whether or not government should act and in what manner.

Journalists and others (political scientists are not fully exempted here) sometimes explain legislative enactments idiosyncratically, as primarily the result of clever actions by this senator or that representative, or the machinations of a particular interest group.[7] Important executive decisions may be attributed to designated officials, acting almost alone and unaided, it would seem. People are important, they do make a difference, but they act within an institutional and societal context that also shapes, directs, and constrains action. The diversity of this context also adds to the complexity of the policy process. If studies of policymaking are complex in substance and uncertain or tentative in findings and conclusions, it is not because political scientists and other policy analysts are at once obtuse and timid. Rather, it is more likely that the subject is complex, conclusive data are scarce, motives are unclear, influence is subtle, and policy impacts uncertain. Accurately explaining human behavior is a tenuous and complicated task.

Third, the policymaking process in the United States tends to be adversarial, featuring the clash of competing and conflicting viewpoints and interests rather than either an impartial, disinterested, objective search for solutions to problems or a cooperative endeavor by interested parties to handle matters.[8] Nowhere is this conflict better illustrated than in the conduct of judicial proceedings, whether trial or appellate; and in the judiciary's extensive involvement in the policy process, which is brought about by those unhappy with decisions made by other governmental actors. Government–business relationships are also notable for their adversarial quality. Although it is occasionally urged that such relationships should be more cooperative, as they are in Japan, so that the United States can compete more effectively in the world economy, not much changes. The adversarial pattern is more congruent with American culture and its self-assertive values.[9] Most Americans prefer a more independent role for government as a guardian of public interest. Also, Americans have the notion that "government is not the solution to our problem. Government is the problem." Uttered by Ronald Reagan in his 1981 Inaugural Address, the mistrust of government that it reflects is an element of American political culture. It is not the stuff from which grow extensive cooperative relationships between government and others. Important interests, including that of the public, may be lost sight of in the clash of adversaries, however.

Fourth, policy analysis has become more widely practiced and its products more heavily drawn upon in the development of policies in the legislative and administrative arenas. Policy evaluation, in its systematic variant, is also much more prevalent. Together these developments have contributed to making the policy process more technocratic. The opposing sides in policy struggles trot out their experts and "objective" policy analyses to support their positions. More and more, policymaking threatens to become the domain of experts, into which ordinary persons ought not to intrude. Debates over arms control, for instance, are loaded with technical data about missiles and other weapons systems. Mathematical models are devised to estimate the likely responses of the erstwhile Soviets or other potential aggressors to possible actions. The average citizen often is baffled by this sort of analysis.

Policy analysis, however, is not the only cause of technocracy in policymaking. In Congress the subcommittee system, which encourages specialization, and the rise of careerist legislators, who have both incentives and opportunity to specialize, have also been contributory.[10] Of course one must also recognize that some policy matters are by their very nature technical and complex. The treatment and disposal of hazardous waste is a good example. On the other hand, issues may be made deliberately to seem more technical than they are in an effort to exclude nonexperts from their consideration. Still worth remembering is the old public-administration adage that the expert should be on tap rather than on top.

Policy decisions ultimately remain political in tone, however, if for no other reason than that they distribute advantages and disadvantages. Sometimes it seems to be assumed that if enough research and analysis are conducted, and enough facts and data are gathered, answers to policy problems will appear upon which all people, or at least all reasonable people, can agree. If policy problems were only scientific or technical this resolution might happen, as when vaccines are developed and generally administered to eradicate childhood diseases. No "pro-poliomyelitis" lobby campaigned against the Salk vaccine, for instance. Conflict may develop, however, over the administration of public vaccination programs.

Most policy problems, and certainly those of any magnitude, generate significant differences of view as to what is socially acceptable, economically feasible, and politically possible. Bargaining, negotiation, and compromise, not simply reliance upon the "facts," are then required to produce decisions. Policy analysis can inform, enlighten, develop alternatives, and even persuade to an extent, but by itself it is unlikely to yield consensus policy decisions. Room still remains in the policy process for generalists, who should be on top, according to the old adage.

Fifth, the notion that policymaking in the United States is essentially incremental is conventional wisdom among political scientists. Incrementalism can mean either that a new policy differs only marginally from current policies, or that it resulted from a decision-making process involving limited analysis of goals, alternatives, and consequences. Some decisions are characterized by more analysis, others by less analysis, and none by complete (i.e., rational–comprehensive) analysis. To say that a policy was based on limited analysis is to say nothing that really differentiates it from other policies. If our attention turns to the amount of change embodied in a policy, we find that many new policies indeed make limited or marginal changes (whether additions or deletions, although, accurately speaking, an increment is an increase) in existing policies. Some new policies, however, are of sufficient magnitude, impact, or variation from the status quo as to be classifiable as basic or fundamental. Examples include the Social Security Act of 1935, the Marshall Plan (which provided extensive economic aid to post–World War II Europe), the interstate highway program, airline deregulation, and the 1986 tax-reform legislation. Although greatly exceeded in number by incremental policies, such basic policies significantly change and shape the content and direction of governmental action. Excessive emphasis on incrementalism therefore obscures the importance of basic policies in the evolution and direction of American public policy.

In time, it is true that significant changes in policies can occur incrementally. The progressive quality of the graduated income tax was gradually reduced by a plethora of laws creating deductions, credits, exclusions, and exemptions, mostly for the benefit of higher-income persons. By 1980 its progressive and redistributive effects were as much symbolic as material. In an incremental manner, a basic change was wrought in income-tax policy, without ever directly being considered on its merit. Incremental action tends to mitigate conflict, but the avoidance of conflict, if conflict helps to clarify issues and focus attention, is not wholly desirable.

Sixth, in the study of public policymaking and in the day-to-day observation of the governmental process, our attention is usually focused on conflict. Conflict attracts attention. Major public policies generate conflict and make news. They also draw scholarly attention. Consequently, one may come to believe that policymaking as a matter of course is always sharply conflictive. One can find some support in this book for such a conclusion, although I have tried to provide a variety of references to less conflictive matters. Environmental protection, tax reform, economic regulation, and Social Security reform have produced much conflict. At the same time, however, there is what Professor Herbert Jacob calls the ongoing "routine policy process."[11] Although not devoid of conflict, it is characterized by such features as a narrow definition of the problem to be solved, low visibility, limited participation, low policy costs, and general compatibility between proposed and existing policies. The policies may be either regulatory or distributive, and they sometimes may be of considerable importance. Examples include the Animal Welfare Act (1966), the Medical Waste Tracking Act (1988), and the Dietary Supplement Health and Education Act (1994), which exempted dietary supplements from most Food and Drug Administration regulation. At the state level, divorce-law reform is an example. Since 1966 all the states, without stirring much controversy, have revised their divorce laws. Now, along with other modifications in divorce law, no-fault divorce can be obtained in every state.

In all, the routine policy process differs from the conflictive process more in degree than in genre. There is, for instance, public participation, but less of it. Disagreement occurs over what should be done on a matter, but efforts are made to muffle it. Much of the work in developing policy takes place at the subsystem level, which contributes to lower public awareness, although adoption occurs in the macro-arena. Of course, routine policy may also be studied using the sequential process framework.

Seventh, change is a constant companion of the policy process. Changes take a variety of forms, including alterations in the number and variety of participants or in their roles and relationships, in the manner in which some issues are handled, and in the procedures or techniques used to deal with problems. When change is deliberately designed and sought, when it takes the form of a deliberate effort to improve the operation of the policy process from some perspective, we often call it *reform*. When, however, it arises undesigned and unintended out of other events, we do not have a distinctive name for it.

Change in the policy process is more likely to be limited or incremental than sudden and sweeping in scope. The efforts of the Reagan administration to redirect the policy process, both in style and output, were soon referred to as the "Reagan Revolution." Changes did occur, but not to an extent sufficient to warrant the label "revolution." More executive control of administrative rule-making was installed, authorized by executive orders and implemented by the Office of Management and Budget. The budget deficit, as a consequence of the large budget deficits incurred during the Reagan years, won a place at the top of the national policy agenda and complicated action on other policy matters. Some argue that large budget deficits were incurred deliberately by the president to make it difficult to adopt new spending programs. Not without a touch of plausibility, this line of argument attributes too much guile and strategic thinking to President Reagan. What actually occurred is better thought of as the unintended consequence of other actions, namely, tax reduction and greater defense spending.[12]

Using causation as the differentiating criterion, changes in the policy process can be placed in three groups: (1) Changes which are designed and which operate generally as intended. The establishment of the Environmental Protection Agency in 1970 to consolidate many environmental programs and enhance environmental protection is an example. (2) Changes in the policy process that are the consequence of changes made for other purposes. The 1974 congressional budget legislation, which set up budget committees in each house of Congress and created a congressional budget process, did bring about some improvement in the rationality of congressional budgetary action. It has also unintentionally helped shift the role of the House Appropriations Committee from that of "defender of the Treasury" to protector of programs favored by committee members. (3) Other changes, because of broad or multiple sources of causation, that can best be thought of as responses to changes in the policy environment. Consider the growing "technocratization" of the policy process. This change stems from, among other factors, the shift in power from congressional committees to subcommittees, increased staff assistance for members of Congress, and the fact that policy problems and issues are becoming more complex and technical. This "technocratization" of the policy process in turn makes meaningful participation by ordinary persons or average citizens more difficult. One cannot point to a particular decision that, intentionally or inadvertently, produced this situation.

The conclusion to be drawn from this discussion is not that change is pernicious but rather that successful and intentional change in the policy process is not easily achieved. Term-limit advocates who suggest that members of Congress should serve for only six years (or twelve years) in order to reduce "careerism" and members' supposed unresponsiveness to the electorate have probably not thought deeply about all the consequences such a change would produce, both in the operation of Congress as an institution and in its participation in the policy process. The political system, systems theory informs us, is composed of interdependent parts. A change in one part will have consequences for the other parts and their roles and activities. Successful reform of the policy process requires adequate knowledge of the process and its operation. Such knowledge is not easy to acquire.

Finally, public policies collectively accomplish a good deal, notwithstanding complaints about "policy failure" (which are not without some validity) and allegations that public problems never get resolved. At the local level, for example, garbage is collected, fires are put out, public order is maintained, traffic moves reasonably well (except during rush hours), water flows from the tap, most children learn to read and write, and parks and recreation facilities exist. If few public problems are entirely resolved by government actions, many are partly or substantially solved or ameliorated. Employment problems remain, but are not as bad as they would be were there no job-training, economic development, unemployment-compensation, and other employment-related programs. Consumers may still be misled and defrauded, but not with the frequently they would be without consumer-protection programs. More wildlife survives than would have in the absence of fish-and-game laws, national and state parks, and wildlife refuges. Public-health and sanitation policies have greatly reduced the incidence of infectious diseases and contributed to greater human longevity. Civil-rights policies have done much to reduce discrimination and expand opportunities for minorities.

The goals of public policies are usually stated in absolute rather than relative language. Thus the streets are to be made safe (rather than safer) for all law-abiding people, or poverty is to be banished (not just reduced) from America. Absolute statements, because they are more appealing than conditional phrasing of goals, are used to garner public and interest-group support for policies. The Clean Water Act of 1972 set a goal of "zero" discharge of pollutants into the nation's streams by 1985. The goal has not been met, although most streams are undoubtedly cleaner than they would have been without the act. Has the act then "failed," as some allege?

Because of the intractability of many public problems, public policies may at best mitigate or reduce the target problems. The prevalence of heart disease can be lessened, for instance, or the amount of juvenile delinquency can be reduced. When goals are stated as absolutes, however, anything less than complete success tends to be constructed as failure. This masks the real accomplishments of many public policies, even those which we may personally disprove of. Whatever their shortcomings, public policies have done much to improve the quality and comfort of modern life.

Notes

1. Cf. Paul A. Sabatier and Hank C. Jenkins Smith, eds., *Policy Change and Learning: An Advocacy Coalition Approach* (Boulder, Colo.: Westview, 1993).
2. David Easton, *The Political System* (New York: Knopf, 1953). Also idem., *The Analysis of Political Structure* (New York: Routledge, 1990), chap. 1.
3. Charles E. Lindblom, *The Policy-making Process*, 2nd ed. (Englewood Cliffs, N.J.: Prentice-Hall, 1980), p. 5.
4. *Wall Street Journal*, July 8, 1996, p. A2; *Federal Register*, Vol. 61 (July 25, 1996), pp. 38806–38989.
5. Hugh Heclo, "The Emerging Regime," in Richard A. Harris and Sidney M. Milkis, eds., *Remaking American Politics* (Boulder, Colo.: Westview Press, 1989), p. 310.
6. John B. Bader, "The 'Contract with America'?: Origins and Prospects." Paper presented at the 1996 meeting of the Midwest Political Science Association, Chicago, April 18–20, 1996.
7. As an example, consider Hedrick Smith's informative work on Washington politics and policymaking, *The Power Game* (New York: Random House, 1988). The power players discussed therein often seem to be acting within an institution-free context.
8. Robert Kagan, "Adversarial Legalism and American Government," in Marc K. Landy and Martin A. Levin, eds., *The New Politics of Public Policy* (Baltimore: Johns Hopkins University Press, 1995), chap. 4.
9. See Steven Kelman, *Regulating America, Regulating Sweden* (Boston: MIT Press, 1981), pp. 133–141, 229–236.
10. Lawrence C. Dodd, "The Rise of Technocratic Congress: Congressional Reform in the 1970s," in Harris and Milkis, op. cit., chap. 4.
11. Herbert Jacob, *Silent Revolution: The Transformation of Divorce Law in the United States* (Chicago: University of Chicago Press, 1988).
12. Cf. David A. Stockman, *The Triumph of Politics: Why the Reagan Revolution Failed* (New York: Harper & Row, 1986).

GLOSSARY

access In group theory, the opportunity for persons or groups to express their viewpoints to decision-makers.

adjudication The application through judicial or judicial-like procedure of existing law or policy to particular cases.

administrative agencies Executive branch organizations that carry out public policies and carry on the day-to-day activities of government.

advocacy coalition A like-minded set of officials, groups, agencies, and others that operates within a political subsystem.

agenda-setting This designates the various ways by which problems can gain a place on an agenda.

antitrust policy A public policy intended to prevent monopoly and maintain competition in the economy.

appropriations legislation Following authorization legislation, this law actually makes money available to support government programs.

authorization legislation Creates government programs and provides legal authority for the outlay of money to carry them out.

backdoor spending Expenditures made by government agencies on the basis of borrowing and contracting authority, and which circumvent the normal appropriations process.

bargaining Decision-making through a process of negotiation, give-and-take, and compromise.

basic decision A decision that makes a major change in the direction or content of public policy.

budget Technically, a statement of estimated revenues and proposed expenditures; it is also a policy statement and a political document.

budget authority This permits agencies to commit or obligate themselves to the later expenditure (or outlay) of funds.

budget deficit The amount by which a government's expenditures exceed revenues in a fiscal year.

bureau A major administrative subunit in a government department or agency, such as the Bureau of Reclamation.

checks and balances The constitutional ability of the branches of the national government to interfere with and to limit the exercise of power by one another.

clientele The set of reasonably distinct or identifiable individuals and groups served or regulated by an agency, such as broadcasters and the Federal Communications Commission.

collective goods Goods such as national defense or clean air that are indivisible and must be provided to all or to none.

command The ability of those in hierarchical positions to make decisions that are binding on subordinates.

congressional oversight Actions by Congress to supervise and control the activities of administrative agencies.

conservative policy A policy emphasizing private action and maintenance of the status quo.

constituency Those groups, officials, and others that an agency or its officials take into account when making decisions.

continuing resolution Congressional action permitting agencies whose appropriations have not been enacted to continue to operate and expend funds.

cooperative federalism All levels of government—national, state, and local—interacting and cooperating in the formation and execution of public policies.

decision-making The process of making a choice among a number of alternatives.

decision rules Guidelines or rules of thumb that simplify decisionmaking on particular topics.

deference A form of decision-making in which a person accepts, or defers to, the judgment of someone else.

delegated powers Those powers assigned to the national government in Article I, Section 8, of the Constitution.

delegation of power Action by Congress authorizing the executive or administrative agencies to take action on specified topics.

deregulation Proposals and actions to eliminate or severely reduce economic regulatory programs.

discretion The capacity of administrative officials to exercise choice on some topic because of authority delegated to them.

discretionary spending Budget authority, other than for entitlements, that is included in annual appropriations acts and subsequent outlays.

distributive policy A policy that provides services or benefits to particular persons, groups, or communities.

dual federalism The theory that the national and state government have distinct and separate spheres of action. Now outdated.

elite theory The view that public policies are determined by a small segment of society, such as an upper-class, uncontrolled by the mass of citizens.

entitlement programs These provide that everyone meeting eligibility requirements is legally entitled to benefit payments on the basis of a formula in the law, for example, Social Security.

executive department A large administrative organization, headed by a secretary, that is a basic component of the executive branch; for example, the Department of Health and Human Services.

executive order A legally-binding policy statement issued by the president on the basis of his constitutional or delegated authority.

federalism The constitutional division of power between a central or national government and a series of state or provincial governments.

fiscal year A twelve-month period, often not coincident with the calendar year, used for budgetary purposes.

formulation The development of proposed courses of action or alternatives for dealing with public problems.

government corporation Established to administer businesslike or commercial activities, this agency has more operating freedom than other agencies.

group theory A theory holding that policies result from conflict and struggle among political groups.

ideology A more or less systematic set of values and beliefs that serve as a guide to action and understanding.

incrementalism A theory of decision-making holding that decisions are usually based on limited analysis and involve marginal changes in existing policies.

independent agency An agency other than an independent regulatory commission or government corporation, formally located outside of the executive departments; for example, the Central Intelligence Agency.

independent regulatory commission A plural-headed agency handling economic regulatory programs that is somewhat free from presidential control, such as the Federal Reserve Board.

informal procedures Agency modes of handling matters that are not specified by laws or other legal documents.

initiative A process available in some states by which a proposed law is put on the ballot by citizen petition for voter approval.

institution A regularized pattern of human behavior that persists over time and that performs an important task.

institutional agenda A set of problems of interest to the member of a particular governmental body, such as a legislature.

institutionalism A theory stressing the importance of organizational arrangements and rules in shaping public policies.

interest groups A private organization or group that strives to influence the actions of governmental officials.

iron triangle A political subsystem comprising a government agency, congressional committees, and some interest groups that is resistant to external influences.

issue A problem or matter on which there is disagreement as to what should be done about it.

issue network A political subsystem marked by its loose amorphous character and the inclusion of many policy experts.

judicial review The power of a court to determine the constitutionality of legislative and executive actions.

laissez faire A term designating government inaction on some aspects of economic activity.

legislative intent The meaning and purpose, not always clear, of a law passed by Congress.

legislative veto The rejection by Congress or its committees of proposed executive or agency actions.

legitimacy The quality of rightness or appropriateness that may characterize a government or a policy and enhance its acceptability and authoritativeness.

liberal policy A policy involving the use of government action to bring about social change.

lobbying The transmission of information to public officials by pressure group representatives hoping to influence government decisions.

logrolling The exchange of support by persons interested in different matters; often called "mutual back-scratching."

macropolitics Policymaking that includes a wide range of important political actors—the president, congressional leaders, interest groups, and others.

majority building The use of bargaining and other means to create numerical majorities needed to pass or kill legislation.

material policy A policy that provides or denies tangible resources or substantive power to those at whom it is directed.

micropolitics Political activity, to gain benefits for particular persons, companies, or communities, characterized by limited participation.

national debt A product of budget deficits, this is the total of financial obligations that the national government owes to others, now over four trillion dollars.

nondecision The failure of government to take action on a problem or condition or to even meaningfully consider it.

outlays The payments made by agencies for goods and services and to meet obligations.

persuasion The use of reason, facts, and logic to convince others of the correctness of one's position on an issue.

pluralism A theory holding that political power in a society is dispersed among many groups or other entities.

policy advocacy Activity to secure what someone identifies as good or proper public policy.

policy agenda A set of problems which public officials feel they should act on in some way.

policy analysis Research drawing upon economic theory that seeks to identify the most efficient way to handle a problem.

policy community A subsystem with quite a few participants that is more stable and determinant in nature than an issue network.

policy decisions Choices made on whether something should be adopted as public policy.

policy demands Requests or calls for action or inaction by government on some matter by individuals, groups, or others.

policy evaluation Concerned with trying to determine the effects or consequences of actual public policies.

policy formation The total process by which public policies are developed and implemented.

policy impact The effects or consequences of a policy, whether intended or unintended.

policy outcomes The ultimate consequences that a policy has for society; for instance, its contribution to social contentment or security.

policy outputs Specific actions taken to carry out policy decisions and statements, such as the collection of taxes or the paying out of benefits.

policy priorities A ranking on some basis of a set of problems or issues from more to less important.

policy problem A condition or situation in society that causes people distress or dissatisfaction and for which relief is sought through government action.

policy statements Formal expressions or articulations of public policies in laws, administrative rules, and other documents.

policy study The effort to systematically explain or account for the adoption of public policies.

political culture Widely shared attitudes, values, and beliefs concerning the nature and use of political power.

political parties Organizations that nominate candidates, contest elections, and seek to gain control of the government.

political system Those interrelated and identifiable institutions and activities in a society that make authoritative allocations of value.

political systems theory This holds that public policies are a political system's responses to demands from its environment.

pollution The discharge of substances into the environment that interfere with or prevent desired uses of the environment.

pork-barrel legislation This authorizes spending on projects such as dams and research facilities located in particular states or localities.

presidential commission A temporary group created by the chief executive to study and make recommendations on a problem.

presidential veto Constitutional authority of the president to reject laws passed by Congress, unless re-enacted by a two-thirds vote of each house.

pressure group See *interest groups*.

primary policy-makers Those who are given constitutional authority to engage in policymaking, for example, the legislature.

private goods Goods that can be divided into units and individually awarded or sold and charged for.

private problems Matters that are of real concern only to one (or a few) person(s).

privatization The transfer of government functions or property into private hands.

procedural policy A policy that specifies how government will handle some matter, such as the conduct of criminal trials.

public interest What is of interest or benefit to people generally rather than particular groups or segments of the population.

public interest groups A group that supports broad causes and goals that are of benefit to society generally.

public opinion Expressions of public attitudes or beliefs on political issues that public officials find it prudent to heed.

public policy A purposive course of action followed by government in dealing with some problem or matter of concern.

public problems These are problems that have a broad effect, including consequences for persons not directly involved.

quantitative data Numerical indicators of social, political, or economic phenomena, such as birth rates, voter turnout, or employment levels.

rational choice theory This holds that public policies result from the pursuit of self-interest by citizens and officials.

rational comprehensive decision-making The theory that decisions should be made on the basis of full analysis of all of the alternatives for a problem.

reconciliation A process by which Congress adjusts the amounts in tax, spending, and debt legislation to conform to ceilings in the budget resolution for a given fiscal year.

redistributive policy A policy that shifts resources among broad groups of people, from the haves to the have-nots.

referendum A vote by citizens on whether a legislative proposal, such as a tax increase, should become law.

regulatory policy A policy that imposes limitations or restraints on persons, groups, and businesses, thus reducing their discretion to act.

rescission Action by the president and Congress to cancel previously granted appropriations authority.

reserved powers Those governmental powers possessed by the states on the basis of the Tenth Amendment.

revenues Taxes, fees, donations, and other sources of government income.

routine decision A comparatively minor or limited decision that falls within the bounds of settled policy.

rule An agency policy statement of general applicability and future effect. Also called a *regulation*.

sanctions Rewards or penalties used to promote compliance with public policies.

self-regulatory policy A policy where those ostensibly being regulated have much influence over the regulation.

separation of power The constitutional allocation of power among legislative, executive, and judicial branches of government.

stare decisis A judicial decision rule which holds that precedents established by previous cases should be followed in deciding current cases.

substantive policy A policy that directly distributes advantages and disadvantages, or costs and benefits, to people.

subsystem politics Policymaking activity involving a limited number of participants that is focused on a particular policy area, such as banking regulation.

sunk costs Previous decisions and actions that limit what one can do in the future.

supplementary policy-makers Those who gain their authority to engage in policy-making from others, namely, primary policy-makers.

symbolic policy A policy that expresses desired values but has little if any material impact on people.

sweeteners Special provisions added to a bill to make it more acceptable to some legislators or other persons.

systemic agenda A set of problems that are of concern generally to the members of a community.

task force A temporary group of citizens and officials set up to investigate and/or propose action on a problem. Used by some presidents.

trust fund Money collected and used by the government only for a particular purpose, such as highway construction.

uncontrollable expenditures Funds that the government is required to spend on the basis of existing laws.

values Strongly held preferences or standards that guide the conduct of people.

ANNOTATED
BIBLIOGRAPHY

Ackerman, Bruce A., and William T. Hassler, *Clean Coal Dirty Air* (New Haven: Yale University Press, 1981). A case study of the Environmental Protection Agency's requirement that new plants use smokestack scrubbers. Good on the decision-making process.

Allison, Graham T., *Essence of Decision: Explaining the Cuban Missile Crisis* (Boston: Little, Brown, 1971). Decision-making during the Cuban missile crisis from the rational actor, organizational process, and governmental politics perspectives.

Art, Robert J., *The TFX Decision: McNamara and the Military* (Boston: Little, Brown, 1968). A case study of the controversy over the decision to select a multipurpose aircraft for the military, contrary to its wishes. Insightful on the decision process in the bureaucracy.

Bailey, Stephen K., *Congress Makes a Law* (New York: Columbia University Press, 1950). A classic case study of the legislative process, showing how ideas, interests, individuals, and institutions contributed to the adoption of the Employment Act of 1946.

Barke, Richard, *Science, Technology, and Public Policy* (Washington, D.C.: CQ Press, 1986). An insightful, informative introduction to science and technology policies and to their impact on policy formation.

Bauer, Raymond A., and Kenneth J. Gergen (eds.), *The Study of Policy Formation* (New York: Free Press, 1968). A series of original essays dealing with theoretical and methodological concerns in the study of public policy.

Baumgartner, Frank R., and Bryan D. Jones, *Agendas and Instability in American Politics* (Chicago: University of Chicago Press, 1993). A systematic, empirical, and challenging examination of how policy issues rise and decline, and the consequences of this for the policy process.

Berman, Larry, *Planning a Tragedy: The Americanization of the War in Vietnam* (New York: Norton, 1982). An outstanding case study of the Johnson Administration's decision in mid-1965 to escalate U.S. involvement in Vietnam.

Bernstein, Marver H., *Regulating Business by Independent Commission* (Princeton: Princeton University Press, 1955). A dated but still useful treatment of independent regulatory commissions as policy formulators and implementors.

Bonser, Charles F., Eugene B. McGregor, Jr., and Clinton V. Oster, Jr., *Policy Choices and Public Action* (Upper Saddle River, N.J.: Prentice Hall, 1996). This text examines a variety of policy areas and is designed to assist students in analyzing issues and making policy choices.

Bosso, Christopher J., *Pesticides and Politics: The Life Cycle of a Public Issue* (Pittsburgh: University of Pittsburgh Press, 1987). A historical and analytical treatment of the pesticides issue and the relevant political institutions and processes.

Brown, Anthony E., *The Politics of Airline Deregulation* (Knoxville: University of Tennessee Press, 1987). An analytical study of the development, operation, and abolition of commercial airline regulation. Several deregulation strategies are discussed.

Browne, William P., *Private Interests, Public Policy, and American Agriculture* (Lawrence: University Press of Kansas, 1988). A thorough and insightful examination of the large number and variety of groups involved in agricultural policy formation.

Browne, William P., *Cultivating Congress: Constituents, Issues, and Interests in Agricultural Policymaking* (Lawrence: University Press of Kansas, 1995). This book probes into the ways in which members of Congress and their staffs interact with constituents in developing public policy.

Bryner, Gary C., *Blue Skies, Green Politics: The Clean Air Act of 1990 and Its Implementation,* 2d ed. (Washington, D.C.: CQ Press, 1995). This study of the background, enactment, and implementation of the 1990 law probes deeply and skillfully into the policy process.

Buck, Susan J., *Understanding Environmental Administration and Law,* 2d ed. (Washington: Island Press, 1996). This book demonstrates how law and the legal process help shape the implementation of environmental policy.

Chong, Dennis, *Collective Action and the Civil Rights Movement* (Chicago: University of Chicago Press, 1991). A challenging and readable application of rational choice theory in the analysis of the civil rights movement in the United States.

Cigler, Allan J., and Burdett A. Loomis, *Interest Group Politics,* 4th ed. (Washington, D.C.: CQ Press, 1994). A collection of original essays that emphasizes the role of groups in the policymaking process.

Cobb, Roger W., and Charles D. Elder, *Participation in American Politics: The Dynamics of Agenda-Building,* 2d ed. (Baltimore: Johns Hopkins University Press, 1983). A leading study of how problems are placed on the systemic and policy agendas in American society.

Conlon, Timothy J., Margaret T. Wrightson, and David R. Beam, *Taxing Choices: The Politics of Tax Reform* (Washington, D.C.: CQ Press, 1990). A lively and balanced account of the enactment of the Tax Reform Act of 1986.

Cubbage, Frederick W., Jay O'Laughlin, and Charles S. Bullock III, *Forest Resource Policy* (New York: Wiley, 1993). This text combines discussion of the politics and process of policymaking, and the content of forest policy.

Dahl, Robert A., and Charles E. Lindblom, *Politics, Economics, and Welfare* (New York: Harper & Row, 1953). A comparison of policymaking by polyarchy, hierarchy, bargaining, and the market system. A classic work.

Davies, J. Clarence, *The Politics of Pollution,* 2d ed. (Indianapolis: Bobbs-Merrill, 1975). A discussion of the formation and implementation of pollution control legislation. Especially good on the administrative aspects thereof.

Derthick, Martha, *Policymaking for Social Security* (Washington, D.C.: Brookings Institution, 1979). A superb analysis of the Social Security program and policymaking process. Views the current program as the product of an incremental, vertical process.

————, and Paul J. Quirk, *The Politics of Deregulation* (Washington, D.C.: Brookings Institution, 1985). A study that focuses on the airline, trucking, and telecommunications industries to make the case that ideas and economic analysis were important contributors to deregulation.

Dror, Yehezkel, *Public Policymaking Reexamined* (Scranton, Pa.: Chandler, 1968). A comparative treatment of policymaking procedures with suggestions for reform. Tough reading and general in approach but useful.

Dye, Thomas R., *Politics, Economics, and the Public: Outcomes in the American States* (Chicago: Rand-McNally, 1966). A leading study that compares the effects of political and socioeconomic variables on state policies, and concludes that socioeconomic variables are more important.

————, *Policy Analysis* (University: University of Alabama Press, 1976). A series of lectures setting forth Dye's ideas on public-policy research.

————, *Understanding Public Policy*, 7th ed. (Englewood Cliffs, N.J.: Prentice-Hall, 1992). A study that discusses a number of models of policy analysis, illustrates them with case studies, and compares their utility for policy analysis.

Edwards, George C., III, *Implementing Public Policy* (Washington, D.C.: CQ Press, 1980). A discussion of communication, dispositions or attitudes, resources, and bureaucratic structure as major forces shaping future policy implementation. Draws on a wide variety of illustrative materials.

————, and Ira Sharkansky, *The Policy Predicament* (San Francisco: Freeman, 1978). Another introduction to the study of public-policy formation, covering such matters as problems in rational decision-making and economic and political constraints on decisions.

Elder, Charles D., and Roger W. Cobb, *The Political Uses of Symbols* (New York: Longman, 1983). A solid, perceptive study of this topic, which has much utility for the study of policy formation as well as politics generally.

Engler, Robert, *The Politics of Oil* (New York: Macmillan, 1961). An analysis of the impact of the petroleum industry on pertinent public policies. Good background reading for the "energy crisis."

————, *The Brotherhood of Oil* (Chicago: University of Chicago Press, 1977). A sequel to *The Politics of Oil* in which Engler remains critical of the industry.

Fiorino, Daniel J., *Making Environmental Policy* (Berkeley: University of California Press, 1995). A fine introduction to national environmental policymaking by a writer with strong academic and practical credentials.

Foreman, Christopher H., Jr., *Plagues, Products, and Politics* (Washington, D.C.: Brookings Institution, 1994). This book examines and evaluates the capacity of the national government to deal with emergent public health problems.

————, *Signals from the Hill* (New Haven: Yale University Press, 1988). A study focusing on congressional efforts to oversee and evaluate social regulatory agencies. Of much value to students of both Congress and the policy process.

Freeman, J. Leiper, *The Political Process*, 2d ed. (New York: Random House, 1965). A brief analysis of the role of executive bureau, congressional committee, and interest-group subsystems in policy formation. An important study.

Fritschler, A. Lee, *Smoking and Politics*, 4th ed. (Englewood Cliffs, N.J.: Prentice-Hall, 1989). A case study of the cigarette controversy that focuses on the role of the bureaucracy in the tobacco subsystem.

Frohock, Fred M., *Public Policy: Scope and Logic* (Englewood Cliffs, N.J.: Prentice-Hall,

1979). A political philosopher combines theory and practice in treating both normative and empirical policy issues and the policy process.

Goggin, Malcolm L., *Policy Design and the Politics of Implementation* (Knoxville: University of Tennessee Press, 1988). An important study of policy implementation, substantively focused on child health care at the state level.

Halperin, Morton H., *Bureaucratic Politics and Foreign Policy* (Washington, D.C.: Brookings Institution, 1974). An analysis of bureaucratic participation and decision-making in American foreign policy in the post–World War II era.

Hansen, John Mark, *Gaining Access: Congress and the Farm Lobby, 1919–1981* (Chicago: University of Chicago Press, 1991). This book traces the rise and decline in influence of farm groups in the congressional policy process.

Harris, Richard A., and Sidney M. Milkis, *The Politics of Regulatory Change,* 2d ed. (New York: Oxford University Press, 1996). A study of deregulation politics during the Reagan administration that focuses on the Federal Trade Commission and the Environmental Protection Agency.

Hayes, Michael T., *Incrementalism and Public Policy* (New York: Longman, 1992). A discussion of several major policymaking models as the sources of incrementalism. Nonincremental policy change is also analyzed.

Heidenheimer, Arnold, Hugh Heclo, and Carolyn Teich Adams, *Comparative Public Policy,* 2d ed. (New York: St. Martin's Press, 1983). A well-done comparative treatment of public policies on health care, housing, education, taxation, and other topics in the United States and Western Europe.

Heineman, Robert A., et al., *The World of the Policy Analyst* (Chatham, N.J.: Chatham House, 1990). An analysis of the role of policy analysis and analysts in the policy process, which takes a broad and positive view of its subject.

Jacob, Herbert, *Silent Revolution: The Transformation of Divorce Law in the United States* (Chicago: University of Chicago Press, 1988). A discussion that develops a theory of routine policymaking to explain action in divorce law and other areas.

Jones, Charles O., *Clean Air* (Pittsburgh: University of Pittsburgh Press, 1975). A study of the formation and implementation of air pollution control policy. Intergovernmental relations are well-treated.

———, *An Introduction to the Study of Public Policy* (Monterey, Calif: Brooks/Cole, 1984). A highly useful volume that presents the sequential, functional approach to policy-formation study illustrated with case studies and other materials.

Katz, Michael B., *In the Shadow of the Poorhouse* (New York: Basic Books, 1986). A history of American welfare policy in which Katz argues that there will always be a need for governmental action in this area.

Katzman, Robert A., *Institutional Disability* (Washington, D.C.: Brookings Institution, 1986). A study of the development of national policy on transportation for the handicapped.

Kettl, Donald, F., *Leadership at the Fed* (New Haven: Yale University Press, 1986). A discussion of policymaking by the Federal Reserve Board that focuses on the role of its chairman.

Kingdon, John W., *Agendas, Alternatives, and Public Policies,* 2d ed. (New York: Harper Collins, 1995). In this important study of agenda-setting, it is argued that separate streams of problems, policies, and politics occasionally converge to create opportunities to set the agenda.

———, *Congressmen's Voting Decisions*, 3d ed. (Ann Arbor: University of Michigan

Press, 1992). A very valuable empirical study of how members of the House of Representatives make decisions and the factors influencing them.

Krasnow, Erwin G., and Lawrence D. Langley, *The Politics of Broadcast Regulation,* 2d ed. (New York: St. Martin's Press, 1978). An analysis, with case studies, of the development of broadcast regulation policy by the Federal Communication Commission.

Landy, Marc K., and Martin A. Levin (eds.), *The New Politics of Public Policy* (Baltimore: Johns Hopkins University Press, 1995). The outstanding collection of essays contained in this volume present a variety of perspectives on public policy formation.

Lester, James P., and Joseph Stewart, Jr., *Public Policy: An Evolutionary Approach* (Minneapolis: West Publishing Company, 1996). This readable text traces the development of policy study, discusses the policy process, and examines some areas of public policy.

Light, Paul C., *Artful Work: The Politics of Social Security Reform* (New York: Random House, 1985). An excellent case study of the 1983 Social Security reform legislation that conveys much insight into the operation of the policy process.

———, *Forging Legislation* (New York: Norton, 1992). The enactment of the legislation that created the Department of Veterans Affairs is ably traced and explained by a participant-observer.

Lindblom, Charles E., *The Intelligence of Democracy* (New York: Free Press, 1965). An examination of bargaining and other forms of mutual adjustment in policy formation.

———, and Edward J. Woodhouse, *The Policy-Making Process,* 3d ed. (Englewood Cliffs, N.J.: Prentice-Hall, 1993). An examination of government institutions, political elites, business, policy analysis, and other social forces in the policy process. Skeptical of rational modes of analysis.

Lindsay, James M., *Congress and the Politics of U.S. Foreign Policy* (Baltimore: Johns Hopkins University Press, 1994). Lindsay focuses on the resurgence of the modern Congress in the formation and control of foreign policy.

Lineberry, Robert L., *American Public Policy: What Government Does and What Difference It Makes* (New York: Harper & Row, 1977). A study that is equally divided between a discussion of how to analyze policy formation and a readable and chatty consideration of four domestic policy problems (e.g., inequality).

Loomis, Burdett A., *Time, Politics, and Policies: A Legislative Year* (Lawrence: University Press of Kansas, 1994). This is an absorbing, detailed, empirically-based, narrative focused on politics and policymaking in the Kansas legislature.

Lowi, Theodore J., "American Business, Public Policy, Case Studies, and Political Theory," *World Politics,* XVI (July, 1964), pp. 667–715. An influential essay that seeks to develop a new framework for policy study. Lowi suggests that the kind of policy (distributive, regulatory, or redistributive) involved in a situation shapes the nature of the policymaking process.

———, *The End of Liberalism: The Second Republic of the United States,* 2d ed. (New York: Norton, 1979). A study that argues that juridical democracy is needed because American public policies no longer are responsive to public needs because of the impact of interest-group liberalism and that legislation delegates too much discretion.

Lunch, William M., *The Nationalization of American Politics* (Berkeley: University of

California Press, 1987). A discussion that asserts that during the last three decades the American political system has become "nationalized" and is now dominated by political ideas rather than material interests.

March, James G., *A Primer on Decision Making: How Decisions Happen* (New York: The Free Press, 1994). Drawing widely on the social sciences, March offers a lot of theory, information, and insight on decision making, but not many empirical illustrations.

McConnell, Grant, *Private Power and American Democracy* (New York: Knopf, 1966). A highly insightful examination of the role of private groups in policy formation and how pluralism and decentralization have often made them the dominant force.

Meier, Kenneth J., *Politics and the Bureaucracy: Policymaking in the Fourth Branch of Government*, 3d ed. (Pacific Grove, Calif.: Brooks/Cole, 1993). A comprehensive and systematic treatment of the national bureaucracy as a policymaking institution. Strong on the political context.

———, *The Political Economy of Regulation: The Case of Insurance* (Albany: State University of New York Press, 1988). A major analysis of insurance company regulation that combines history, politics, and economics.

Melnick, R. Shep, *Regulation and the Courts* (Washington, D.C.: Brookings Institution, 1983). An analysis of the impact of judicial decisions on clean air policy and of the interaction between the courts and other political institutions.

Mezey, Michael L., *Congress, the President, and Public Policy* (Boulder, Colo.: Westview, 1989). A discussion of presidential-congressional relations which argues that conflict between the two bodies reduces the yield of good public policy.

Mucciaroni, Gary, *Reversals of Fortune: Public Policy and Private Interests* (Washington, D.C.: Brookings Institution, 1995). The author strives to explain why the success of interest groups may vary over time and from one policy area to another.

Nachmias, David, *Public Policy Evaluation: Approaches and Methods* (New York: St. Martin's Press, 1979). An analysis and comparison of various conceptual models for evaluatory policies and statistical techniques useful in evaluation research.

Nadel, Mark V., *The Politics of Consumer Protection* (Indianapolis: Bobbs-Merrill, 1971). A good analysis of the formation and adoption of consumer protection legislation.

Nathan, James A., and James K. Oliver, *Foreign Policy Making and the American Political System*, 3d ed. (Baltimore: Johns Hopkins University Press, 1994). This book surveys American foreign policy since World War II and analyzes its formation from an institutional perspective.

Nathan, Richard P., *Social Science in Government: Uses and Misuses* (New York: Basic Books, 1989). A discussion of the roles and uses of applied social science research in the development and evaluation of public policies.

Nelson, Barbara J., *Making an Issue of Child Abuse* (Chicago: University of Chicago Press, 1984). A perceptive and absorbing analysis of how child abuse became an important social welfare issue in the United States.

Neustadt, Richard E., *Presidential Power: The Politics of Leadership from FDR to Carter* (New York: Wiley, 1980). A classic study of presidential power and leadership in the policy process that finds that the effective influence of the president is limited.

———, and Harvey v. Fineberg, *The Swine Flu Affair* (Washington, D.C.: U.S. Department of Health, Education, and Welfare, 1978). An examination of the abortive effort of the Ford administration to combat an expected swine flu epidemic.

Olezak, Walter J., *Congressional Procedures and the Policy Process*, 4th ed. (Washington, D.C.: CQ Press, 1996). A thorough treatment of congressional legislative procedures and how they can affect the course and content of legislation.

Pertschuk, Michael, *Revolt Against Regulation: The Rise and Pause of the Consumer Movement* (Berkeley: University of California Press, 1982). A spirited analysis of consumer policy and politics by a former Federal Trade Commissioner.

Peters, B. Guy, *American Public Policy*, 4th ed. (Chatham, N.J.: Chatham House, 1996). An introduction to the policy process that also examines several areas of substantive policy.

Peterson, Paul E. (ed.), *The President, the Congress, and the Making of Foreign Policy* (Norman: University of Oklahoma Press, 1994). The essays in this compendium look at the relative power of the executive and legislative branches in the development of American foreign policies.

Pierce, Lawrence C., *The Politics of Fiscal Policy Formation* (Pacific Palisades, Calif.: Goodyear, 1971). A political scientist's analysis of the process and politics of fiscal policy formation. Especially strong in its treatment of the development of policy proposals by fiscal agencies.

Piven, Frances Fox, and Richard A. Cloward, *Regulating the Poor* (New York: Pantheon Books, 1971). A normative evaluation of welfare policies that finds them to be a means more for controlling the poor than for meeting their substantive needs.

Pleck, Elizabeth, *Domestic Tyranny* (New York: Oxford University Press, 1987). A historical treatment of the problem of family violence and American social policy thereon since colonial times.

Pressman, Jeffrey L., and Aaron B. Wildavsky, *Implementation* (Berkeley: University of California Press, 1973). An account of the problems of implementing the public-works program of the Economic Development Act of 1965 in the Oakland area.

Quirk, Paul J., *Industry Influence in Federal Regulatory Agencies* (Princeton: Princeton University Press, 1981). An empirical examination of some theories on the influence of industry on regulatory agencies' policy incentives. A very valuable study.

Ranney, Austin (ed.), *Politics Science and Public Policy* (Chicago: Markham, 1968). An uneven collection of essays on issues, problems, and theoretical concerns in the analysis of policy and policy outcomes.

Reagan, Michael, *Regulation: The Politics of Policy* (Boston: Little, Brown, 1987). An excellent, succinct treatment of governmental regulation of private economic policy from a political perspective.

Redford, Emmette S., *Democracy in the Administrative State* (New York: Oxford University Press, 1969). An insightful examination of the role of administration in the policy process together with concern for democratic control of administration.

———, *The Regulatory Process* (Austin: University of Texas Press, 1969). An analysis of the economic regulatory process with emphasis on administrative agencies and commercial aviation regulation.

Regens, James L., and Robert W. Rycroft, *The Acid Rain Controversy* (Pittsburgh: University of Pittsburgh Press, 1988). A discussion of the acid rain problem; its scientific, economic, and political dimensions; and the policymaking process as it centers on the issue.

Reich, Robert B. (ed.), *The Power of Public Ideas* (Cambridge, Mass.: Ballinger, 1988). An anthology of integrated essays that collectively argue that ideas about the public good are important in shaping public policy.

Ripley, Randall B., and Grace A. Franklin, *Policy Implementation and Bureaucracy*, 2d ed. (Homewood, Ill.: Dorsey Press, 1986). An empirical discussion of distributive, competitive regulatory, protective regulatory, and redistributive programs.

Robyn, Dorothy, *Breaking the Special Interests* (Chicago: University of Chicago Press, 1987). An analysis of the deregulation of the motor carrier industry that covers topics such as coalition building, economic analysis, and presidential bargaining.

Rochefort, David A., and Roger W. Cobb (eds.), *The Politics of Problem Definition* (Lawrence: University Press of Kansas, 1994). Following an introductory chapter, problem definition is analyzed and illustrated in this volume by a series of case studies.

Rogers, Harrell R., Jr., and Charles S. Bullock III, *Law and Social Change* (New York: McGraw-Hill, 1972). An evaluation of the impact of the civil rights legislation of the 1960s.

Rosenbaum, Walter A., *Environmental Politics and Policy*, 3d ed. (Washington, D.C.: CQ Press, 1995). A comprehensive survey of environmental policies and politics, that includes solid chapters on science and energy and their relationship to environmental policy.

———, *Energy, Politics, and Public Policies*, 2d ed. (Washington, D.C.: CQ Press, 1987). A survey of energy policies and the policymaking processes that explores major shifts in energy policy.

Rothenberg, Lawrence S., *Regulation, Organizations, and Politics* (Ann Arbor: University of Michigan Press, 1994). The regulation of motor carriers by the Interstate Commerce Commission is examined from a political economy perspective in this volume.

Rourke, Francis E., *Bureaucracy, Politics, and Public Policy*, 3d ed. (Boston: Little, Brown, 1983). A discussion of administrative agencies and their role in the formation of public policy.

Sabatier, Paul A., and Hank C. Jenkins-Smith (eds.), *Policy Change and Learning* (Boulder, Colo.: Westview, 1993). The advocacy coalition approach to policy study is discussed and then applied to a number of policy areas in this collection of essays and case studies.

Schattschneider, E. E., *The Semi-Sovereign People* (New York: Holt, Rinehart and Winston, 1960). A critique of group theory and an influential discussion of the impact of conflict on political decision-making.

Schick, Allen, *The Federal Budget: Politics, Policy, Process* (Washington, D.C.: Brookings Institution, 1995). Anyone wanting to understand the national budget and how it is constructed will find this an invaluable guide.

Schneier, Edward V. (ed.), *Policy-Making in American Government* (New York: Basic Books, 1969). An anthology organized under the headings of policy formulation, articulation, mobilization, codification, application, and redefinition.

Schultze, Charles L., *The Public Use of Private Interest* (Washington, D.C.: Brookings Institution, 1977). An analysis of how market incentives can be used to improve governmental intervention in the economy.

Skrentny, John David, *The Ironies of Affirmative Action* (Chicago: University of Chicago

Press, 1996). The evolution of affirmative action programs, their politics and problems, are analyzed in this insightful book.

Smith, James A., *The Idea Brokers: Think Tanks and the Rise of the New Policy Elite* (New York: Free Press, 1991). A balanced look at the rise and proliferation of private research organizations as a force in the policy process.

Smith, T. Alexander, *The Comparative Policy Process* (Santa Barbara, Calif.: Clio Books, 1975). A distinctly comparative treatment of policy formation employing case studies from Western democracies and organized around the categories of distribution, sectoral fragmentation, emotive symbolism, and redistribution.

———, *Time and Public Policy* (Knoxville: University of Tennessee Press, 1989). A carefully reasoned, profound study that focuses on the effect of time and time horizons on politics and public policy.

Sorensen, Theodore C., *Decision-Making in the White House* (New York: Columbia University Press, 1963). A short analysis of presidential decision-making by the former counsel to President John Kennedy.

Spanier, John, and Eric M. Uslaner, *How American Foreign Policy Is Made,* 4th ed. (New York: Holt, Rinehart and Winston, 1985). An introduction to foreign policy formation that deals with the interaction of president and Congress, and with foreign and domestic policy.

Steiner, Gilbert Y., *Social Insecurity: The Politics of Welfare* (Washington, D.C.: Brookings Institution, 1966). An analysis of welfare policymaking that illustrates the relationship between the nature of the policy process and the substance of policy.

Stevenson, Gordon McKay, Jr., *The Politics of Airport Noise* (North Scituate, Mass.: Duxbury, 1972). A systematic analysis of the participants in and process of the development of noise abatement policies. Good on the details of policy action.

Stimson, James A., *Public Opinion in America: Moods, Cycles, and Swings* (Boulder, Colo.: Westview Press, 1991). An empirical investigation of the impact of policy moods (general public dispositions) on political activity and policymaking.

Stoker, Robert P., *Reluctant Partners: Implementing Federal Policy* (Pittsburgh: University of Pittsburgh Press, 1991). An examination of cooperation and conflict in the state and local implementation of federal programs.

Stokey, Edith, and Richard Zeckhauser, *A Primer for Policy Analysis* (New York: Norton, 1978). A useful and comprehensive treatment of quantitative approaches to policy analysis and decision-making.

Stone, Alan, *Economic Regulation and the Public Interest* (Ithaca: Cornell University Press, 1977). A thorough, insightful, and critical examination of the Federal Trade Commission and trade regulation policies.

———, *Regulation and Its Alternatives* (Washington, D.C.: CQ Press, 1982). A wide-ranging, insightful analysis of the nature, justifications, and politics of economic regulation.

———, and Edward J. Harpham, *The Political Economy of Public Policy* (Beverly Hills: Sage, 1982). A critical and challenging collection of essays dealing with various major issues in policy formation and public policy.

Stone, Debra, *Policy Paradox and Political Reason* (Boston: Little, Brown, 1988). An insightful, engaging, theoretical, and somewhat unconventional look at goals, problems, and solutions in the policy process, which is portrayed as full of paradoxes.

Sundquist, James L., *Politics and Policy: The Eisenhower, Kennedy and Johnson Years* (Washington, D.C.: Brookings Institution, 1968). Highly informative case studies of several major areas of domestic policy are combined with a general explanatory analysis.

Tatalovich, Raymond, and Byron W. Daynes (eds.), *Social Regulatory Policy* (Boulder, Colo.: Westview Press, 1988). A collection of case studies of policies on school prayer, pornography, crime, gun control, affirmative action, and abortion, plus theoretical chapters on social regulatory policy.

Tobin, Richard, *The Expendable Future: U.S. Politics and the Protection of Biological Diversity* (Durham, N.C.: Duke University Press, 1990). This is a thorough analysis and evaluation of the Endangered Species Act.

Truman, David B., *The Governmental Process* (New York: Knopf, 1951). A classic treatment of the role of interest groups in the American political process. Indispensable for an understanding of group therapy.

Tufte, Edward R., *Political Control of the Economy* (Princeton: Princeton University Press, 1978). A carefully prepared comparative study that contends that economic policy is substantially shaped by the quest for partisan political advantages.

Van Horn, Carl E., Donald C. Baumer, and William T. Gormley, Jr., *Politics and Public Policy*, 2d ed. (Washington, D.C.: CQ Press, 1992). A view of public policymaking as it occurs in six arenas: the boardroom, the bureaucracy, the cloakroom, the chief executive, the courtroom, and the living room.

Vig, Norman J., and Michael E. Kraft, *Environmental Policy in the 1980s* (Washington, D.C.: CQ Press, 1984). Seventeen original essays that yield much information on environmental policies generally while providing critical appraisals of Reagan administration environmental actions.

Vogel, David, *National Styles of Regulation* (Ithaca: Cornell University Press, 1986). A comparative treatment of environmental regulation in the United States and Great Britain that finds that differences reflect each nation's "regulatory style."

Wade, Larry L., *The Elements of Public Policy* (Columbus: Merrill, 1972). An introduction to policy analysis that focuses on decision-making and policy costs and benefits.

——, and R. L. Curry, Jr., *A Logic of Public Policy* (Belmont, Calif.: Wadsworth, 1970). An examination of American public policy from the "new political economy," or public-choice, perspective.

Walker, Jack L., Jr., *Mobilizing Interest Groups in America* (Ann Arbor: University of Michigan Press, 1991). A major treatment of the origins, maintenance, and influence of interest groups in American politics.

Wasby, Stephen L., *The Impact of the United States Supreme Court* (Homewood, Ill.: Dorsey, 1970). A nonquantitative analysis of the Court's impact on public policy that attempts to develop a theory of impact.

Waste, Robert J., *The Ecology of City Policymaking* (New York: Oxford University Press, 1989). A complex theoretical framework for analyzing urban policymaking.

Weiss, Carol H., *Evaluation Research* (Englewood Cliffs, N.J.: Prentice-Hall, 1972). A short but valuable treatment of the methodology of evaluation research.

Welborn, David M., *Governance of Federal Regulatory Agencies* (Knoxville: University of Tennessee Press, 1977). A perceptive study of the organization, operation, and decision-making of the "big seven" independent regulatory commissions.

Wholey, Joseph S., et al., *Federal Evaluation Policy* (Washington, D.C.: Urban Institute,

1970). A survey and assessment of the extent and quality of social policy evaluation by federal administrative agencies.

William, Walter L., *Social Policy Analysis and Research* (New York: American Elsevier, 1971). A solid introduction to the systematic evaluation of social policies.

Wolman, Harold, *Politics of Federal Housing* (New York: Dodd, Mead, 1971). A succinct analysis of the formation and implementation of public housing policies.

Young, James Harvey, *Pure Food: Securing the Federal Food and Drugs Act of 1906* (Princeton: Princeton University Press, 1989). An informative and thorough historical account of the enactment of food and drug and meat inspection legislation.

INDEX